SETTING NATIONAL PRIORITIES
The 1979 Budget

JOSEPH A. PECHMAN *Editor*

SETTING NATIONAL PRIORITIES
The 1979 Budget

Martin E. Abel
David W. Breneman
Anthony Downs
Robert W. Hartman
Herschel Kanter and Others
Joseph J. Minarik
John L. Palmer
Joseph A. Pechman
Charles A. Sorrels and Others

THE BROOKINGS INSTITUTION
Washington, D.C.

Copyright © 1978 by

THE BROOKINGS INSTITUTION

1775 Massachusetts Avenue, N.W., Washington, D.C. 20036

ISBN 0-8157-6984-9 (cloth)
ISBN 0-8157-6983-0 (paper)

Library of Congress Catalog Card Number 77-91837

9 8 7 6 5 4 3 2 1

THE BROOKINGS INSTITUTION is an independent organization devoted to nonpartisan research, education, and publication in economics, government, foreign policy, and the social sciences generally. Its principal purposes are to aid in the development of sound public policies and to promote public understanding of issues of national importance.

The Institution was founded on December 8, 1927, to merge the activities of the Institute for Government Research, founded in 1916, the Institute of Economics, founded in 1922, and the Robert Brookings Graduate School of Economics and Government, founded in 1924.

The Board of Trustees is responsible for the general administration of the Institution, while the immediate direction of the policies, program, and staff is vested in the President, assisted by an advisory committee of the officers and staff. The by-laws of the Institution state: "It is the function of the Trustees to make possible the conduct of scientific research, and publication, under the most favorable conditions, and to safeguard the independence of the research staff in the pursuit of their studies and in the publication of the results of such studies. It is not a part of their function to determine, control, or influence the conduct of particular investigations or the conclusions reached."

The President bears final responsibility for the decision to publish a manuscript as a Brookings book. In reaching his judgment on the competence, accuracy, and objectivity of each study, the President is advised by the director of the appropriate research program and weighs the views of a panel of expert outside readers who report to him in confidence on the quality of the work. Publication of a work signifies that it is deemed a competent treatment worthy of public consideration but does not imply endorsement of conclusions or recommendations.

The Institution maintains its position of neutrality on issues of public policy in order to safeguard the intellectual freedom of the staff. Hence interpretations or conclusions in Brookings publications should be understood to be solely those of the authors and should not be attributed to the Institution, to its trustees, officers, or other staff members, or to the organizations that support its research.

Foreword

EACH YEAR, the federal budget presents in great detail the programs of the national government and their costs. It explains the tax policies the administration proposes and how the budget will affect the economy. In recent years, it has also provided estimates of the future costs of continuing federal programs and of new ones proposed by the President. Yet the budget reflects only the final decisions the President makes—it does not discuss alternative ways of achieving the same objectives—and it is formidably complex. Hence public understanding of it is limited.

President Jimmy Carter began his budget message for fiscal year 1979 with the following words: "The first complete budget of any new administration is its most important. It is the administration's first full statement of its priorities, policies, and proposals for meeting our national needs." This book, the ninth in an annual series, is intended to help the general public understand the problems addressed in the budget and the options considered by the President in trying to solve them. It analyzes President Carter's major initiatives, compares them with alternative policies, and evaluates the budgetary implications of the decisions.

The contributors discuss the budget for fiscal year 1979 and deal with several major policy issues: education, employment and income security, taxation, urban policy, agriculture, and defense. The final chapter is devoted to an analysis of the budget outlook over the next five years. The three appendixes discuss the reasons for which outlays have fallen below official estimates in recent years, the new system of multiyear budgeting that will be implemented by the administration with next year's budget, and the nature and significance of tax expenditures.

The work on this volume was undertaken jointly by the Brookings Economic Studies and Foreign Policy Studies programs. Joseph A. Pechman is director, and Robert W. Hartman, David W. Breneman, John L. Palmer, Joseph J. Minarik, and Anthony Downs, are members of the staff, of the Economic Studies program. Charles A. Sorrels and Herschel Kanter are members of the defense analysis staff of the Foreign Policy Studies program, which is under the direction of Philip H. Trezise. Martin E. Abel is a member of the staff of Schnittker Associates.

Karen Brown, Elizabeth H. Cross, Barbara P. Haskins, and Diane Hammond edited the manuscript of this book; Diane Hammond prepared it for publication. The risk of factual error was minimized by the work of Evelyn P. Fisher, Penelope S. Harpold, and Judy Conmy.

Grants from Carnegie Corporation of New York and the Ford Foundation principally supported the research for this volume. Research underlying the chapters on the defense budget was supported by grants from the Ford Foundation and the Charles E. Herrill Trust. The simulations of the revenue and distributional implications of the administration's tax policies were financed by a grant from the RANN program of the National Science Foundation. The Brookings Institution is grateful to these foundations for their support.

As in all Brookings books, the views expressed here are those of the authors and should not be ascribed to the trustees, officers, or other staff members of the Brookings Institution, or to the foundations that contributed to the support of this project.

BRUCE K. MACLAURY
President

May 1978
Washington, D.C.

Contents

Text Tables

Text Figure

Appendix Tables

SETTING NATIONAL PRIORITIES
The 1979 Budget

CHAPTER ONE

Introduction and Summary

JOSEPH A. PECHMAN

PRESIDENT CARTER'S BUDGET for fiscal year 1979 calls for out-lays of $500.2 billion, receipts of $439.6 billion, and a deficit of $60.6 billion. The budget itself contains no spending proposals beyond those that were part of the 1977 economic stimulus program or were announced in 1977. But since the budget was submitted, the administration has recommended new programs for higher education and the cities. Receipts allow for a new tax cut—equaling about 1 percent of the gross national product—to promote continued economic recovery. For the longer run, the President plans to adhere to his campaign promise to reduce outlays to 21 percent of the gross national product by 1981.

The major elements of the 1979 budget are:

- An $8 billion increase in outlays. This is 2 percent more than the amount needed to finance current federal programs and activities at 1978 levels.

- A $25 billion decrease in receipts. Gross tax cuts of $34 billion are partially offset by $9 billion of increased receipts from tax reforms.

The President's basic strategy is to provide enough of a fiscal stimulus to keep the economy growing at about 4.75 percent a year and, at the same time, to restrain the growth in federal spending so that it will amount to 21 percent of gross national product by 1981. The administration believes that this strategy will not worsen the underlying inflation rate, which reflects mainly the momentum of past price and wage increases. The President hopes to decelerate in-

1

flation by holding 1978 price and wage increases below the average increases in the prior two years.

Although the budget proposes significant increases in outlays for employment and training, welfare, education, urban aid, agriculture, and defense over the next five years, there is pressure to raise outlays and reduce taxes even more. The condition of the budget and the economy in the years ahead will depend heavily on the reaction of the administration and the Congress to this pressure.

The Economy

Shortly after taking office in 1977, President Carter revised the 1978 budget of the outgoing Ford administration. His revisions— most of which were enacted—were intended to provide about $20 billion in economic stimulus by early 1978. During most of the year the economy did grow at about a 5 percent real rate, as forecast, but growth tapered off toward the end of the year.

The President's plan for the coming year is to offset the tendency of fiscal policy to become automatically more restrictive as federal tax receipts rise much faster than federal outlays. The divergence would be even greater in 1979 when a large payroll tax increase goes into effect. Without changes in policy, the budget would automatically be about $30 billion more restrictive at the end of 1979 than it was two years earlier. With the proposed $25 billion tax cut and $8 billion spending increases, the situation at the end of fiscal year 1979 will be about where it was at the end of 1977. By past standards, the proposed deficits are large, but the administration argues that they are necessary to keep the expansion going.

The administration's plan leaves economic growth essentially to the nonfederal sectors of the economy: consumers, investors, state and local governments, and foreigners. When the budget was prepared, the administration expected a weakening in the growth of consumer demand (on the assumption that personal saving would rise from its low level in 1977) and of housing (which had been unusually strong). These would be counterbalanced by federal deficits in the first half of 1978 and stronger business investment, state and local government spending, and foreign trade later in the year.

Unanticipated events, which occurred after the budget was submitted, will affect economic developments during the remainder of

1978. First, there will be a spending shortfall of $8.7 billion below the estimates, which means there will be no net fiscal stimulus in 1978. Second, prices rose faster early in the year (because of a variety of factors, including a surprisingly large increase in food prices), and this quickening of inflation may mean tighter credit markets and growing business pessimism. Finally, the coal strike and the hard winter slowed production growth. And although the drop in the exchange rate of the dollar should spur exports, the effect will be felt only gradually. For these reasons, the administration's forecast for real growth in 1978 may be a bit on the high side. However, employment is rising sharply, and there is little reason to anticipate a serious decline in economic activity before the end of the year.

For 1979, the prospects depend on how the private economy and federal fiscal policy develop. Business investment and exports are expected to go up and state and local government surpluses to go down—which will spur business activity. If the federal fiscal program offsets rising tax receipts, the official forecast of 4.75 percent growth in 1979 seems reasonable. However, if the spending shortfall continues or the tax cut is significantly smaller than the President proposes or monetary policy tightens, the economy could slow down in 1979.

Inflation is considerably worse than the administration expected when the budget was prepared. The forecast of 6 percent inflation in 1978 assumed that food and fuel prices would not add to the underlying inflation rate and that the deceleration program would have some effect on wages and prices. However, food prices rose much more than expected, a protectionist measure was adopted for steel, a price-raising farm program was adopted, and the wage agreement in the coal industry may trigger more price increases and large wage increases in upcoming union settlements. Moreover, the decline of the dollar raised the prices of imports and heightens the possibility of a hike in petroleum prices by the Organization of Petroleum Exporting Countries. And the administration's failure to push its wage-price program early in the year does not bode well for deceleration. As this book goes to press, the President is taking a tougher stance on inflation, but the outlook is not encouraging because he does not have a politically acceptable policy to moderate price and wage decisions. If his anti-inflation policy fails, the Federal Reserve may intervene to reduce economic growth.

The Budget

Much federal spending is the result of past congressional actions and commitments, which are always very hard to reverse. Thus just to maintain the 1978 programs will cost $492 billion in 1979, $32 billion more than in 1978. This built-in growth leaves little margin for new programs, especially since President Carter is committed to restraining outlay growth.

Other administrations have tried to increase dollars for new programs by proposing cutbacks in current programs. Despite the fact that President Carter instituted zero-based budgeting—a process that in principle makes every old program compete for dollars on an equal footing with new proposals—there are virtually no reductions in outlays for old programs in the President's proposal for 1979. New spending will add $8 billion in 1979, raising spending to $500 billion, or about 22 percent of the gross national product forecast for that year.

The $8 billion addition to current programs shows little resetting of national priorities. Spending for most current programs is increased by at least small amounts, and several of them will grow substantially: rebates of energy taxes; the acquisition of petroleum for a strategic reserve; aid to elementary and secondary education; and youth employment and public service jobs. After the budget was presented to the Congress, the President made two major policy proposals that will add $1 billion to the 1979 budget; the contingency allowance in the budget will cover part of the addition. These proposals—for expanded aid to college students and for new urban programs—are discussed later in this chapter. The March budget revision reduced expected 1979 outlays by about $1 billion, so the $500 billion figure is still a reasonable estimate for the year, provided the shortfall does not continue.

The Budget Outlook

The budget in the years ahead depends on economic developments as well as on future spending and tax decisions. When President Carter came into office, the economy was still recovering from the deep recession of 1974–75. The federal government was running a large deficit and, to keep the economic recovery going, it was necessary to continue the budget deficit. But it was also necessary to plan to bring spending and taxes into rough balance when full employment is reached. Thus, the problem of fiscal management is to provide enough stimulus in the short run to maintain the desired rate of economic growth, but to keep an eye on the long run so that federal spending and taxes will come roughly into balance when full employment is reached.

The budget for fiscal year 1979 shows evidence that the President has both the short-run and long-run considerations in mind in his legislative program. Although the planned 1979 deficit is about $60 billion, the President proposes to restrain spending so that by 1981 outlays will be less than 21 percent of the gross national product. If the economy should grow by about 4.75 percent a year, 1981 receipts would slightly exceed outlays for present and proposed programs, giving not only a balanced budget but a margin for small increases in outlays or further reductions in taxes.

This outcome seemed unlikely even at the time the budget was submitted, and developments since then make it more doubtful: the administration's later decisions will increase outlays, and Congress may raise them even more. Furthermore, projected expenditures for education, health, welfare, and farm commodity programs are probably underestimated. These changes alone would make 1981 outlays more than 21 percent of the gross national product.

The receipts side of the budget is even less certain. Many in Congress oppose the administration's tax reforms and want to reverse at least part of last year's social security payroll tax increases. If Congress accepts the President's proposed tax cuts but rejects two-thirds of his tax reforms and eliminates half the payroll tax increases, 1981 outlays will exceed receipts by $30 billion. It may be that a deficit will be appropriate in 1981, but the administration is trying to avoid creating the conditions now under which a deficit would be a certainty in that year. A deficit of this size would be especially disturbing because it makes no allowance for tax reductions to offset the rise in real taxes resulting from inflation. Such reductions have been made in the past decade.

Although receipts will rise more than $80 billion a year during 1981–83 there will not be much left for new programs or for further tax cuts. By 1983, if outlays are held to 21 percent of the gross national product, they would be $722 billion. And under the President's tax program, receipts would be $747 billion, leaving a margin of $25 billion—enough for only small reductions in taxes. For example, assuming the 1978 tax cut equals $25 billion, the 1981 margin could be used to reverse the 1977 payroll tax increases, but for little else. Even if the entire margin were used to reduce the income taxes of individuals, the individual income tax would still be over 11.5 percent of personal income, nearly the highest since the end of the Second World War.

One percent of the gross national product in 1983 will be almost $35 billion. Thus, if outlays are 22 percent of the gross national product in that year, there would be no room for tax cuts beyond the 1978 cut of $25 billion. Alternatively, if outlays are 20 percent of the gross national product, some additional tax cuts could be made, but they would be small: for example, half.the payroll tax increase could be reversed, but the corporation tax could not be cut. (This assumes that the individual income tax stays below 11 percent of personal income; under the present tax laws it is 10.7 percent this year, and under the President's tax program it is 10.3 percent this year and will be 10.5 percent in 1979.)

The budget outlook is therefore not rosy. It will be difficult to keep outlays to 21 percent of the gross national product in 1983. But given success in reaching that goal, the margin for tax reductions (beyond those proposed for this year) would be slim. Since a budget deficit is dangerous during full employment, the cautious approach is to avoid more outlays or lower taxes than the President proposes. Any significant tax reduction in the early 1980s will require either substantial spending cuts or large deficits, which might be extremely inflationary in the economy projected for those years.

Tax Reduction and Reform

Beginning with his 1976 election campaign, President Carter has repeatedly stressed the need for tax reform. His first reform proposals were almost one year in the making and bear the scars of intensive debate within the administration and extensive criticism from without.

A statement of tax reform options prepared by the Treasury in September 1977 was shortly leaked to the press. The options called for significant structural changes in income taxes: full taxation of long-term capital gains; elimination of tax shelters; narrowing of personal deductions; integration of the individual and corporate income taxes; reduction of the maximum individual income tax rate to 50 percent; an increased and enlarged investment credit; and reductions in the corporation tax rates. The tax cuts for individuals were meant to compensate for higher tax rates caused by inflation; and the tax cut for business was meant to encourage investment. Public reaction to the leaked proposals was mostly negative; those who benefited from the tax preferences slated for revision or elimination argued vigorously for their continuation. Debate over capital gains and the business tax proposals was especially intense.

The proposal that emerged is considerably narrower than the September options. It calls for a larger net tax reduction with significantly fewer changes in the tax structure. The tax cuts are relatively the largest in the lowest income classes and taper off as income increases up to $100,000; above that level, taxpayers actually face small tax increases on average. The individual income tax rates would run from 12 to 68 percent instead of the present 14 to 70 percent. The most important revisions in the individual income tax were elimination of the deductibility of state taxes on sales, gasoline, and personal property, and consolidation of the medical and casualty deductions with a floor of 10 percent of income. These revisions were intended to simplify the tax return form as well as to raise revenue, but the response to even these modest changes was negative, and they were given little chance of passing the Congress.

The income tax reduction was designed to offset, at least in the aggregate, the effects of the 1977 payroll tax increases. The higher rates affect low-income households most, and the higher wage base ceiling hits those earning that amount the hardest. But in conjunction with the income tax proposals for 1979, the net result would be modest tax cuts for all households except those at the very highest and lowest income levels. About 7 percent of households with incomes of more than $50,000 and almost 10 percent of households with incomes of $100,000 and above would have "significant" tax increases, that is, increases of at least $100 or 5 percent of their previous liability.

Apart from tax increases through legislation, there are tax increases through inflation, which increases nominal incomes faster than exemptions, deductions, or exclusions. For many households the tax increases from the 1977–78 inflation and from the payroll tax increases are not offset by the President's proposed tax cuts. They would reduce taxes only for households with incomes under $15,000, but 15 percent of all households would have significant tax increases, including almost half the households with incomes of $30,000 or more. Inflation and the new payroll tax law will continue to raise taxes, and the President has said that additional tax cuts might be needed early in the 1980s.

One of the administration's goals is to promote saving and the formation of capital; hence, tax cuts for business are an important part of its program. The President recommends reducing corporate tax rates and broadening the investment tax credit, which would reduce business taxes more than $10 billion by 1980. This program has the virtue of being relatively simple, but it probably would have greater impact on investment if it concentrated more heavily on increasing investment incentives. Partially offsetting the $10 billion tax cut is an almost $4 billion increase through tax revisions. Among the revenue-raising proposals are restrictions on the deductibility of meals and entertainment and the elimination of the deferral of taxes on earnings from exports and on profits earned abroad. Again the proposed revisions aroused considerable opposition and are given little chance of survival.

The controversy in Congress continues. Some favor a bigger tax cut to stimulate the economy, others a smaller one (or none at all) and higher spending. Some propose a bigger tax cut with restrictions on federal spending, and others a smaller one to reduce the budget deficit immediately. Members of both parties favor a rollback of payroll tax increases, although there is no consensus on how this is to be done and how the social security trust funds are to be reimbursed. The proposed petroleum wellhead tax, including at least a partial refund to consumers, is still under consideration. With these crosscurrents in Congress, the outcome is hard to predict; but, given the opposition to the proposed tax reforms, what emerges will be different from the President's tax program.

Employment and Income Security

The Carter administration has proposed or supported major—and controversial—legislation affecting employment and income security.

In three cases—increases in the minimum wage, revision of the food stamp program, and financing of social security—legislative action has been completed. The first two do not affect the budget greatly; the third does. The administration proposed to deal with the projected deficits in the social security system by eliminating the over-adjustments of benefits to inflation, increasing payroll taxes (principally for employers), and using general revenues to a limited extent. Congress rejected the financing proposals in favor of a much larger payroll tax hike, increasing the tax rate and the applicable wage base for employees and employers alike. Public opposition to this new law has been mounting ever since it was passed because it will ultimately push payroll taxes very high. In addition, economists have urged a reduction of the payroll tax to reduce employer costs and thus to moderate inflation. As a result, Congress is considering revising some of the recent payroll tax increases and possibly substituting general revenue financing.

Although there is strong support in Congress for most of the objectives embodied in the administration's welfare proposal, its prospects for passage are poor, partly because of its large incremental cost (about $17 billion by 1982) and partly because of skepticism about major departures from the current system (cash payments for the entire low-income population and public service jobs for primary earners in families with children). Modest reforms with lower price tags have been proposed by various members of Congress. If congressional priorities do not push welfare reform to the background and if the administration is willing to negotiate, many of its welfare objectives may be achieved.

Several pending initiatives are central to federal employment and training policy. The Comprehensive Employment and Training Act (CETA) is the primary legislation in this area. Largely as a result of the expansion of public service employment and youth programs, outlays under CETA nearly doubled between the 1976 and 1978 budgets (to $9.6 billion). The 1979 budget calls for maintaining CETA's 1978 service levels but increasing the youth programs, funding pilot demonstrations of the welfare reform jobs program, and introducing a program to increase jobs in the private sector for CETA target groups. The President is also requesting a four-year reauthorization of CETA, starting in 1979. It would change eligibility requirements and consolidate several existing public service employment programs into one in which the number of subsidized jobs would vary automatically with the aggregate unemployment rate. In addition, the President's urban program includes a tax credit for hiring disadvantaged youths and a labor-intensive public works program, and the administration supports the bill for full employment and balanced growth (Humphrey-Hawkins), which sets ambitious employment goals and mandates the federal role for achieving them.

The administration wants its manpower policies to promote long-term employment by focusing on training and jobs for the private sector rather than public service employment. Yet 80 percent of CETA outlays and jobs are devoted to public service employment and work experience for youth—which promote short-term employment—and this percentage would increase under proposed administration policies. As the economy continues to recover, those who suffer from structural unemployment can and should be part of the regular labor force; and employment and training programs must emphasize jobs in the private and regular public sectors.

If all the administration's employment and income security initiatives were enacted, federal programs would change in many ways. First, there would be some simplification and streamlining of administrative procedures. Second, the federal role would be stronger vis-à-vis state and local government roles. Third, including the proposed income tax cut, there would be a minor redistribution of income from those above the median to those below, with lower middle-income families faring somewhat better than low-income families. Fourth, employment programs would expand greatly, with heavy emphasis on subsidized public sector jobs, even when unemployment is low. Finally, during 1977–82, outlays would be a little more than $20 billion in excess of those predicated on the 1977 current policies budget inherited by President Carter. While this is a sizable expansion in dollar terms, it is not large relative to the size of the economy and in fact would be roughly constant as a share of the gross national product over the five-year period, in contrast to its approximate 75 percent growth over the previous decade.

Education

In marked contrast to the Nixon and Ford requests, the Carter administration's 1979 education budget calls for substantially increased budget authority—14 percent over the preceding year in current dollars for elementary and secondary and 12 percent for post-secondary programs. Several new legislative proposals, plus the President's decision to press for a cabinet-level department of education, made the new administration's first year an active one for federal education policy.

While the administration's press releases stress its interest in improving basic skills, changes in these programs are mainly administrative. Emphasis is on elementary and secondary education programs that serve children who are economically or educationally disadvantaged. The largest program, compensatory education (title I of the Elementary and Secondary Education Act of 1965), increases from $2.7 billion to $3.4 billion, including $400 million for targeting on inner-city and rural districts. Grants to states for the education of handicapped children increase to $800 million, 50 percent over the 1978 level. (Federal payments for providing all handicapped children with free, appropriate public education are authorized to reach nearly $4 billion a year by the early 1980s, but appropriations are not likely to reach that level.)

Education's largest pork barrel, impact aid (assistance to school districts "burdened" by the presence of federal installations), was slated for modest reform through legislative proposals that would eliminate the most egregiously undeserved payments. Congress has resisted any reform of this program in the past and there is little evidence that it will change its mind this year.

Congress must also decide whether to change the formula for allocating title I compensatory education dollars. The current procedure uses 1970 census data to determine the number and location of children in poverty. If more recent survey results were used, funds would shift from southern states to the industrial states of the Northeast and Midwest. The administration has not proposed using the newer data, but a strong case can be made for doing so.

Modest increases were initially proposed for higher education programs in the President's budget, but the pressure on Congress for middle-income relief in the form of tuition tax credits forced the administration in February to advance an alternative to increase direct student aid. If this proposal were enacted, budget authority for Office of Education student aid programs would rise from $3.8 billion in 1978 to $5.3 billion in 1979. Some of the increase would be offset by a fall in the cost of the GI bill program (the declining number of eligible veterans cuts estimated outlays to $2 billion in 1979, down from $3.5 billion in 1975). Education benefits to dependents of social security recipients continue to edge upward, however, and are budgeted at $1.5 billion.

Between 1967 and 1975, federal expenditures for basic research dropped by roughly 20 percent in real terms, but the 1979 budget continues President Ford's policy of reversing this trend. Since universities are the recipients of much of this money, federal policies toward scientific research are of particular importance to them. Federal support for research and development at colleges and universities is budgeted at $3.6 billion, up 8 percent from the previous year. The budget also requests $50 million to help colleges modify their buildings to provide access for physically handicapped people. Although this amount is small relative to potential conversion costs, it is evident that Washington intends to help pay the costs of social regulations.

Tax credits for tuition dominated education discussion in late 1977 and early 1978. More than 100 bills have been introduced in the Ninety-fifth Congress; the original proposals were limited to college education expenses, typically providing a maximum of $250 credit. Costs to the Treasury in forgone revenues are estimated at $1.4 billion if the credit is nonrefundable (limited to those who have at least $250 in federal tax liability) or $1.9 billion if payments are made to families with less than $250 tax liability. The administration opposes tax credits: they do not encourage additional investment in higher education, they are windfalls to those with children in college, and they are regressive, since a large share of the benefits would go to high-income families. An estimated 45 percent of benefits from a $250 nonrefundable credit would go to the 14 percent of the population with incomes over $25,000. Faced with the political need to advance an alternative, the administration made two proposals: an increase in basic opportunity grants of $1 billion, targeted primarily on families with incomes of $16,000 to $25,000; and interest subsidies for high-income families borrowing under the student loan program.

In February, the Senate Finance Committee approved a tuition tax credit program for private elementary and secondary schools as well as for higher education. Sponsored by Senators Robert Packwood and Daniel P. Moynihan, this decision would credit 50 percent of tuition up to a maximum of $500, at a cost estimated between $4 billion and $5 billion a year when fully implemented. Unlike the higher education credit, which would have little effect on decisions, this credit could be expected to alter the choice between public and private schools for significant numbers of parents. Proponents argue that this legislation would provide competition for public schools and enhance diversity and choice; opponents argue that it would contribute to further separation of public and private school enrollments along economic-class lines (a family must spend $1,000 to earn the $500 credit) and would undermine the national commitment to tax-supported public education. More than any other education budget issue, tax credits for private elementary and secondary school tuition involve fundamental social values.

In endorsing a department of education at the cabinet level, President Carter honors a campaign commitment but faces a political and organizational dilemma. Simply to elevate the Office of Education to cabinet status would serve little purpose except to mollify the politically active education organizations. Any department worth creating should include a number of education-related activities now scattered throughout the government. However, the political opposition to such reorganization is intense. This dilemma may explain why the administration is moving slowly in developing a specific proposal for the department.

Urban Policy

Recent population and economic developments have generated a steady shift of both jobs and households out of older central cities into surrounding suburbs, and away from the Northeast and Midwest toward the Sunbelt. As a result, over 60 percent of the nation's 153 largest cities have been losing population since 1970. People move because housing, environments, and work places in the suburbs and in the South and West are more attractive and more efficient than those in the old central cities of the Northeast and Midwest. Thus, the movement simultaneously improves the homes and environments of millions of households and leaves older cities with disproportionate shares of both low-income households and the high costs of caring for them. This burden created a demand for a national urban policy from big-city leaders.

To be effective, a national urban policy must be flexible enough to adapt to each of the nation's 281 metropolitan areas and many decisions must be made at local levels. The complexity of working out a truly comprehensive urban policy led the administration to focus its first policy statement on the most pressing problems: improving the lot of distressed people (the poor and unemployed in cities) and distressed cities (those with the most acute fiscal problems).

A crucial decision is what the underlying strategy should be, adjustment or revival. An adjustment strategy accepts the inevitability of falling population and helps alleviate only the most severe problems, providing temporary aid as services and municipal work forces are reduced and helping the unemployed move to better jobs. No federal funds would be invested as long-term capital, but states might be encouraged to help their cities cope with fiscal problems.

A revival strategy works to reverse population loss and to restore to declining cities their past significance. It calls for large, long-term investment in improvements and temporary subsidies to attract businesses and residents. Whether revival is a realistic strategy depends on whether the main cause of big-city decline is biased federal urban policies or whether it is a fundamental American preference for living in uncrowded areas. Since revival runs counter to this powerful trend, whatever its cause, suburban growth would need to be limited. But that poses a dilemma, because slowing overall suburban growth would injure the building industry and reduce housing choices. One possible way to resolve this dilemma is to apply strategy at the neighborhood level. That means encouraging the revival of many neighborhoods, both residential and commercial, while helping others to adjust to population losses.

In any case, the programs themselves will be administered by dozens of different agencies, with none dominant, and it is important that they coordinate. Federal agencies need to agree what programs to offer, and local agencies need to agree what programs to use. The first will require a strong interagency coordinating group attached to the presidential staff or to the Office of Management and Budget. The second is best left to each local government.

President Carter's urban policy can be measured by his 1979 budget requests and his later policy statement. Rough estimates of spending for all programs with urban orientation show that about $92 billion will go to central cities, about $67 billion for person-oriented programs (such as social security, welfare, unemployment assistance,

Medicare, Medicaid, and food stamps), and $25 billion for place-oriented programs (such as community development block grants, employment and training grants, transportation assistance, and construction and education aids). Outlays for all urban-oriented programs equal 18 percent of all 1979 federal outlays—or 24 percent of all nondefense outlays. Place-oriented federal spending for 1979 is equivalent to 40 percent of all central-city government expenditures. In fact, since federal funds in effect underwrite state aid to city governments, the federal government will pay for over 40 percent of central-city government activities in 1979—about as much as are funded by local revenues. Roughly 42 percent of 1979 place-oriented spending and 36 percent of all federal urban spending will go to the residents and governments of central cities, which contain about 29 percent of the total population.

In March 1978, President Carter announced the administration's national urban policy. The program would improve the administration of existing urban-oriented activities and add several new ones, including a national development bank, a labor-intensive public works program, and tax credits for hiring young workers or investing in central cities. The strategy is apparently revival, but the program offers no means of slowing suburban growth. Its overall cost (including forgone revenues) would be about $2.5 billion in 1979 and about $4.6 billion in 1980—not as high as the programs already in the 1979 budget. Making those work more effectively is actually more important than enacting new programs, and the President proposed a new interagency coordinating council for that purpose, but he did not specify the staff's powers or location within the government.

To be at all effective, the new urban policy must improve the efficiency of government urban actions. It is too early to tell whether the administration's effort to form a comprehensive policy will achieve even that modest goal.

Agriculture

The costs of agricultural commodity programs are of special significance to federal budget planning, because they can be very high, hard to predict, and quite unstable. In the 1960s and early 1970s, when commodity prices were low and production was high, federal program costs were also relatively high. They fell during 1974–76 as a result of a tight world food supply and high commodity prices. Recent substantial increases in U.S. and world grain production have significantly lowered commodity prices and raised the costs of federal price-support and income-support programs. The long-term outlook depends very much on whether or not the current surpluses persist.

The Food and Agriculture Act of 1977 was a response to a situation of oversupply and low prices. By directing income support payments to producers, the act not only provides producers a "fair" return for their labors but also ensures that U.S. commodities remain competitive in world markets. If production outpaces demand and food prices fall, the rise in direct payments to producers will substantially increase the costs of commodity programs. On the other hand, if demand exceeds supply and market prices rise, commodity program costs will decline.

One trade-off that the Food and Agriculture Act imposes is between high budget outlays with stable food prices and low budget costs with high food prices. Another trade-off is between high and low inflation rates, because rising food prices are a major component of consumer spending. The fact that many other components of the federal budget are adjusted for inflation makes the effects of agricultural budget policy far-reaching and complex.

In 1979, land set-aside programs for wheat and feedgrains may reduce both payments to producers and the operating costs of the Commodity Credit Corporation. The administration estimated in January that this would lead to a drop of $3 billion in the 1978 outlay figure. However, target-price payments for wheat are higher, price supports for soybeans continue at the same rate, the cost of dairy programs is up slightly, and costs of export credit, storage, and interest payments have declined very little. Therefore, though commodity program costs in 1979 should be lower than in 1978, they could be nearly a billion dollars higher than the official estimate.

It is impossible to estimate future commodity costs beyond 1979 with any precision. Crop production is as uncertain as weather and crop conditions. However, there are limits—dictated by commodity prices—within which program costs might fall. If market prices fall to the level of support prices (if, that is, weather is favorable and production large), budget expenditures will be at their maximum, reflecting increased target-price payments and increases in price-support levels. If, however, market prices rise to or above target prices following a period of poor crops and tight supplies, the cost of commodity programs would be minimal. For 1982, these budgetary extremes are estimated at $1.5 billion and $8.8 billion, a difference of $7.3 billion.

The maximum commodity program cost projected for 1982 would be associated with stable commodity prices, meaning that the prices of agricultural products would contribute to a reduction of the general rate of inflation. On the other hand, high agricultural prices—and minimum budgetary costs—could raise the general price level nearly 2 percent during the year in which the price rise occurred. These projections are, of course, extremes. Actual figures will probably be somewhere between them. Even so, the range is significant and emphasizes the degree to which the costs of commodity programs are unpredictable and uncontrollable.

The 1977 act provides the administration with considerable flexibility. If the administration emphasizes building reserves and keeping prices low, budget expenditures will be high in most years. On the other hand, if it supports farm prices by maintaining smaller reserves and withholding land from production, budget costs will be reduced but food prices will be higher. It remains to be seen whether the administration opts to use its legislative authority as a price-stabilization or as a price-support device.

Defense

The administration's 1979 defense budget represents both continuity and change: continuity, because the country's principal security interests and the now traditional means of protecting them have been reaffirmed· change, because the budget would cut some previously planned programs (notably Navy) and would hold constant some that had been scheduled for acceleration (most importantly those involving the strategic nuclear forces).

The budget request is $126 billion, above the 1978 budget by 1.8 percent, or $2.3 billion in constant 1979 dollars. At 5.1 percent of expected gross national product, it will be at the lowest relative level since 1950. Administration budget projections call for annual increases in real terms of 2.7 percent through 1983. At this rate of growth, outlays will fail to cover the projected Defense Department programs by about $24 billion, a discrepancy that will have to be reconciled by program reductions or larger budgets in fiscal years 1980–83.

The European orientation of general-purpose ground forces and land-based air forces will be further emphasized by the planned withdrawal of the Second Division from South Korea and by continuing programs to store—pre-position—Army equipment in Europe and to increase airlift capabilities. Under current plans, virtually all ground forces deployed overseas by the end of 1982 will go to Europe, and twenty-four air force squadrons equipped with the most advanced aircraft will be stationed in the European theater (nine will go to Asia). Spending on ground forces and land-based air forces in 1979 will rise by 30 percent in current dollars if the budget request is approved.

In contrast, the budget for general purpose—nonstrategic—naval forces will go up only slightly in current dollars and will go down in real terms, a reduction that will be accomplished by a cut in ship construction. Over the five-year period 1979–83, the shipbuilding program proposed in the previous administration's 1978 budget would be cut from $44 billion to $20 billion. At the same time, the Navy's structure, which is centered on and basically determined by the large aircraft carrier, is to be unchanged, even though the missions assigned to the carrier have come increasingly into question. The administration's building and modernization program would lead to a 1990 Navy with thirteen carriers, the same number as today, and a supporting cast of ships not greatly different from the present.

In 1977 the administration obtained congressional approval for the cancellation of the B-1 bomber, the savings from which have permitted a budget request for spending on strategic nuclear forces that is the same in current dollars as the 1977 request and is 11 percent less in real terms. Additional but much smaller savings would be realized from the proposed slowing of development of a new land-based intercontinental ballistic missile, the M-X. Further decisions about the nuclear deterrent force are to be made in later budgets.

The most controversial decision is likely to be on the M-X as a supplement and eventually a replacement for the 1,000 Minuteman intercontinental ballistic missiles now in place. The Soviet ICBM force has been substantially modernized; by the early 1980s it may be able to destroy Minuteman missiles in their silos in one massive attack. The M-X is potentially a much more powerful and more accurate missile than the Minuteman; one proposal is to put these missiles in covered trenches where they could be shuttled from point to point to minimize vulnerability. The costs of buying, siting, and operating 200 M-Xs for ten years is estimated at $20 billion to $30 billion in 1979 dollars. But many uncertainties and problems about the M-X remain. And possible alternatives, particularly an advanced submarine-launched missile and an air-launched cruise missile, are in prospect within the time period needed to deploy a new land-based missile in less vulnerable sites than those of the Minuteman.

Negotiations for strategic arms limitations are linked to decisions about the strategic nuclear forces. It appears unlikely, however, that even a successful SALT II will greatly influence strategic-force budgets for the next two or three years, since approved development or modernization programs will not be affected. On the other hand, failure of the SALT negotiations might set off a costly competition in building nuclear weapons in the early 1980s.

Performance and Prospects

In a little over a year, President Carter has proposed significant changes in a wide variety of federal programs: energy, social security, food stamps and welfare, employment and training, education, hospital cost control, urban policy, defense, and taxation. Judged solely on the basis of whether the administration has identified major issues and made difficult choices, its performance must be regarded as courageous. But few of the proposals have received congressional approval; some will be substantially modified and others will be completely rejected. On this basis, the performance is disappointing. Where the administration falls short is in carrying its initiatives through the legislative process—whether by overloading the congressional calendar or by misjudging the balance of political forces on major issues.

The record of the administration on the economic problems of the nation is mixed. Last year's economic stimulus program helped to prolong the economic expansion; employment, personal income, and corporate profits rose, and unemployment declined. The prospect is that these trends will continue in 1978 and 1979. But inflation is still a major problem. Consumer prices rose 6.5 percent in 1977 and they are likely to rise at least as much in 1978. The administration can be faulted for giving inflation control little emphasis in its various initiatives and for not dealing with the wage-price problem. But the blame must be shared by other groups: business, labor, farmers, and consumers. Inflation control requires everyone to modify their demands, but history indicates that political leaders find it difficult to persuade them of the need for constraints.

President Carter can achieve some, but not all, of his budget objectives by 1981. If he is able to keep Congress from adding to the overall budget, outlays will gradually decline to about 21 percent of the gross national product. Still, a balanced budget is feasible only if there is unusual growth of demand in the nonfederal sectors of the economy. If business fixed investment goes up and state and local surpluses and the deficit with the rest of the world are reduced, the economy can grow at the desired 4.75 percent annual rate, and the budget can be balanced. All these developments are not likely to occur at the same time or in the required degree, which means that some deficit—but much less than one of $60 billion—would be needed in 1981 to stimulate the economy.

The possible incompatibility of fiscal and monetary policy also risks cutting short economic expansion. The Federal Reserve's money growth targets may not be adequate to finance the 11 percent growth rates of gross national product envisioned by the administration for 1978 and 1979. If the result should be an increase in interest rates that triggers off disintermediation and a mortgage credit crunch, the current expansion would be in jeopardy.

For the longer run, the achievement of a balanced budget after full employment is reached will depend on the ability of the administration and Congress to restrain the growth of federal spending and to curb the public's appetite for tax cuts. Even if the ratio of federal spending to gross national product continues to decline after 1981, there will be little room for tax cuts in 1979–83 over the tax cut requested this year by the administration.

President Carter's decisionmaking process for the 1979 budget was a departure from past procedures. In recent years, the annual budget review has been the occasion for pitting new initiatives against one another and for searching for inefficiencies in existing programs. President Carter's 1979 budget shows little evidence of such a competition. No significant new proposals for economizing were put forward. Most of the major initiatives of the President's first fifteen months in office were developed independently of budget reviews. Although program development is divorced from the budget review, the outlays proposed will seriously impinge on the administration's future budget margins. Early in 1978, President Carter issued an order calling for a multiyear planning system to encompass all proposals developed in the executive branch. It remains to be seen whether this new process will integrate policy development in the administration and restore the discipline previously supplied in budget reviews.

CHAPTER TWO

The Budget and the Economy

ROBERT W. HARTMAN

THE DECISIONS underlying President Carter's proposed budget for 1979 were dominated by considerations of its effect on the economy. The economy was slowly recovering from the 1975 recession and no breakthrough for decelerating inflation was in sight. The budget and economic plan try to maintain economic recovery without boosting the economy so much that inflation is accelerated. This is to be accomplished primarily by stimulating the private sector through tax reduction and by curbing inflation through a voluntary response to federal guidance.

The programmatic emphases in the administration's 1979 budget proposals can best be described as a holding action. In 1977, the new administration was very active, proposing substantial revisions in President Ford's 1978 budget, most of which were accepted, and legislation for a major revision of social security, a new energy program, and welfare reform to take effect in 1981–82. But aside from a few small initiatives, the 1979 budget mainly continues the 1978 programs. There is no evidence that the administration plans to reset national priorities.

Economic Background

To formulate overall budget policy, the health of the economy must be assessed. For its budget policy for fiscal year 1979, the administra-

For helpful comments on drafts of this chapter, the author thanks William Beeman, Roger Brinner, Darwin Johnson, Joseph Minarik, Arthur Okun, and John Palmer. Research assistance was provided by James Altman.

tion had to make this assessment in the last part of calendar year 1977, just before submitting the 1979 budget. Therefore, the prospective state of the economy as it looked at the end of 1977 is reviewed here.

The levels of both unemployment and inflation were widely viewed as far from desirable. Although recovery from the deep 1975 recession was nearly three years old, the unemployment rate seemed stuck at about 7 percent, well above what most leaders regard as full employment. Inflation, aside from seasonal variations, seemed to have settled at about 6 percent a year, again a politically unacceptable rate. Moreover, most private economic forecasts at the end of 1977 predicted little relief. Without government action, the growth of real GNP in 1978 was expected to be about 4 percent, which would reduce unemployment by less than one-half of a percentage point. Built-in inflation for 1978 would be exacerbated by price-raising legislation, so the economy was expected to enter fiscal 1979 with inflation of at least 6 percent. Thus, while the administration could not credibly propose instant achievement of long-term employment and inflation goals, it was under increasing pressure to show that its program was at least pointing more surely in the right direction.

The right direction toward full employment implies a more rapid rate of economic growth than the 4 percent rate of late 1977. For example, to reach a 5 percent unemployment rate by 1981 requires that real GNP grow by almost 5 percent a year from 1978 to 1981. Many policy choices—both budgetary and others—are available to raise the economy's growth rate into this higher range. Which options to adopt depends in part on an examination of recent U.S. economic history.

Recent History of Aggregate Economic Activity

Table 2-1 puts the present state of the economy into historical perspective by showing a broad measure of the loss of real income when GNP is below its potential level.[1] This underutilization of re-

1. Potential GNP was defined by the Council of Economic Advisers in 1977 as the level of real GNP that would obtain if labor and capital were "fully employed." Full employment of capital was assumed to exist when the Commerce Department's capacity utilization index was 86 percent. Full employment of labor was assumed to correspond to an unemployment rate of 4.1 percent in 1960 rising gradually to 4.9 percent in 1977–78 as the composition of the labor force changed. See *Economic Report of the President, January 1977*, pp. 45–57, for a discussion of these estimates. President Carter's advisers have adopted this potential GNP series.

Table 2-1. Potential and Actual Gross National Product, Calendar Years 1960–77
Amounts in billions of 1972 dollars

Year	Potential GNP	Actual GNP	GNP gap		Full-employment unemployment rate (percent)
			Amount	As percent of potential GNP	
1960	771.9	736.8	35.1	4.5	4.1
1961	798.6	755.3	43.3	5.4	4.1
1962	826.4	799.1	27.3	3.3	4.1
1963	857.1	830.7	26.4	3.1	4.2
1964	890.3	874.4	15.9	1.8	4.3
1965	925.0	925.9	−0.9	−0.1	4.4
1966	960.8	981.0	−20.2	−2.1	4.5
1967	996.3	1,007.7	−11.4	−1.1	4.4
1968	1,031.7	1,051.8	−20.1	−1.9	4.4
1969	1,068.3	1,078.8	−10.5	−1.0	4.4
1970	1,106.2	1,075.3	30.9	2.8	4.5
1971	1,145.5	1,107.5	38.0	3.3	4.6
1972	1,186.1	1,171.1	15.0	1.3	4.7
1973	1,228.2	1,235.0	−6.8	−0.6	4.8
1974	1,271.7	1,217.8	53.9	4.2	4.8
1975	1,316.9	1,202.1	114.8	8.7	4.8
1976	1,363.6	1,274.7	88.9	6.5	4.9
1977	1,412.0	1,337.5	74.5	5.3	4.9

Sources: *Economic Report of the President, January 1978*, p. 84; *Survey of Current Business*, vol. 58 (February 1978), p. 2.

sources averaged about $30 billion in constant 1972 dollars (about 4 percent of potential output) in the early 1960s but was more than eliminated in the boom of the late 1960s. In the 1970s, the economy has been more unstable. Between 1970 and 1972, economic activity was about 2 percent below its full-employment level. In 1973, full employment was briefly restored. Then in 1974–75 came the worst economic recession of the postwar period, with the economy operating almost 9 percent below potential. By 1976 and 1977, the recovery had restored part of the gap between potential and actual output, but GNP was still more than 5 percent below full employment, and forecasts for 1978 indicated only limited improvement.

The major components of GNP for 1977 are shown in table 2-2. Consumption expenditures, which constitute nearly two-thirds of the total, represent the production of consumer goods such as food, shelter, and clothing. Investment expenditures, which account for

Table 2-2. Gross National Product, by Major Component, Calendar Year 1977

Component	Amount (billions of dollars)	Percent of total
Consumption	1,211.4	64.1
Investment	293.9	15.5
Residential	91.0	4.8
Other	202.9	10.7
Government expenditures on goods and services	394.9	20.9
Federal	145.5	7.7
State and local	249.5	13.2
Net exports	−10.1	−0.5
Exports	175.5	9.3
Imports	−185.6	−9.8
Total	1,890.1	100.0

Source: *Survey of Current Business*, vol. 58 (February 1978), p. 2. Figures are rounded.

about one-seventh of national output, consist of the construction of residences and business spending for plant, equipment, and inventory accumulation. Government expenditures on goods and services account for one-fifth of national output, with state-local government salaries and purchases considerably larger than those of the federal government. About 9 percent of output is devoted to exports of goods and services. Finally, since imports are included in the previous accounts (for example, Japanese automobiles bought by Americans are part of consumption) but are not part of U.S. output, they are subtracted to arrive at total GNP.

Thus the federal government directly purchases a very small part of the nation's output. Moreover, as is shown in table 2-3, only about one-third of federal expenditures are for goods and services. The federal government's fiscal program is transmitted to the nonfederal demand sectors largely through more indirect forms of expenditure such as transfer payments and grants to state and local governments and through federal taxes.

Federal Policy and Nonfederal Demand

INVESTMENT. Real expenditures for residential construction have shown the widest swings of any major component of GNP in recent years. From the last business cycle peak at the end of 1973, residential investment had fallen about one-third by early 1975. From that depressed base, the construction of homes grew sharply, con-

Table 2-3. Expenditures of the Federal Government, Calendar Year 1977

Item	Amount (billions of dollars)	Percent of total
Purchases of goods and services	145.5	34.4
National defense	94.3	22.3
Nondefense	51.2	12.1
Transfer payments	173.1	40.9
Grants-in-aid to state and local governments	67.6	16.0
Net interest paid	29.6	7.0
Other	7.7	1.8
Total	423.5	100.0

Source: *Survey of Current Business*, vol. 58 (February 1978), p. 6. Figures are rounded.

tributing to the economic recovery. By late 1977, housing starts were running at the high annual rate of 2 million; consequently, relatively little further impetus to aggregate demand could be expected. Most forecasts in late 1977 predicted that real residential construction would grow at less than a 3 percent annual rate over the 1978–79 period, as the number of units built dropped off slightly but the average value per unit continued to rise.

Although the federal government affects the construction of houses in many ways, monetary policy is probably the crucial variable. The principal risk to slow but steady growth in residential building is that mortgage funds will become too scarce or costly to sustain the market. In the past, such mortgage crunches have resulted from disintermediation. Simply put, disintermediation occurs when savers put their money directly into income-producing securities such as short-term government bonds or money-market mutual funds rather than into financial intermediaries such as savings and loan associations or mutual savings banks, which currently account for about two-thirds of mortgage commitments. By one measure, such switches have occurred in the past when interest rates on three-month Treasury bills exceeded ordinary passbook rates at savings institutions by over 1.5 percentage points. By late 1977, this difference was about 0.7 percentage point, and deposit inflows were weak. The response of the Federal Reserve System in 1978–79 to economic developments will be a major determinant of whether interest rates rise so much that inflows to savings institutions drop off sharply, forcing them to raise mortgage interest rates and limit commitments.

The other major component of investment is business fixed investment: the purchase of machinery, equipment, factories, trucks, and the like by business. This component had not recovered by the end of 1977 from the 1974–75 recession; real expenditures were still below the 1973 peak level. Weakness was particularly pronounced in business construction.

The disappointing recovery in business fixed investment has spawned a great many theories on why it is so weak. Some analysts contend that it is because of lower rates of profit or because the "quality" of profits has been eroded by accounting practices that greatly underestimate the cost of replacing depreciating capital. Looking at it another way, some economists contend that people with investable funds can always invest in paper representing old assets rather than in newly produced real capital. As long as paper—common stock—has low prices (high yields), the flow of funds into investment goods will be impeded. Other explanations name a lack of business confidence as the culprit: before investing in a factory that will last thirty years, businesses want some basis for believing that new federal environmental, fuel, tax, or wage-price provisions will not change the ground rules. Recent history also may have played a role. The last decade included a war, a presidential resignation, several devaluations of the dollar, business liquidity crises, growing competition from imports, record federal deficits, an oil embargo, and the deepest recession with the highest inflation rate that many business leaders have ever experienced. These traumatic events doubtless raised the rate of return that investors require to commit their money. Higher energy prices have also been implicated in the weak capital recovery. When producers choose among alternative production methods nowadays, capital-intensive processes look more expensive than in the past: vast buildings must be heated and illuminated and big machines use a lot of expensive power.

While these factors undoubtedly have slowed the recovery in business investment, a fundamental determinant of investment—the degree of capacity utilization—cannot be ignored. Businesses do not invest in output-expanding capacity unless existing capacity is reasonably close to being fully used regardless of other factors. The severity of the 1974–75 trough drove capacity utilization in manufacturing down from its 1973 level of about 88 percent to about 71 percent. By late 1977, it was back up to a rate of about 83 percent.

One interpretation of the outlook for the future, then, is that utilization rates by 1978–79 will be back in the range where a significant upturn in business fixed investment is a possibility—unlike the 1975–77 period, when it was impossible.

Federal policies can have a bearing on whether an investment upturn becomes a reality. Of overriding importance is that real GNP growth be strong enough to push up capacity utilization levels; such growth depends in part on overall federal fiscal and monetary policies.

Policies specific to the capital goods sector are, of course, also significant. For example, all else being the same, the federal corporate profits tax has a bearing on whether an investment will be undertaken; a lower profits tax rate raises the after-tax rate of return on plant and equipment, thereby making worthwhile some investments that would not otherwise be undertaken. Similarly, the investment tax credit, which allows firms to reduce their tax liability (up to a limit) by 10 percent of the investment in equipment (not structures) undertaken in a given year, has the same effect as would a cheaper price of capital goods—it increases the quantity bought. Finally, monetary policy affects the volume of business investment in several ways. Lower interest rates mean that firms can issue bonds with lower coupon rates. Similarly, lower interest rates tend to strengthen the market values of common stock. An easier money policy thus tends to reduce the costs of investment, whether financed through debt or equity (new stock issues), and to stimulate business investment. Even without an explicit attempt to ease credit, monetary policy may be an important adjunct to fiscal policy. As the economy expands under fiscal policy, interest rates, without an expanding money supply, would rise and discourage some investment.

EXPORTS. Although exports maintained their share of GNP early in the economic recovery, their growth slowed considerably in 1977; in real terms exports grew only 2.2 percent, less than half as fast as GNP.

America's share of world exports has been declining ever since the postwar recovery of the European and Japanese economies. In 1960, its exports accounted for 21 percent of world exports (excluding exports to the United States). By 1973, this fraction had fallen to 15.8 percent and, in 1977, it was running at 13.9 percent. Growth in U.S. exports over the years has been due to a rapid growth in international trade rather than to an improving U.S. competitive position.

The export performance of the United States depends in theory on the relative price of its exportable goods and on the growth of demand in foreign countries. In the last few years, these factors have undergone major changes.[2]

For manufactured items, U.S. export prices went down relative to world export prices between 1972–74 from a combination of exchange rate changes and relatively slower inflation in the United States than in competing countries. This advantage was wiped out by an appreciation of the dollar from early 1975 to early 1976, and this probably explains some of the weakness in U.S. exports in 1977. By 1977, however, relative prices once again began turning to the United States' advantage, which should aid export volume in the future.

The growth of national income of U.S. trading partners shows clearly what has been happening to U.S. exports in the current recovery. For example, in 1973, real income grew at between 5 and 6 percent in France and Germany, over 7 percent in Canada, and nearly 10 percent in Japan. In 1977, France and Germany experienced growth below 3 percent, Japan's real growth was 5 percent, and Canada (the main importer from the United States) grew slightly more than 2 percent. This sluggish recovery in the rest of the world has limited the growth of demand for U.S. exports, and it seems unlikely that exchange rate adjustments could fully compensate for continued slow growth abroad.

But continued sluggishness abroad is what forecasters were predicting for 1978. In late 1977, the Organisation for Economic Cooperation and Development expected Western European growth of no more than 2.5 percent for 1978; the outlook for Japan was 5 percent and for Canada, 3.75 percent. Under these circumstances, exports of American goods could give no real thrust to GNP (aside from some help from agricultural exports, which depend on foreign harvests).

Federal budget policy has little to contribute directly to export performance. Rather, the main vehicles for influencing export growth are reducing domestic inflation, encouraging economic stimulus abroad, and pressing for a reduction of barriers to the exports of the United States by some of its trading partners.

2. For an extended discussion of recent U.S. international trade, see Robert Z. Lawrence, "An Analysis of the 1977 U.S. Trade Deficit," *Brookings Papers on Economic Activity, 1:1978,* pp. 159–86.

STATE AND LOCAL GOVERNMENTS. Purchases of goods and services by state and local governments held up remarkably well as the economy sank between 1973 and 1975. But between mid-1975 and the beginning of 1977, there was virtually no real growth in state and local demand. As 1977 unfolded, however, state and local spending picked up sharply and was rising at a rate of nearly 5 percent by the end of the year. Most forecasts for this sector's demand in 1978–79 were quite bullish, with real growth expected to continue at 5 percent or more a year.

Between 1973 and 1977, state and local budgets underwent several unusual changes. Total receipts grew 52 percent over the four-year period, somewhat in excess of the growth in GNP of 45 percent. Receipts were swelled by rapid increases in grants-in-aid from the federal government, which grew 67 percent during the period. In 1977, these grants accounted for 23 percent of total receipts available to state and local governments (see table 2-4).

Expenditures of state and local governments grew by only 47 percent between 1973 and 1977. Spending was relatively strong for

Table 2-4. Receipts and Expenditures of State and Local Governments,
Calendar Years 1973–77

Amounts in billions of dollars

Item	1973	1974	1975	1976	1977	Percent change, 1973–77
Receipts	**193.5**	**210.4**	**235.7**	**264.7**	**294.5**	**52.2**
Federal grants-in-aid	40.6	43.9	54.6	61.0	67.6	66.5
All other	152.9	166.5	181.1	203.7	226.9	48.4
Expenditures	**180.5**	**202.8**	**229.8**	**246.2**	**265.2**	**46.9**
Purchases of goods and services	167.3	191.5	215.6	231.2	249.5	49.1
Compensation of employees	97.1	106.5	119.2	129.2	139.4	43.6
Structures	28.4	33.8	34.7	31.7	30.1[a]	6.0
Other[b]	41.8	51.2	61.7	70.3	80.0	91.4
Transfer payments	20.3	20.5	23.8	25.9	28.0	37.9
All other[c]	−7.1	−9.2	−9.6	−10.9	−12.2	71.8
Deficit (−) or surplus	**13.0**	**7.6**	**5.9**	**18.4**	**29.3**	**125.4**
Social insurance funds	8.9	10.5	12.1	14.5	15.5	74.2
Other	4.1	−2.9	−6.2	3.9	13.7	234.1

Source: *Survey of Current Business*, vol. 58 (February 1978), p. 6, and previous issues. Figures are rounded.
a. Unpublished Bureau of Economic Analysis estimate.
b. Purchases of durable and nondurable goods and of services (including Medicaid).
c. Net interest received and net earnings of government enterprises.

employee compensation and purchases of other goods and services (such as Medicaid vendor payments) but was dragged down by the slow growth of public construction. Transfer payments by state and local governments leveled off, and the excess of interest earned over interest paid grew rapidly.

The more rapid growth of receipts than of expenditures has caused an enormous rise in the budget surpluses of state and local governments. In 1977, an all-time record of some $29 billion in surplus accrued, more than twice the 1973 annual surplus. While much of this is attributable to the faster growth of premiums and earnings than of benefits to retirees in public-employee retirement systems,[3] most of the growth in the state-local surplus accrued in the accounts of general governments. In part, this general government surplus probably represents a desired rebuilding of financial assets whose growth was slowed in the recession, but some of it probably represents unexpected accumulation.[4]

These large general government surpluses will not automatically disappear in 1978–79. Federal grants-in-aid are projected to rise by 13 percent in 1978, and other sources of receipts, under current tax laws, will probably rise at nearly the same rate, especially at the state government level. Such increases could more than support ordinary increases in operating costs and trust fund surpluses and even a rapid expansion in public construction.

State and local governments will therefore have to choose in the coming years between allowing a large general government surplus to accumulate (which they seem unlikely to do once financial assets have been rebuilt) and more fully funding retirement trust funds (neither of which add to GNP demand) or lowering taxes. If taxes are lowered, the main impact will be on the growth of demand in the consumer sector of the economy.

Federal policy affects the state-local sector in several ways, most directly through grants-in-aid. Whether such grants have a substantial influence on state-local spending or result chiefly in reduced state-

3. But not fast enough to fund these programs fully. See Alicia Munnell and Ann Connolly, "Funding Government Pensions: State-Local, Civil Service and Military," in *Funding Pensions: Issues and Implications for Financial Markets* (Federal Reserve Bank of Boston, 1976).

4. See Edward M. Gramlich, "State and Local Budgets the Day after It Rained: Why Is the Surplus So High?" *Brookings Papers on Economic Activity, 1:1978*, pp. 191–214.

local taxes is a matter of some controversy. Some recent estimates suggest that a $100 increase in federal grants in the short run may only increase state-local spending by between $1 and $18 and reduce taxes by no more than $7.[5] This same analysis expects that over the long term the initial grant would result in $16 to $32 in increased state-local spending and $84 to $68 in reduced taxes.[6]

The other major effect of federal policy on state-local behavior is on the credit and monetary policy side of the ledger. Some state and local spending—especially for construction—is dependent on interest rates of state-local (municipal) bonds, which move with overall interest rates. In recent years, federal credit policies toward New York City, whose financial woes affected the ability of other governments to raise funds at reasonable rates, have also been of some importance.

PERSONAL CONSUMPTION. Fortunately, personal consumption, by far the largest component of demand for U.S. output, has maintained a fairly constant share of GNP for a long time; since 1960, it has never fallen below 60 percent of GNP in peacetime and it has never risen above 66 percent. This stability derives from two underlying relations that explain a lot about this source of demand.

Personal consumption is largely determined by the after-tax income received by individuals. The ratio of consumption to disposable personal income has hovered around 90 percent for two decades. Disposable personal income is essentially what consumers receive in their paychecks after net taxes and retained profits are deducted from the market value of goods and services produced (GNP). This income concept, in turn, has remained remarkably stable in relation to GNP over the last two decades, staying at around 70 percent of GNP.

Table 2-5 shows in greater detail the recent movements of the factors affecting consumption. Note particularly the 1976 and 1977 increase in the fraction of disposable income spent by consumers. By raising this fraction from about 90 percent in the early 1970s to over 92 percent, consumers gave a $20 billion boost to the economy during the recovery from the recession. A major question for the future is

---

5. This implies that in the short run $75 more than the federal grant may simply go into financial asset accumulation (such as states buying up the federal bonds issued to finance the grants!) or reduced state and local borrowing.
6. Gramlich, "State and Local Budgets the Day after It Rained," p. 202.

Table 2-5. Relation of Disposable Personal Income to GNP and Disposition of
Disposable Personal Income, Calendar Years 1973–77

Item	1973	1974	1975	1976	1977
	Billions of dollars				
Gross national product	1,306.6	1,412.9	1,528.8	1,706.4	1,890.1
Less:					
Gross business saving	140.3	137.9	179.2	206.6	226.3
Taxes	411.2	455.1	468.0	536.0	600.5
Plus:					
Government transfer payments	113.5	134.9	169.8	184.8	197.9
Other receipts and adjustments	33.1	29.8	32.9	37.2	48.1
Equals:					
Disposable personal income	901.7	984.6	1,084.4	1,185.8	1,309.2
	As percent of GNP				
Gross business saving	10.7	9.8	11.7	12.1	12.0
Taxes	31.5	32.2	30.6	31.4	31.8
Government transfer payments	8.7	9.5	11.1	10.8	10.5
Other receipts and adjustments	2.5	2.1	2.2	2.2	2.5
Disposable personal income	69.0	69.7	70.9	69.5	69.3
Addendum:					
Disposition of disposable personal income (percent)					
Consumption expenditures	89.8	90.4	90.4	92.2	92.5
Consumer interest payments and foreign transfers	2.4	2.4	2.2	2.2	2.4
Personal saving	7.8	7.3	7.4	5.6	5.1

Source: *Survey of Current Business*, vol. 58 (February 1978), pp. 2, 5–7, and previous issues. Figures are rounded.

whether this upswing in the propensity to spend for consumption is temporary.

Those who think consumption will return to lower levels in relation to disposable income believe that consumers were affected by special factors in 1976–77. One explanation is that consumers adjusted so slowly to the slower real income growth (and higher inflation) of recent years that they tried to maintain rapidly growing consumption levels and decreased personal saving. Also, 1976 and 1977 were exceptionally strong years for new automobile purchases. To the extent that buying new cars and saving are substitutes, for which there is some evidence, one would expect saving rates to rise when automobile buying slows down, as it may do in the near future if only because consumer installment debt had reached, by the end of 1977, its highest ratio to income since 1973. Finally, the quarterly pattern of personal saving in 1977 indicates that families may have paid their high fuel bills in the unusually cold winter with money they would normally save.

Most forecasts for 1978–79 show some increase in personal saving rates, though they are not back to the level of the early 1970s. In fact, consumption and saving have become increasingly difficult to forecast in the short run.[7]

The federal government affects consumption primarily through its tax and transfer payment policies. Transfer payments (over 85 percent of which are federal) now account for about 15 percent of disposable personal income and act as an important stabilizer of consumer spending in times of recession (table 2-5). The rapid growth of these transfers—especially for social security and Medicare, which account for more than half of all transfers—has helped stabilize personal income. In the 1970s, federal taxes as a percentage of GNP have been shrinking just enough to offset a growing rate of state-local taxes. This shrinkage would not have come about had the tax laws remained unchanged; federal taxes would have risen as a proportion of GNP because inflation and real growth pushed individuals into higher income tax brackets and because payroll tax rates and bases increased. Federal income taxes were reduced in 1975, 1976, and 1977 to hold down this automatic tendency for taxes to rise faster than GNP.

Monetary policy also influences consumer expenditures. For one thing some purchases of durables are related to house-buying, so the effect of credit policy on residential construction affects consumption as well. The terms of automobile loans also move with other credit market instruments. When monetary policy tightens, it becomes less

7. In the longer run, the outlook for saving is confounded by the changes that have taken place in the social security system. In legislation passed in 1972 and 1977, social security benefits were extended to cover a much larger fraction of income than previously, and they were indexed for inflation. Social security taxes were correspondingly increased. The question is how individuals' private saving behavior will respond to these changes. There is little doubt that providing for retirement is a major motive for personal saving. If people now regard their retirement income as being better provided for by social security, a significant drop in the personal saving rate can be expected, although this will occur gradually.

easy and more expensive to borrow money to buy a car. Tight money policy also depresses the stock market, reducing consumer wealth and discouraging consumption.

IMPORTS. A final factor affecting the demand for output is the volume of imports. All else being equal, a shift toward imported goods and services lessens the demand for domestic output and reduces GNP. Aside from petroleum, no such significant shift has taken place. Between 1973 and 1977, imports of nonpetroleum goods and of services remained a fairly constant fraction of GNP, although the ratio has grown since 1975 (see table 2-6).

Petroleum imports, however, rose sharply. Between 1973 and 1977, they went up by $37 billion—even more than the $16 billion shift in the net export of goods and services. A great deal of this change is of course due to the substantial increase in petroleum prices, but since 1975, the physical volume of oil imports has grown rapidly as a result of the combined effect of economic recovery in the United States, the absence of an effective energy conservation program, and declining domestic production of oil. Oil imports are likely to increase for the next five years, even if President Carter's

Table 2-6. Imports and Exports of Goods and Services, Calendar Years 1973–77
Billions of dollars

Item	1973	1974	1975	1976	1977	Change, 1973–77
Imports of goods and services	**94.4**	**131.9**	**126.9**	**155.1**	**184.7**	**90.3**
Merchandise	70.5	103.7	98.0	124.0	150.5	80.0
Petroleum	8.4	26.6	27.0	34.6	45.2	36.8
Nonpetroleum	62.1	77.1	71.0	89.4	105.2	43.1
Other	23.9	28.2	28.9	31.1	34.2	10.3
Exports of goods and services	**101.6**	**137.9**	**147.3**	**162.9**	**175.6**	**74.0**
Net exports	**7.1**	**6.0**	**20.4**	**7.8**	**−9.0**	**−16.1**
Addenda						
Imports as percent of GNP	7.1	9.4	8.3	9.0	9.8	2.7
Merchandise						
Petroleum	0.6	1.9	1.8	2.0	2.4	1.8
Nonpetroleum	4.7	5.5	4.6	5.2	5.6	0.9
Other	1.8	2.0	1.9	1.8	1.8	0.0

Sources: *Economic Report of the President, January 1978*, pp. 257, 368, 370; *Survey of Current Business*, vol. 58 (January 1978), pp. 1, 6. Figures are rounded.

energy program is enacted and despite increased oil production in Alaska. Thus the relatively high percentage of national income spent on imports is likely to continue.

The outlook for the immediate future, however, is a bit brighter. A number of special factors may have caused imports to grow unusually rapidly in 1976 and 1977. One was the enormous increase in the price of coffee and coffee substitutes resulting from a frost in Brazil and a war in Angola. These prices have begun to fall. There is also some evidence that petroleum imports in 1977 were above trend because of unusual weather. The cold winter of 1976–77 and low rainfall in the Northwest, which reduced hydroelectric power, spurred imports of oil. One estimate is that these special factors may have increased imports by over $6 billion in the first half of 1977.[8]

The reduction in the exchange value of the dollar should also contribute to lower imports, although the timing of this effect is uncertain. When the exchange value of the dollar declines, it takes some time for foreign firms to raise their dollar prices. Once the dollar prices go up, moreover, there is usually a lag before U.S. buyers respond to the change. (During this period, the dollar value of imports would actually rise.) Eventually, however, the volume of imports should turn down and under normal circumstances so should dollar values.

Federal fiscal policy influences imports indirectly through its effect on domestic inflation and incomes. Under a fixed exchange rate regime, monetary policy was thought to have a special role in offsetting disequilibrium in international payments. When imports exceeded exports, the institution of monetary restraint could help attract to the United States capital seeking a higher yield. But under free exchange rates, there is less consensus that monetary policy should abandon its domestic objectives for balance-of-payments reasons. In the present state of world trade, the proper policy for a trade-deficit country might be to shift the mix of monetary policy (toward restraint) and fiscal policy (toward ease), provided domestic goals are not thereby thwarted. However, for the United States, the need to supply incentives for domestic business investment renders this prescription inappropriate.

SUMMARY. One way of looking at the relation of nonfederal sources of demand to the federal sector is to think of the national

8. Lawrence, "An Analysis of the 1977 U.S. Trade Deficit," p. 182.

economy as a huge plumbing system in which the flow of national product is reduced by drains from the system and enlarged by injections into the system. The nonfederal drains discussed in this chapter can be summarized as:

—personal saving and the surplus of social insurance trust funds of state and local governments;[9]

—business saving, mainly the retained earnings and depreciation allowances of firms;

—operating surpluses of state-local governments; and

—imports.

These drains are shown in table 2-7 for selected full-employment years and for 1977.

The principal nonfederal injections into the flow of national production are domestic investment and exports. At any level of economic activity the federal budget deficit (surplus) must offset any excess (inadequacy) of drains in relation to injections. Thus, in the peak years of 1955–56, a federal surplus was needed at high employment to offset the excess of nonfederal injections over drains. In the 1960s, the prosperity period showed a balance between drains and injections allowing the federal budget to show a balance at full employment. By 1972–73, the nonfederal sectors were saving more than they were investing at full employment, leading to a small federal deficit at full employment.[10]

A major problem for the administration, therefore, was to determine what the balance of drains and injections will be as the economy moves closer to full employment over the next few years. Although there is reason to believe that the drain from personal saving will rise in proportion to GNP from the low levels of 1977, state-local operating surpluses and imports were atypically high in 1977; a small

9. These have been grouped together because they play a similar role in the economy. When a person is employed in the private sector, surpluses that accumulate in a company-sponsored pension program are counted as "personal saving" in the national income accounts. When, however, the person is employed—say, as a teacher—by a state or local government that participates in a public pension program, any surpluses in those funds are counted as a component of the state-local sector's surplus. With the state-local government work force growing more rapidly than that in the private sector for the last twenty years (state-local employees accounted for 9.3 percent of employees on nonfarm payrolls in 1955 and 15.2 percent in 1977), a spurious reduction in the personal saving rate will appear in the national income accounts. Adding together personal savings and state-local social insurance surplus removes this bias.

10. There is reason to believe that fiscal (and monetary) policy was too stimulative in 1972–73, resulting in excessive demand for goods and services.

Table 2-7. Drains from and Injections into the National Economy as a Percentage of
GNP, Selected Calendar Years, 1955-77[a]

Item	1955-56	1965-66	1972-73	1977
Drains				
Personal saving plus state-local social insurance fund surplus	4.55	4.91	5.49	4.37
Business saving[b]	11.95	12.48	11.13	12.03
State and local other funds surplus[c]	−0.61	−0.48	0.40	0.72
Imports[d]	5.17	5.30	7.43	10.34
Total	21.06	22.20	24.48	27.48
Injections				
Domestic investment[e]	17.00	16.41	16.46	15.55
Exports[f]	5.34	5.71	7.02	9.29
Federal deficit	−1.28	0.08	1.00	2.64
Total	21.06	22.20	24.48	27.48

Sources: *Economic Report of the President, January 1978*, pp. 257, 266–67, 343; Bureau of Economic Analysis, *The National Income and Product Accounts of the United States, 1929–74 Statistical Tables* (GPO, 1977), pp. 108–09; *Survey of Current Business*, vol. 57 (July 1977), p. 32; *Survey of Current Business*, vol. 58 (February 1978), pp. 2, 6–7. Figures are rounded.
a. Average of percentages for each year.
b. Gross retained earnings plus statistical discrepancy.
c. State-local surplus in the national income and product accounts, excluding surplus of social insurance funds.
d. Imports of goods and services plus net transfers and interest paid to foreigners.
e. Residential construction, business fixed investment, and inventory investment.
f. Includes net capital grants of $0.7 billion received by the United States in 1972.

reduction in these drains, relative to GNP, could be expected in 1978 and 1979. On balance, then, the unusually high ratio of drains to GNP of 1977 were forecast to remain about the same for the next few years.

The outlook for nonfederal injections relative to GNP was not very optimistic. Residential construction, already at a peak level in 1977, would do well to maintain its share of GNP. Exports, which depend heavily on real economic growth among U.S. trading partners, seemed to have little near-term potential for injecting demand into the economy. Business investment, though showing signs of life, gave little evidence of a dramatic upturn.

It thus seemed unwise to allow the historically high federal deficit of 1977—about 2.6 percent of GNP—to fall.[11] If this deficit, which

11. Naturally, if exports or domestic investment were to rise, there would be an automatic reduction in the federal deficit as higher incomes drove up federal receipts. The presentation of the federal deficit as an offset to nonfederal drains in table 2-7 does not distinguish between such a passive adjustment in the deficit and a deliberate attempt to use the deficit to maintain or enlarge aggregate demand. This distinction is made in the discussion of fiscal policy later in this chapter.

seemed necessary to maintain real national product growth at 5 percent in 1977, were to be reduced without any offsetting increases in domestic investment or exports, the rate of output growth would be reduced, making the ascent to full employment that much longer and less certain.

Inflation

Since the late 1960s, the United States (and most of the rest of the world) has experienced a persistent rise in the general price level. The explanation for inflation in the late 1960s is the classic case of excessive demand. As Vietnam War expenditures expanded on top of an economy already fully employed, prices were driven up.

In the 1970s, the causes of inflation have become much more complex. In 1971–72 a wage-price freeze followed by a period of milder controls kept inflation under 4 percent a year. But in 1973–74, nearly everything went wrong. Early in the period fiscal and monetary policy were too stimulative. Controls were removed just as the economy reached full employment. Devaluation of the dollar and a simultaneous economic expansion of the world's major economies meant pressure on domestic capacity and on industrial commodity prices. Shrinking grain reserves and a series of poor harvests caused food prices to surge. Finally, the Organization of Petroleum Exporting Countries (OPEC) imposed a steep rise in petroleum prices in late 1973 that soon spread to all other energy sources.

These shocks combined to produce double-digit inflation—consumer prices rose 12 percent in 1974, for example—and the economy has not fully recovered from the experience. The initiating round of inflation was so severe that since 1975 wages and prices have been trying to recover from losses and imbalances generated in earlier periods. Some large wage increases were granted when prices were expanding rapidly. These increases subsequently spread to other labor markets as workers tried to maintain their relative wage positions. Businesses found that they were able to pass through cost increases, and they began to believe that inflation was a permanent condition. This encouraged further price rises and a lenient attitude toward wage increases.

The upshot is that inflation has been stuck at an underlying rate of about 6 percent since 1975 (table 2-8). Variations in the prices of energy and especially of food have made consumer prices rise

Table 2-8. Annual Rates of Change in Selected Components of the Consumer Price Index and Employment Costs, Calendar Years 1960–77

Item	1960–65	1965–70	1970–75	1976	1977
Consumer prices					
All items	1.3	4.5	6.9	4.8	6.8
Food	1.5	3.7	9.4	0.6	8.0
Energy	0.4	2.5	10.9	6.9	7.2
All items less food and energy	1.4	5.0	5.7	6.1	6.4
Private nonfarm business					
Compensation per hour	4.0	6.5	7.9	9.2	8.6
Productivity	4.0	1.2	1.4	3.2	2.7
Unit labor costs	0.0	5.2	6.4	5.8	5.7

Source: *Economic Report of the President, January 1978*, p. 155.

above or below this rate, but the remainder of the items in the consumers' market basket seem to have adjusted to a steady upward trend of about 6 percent.

This inflation has continued despite prolonged and severe weakness in the economy. The classic medicine for inflation—a planned reduction in aggregate demand—was administered in 1974–75, but inflation continued at its high underlying rate. The drop from double-digit rates after 1974 was caused primarily by the moderation of the special factors that had driven up the prices of food, other commodities, and energy.

That the recession and the generally underemployed economy since 1975 seem to have had little effect on inflation can be seen in the course of wages. Hourly compensation rose for three years at an average rate of 8–9 percent. Even though productivity improved rapidly from its 1975 level—as it usually does in the early stages of a recovery—unit labor costs (labor cost per unit of output) rose steadily at about 6 percent a year (table 2-8). This is not what one would expect in an economy with idle capacity and high unemployment: clearly something has happened to entrench inflation in the economy.

As the Carter administration considered economic policy for 1978–79, the inflation outlook was thus not good. First, there was no evidence of deceleration in wage increases. The prospect of a further slowdown in the growth of productivity, which is likely as the recovery enters its fourth year, implies that there will be pressure on unit labor costs to rise above 6 percent a year. Second, costs may begin to accelerate even more than in past periods when full employment was almost achieved because of the recent very low rates of investment, much of which went for pollution control and other purposes unrelated to output expansion. Although capacity utilization was quite low as 1978 began and ample capacity exists in other industrialized countries, it is possible that the United States will reach full employment of capital before reaching full employment of labor unless private investment turns up sharply in the next two years.[12] Third, the federal government has instituted several policies, which will come into effect in 1978–79, that will add inflationary points to the underlying rate. Among these are significant increases in social security payroll taxes (small in 1978, large in 1979); an increased minimum wage (from $2.30 an hour to $2.65 in 1978 to $2.90 in 1979); a new agriculture program; and the proposed energy taxes. The Council of Economic Advisers estimates that the payroll tax and minimum wage increase alone will add 1 percent to labor costs in the private sector in 1978, and the energy tax proposals would add another 0.2 percent.[13] Fourth, the significant decline of the exchange value of the dollar during 1977 and early 1978 could eventually add another 0.75 percentage point to inflation by driving up the dollar price of U.S. imports and import-competing goods.[14]

Since the administration was committed to a policy of continued growth of aggregate demand, it explicitly rejected the traditional cure of starving the economy to curb inflation. This meant that the only means of restraining inflation were nonmacroeconomic. These include avoidance of government actions that raise private sector costs and a variety of options, usually called "incomes policy," that range from strict wage-price controls to voluntary processes for giving government a role in wage-price setting.

Fiscal Policy in the President's Budget

The fiscal policy implied by the Carter administration's 1979 budget is designed with two apparent goals in mind: first, to offset the

12. For a discussion of the relation between the capacity utilization of capital and full employment of labor, see *Economic Report of the President, January 1978*, pp. 157–61. For a discussion of pollution control and related items and their impact on productivity, see Edward F. Denison, "Effects of Selected Changes in the Institutional and Human Environment Upon Output Per Unit of Input," *Survey of Current Business*, vol. 58 (January 1978), pp. 21–44.

13. *Economic Report of the President, January 1978*, p. 80.

14. The estimate is that of William Miller, Chairman, Federal Reserve Board, reported in *New York Times*, March 19, 1978.

tendency toward growing fiscal restraint under existing tax and spending programs; and second, to begin a long-term program of reducing the relative size of the federal budget.

The Fiscal Policy Proposals

In discussing the impact of fiscal policy on the economy, attention is often paid to the budget deficit or surplus. However, the budget deficit incorporates two quite different aspects of federal fiscal activities: first, the automatic response of the budget (especially receipts) to swings in economic activity, and second, discretionary actions undertaken to affect the economy. To focus on the second of these, economists often rely on a measure called the full-employment surplus, which is the difference between receipts and expenditures of the federal government measured at full-employment GNP.[15] Changes in the full-employment surplus can measure the federal budget's effects on the economy undistorted by the budget's response to the economy. An increase in the full-employment surplus indicates that the federal budget is becoming more restrictive; a decline in the full-employment surplus (or a larger full-employment deficit) signifies increasing stimulation of the economy by the federal government. An unchanged full-employment surplus means that fiscal policy is, in effect, neutral—it is neither adding to nor restraining the rate of growth implicit in the nonfederal sector.

Historically, the full-employment surplus was positive (receipts exceeded outlays at full employment) in the 1950s and early 1960s. But since 1965, the full-employment budget has been in surplus in only two years (1969 and 1974), and the full-employment deficit averaged about $7 billion (0.7 percent of full-employment GNP) in the decade 1966–75.[16] In relation to 1978 estimates of full-employment GNP, this average would translate into a full-employment deficit of about $15 billion.

Table 2-9 summarizes the course of the full-employment surplus over the six half-years that make up fiscal years 1977–79. The first thing to note is that the federal budget swung sharply toward stimulus between the first half of fiscal 1977 and the first half of 1978. This

15. The concept of full-employment GNP is the same as potential GNP (see table 2-1). In 1977–79, this corresponds to the GNP that would be produced if the unemployment rate were 4.9 percent.
16. The full-employment budget data on which this discussion is based are from *Economic Report of the President, January 1978*, p. 55, and unpublished data from the Council of Economic Advisers.

Table 2-9. Full-Employment Surplus under Current Law and as Proposed by the Administration, Fiscal Years 1977–79[a]

Billions of dollars

Item	Fiscal year[b]					
	1977:I	1977:II	1978:I	1978:II	1979:I	1979:II
Full-employment surplus under current law[c]	−9.1	−19.1	−27.2	−15.4	−3.4	12.5
Effect of administration proposals[d]	...	...	−1.6	−5.5	−31.0	−33.4
Spending initiatives	...	...	...	−2.6	−5.0	−5.2
Energy proposals	...	...	−0.2	−0.2	−1.5	−0.4
Tax simplification and reform	...	...	−1.4	−2.7	−22.5	−25.5
Excise tax and unemployment tax changes	...	...	0.0	0.0	−2.0	−2.3
Full-employment surplus as proposed	−9.1	−19.1	−28.8	−20.9	−34.4	−20.9

Sources: Unpublished quarterly data from the Council of Economic Advisers; *Survey of Current Business*, vol. 58 (February 1978), pp. 25–27; and author's estimates.

a. National income accounts basis; semiannually at seasonally adjusted annual rates.

b. The Roman numerals after the year designate the first and second halves of the year; for example, 1977:I stands for the first six months of fiscal 1977, or October 1, 1976, to March 31, 1977.

c. The full-employment surplus is the difference between full-employment receipts and expenditures. Full-employment receipts under current law means receipts that would accrue at full employment, under the tax laws existing on January 1, 1978, with temporary provisions extended. Full-employment expenditures are equivalent to those that would prevail at full employment under the Office of Management and Budget's concept of a current services budget.

d. Estimated for actual gross national product.

$18 billion swing was attributable to rapid expenditure growth and a small income tax cut in calendar 1977 that more than offset growing income taxes and a payroll tax increase in early 1978.[17]

Under current tax and spending laws, however, this fiscal position of the government would more than reverse itself between 1978:I and 1979:II. The underlying fiscal policy would move from a $27 billion full-employment deficit in 1978:I to a $13 billion full-employment surplus eighteen months later. The reason for this growing "fiscal drag" is that even at a continuous full-employment level (that is, trend real economic growth of 3.5 percent) tax receipts rise proportionately much more than expenditures under current law; receipts rise fast generally because income tax rates on increments to income are greater than the tax rate on previous dollars of income

17. This discussion does not take into account revisions in the budget for a spending "shortfall." See the final section of this chapter and appendix A.

and, in this case, because payroll taxes are scheduled to rise much faster than income beginning in 1979.

The administration's long-term fiscal plan may be readily discerned by looking at the changes in current law it proposes and their effect on the full-employment surplus. The salient fact is that the proposed full-employment deficit for the last half of fiscal 1979 ($21 billion) is almost the same as the full-employment deficit two years earlier ($19 billion in 1977:II). In effect, the administration's fiscal plan for the 1977–79 period as a whole can best be characterized as one of neither restraint nor stimulus compared to policies whose effect was being felt at the time the budget was being drawn up. The idea, in other words, is to end the period with a fiscal policy no more stimulative than at the start, making it possible to shift toward restraint as full employment is reached in the near future. This broad fiscal prescription is a passive one, designed to offset only the federal government's own tendency to slow the economy and to leave economic growth to the forces in the nonfederal sectors of the economy.

The proposed fiscal policy is slightly more stimulative than that of the past decade. The full-employment deficit for 1978 and 1979 averages about 1.1 percent of full-employment GNP. The administration's justification for this is twofold. First, the unemployment rate is well above the average for the past decade. Second, nonfederal drains on the economy—especially the international trade deficit and state-local government surpluses—are high, necessitating an unusually high injection of demand by the federal government until these drains are reversed or private investment picks up steam.

For 1978 and 1979, the administration's fiscal policy mostly reflects a transition from the 1977 stimulus program to its new proposals. In the first half of 1978, spending from the stimulus program enacted in 1977 peaks. For the second half of 1978, the administration seems willing to allow a slight tightening of fiscal policy. In the first half of fiscal 1979, there is a sharp increase in the full-employment deficit as the proposed tax cuts go into effect.[18] By the second half of 1979, the underlying fiscal drag restores fiscal policy to where it was two years earlier. Thus, the essence of the administration's

18. Not too much should be made of semiannual swings in fiscal policy because it takes time for the nonfederal sector to adjust. For example, although the full effect of the cut in tax liabilities is shown in the first half of 1979, it will probably influence spending before that and the full effect on spenders will not be complete for some time beyond 1979:I.

short-run plan is the expectation that nonfederal demand will strengthen somewhat over the course of 1978 so that it will supplant the slight reduction in fiscal stimulus. For fiscal 1979, the administration's bet is that real growth can be maintained at the previous year's level by adopting a policy of neutralizing the built-in fiscal drag.

Composition of the Fiscal Program

The decision to aim for an offset to fiscal drag in fiscal 1979 meant that the administration had to choose among alternative tax cuts or spending initiatives amounting to about $30 billion.[19]

Table 2-10 shows that the administration proposed most of the offsetting on the tax side—about three-quarters of the total new fiscal action consists of tax cuts. Spending programs were boosted less than 2 percent above the current services level of fiscal 1979.

Table 2-10. Outlays and Receipts in the Administration's Proposed Budget, Fiscal Years 1977–79[a]

Billions of dollars

			1979		
Item	1977	1978	Current services	Proposed	Difference
Outlays	401.9	462.2	492.4	500.2	7.8
Receipts	356.9	400.4	463.8[b]	439.6	−24.3
Deficit	45.0	61.8	28.6[b]	60.6	32.0

Source: *The Budget of the United States Government, Fiscal Year 1979*, p. 11; *Special Analyses, Budget of the United States Government, Fiscal Year 1979*, p. 19. Figures are rounded.

a. This table and subsequent ones in this chapter are on a unified budget basis. This differs from the national income and product accounts basis used in previous tables primarily by including financial transactions in the outlay estimates and by estimating receipts on a cash, rather than a liability, basis. See *Special Analyses, Budget of the United States Government, Fiscal Year 1979*, pp. 45–68, for a description of these differences.

b. These are the receipts and deficit that would accrue if the economy were to reach the levels forecast by the administration and if tax laws of 1978, including temporary provisions, were extended.

Why tax cuts to offset fiscal drag? There seem to be several reasons. One of these is President Carter's promise to limit the size of the federal government. This has led to an emphasis in the long-range fiscal plan on the goal of limiting outlays to 21 percent of GNP by fiscal 1981. In 1977, outlays were 21.9 percent of GNP. With the sharp increases in President Carter's stimulus program (and signifi-

19. Yet another alternative would have been a planned easing of monetary policy, accompanied by less fiscal stimulus. Whatever might have been the merits of such an approach, it had an insuperable shortcoming. The weakness of the U.S. balance-of-payments position made it incautious to lower interest rates—such an action drives funds out of the United States and its international accounts suffer.

cant inherited growth in national defense spending), the ratio in 197
rises to 22.6 percent. By limiting spending increases in 1979, th
administration is able to project federal spending of 22.0 percent o
GNP in 1979, which is a step in the intended direction.[20]

Also discouraging the use of federal spending to offset drag i
the apparent political difficulty of instituting truly temporary spend
ing programs. The administration's economic stimulus program o
1977, for example, featured a sharp rise in the number of publi
service employment slots. This was defended both within the govern
ment and publicly as a temporary measure that would phase down a:
the economy recovered. In the 1979 budget, proposed for a perioc
in which unemployment is expected to be about 1.5 percentage point:
below its level at the time temporary public service employment wa:
first boosted, the administration has proposed no phasing down ai
all.[21] This lesson must have sunk in: most spending programs, regard·
less of their special nature at inception, are hard to pare. This implie:
that, although a case could be made for additional temporary spend·
ing in fiscal 1979, acceptance of the case by the administration would
mean removing spending items from its long-run agenda because the
temporary programs would persist. As pointed out in chapter 10,
the agenda for spending programs is already quite full (especially
if 21 percent of GNP in fiscal 1981 is regarded as a rigid commitment), and the administration would be squeezing out preferred
spending programs if it accepted "permanent temporary" ones.

A third argument for emphasizing tax cuts is that they can be
carried out quickly. As indicated in table 2-9, fiscal drag begins during the second half of fiscal 1978 and then becomes sharply restrictive in the first half of fiscal 1979 (in large part because of an increase
in payroll taxes on January 1, 1979). Most spending stimulus programs could not be put into effect quickly enough to offset forces of
such magnitude. The local public works program, as an example of
federally assisted stimulus, would not peak until about a year and a
half after federal allocations were made, which would be about one
year too late.[22] A tax cut, on the other hand, can be put into effect
quickly. During the administration's deliberations over tax cuts, the

20. See chapter 10 for whether the 1981 goal is likely to be reached.
21. New proposals under the Comprehensive Employment and Training Act
would bring the level down in later years. See chapter 3.
22. The public service employment program, however, was carried out quite
rapidly, as promised. See chapter 3.

newspapers reported that it would seek an effective date of July 1, 1978, for its program. However, the congressional budget process would have made such an early start difficult, so the effective date for individual income tax cuts was pushed ahead to October 1.[23] The administration clearly hopes that enactment of its tax legislation in the summer of 1978 will begin to affect spending right away, even if the effective date is October. While that hope may be ambitious, it is almost certain that tax changes will affect spending before any feasible expenditure program could.

Finally, and probably most important for calculating the politics of any fiscal proposal, were the facts that a combination of factors has been raising personal taxes and that members of Congress, many up for reelection in 1978, have been receiving complaints from constituents about the need for tax relief. The most visible tax change, of course, is the sharp rise in the social security tax slated for 1979. Fashioning an income tax cut that is progressive and at the same time offsets the social security tax increase for most workers necessitates a personal tax cut on the order of the $18 billion reduction proposed by President Carter.[24]

Although there is economic sense in trying to offset fiscal drag in general, there is little economic sense in offsetting the increase in one tax by a decrease in another tax. People's real incomes are also affected by many things besides the payroll tax hike, such as inflation (which raises taxes disproportionately), expanding federal grant programs (some of the grants-in-aid to state governments are resulting in tax cuts by states), growing transfer programs (the large increase in student aid discussed in chapter 4 is initially the equivalent of reduced tuition for a large segment of the population), new excise taxes (such as those proposed for energy), and so on. However, from a political point of view, there is obvious appeal in emphasizing direct comparisons showing that income tax gains offset payroll tax losses.

TAX CHANGES. The tax cuts proposed by the administration amount to about 5 percent of total federal taxes (table 2-11). The program has three principal components.

---

23. Under the congressional budget process the second concurrent resolution for fiscal 1978 set a floor on tax receipts of $397 billion. Any tax legislation that would reduce receipts below that level in 1978 requires passage of a third concurrent resolution, just as President Carter's 1977 stimulus package did. Members of Congress seem reluctant to consider third concurrent resolutions every year.

24. See chapter 5 for a full discussion of the incidence of recent tax changes.

Table 2-11. The Administration's Tax Reduction Program, Fiscal Years 1978-79
Amounts in billions of dollars

| Tax | 1978 | 1979 | | Difference between 1979 proposal and current services | |
		Current services	Proposed[a]	Amount[a]	Percent
Individual income	178.8	214.0	195.7	−18.3	−8.6
Corporation income	58.9	68.8	63.7	−5.1	−7.4
Excise	20.2	18.7	17.6	−1.1	−5.9
Social insurance	124.1	142.5	141.9	−0.6	−0.4
Other	18.3	19.8	19.7	−0.2	−1.0
Total	400.4	463.8	438.6	−25.3	−5.5
Addenda					
Tax reduction[b]					
Individual				−22.5	−10.5
Corporation				−6.3	−9.2
Tax reform[b]					
Individual				4.2	2.0
Corporation				1.1	1.6

Sources: *The Budget of the United States Government, Fiscal Year 1979*, p. 49; *Special Analyses, Budget of the United States Government, Fiscal Year 1979*, pp. 11, 19; Congressional Budget Office, *An Analysis of the President's Budgetary Proposals for Fiscal Year 1979* (CBO, 1978), p. 12. Figures are rounded.
    a. Excludes energy tax proposals, which would lower individual income taxes by $5.6 billion and corporation income taxes by $1.2 billion, and raise excise taxes by $7.9 billion, for a net tax increase of $1.1 billion.
    b. Excludes energy tax, excise tax, and social insurance tax proposals.

Individual incomes taxes are reduced by about 9 percent in fiscal 1979 by means of a cut of about 11 percent in tax rates and a revenue gain of about 2 percent from a reform package. The cuts are the result of replacing personal exemptions with a tax credit of $240 per person and a reduction in the marginal tax rate for each income bracket from 14–70 percent to 12–68 percent. Most of the revenue increases in the reform package derive from the elimination of the deductibility of state sales taxes and gasoline taxes and a tightening of the rules for deducting medical and casualty expenses.

As noted in chapter 5, where the tax changes are discussed in greater detail, these tax reductions are heavily tilted toward taxpayers with incomes under $30,000. Since these consumers are normally ones who spend a large fraction of the income they receive, they might be expected to consume more after the tax reduction.

Corporation income taxes are cut by 7.4 percent. (But because the proposed changes are phased in, this fraction rises to 9 percent in 1980.) The largest reduction by far is accomplished through a cut in the corporation tax rate from 48 percent to 45 percent (with corresponding reductions in the rates on profits of less than $50,000) effective in October 1978. Furthermore, the 10 percent investment tax credit would be extended to cover new structures, and the maximum credit available to a corporation would be increased so that it could offset up to 90 percent of the tax liability otherwise owed. These reductions are partly offset by proposed business tax reforms (table 2-11). The most important of these are limitations on the deductibility of corporate yachts, business meals, and other entertainment expenses and a phasing out of the deferral of tax on export earnings and on profits from abroad. While the extension of the investment tax credit to structures should strengthen this particularly weak component of investment, the corporate rate cut is probably not as effective an investment stimulant as other business tax changes (mainly those allowing more liberal treatment of depreciation).

The administration proposes a small reduction in two other taxes. Repealing the telephone excise tax and reducing the payroll tax on unemployment insurance is a token gesture toward reducing government taxes that feed directly into private sector costs. As the combined revenue loss is $1.6 billion in a $2 trillion economy, such a measure is a droplet in a sea of other changes.

SPENDING CHANGES. The proposed overall spending increase for fiscal 1979 over 1978 amounts to about $40 billion. Only $7.8 billion of this represents an increase from the 1979 level of current services. Most of the increase in spending, in other words, results from more or less automatic increases in entitlement payments (such as social security, federal employee retirement, Medicare, and Medicaid), in interest on the federal debt, in annual pay raises for federal workers, and in military procurement spending as a result of past increases in the defense budget (see table 2-12).

The $7.8 billion increase above current services represents only about 1.5 percent of the budget. When the budget was introduced, there were only three domestic initiatives listed that involved substantial expenditures in fiscal 1979.

First, the President's energy proposal contained two large spending items. One was the accelerated development of a strategic petroleum reserve, scheduled to reach 1 billion barrels by 1985. The other was

Table 2-12. Composition of Changes in Outlays from Fiscal Year 1978 to
Fiscal Year 1979

Billions of dollars

Item	Amount
Outlays, fiscal year 1978	462.2
Increases mandated under current law	30.2
Social security	10.6
Medicare and Medicaid	5.5
Pay and retirement for federal employees	5.6
Defense (excluding pay and retirement)	5.9
Net interest	4.4
Farm price supports	−3.7
All other	1.9
Current services outlays, fiscal year 1979	492.4
Initiatives of the President	7.8
Energy programs	3.4
Education, training, employment, and social services	1.0
Defense	1.0
Allowance for contingencies	1.7
All other increases	2.5
Hospital cost increase limitations	−0.7
Social security changes	−0.6
All other reductions	−0.5
Outlays proposed by the President, fiscal year 1979	500.2

Sources: *The Budget of the United States Government, Fiscal Year 1979*, pp. 456–69; *Special Analyses, Budget of the United States Government, Fiscal Year 1979*, pp. 17, 20, 33–34.

a variety of rebates to offset the administration's proposed taxes on crude oil and on "gas guzzler" automobiles.[25]

Second, the administration proposed a number of initiatives in education and training. The most significant increases in outlays are for a private sector manpower program ($250 million) and for youth employment programs ($273 million). Less significant in 1979, but presaging large spending increases in future years, are the administration's education proposals. Substantial increases were announced in the budget for aid to disadvantaged children (title I of the Elementary and Secondary Education Act) and other elementary and secondary education programs (training and education programs are discussed in chapters 3 and 4).

The other major "initiative" was carried in the budget as a $1.7

25. These are discussed in Joseph A. Pechman, ed., *Setting National Priorities: The 1978 Budget* (Brookings Institution, 1977), chap. 10.

billion "allowance for contingencies" (table 2-12). By early spring, the contingencies had arrived. First, in an attempt to head off a tuition tax credit plan gaining momentum in Congress, the administration proposed a student grant and loan alternative, with estimated outlays of $200 million in 1979 (see chapter 4 for details). Second, in March the President announced his national urban policy, which implied additional spending in 1979 of $742 million spread among a variety of programs. (Tax reductions of $1.7 billion were also proposed; see chapter 6.)

Beyond these initiatives, the administration supported small increases above current service levels in hundreds of different programs, but there are few cutbacks from current service levels. The most significant of these are listed in table 2-12: a repeat of the administration's request for legislation to control hospital costs and some previously tendered proposals to curb social security benefits. A modest effort to reduce impact aid for education and to reduce pay increases for federal blue-collar employees are also part of the President's program.

Program Choices in the Budget

Perhaps the most interesting aspect of the $7.8 billion spending increase is how little it reflects any attempt to reallocate funds among various government functions. Table 2-13 shows the uniformity of the proposed increases in the various outlay functions, except energy. (And part of the increase in energy was largely pro forma: the administration knew its tax proposals were in jeopardy.)

Of course, the administration was trying to limit outlays in line with its long-run spending target, and built-in costs did eat up most of the available spending margin. But even if the administration felt limited to a $500 billion outlay level, it could have proposed several substantial initiatives for 1979, provided it could have found savings in the budget's $492 billion for current services. Past administrations have proposed cutbacks in existing programs to gain room for new spending initiatives (or to demonstrate their devotion to efficiency). Such efforts have not been notably successful in Congress, but a major reason was that Republican presidents were proposing cuts in social programs to a Democratic Congress and offering little that Congress wanted in return. For 1979, a Democratic president pre-

Table 2-13. Current Services and Proposed Outlays, by Function, Fiscal Year 1979
Amounts in billions of dollars

Function	Current services	Proposed	Increase (percent)
National defense	116.8	117.8	0.8
International affairs	7.4	7.7	3.8
General science, space, and technology	5.1	5.1	0.2
Energy	7.6	9.6	27.1
Natural resources and environment	12.0	12.2	2.0
Agriculture	5.5	5.4	−1.4
Commerce and housing credit	3.1	3.0	−4.4
Transportation	17.1	17.4	1.7
Community and regional development	8.5	8.7	2.0
Education, training, employment, and social services	29.4	30.4	3.6
Health	50.3	49.7	−1.3
Income security	159.2	160.0	0.5
Veterans' benefits and services	18.9	19.3	2.0
Administration of justice	4.1	4.2	3.8
General government	4.2	4.3	2.9
General purpose fiscal assistance	9.5	9.6	1.5
Interest	48.7	49.0	0.6
Allowance for contingencies	1.1	2.8[a]	b
Undistributed offsetting receipts	−16.0	−16.0	0.0
Total	492.4	500.2	1.6

Sources: *The Budget of the United States Government, Fiscal Year 1979*, pp. 456–68; *Special Analyses, Budget of the United States Government, Fiscal Year 1979*, pp. 33–44. Figures are rounded.
a. Allowance for contingencies includes amounts subsequently reallocated to higher education and urban programs.
b. No meaning.

sumably willing to offer some programs that Congress would like (such as the urban and higher education programs announced later) proposed virtually no new economizing measures.

The failure of the administration to find such efficiencies is all the more remarkable in that it introduced a new budgeting technique—zero-base budgeting—which is designed to focus equal attention on the budget "base" and on the increments to that base. As it turned out, this budgeting technique seems to have led to little restructuring of the budget base. To the extent that zero-base budgeting had any effect at all, it was on low-level improvements in the operation of programs (for example, consolidation of several administrative support operations within an agency). But such a focus comes at considerable cost. As Allen Schick noted, "A preoccupation with the routines of operation drives out a consideration of program objectives and effectiveness. . . . An agency cannot devote itself to the managerial routines of ZBB while deploying its budget process for program planning and analysis."[26] Some part of the administration's failure to reallocate funds would seem to have derived, ironically, from its implementation of a process that was heralded as demanding "a total rejustification of everything from zero."[27]

As for the major administration initiatives, it is notable that most of them were developed entirely outside the new budget procedures. The energy and welfare reform initiatives antedate zero-base budgeting, and the urban policy and higher education proposals were developed after the budget was put together. None of these initiatives seem to have been made to compete with other programs in the way that an integrated budget review process requires. These developments raise the question of whether budgetary decisions—once the crucible for setting national priorities—will play a smaller role in such policy-setting in the future. By early 1978, the Carter administration showed some signs of taking action to strengthen coordination by announcing a new governmentwide multiyear planning system. Prospects for this system are discussed in appendix B.

The Anti-inflation Program

Since the administration disavowed using aggregate fiscal policy to starve the economy in order to curb inflation, it was forced to turn to other means to "contain and reduce the rate of inflation as we move toward a more fully employed economy," one of the four objectives set out by President Carter in his economic message.[28]

Several alternative policies for dealing with inflation have been debated in recent years. At one extreme are the measures instituted under the Nixon administration in the early 1970s. First, a short wage-price freeze attempted to moderate inflationary expectations and habits. This was followed by a gradual reduction of wage-price

26. Allen Schick, "The Road from ZBB," *Public Administration Review,* vol. 38 (March–April 1978), pp. 177–80. For a description of zero-base budgeting, see Pechman, ed., *Setting National Priorities: The 1978 Budget,* chap. 11.
27. Jimmy Carter, "Zero-Base Budgeting," *Nation's Business,* vol. 65 (January 1977), pp. 24–26.
28. *Economic Report of the President, January 1978,* p. 5. The other three goals were high employment, emphasis on the growth of the private sector, and strengthening the world economy.

controls, including a period in which the government was an active participant in major wage bargains and price changes. The evidence on the effectiveness of these policies is mixed;[29] but business and labor are in unified opposition to any reintroduction of a mandatory control program. Labor leaders feel that controls are effective in holding down union wages but not in restraining nonunion wages and prices. Business contends that controls thwart the ability of prices to allocate resources, create an unnecessary bureaucracy that inevitably writes more and more detailed regulations, and, in general, impede businessmen's freedom.

This strong opposition to mandatory controls forces consideration of several less strict anti-inflation plans. All try to use the federal government's leverage to induce a deceleration of inflation in the nonfederal sector. Some examples are proposals that the federal government make grants to states that lower sales taxes or that federal taxes be cut on the condition that labor will restrain wage gains in exchange for such cuts.

A recent proposal by Arthur Okun, which is receiving much attention, would establish a standard for wage-rate increases. Any firm that kept pay increases below the standard would qualify its employees for tax rebates, and if prices were restrained, the firm itself would qualify for a lower corporate profits tax. While this proposal is attractive in that it allows firms and their employees to refuse the tax-reduction carrot—something that would require special appeals to a government board under a mandatory controls system—it is also complicated. The provisions of the tax code would have to define the wage and price standards precisely, and regulations would have to be written on how to compute whether such standards were met. Such provisions could again arouse the opposition of business and labor.[30]

Another point of federal leverage is the panoply of government actions that add to private costs. Among those usually cited are paper-

29. The raw facts are that inflation slowed during the period of controls, but skyrocketed afterward. How much of this was due to the controls having bottled up inflationary forces whose eruption was inevitable once the controls were removed is impossible to tell because so many other factors also contributed to postcontrol inflation.

30. For the Okun proposal, see Arthur M. Okun, "The Great Stagflation Swamp," *Challenge*, vol. 20 (November–December 1977), pp. 6–13. Related proposals are found in Henry C. Wallich and Sidney Weintraub, "A Tax-Based Incomes Policy," *Journal of Economic Issues*, vol. 5 (June 1971), pp. 1–19; and Abba P. Lerner, "Stagflation—Its Cause and Cure," *Challenge*, vol. 20 (September–October 1977), pp. 14–19.

work requirements; health, safety, and environmental regulations; minimum wage laws; import restrictions; farm price supports; and restraints on natural resource development on federal lands. Similarly, many laws governing competition in both product and labor markets can be shown to raise costs. Although adjustment of these laws and requirements could ease inflationary forces, they are difficult to change quickly and each has a strong constituency to argue that the goal supported by the requirement is more important than any small anti-inflation gain to be achieved by revision.

The composition of federal taxation is another potential instrument for fighting inflation. Federal payroll taxes—particularly the employers' share of the large tax supporting social security, disability, and Medicare—are directly passed through to consumers in higher prices in the short run. A substantial replacement of such taxes with less cost-increasing ones such as income taxes could help restrain inflation. However, there is considerable opposition to the use of other taxes to finance social security programs.

A final point of federal leverage is the power of the presidency as an educational and leadership pulpit. If inflation is due primarily to a self-perpetuating process of labor and management trying to make up for past—or anticipated—losses, one part of a program to decelerate inflation should be to make sure that everyone understands the futility of such efforts. Carrying out this strategy would mean the government's first setting a goal for the deceleration of inflation, then becoming involved in major wage and price negotiations, publicizing which agreements were out of line with the goal, and efforts by the President to demonstrate to the private sector, by his actions on government programs, how inflation could be brought under control.

In its January economic message, the administration took a first step in the presidential leadership strategy. President Carter asked business and labor "to participate in a voluntary program to decelerate the rate of price and wage increase." He set "a standard of behavior for each industry for the coming year: every effort should be made to reduce the rate of wage and price increase in 1978 to below the average rate of the past two years."[31] Unfortunately, this announcement was followed by several months in which the administration failed to follow up its goal-setting. During those early months,

31. *Economic Report of the President, January 1978*, pp. 19–20.

moreover, it participated in several price-raising decisions: an agreement to protect the steel industry from foreign competition, settlement of the coal strike with very high wage increases, and promulgation of a set-aside program that will raise prices on several farm products.

Finally, on April 11, 1978, the President announced his follow-up program. It emphasized steps the government itself could take to decelerate inflation. These included a 5.5 percent "cap" on October 1978 pay raises for white-collar federal employees (about one percentage point below the pay raise envisioned in the January budget), a freeze on the salaries of executive-level employees in the administration, a reduction of regulations that impose "unnecessary costs" on the private sector, and a promise to explore ways to expand timber harvests. President Carter encouraged Congress to pass hospital cost containment and airline deregulation legislation.

The President made it very clear that he expected these federal actions to elicit similar restraint in other parts of the economy. Mayors and governors were asked to "follow the Federal example and hold down their pay increases." American workers were asked to "accept a lower rate of wage increase." And business was asked to show "a comparable restraint in price increases." At the time this book went to press, the exact nature of these requests and the procedures to be followed in monitoring private decisions were not available.

Evaluation of the Economic Program

One of the perils faced by every administration's economic plan is that the assumptions on which it is based will be overturned by events that are difficult to forecast. Since the President's budget has to make assumptions about the economy as much as two years in advance, such unanticipated events are guaranteed to occur. But even by the spring of 1978, there were an uncommon number of surprises. Among these were (1) an abnormally cold, wet winter that reduced production and sales in the first two months of 1978; (2) a sharp lowering of the exchange value of the dollar in the early months of 1978, which led to an increase in short-term interest rates; (3) a prolonged coal strike, which was settled in late March only after wage concessions that by any measure are inflationary were granted; (4) a revision of unemployment statistics by the Department of Labor showing that unemployment had declined substantially throughout 1977 instead of being stuck at a fixed rate after April as the earlier data had showed (the revised series showed an unemployment rate in February 1978 of 6.1 percent, *below* the administration's goal of 6.2 percent for the end of 1978); and (5) in March 1978, the Office of Management and Budget lowered its estimates of federal spending in fiscal 1978 by about $9 billion on the basis of actual spending in the first few months of that year, which showed another "shortfall" developing (see appendix A).

Even without these postbudget events, the administration's inflation forecast was dubious. It predicted consumer price increases in 1978 and 1979 at a 6 percent rate, despite the several special factors —payroll tax increases, minimum wage increases, dollar devaluation —that were known to be putting upward pressure on prices. This forecast could be correct only with a substantial deceleration of food prices, a very modest rise in energy prices, and some success with the voluntary wage-price program.[32] All of these seem overoptimistic.

As indicated in chapter 7, food prices are likely to rise faster than the administration assumed. Moreover, by early spring Congress was considering farm legislation that would raise prices further. (President Carter indicated he would veto such a measure.)

Energy prices may be affected by the decline in the exchange rate of the dollar. The OPEC cartel sets prices in dollars and the portfolios of the major OPEC holders of surpluses are primarily in dollar form. The deterioration of the buying power of oil-production income caused by the decline in the dollar's value gives OPEC an "excuse" for another round of price increases. These would presumably be tempered by OPEC's assessment of the demand for oil and the consequences of a price raise.

Equally in doubt is the contribution of the voluntary anti-inflation program. For such a program to have any chance of moderating wage and price increases, an administration would have to demonstrate by word and deed that it was serious about making deceleration of inflation a high-priority goal for government actions, and it would have to take steps to ensure that the private sector modified its behavior. Although the April anti-inflation message started the ball rolling on government actions, the response of the private sector is the

32. See *Economic Report of the President, January 1978*, pp. 80–81.

key to the voluntary anti-inflation strategy. It is too early to tell what that response will be.

The postbudget news that unemployment is closer to the full-employment range than previously believed and that the cost of imports will rise even more as a result of further devaluation leads to the conclusion that inflation for 1978 is likely to be higher than the forecast rate. By April, some private forecasting services were predicting a rise of nearly 7 percent in consumer prices for 1978. For 1979 and the years beyond, the chances of a decelerating inflation rest on whether the administration's anti-inflation program succeeds.

The administration's forecast of real economic growth of about 4.75 percent for both 1978 and 1979 seems to be consistent with the fiscal policy it advanced, which would raise expenditures and cut taxes just about enough to offset what otherwise would be a restrictive change in the federal budget. Thus the administration's forecast of real growth depends primarily on the expectation that accelerated growth in business fixed investment and net exports will offset a somewhat slower growth in consumption and a leveling off of housing expenditures. Although the forecast was at the optimistic end of the range of private forecasts, it was not considered seriously out of line.

Postbudget events do not significantly change this evaluation. The budget shortfall in 1978 does raise some doubts about growth in the second half of 1978, but these may be offset if production makes up for winter delays and the coal strike and if stronger net exports result from the decline in the exchange value of the dollar.

The inflation-raising consequences of early developments in 1978 may, however, affect real growth in 1978 and 1979 by changing monetary policy or expectations. If inflation accelerates, and especially if it is accompanied by only a gradual improvement in the U.S. balance of trade, there will be strong pressure on the Federal Reserve to "do something." If the Fed responds by slowing monetary growth and allowing interest rates to rise, the administration's real growth forecast will prove too high. Business investment and construction will fall short of the forecast growth. And even if the Federal Reserve were to maintain credit flows, an acceleration of inflation might discourage investment if corporate leaders regarded it as worsening the long-term economic outlook. In all, the real growth forecast seems more fragile than when the budget was formulated.

But the improved unemployment picture may make the administration accept some slowing in its forecast growth.

The President's budget is by no means the last word on fiscal policy. Congress must pass on all the proposed changes in the budget, and it may well differ on both the overall fiscal plan and the details. Indeed, for the budget to emerge from Congress in an election year with the modest spending increases proposed by the President would be quite unusual. All the evidence, moreover, indicates that most of the administration's proposed tax reforms are unpopular. These factors point to a more stimulative budget. Nonetheless, it is hard to imagine that Congress will show an even larger deficit than the President proposed at a time when inflation is quickening. This problem may be solved in 1978 by projecting spending shortfalls into the 1979 budget, which would allow Congress to increase spending for some programs more than the President proposed without taking the unpopular action of raising the deficit. But as the economy moves closer to full employment, some politically unpopular budget choices will have to be made.

CHAPTER THREE

Employment and Income Security

JOHN L. PALMER

THE EMPLOYMENT and training and income security programs account for one-third to one-half of the federal budget, depending upon how broadly those programs are defined. More than any other function, except the management of macroeconomic policies, they determine the role of the federal government in promoting the economic security of Americans. This is especially true for groups such as the elderly and disabled, the unemployed, and low-income families.

From the beginning of President Carter's term through his 1979 budget submission and urban policy statement, he has proposed or supported several major controversial initiatives in these areas. In some cases congressional action is completed; in others it is still pending. This chapter opens with a brief discussion of legislation already enacted by Congress concerning reforms of the food stamp programs, increases in the minimum wage, and the financing of social security. Then welfare reform and employment and training policy are explored in more detail. Pending initiatives, the issues they raise, and some alternative approaches are considered. An attempt is made to assess the overall direction of the Carter administration with respect to these social welfare policies in the final section.

The author thanks Barry White for providing much of the data in the employment and training section and for reviewing the section for factual accuracy. Helpful comments on a draft were supplied by Robert W. Hartman, Robert Lerman, Robert D. Reischauer, and John E. Todd. Research assistance was provided by James Altman.

Completed Legislation

Before disposing with the 1978 budget in 1977, Congress passed legislation revising the food stamp program, raising the minimum wage, and increasing payroll taxes to finance social security. In each case the Carter administration had put forward a proposal, although Congress had planned to take action even in the absence of any executive branch initiative.

Food Stamps

The food stamp program has been controversial since it expanded in the early 1970s from a minor budgetary item providing benefits for a few million people to a $5.7 billion program reaching 18 million recipients. Criticism has been directed at its administrative complexity and high costs, at the large number of recipients with incomes above the poverty level, and at the low participation rates among those with incomes near or below the poverty level. In addition, the elimination of food stamps in favor of direct cash payments has often been considered as part of welfare reform.

In action that generally conformed with an administration proposal submitted in early 1977, Congress passed a bill in the fall of that year addressing many of these concerns. Prominent among the changes are the elimination of the requirement that most households pay some cash to receive a larger value in food stamps; simplification of deductions from gross income to derive a net figure on which benefits are based; generally reduced administrative procedures and tightened eligibility that restricts recipients to households whose income after allowable deductions is below the poverty level.

When its full impact is felt in 1980, the new law is expected to increase recipients of the program by approximately 1.7 million people and costs by about $265 million above what they otherwise would have been. (Congressional Budget Office estimates for 1979 are 16.5 million participants and $6.0 billion in expenditures.) This is the net effect of the 1977 changes outlined above. Although many of those changes make the program much like one that provides cash income supplements, the administration's initial proposal was independently formulated before its welfare reform proposal.

Minimum Wage

In October of 1977, Congress approved a four-step increase in the minimum wage, from $2.30 to $2.65 in 1978, $2.90 in 1979, $3.10 in 1980, and $3.35 in 1981. The Carter administration initially proposed only a $.20 increase for 1978, but subsequently joined forces with a coalition including labor and civil rights groups to advocate an increase to $2.65 in 1978, with annual increases thereafter pegged to the rate of growth of the average manufacturing wage. Over five million workers are estimated to be directly affected by the higher minimum and the total wage bill directly increased by 0.4 percent for each year during the period 1978–81.

Two issues of major importance for minimum wage increases are their effects on increasing prices and on reducing the employment of low-wage workers. Of particular concern is whether the effects on employment will outweigh the wage gains for any groups of workers.

Increases in the minimum wage have both direct and indirect effects on the total wage bill.[1] Since these effects are estimated to be roughly equivalent for an increase the size of the recent one, the overall consequences are likely to be a total wage bill that is about 0.8 percent higher for each of the years in question. An equivalent increase in the general price level should follow. This is an undesirable consequence that has to be weighed against the potential benefits of increased earnings for workers earning low wages.

In a recent study examining the wage and employment consequences of an increase in the minimum wage, Edward M. Gramlich concluded that, despite a modest negative employment effect, adult males as a group appear to increase their overall earnings.[2] The net favorable effect for adult women is more pronounced. However, "the most reasonable verdict is that teenagers have more to lose than to gain from higher minimum wages: they appear to be forced out of the better jobs, denied full-time work, and paid lower hourly wage rates; all these developments are probably detrimental to their income

1. The indirect effects come either from increases in wage rates above the new minimum that reinstitute preexisting wage differentials or from the substitution of skilled for unskilled workers because of the shift in their relative cost to employers.

2. Edward M. Gramlich, "Impact of Minimum Wages on Other Wages, Employment, and Family Incomes," *Brookings Papers on Economic Activity*, 2:1976, pp. 409–51.

prospects in both the short and the long run."[3] It is evidence of this type that is cited by supporters of a special lower minimum wage for teenagers or some other policy to offset the negative employment effects. A two-tier minimum-wage structure received serious attention in Congress in the 1977 debate, but was ultimately rejected.

Social Security

The status of the social security system was often in the news in 1977. The insolvency of the old age, survivors, and disability (OASDI) portion of the program was predicted for the early 1980s, largely as a result of the shortfall in revenues due to the 1974–75 recession and a continued unexpected rise in disability applications. Larger long-term deficits were projected, primarily because of a feature in the 1972 social security amendments that overadjusted the expected future benefits of current workers to inflation and a shift in the age distribution of the population that will result in a major increase in the ratio of the elderly to the working population early in the next century. Among the other issues that received attention were the treatment of women, the earnings requirement, and mandatory coverage of all workers.

Shortly after taking office, President Carter sent Congress a major social security proposal focusing on financing.[4] Its major elements were a transfer of general revenues to the OASDI trust funds to make up the revenue shortfall caused by any excess of the aggregate unemployment rate over 6 percent during the recent recession; a shift of already scheduled Medicare tax rate increases to the OASDI program; a gradual elimination of the wage-base ceiling on which employers' payroll taxes are paid; and a series of small increases (totaling $2,400 by 1985) in the wage-base ceiling for employees.

Congress approved the President's proposal to eliminate the overadjustment to inflation and made certain minor changes. However, it largely rejected the financing methods proposed by President Carter in favor of a more traditional approach consisting of increases in the

3. Ibid., p. 443. The lower hourly wage rates result from the exclusion of teenagers from the sector covered by the minimum wage. This highly differential effect for teenagers should not be surprising; in 1975 when the minimum wage was 46 percent of average hourly earnings in the private nonagricultural sector, it was 94 percent of the median wage for all teenagers. The new law raises both percentages.

4. The President's budget for 1979 contains several minor social security initiatives. Chief among these are some benefit reductions that have little chance of passage. They are not discussed here.

payroll tax rates and in taxable wage bases for both employers and employees. Both increases are large and will phase in gradually between 1979 and 1990.[5] In addition, Congress liberalized the earnings test and made several other changes in eligibility and benefits.[6] President Carter strongly endorsed the final bill.

Both the proposal by President Carter and the final outcome would essentially preserve the relationship between benefits and earnings histories for future retirees that existed before the overadjustment to inflation had any effect, eliminate entirely the projected deficits through the end of this century, and reduce by over three-fourths the projected deficit for the first half of the next century. There are two major differences, however. First, because of its primary reliance upon general revenue financing and greatly increased payroll taxes for employers of workers earning high wages and salaries, the tax burden would have been more progressively distributed by the administration's tax proposal than by the congressional substitute. Second, the new law will result in a larger and far more visible tax increase for most taxpayers, particularly those in the upper-middle income range.[7] This is because the tax increase under the new law is greater and more immediate and, more importantly, because it will result in much higher tax payments that are *earmarked* for social security by virtually all covered wage earners and businesses.

The macroeconomic consequences of tax increases to finance social security are also considerable. Two that are most important in the near future—the drain on the economy and the resulting increase in price levels—are discussed in chapter 2. Both the administration's

5. The combined employer-employee tax rate will rise to 15.3 percent and the wage base to approximately $50,000 in 1990 rather than 12.9 percent and approximately $36,000 as previously scheduled. (The wage base automatically increases as wages increase.) The 1978 levels are 12.1 percent and $17,700.

6. Social security benefits for all recipients under age 72 previously were reduced by 50 percent of all earnings over $3,500. This limit has now been eliminated for those seventy years and over; for others it will be raised to $6,000 by 1982 and indexed to general wage levels thereafter. Other major provisions prevent the loss of benefits due to marriage after the age of sixty, permit persons to qualify for benefits based on their spouses' earnings after ten years rather than twenty years, freeze the minimum-benefit level, and increase the bonus in benefit levels for the postponement of retirement beyond age 65.

7. When fully implemented in 1990, the *increase* in payroll taxes relative to the previous law will be about 20 percent for all earners below the wage ceiling according to the previous law and range up to 62 percent for earnings at the wage ceiling of the new law (approximately $50,000). The maximum combined employer-employee tax burden will be approximately $7,700. See chapter 5 for details on the distribution of the payroll tax increase.

proposal and the bill approved by Congress would have these unfavorable effects, although their magnitude would be greater under the new law.

Since its passage, the massive increase in payroll taxes has evoked a strong and generally negative public response. This has led Congress to reassess its opposition to alternatives to the payroll tax for additional sources of revenue, and it may lead to greater pressure for changes in the coverage and the benefit structure of the system.[8] It is clear that controversy over the social security system is likely to remain at center stage in federal policy debates for many years to come.

Welfare Reform

In September 1977 the Carter administration proposed an overhaul of the welfare system, which has long been criticized for inadequate and inequitable coverage, strong work disincentives, and unnecessary administrative inefficiency and complexity.[9] A program for better jobs and income would substitute for three current major welfare programs: aid to families with dependent children (AFDC), supplemental security income for the elderly and disabled (SSI), and food stamps. In their places would be a system of nationally uniform cash payments to the low-income population (with optional state supplementation), extensive employment and training assistance, and an expansion of the current earned income tax credit. While many elements of the administration's initiative are characteristic of most welfare reform proposals, it is notable for the comprehensiveness of its coverage, its integration of a large public service employment program with the income maintenance system, and its interrelationship with the tax system.

Program Structure

The basic features of the proposed federal cash-assistance benefit structure are illustrated in table 3-1. Benefits would vary by family

8. Within two months of passage of the tax increase, several proposals to roll it back or to cut payroll taxes below their current level have been made in Congress. The substitution of general revenue financing generally is advocated for whatever deficit is thus created.

9. For a discussion of the problems of the current welfare system and the objectives of reform, see George J. Carcagno and Walter S. Corson, "Welfare Reform," in Joseph A. Pechman, ed., *Setting National Priorities: The 1978 Budget* (Brookings Institution, 1977), pp. 249–81.

Table 3-1. Benefit Structure for Federal Cash Assistance under President Carter's Welfare Reform Proposal, 1978

Amounts in 1978 dollars

Recipient	Basic benefit[a]	Disregard[b]	Benefit reduction rate (percent)[c]	Phase-out level[d]
Elderly or disabled				
Individual	2,500	...	50	5,000
Couple	3,750	...	50	7,500
Single-parent family[d]				
Youngest child under fourteen	4,200	...	50	8,400
Youngest child fourteen or over				
Job available	2,300	3,800	50	8,400
No job available	4,200	...	...	...
Two-parent families[e]				
Job available	2,300	3,800	50	8,400
No job available	4,200	...	...	...
Single individual				
Job available	0	...	...	...
No job available	1,100	...	...	...

Source: "Statement by Joseph A. Califano, Jr., Secretary of Health, Education, and Welfare, before the Subcommittee on Welfare Reform of the House of Representatives" (HEW, September 19, 1977; processed).

a. Amount received by the individual or family if there is no other income.

b. Amount of earnings that is disregarded before benefits are reduced.

c. Rate at which benefits are reduced as earnings increase. A 50 percent rate implies that benefits are reduced $1 for each $2 of earnings. An 80 percent benefit reduction rate is applied to nonemployment income.

d. Level of earnings at which the amount of cash assistance becomes zero. At $2 less earnings, the benefit would be $1.

e. Based on a family of four members.

size and type. Several features are designed to improve its equity and efficiency relative to current welfare programs, including the way in which income would be measured for eligibility purposes. Most adults who are neither elderly nor disabled nor have preschool-age children would have to satisfy a work requirement (that is, register and search for employment and accept any suitable job offer). To promote work incentives, most families with such an adult would be placed initially at a lower benefit level; however, if a family's primary earner were unemployed and not offered suitable employment within eight weeks of becoming eligible for cash assistance, the family would move to a higher benefit level.

Because approximately forty states now have combined welfare and food stamp benefits that exceed the proposed federal cash-assis-tance benefit levels, a large number of them probably would want to establish a supplementary program. This would be encouraged by 75 percent federal matching of state supplements up to three-fourths of the poverty level and, for most families, 25 percent matching above that up to the official poverty line (approximately $6,560 in 1978 for a family of four). For states to receive this cost sharing and benefit from various (hold-harmless) provisions that limit their total financial liability, their supplements would have to meet certain federal requirements.

A long-standing dilemma of welfare reform is how to provide adequate assistance to families with adults who are able to work (particularly in two-parent families) without creating either strong work disincentives through high benefit-reduction rates or incurring the higher costs and coverage that accompany low benefit-reduction rates. The administration's proposal partially sidesteps this problem by integrating a large employment program with the cash-assistance structure, as indicated in table 3-1. Under a new title of the Comprehensive Employment and Training Act (CETA), any unemployed primary earner of a family with children would become eligible for federally subsidized training or public service employment after five weeks of unsuccessful job search. The jobs would be in special projects administered by CETA local prime sponsors under the Department of Labor oversight.[10] The content of the jobs would be determined by the local prime sponsors in accordance with federal guidelines. Basic pay would be at the minimum wage in states that do not supplement the program and up to 10 percent higher in those that do.

By 1982, the planned first year of full implementation of the program, the program would provide for a maximum of 1.4 million annual slots, which could serve 2.5 million adults. According to administration estimates, this would accommodate those who are subject to the work requirement and cannot locate suitable unsubsidized employment and allow for several hundred thousand volunteers not subject to the work requirement.[11] The jobs would be temporary for most; after one year in the program, participants would be required to undergo an intensive five-week job search before being readmitted.

10. Prime sponsors are the state and local governments, or consortia thereof, eligible to receive funds under CETA. They would have the discretion to provide participants with either training or public service employment. The expectation is that the majority of slots would be in the latter.
11. This assumes an unemployment rate of no more than 5.6 percent in 1982.

The earnings of most families that have children and are below the median income level would be supplemented through an expanded version of the current earned income tax credit. To create a financial incentive to seek or hold regular low-wage jobs in both public and private sectors rather than in subsidized public service employment, the latter would not be supplemented. The amount of supplementation of regular employment would be 10 percent of the first $4,000 of earnings and 5 percent of the remainder between $4,000 and the maximum level of federal financial participation in state supplementation (about $9,000 for a family of four). It would be phased out at a 10 percent rate for higher levels of income. The program would be administered in conjunction with the federal personal income tax system.

Table 3-2 shows various circumstances for a family of four under the proposed program, assuming it is in effect in 1978. For simplicity, no state supplementation is included.

Table 3-2. Total Income by Source for a Family of Four in Various Circumstances under President Carter's Program for Better Jobs and Income

1978 dollars

	Annual family income				
Family circumstance	Cash benefit[a]	Social security	Earnings	Earned income tax credit	Total
One adult, three children					
No other income	4,200	...	...	...	4,200
Eligible for $100 a month social security	3,240	1,200	...	...	4,440
Adult works half time in public service employment and is eligible for $100 a month social security	1,862	1,200	2,756	[b]	5,818
Two adults, two children					
One adult works full time in public service employment	1,444	...	5,512	[b]	6,956
One adult works full time in regular employment at minimum wage	1,444	...	5,512	476	7,432

Source: Same as table 3-1.

a. Assumes no state supplementation. In calculating the cash benefit, a reduction rate of 80 percent is applied to nonearnings income (in this case, social security in the second column).

b. The earned income tax credit does not apply to the earnings from public service employment.

Table 3-3. Administration and Congressional Budget Office Estimates of Cost
of President Carter's Welfare Reform Proposal, Fiscal Year 1982
Billions of dollars

Item	Administration estimate	Congressional Budget Office estimate	Difference
Gross cost	38.8	42.3	3.5
Cash assistance	26.0	28.1	2.1
Jobs	9.9	11.5	1.6
Earned income tax credit	3.0	2.6	−0.4
Offsets	30.0	24.9	5.1
Net cost	8.8	17.4	8.6

Sources: *The Budget of the United States Government, Fiscal Year 1979*, p. 198; and tabulations prepared by the Congressional Budget Office. Figures are rounded.

Cost and Impact

Even if the program were passed immediately, the new system would take several years to implement.[12] Assuming early enactment, the program's net cost to the federal government for fiscal year 1982 has been estimated as $17.4 billion by the Congressional Budget Office and $8.8 billion by the administration (table 3-3). The former figure is probably closer to the appropriate number than the latter because the administration's estimate is based on several dubious offsets.[13]

About $3.4 billion of the net cost estimate by the Congressional Budget Office reflects reduced costs (fiscal relief) to state and local governments; the fiscal relief is about one-third lower for the administration's estimate. In both cases the remainder (excluding overhead) reflects greater benefits to individuals—through refundable tax credits, direct cash payments, or public service employment.

The distributional impact of the administration's proposal is diffi-

12. The employment component would be tested on a pilot basis beginning in 1979 ($125 million in outlays are anticipated) and would be phased in by 1983.

13. Such estimates require a complex set of assumptions. Most noteworthy is that states provide supplementation to approximate expected 1982 SSI, AFDC, and food stamp benefits for the SSI and AFDC populations.

The $8.6 billion discrepancy between estimates of the Congressional Budget Office and the Carter administration is a result of many differing assumptions. A large part of it, however, is attributable to two offsets that the administration included and the Congressional Budget Office did not—$1.5 billion for the crude oil tax rebate (part of the President's energy proposal) and $3.9 billion for CETA public service jobs, which are scheduled to phase out with economic recovery.

cult to ascertain with precision. Nevertheless, the following general observations can be made:[14]

1. The aggregate of federal expenditures for income assistance would be more concentrated on those with income below or near the poverty level.

2. The majority of people who otherwise would have been eligible for current income assistance programs will have higher incomes. Of the minority whose incomes would be lower under the current system, many would be in the upper income range of those assisted but would have either temporary drops in income or large allowable deductions from income that would make them eligible for greater assistance under the current system.

3. Those who would gain the most under the President's proposal would be two-parent families who presently are largely excluded from cash-assistance programs and would have access to a combination of earnings and cash supplementation that would provide an income above the poverty level. Single-parent families residing in states with low benefits also would have their incomes raised substantially, especially if they take advantage of the public employment.

Current Status and Prospects

Because of its wide-ranging implications for current programs, the administration's proposal must be considered by several committees in both houses of Congress. A special House subcommittee, constituted to facilitate the process, marked up the bill during winter 1977 and reported it to the three parent committees—Ways and Means, Agriculture, and Labor and Education. The subcommittee left the broad outline of the administration's program intact, but made several alterations, including reduction of the work incentives for many families. The bill is estimated by the Congressional Budget Office to increase the net cost to the federal government for fiscal year 1982 by an additional $2.9 billion.[15]

14. These observations assume state supplementation for current categories of recipients to reflect combined AFDC or SSI and food stamp benefit levels and ignore the part of the earned income tax credit that results in a reduced income tax liability as opposed to a direct cash payment.

15. This is net additional cost after changes made by the subcommittee in the administration's proposal, which reduced costs by about $7 billion. Chief among those changes were a large cutback in the earned income tax credit and elimination of independent eligibility for single individuals under age 25. The main factors accounting for the increase are (1) indexing the basic federal cash benefits to inflation after the year of implementation; (2) increased eligibility for and participation in

Although the bill was initially well received the prospects for congressional passage of the administration's welfare reform program—in either its original form or the House subcommittee version—appear poor. This is probably due more to the discomfort of Congress with the program's high net cost than with its basic objectives.

After a decade of intense controversy over welfare, a growing consensus is emerging regarding the directions that any new major reforms should take. Among these are some consolidation and streamlining of existing programs; greater national uniformity in levels of assistance; an increased and more nationally uniform federal financial role, thereby providing fiscal relief to some state and local governments; greater comparability in levels of assistance for different demographic groups within the low-income population; and greater reliance upon work incentives and employment assistance for those expected to work. This reflects a considerable evolution in congressional and public attitudes.

The administration's program would result in a considerable change from current welfare program structures in all the directions indicated above. There is resistance to such major change. The alternatives that are likely to receive serious congressional consideration, therefore, are those that involve less movement along some or all of those dimensions and have lower net costs. Although there are an infinite number of possibilities, most "incremental" approaches to welfare reform are likely to have most or all of the following characteristics:

1. A substantially altered AFDC program, including nationally uniform eligibility criteria and streamlined procedures for benefit calculations, broader coverage for two-parent families, a national minimum-benefit level, and greater federal financial participation.

2. Maintenance of the separate SSI program for the elderly and disabled, perhaps with elimination of food stamps in favor of higher benefit levels.

3. Retention of the food stamp program for all other (non-SSI) currently eligible families, possibly integrated administratively with AFDC.

---

the cash-assistance component (of 7 to 8 million more persons) resulting from the substitution of a shorter prior time period over which income would be measured; (3) higher limits to federal participation in state supplements; (4) reduction in work effort and earnings; and (5) higher wage rates in the public service employment jobs.

4. Provision of several hundred thousand public service employment jobs for welfare recipients.

5. Retention of the earned income tax credit with higher benefit levels.

6. Expanded use of subsidies to private and nonprofit employers to promote job opportunities for those who are, or are likely to become, welfare recipients.[16]

Depending on the level of the national minimum, the extent of coverage of two-parent families, and the size of the jobs program, such approaches could have net costs from $5 to $15 billion in fiscal year 1982.[17]

Some broad generalizations can be made about the merits of incremental and comprehensive approaches. Incremental reforms can be designed to cost less and be less disruptive of current delivery systems and recipients, offer more flexibility for differential treatment of various subgroups within the low-income population, and are less likely to have unexpected undesirable consequences. Comprehensive approaches generally provide more equitable treatment (at least with respect to federal dollars) of people with similar economic needs, are more efficient administratively, result in a more consistent and appropriate differentiation of federal and state roles, and are more easily coordinated and integrated with other programs and policies that affect the same target population (such as health insurance and the tax system).

A detailed debate on the pros and cons of incremental and comprehensive approaches has been carried on for the past several years and will not be repeated here.[18] However, one issue arises under both

16. A small employer-subsidy program exists for AFDC recipients under the work incentive (WIN) program.

17. The Congressional Budget Office has estimated the net cost of mandating nationwide provision of the AFDC unemployed fathers program, combined with a national minimum AFDC and food-stamps benefit at 75 percent of the poverty level, to be $3.5 billion in 1978 and $5.6 billion in fiscal 1982. Chairman Al Ullman of the House Ways and Means Committee has a proposal that would go further than this, including expanding the earned income tax credit and providing half a million public service jobs, which is estimated to have a net cost of $7.5 to $9.0 billion in 1982. Senators Howard H. Baker, Jr., Henry L. Bellmon, and Abraham A. Ribicoff are preparing a proposal with many similar elements, but with less reliance on public service employment. It includes a categorical wage subsidy to private employers for welfare recipients and other disadvantaged workers. A preliminary version of that proposal was estimated by the Congressional Budget Office to have a net cost of $6.3 billion in fiscal year 1982.

18. See Carcagno and Corson, "Welfare Reform"; Mark D. Worthington and Laurence E. Lynn, Jr., "Incremental Welfare Reform: A Strategy Whose Time Has

that is relatively new—the design of a jobs program to accompany welfare reform; it is discussed in the next section entitled "Employment and Training Policy."

Because energy and tax legislation take much of the time of the House Ways and Means and Senate Finance Committees, progress in 1978 on welfare reform promises to be slow. However, several incremental reform proposals have common elements and are often consistent with administration objectives, so favorable congressional action in 1978 or 1979 is possible. The willingness and flexibility of the administration and various congressional factions regarding negotiations will be crucial to the outcome.

Employment and Training Policy

Considerable progress was made on both the employment and unemployment fronts in 1977 and in the first quarter of 1978 when economic growth was generally strong. There was an unprecedented rapid rate of growth in total employment, with a rise of about two percentage points in the number of employed. Because this was accompanied by a large increase in the labor force, it translated into a more modest, but still quite substantial, drop in the overall unemployment rate from 7.8 at the beginning of 1977 to 6.2 percent by the end of the first quarter of 1978. Consistent with past experience, however, the unemployment rates of some groups remained far above the average. Of particular concern currently are nonwhites and youth, whose rates are approximately two and three times, respectively, that of the aggregate unemployment rate.

The administration's economic strategy calls for a continued decline in the overall unemployment rate over the next five years to 5.0 percent in 1981 and 4.0 percent by the end of 1983—and its budgetary policy is designed with this in mind.[19] Achieving even this gradual reduction in unemployment without increasing upward pres-

Passed," *Public Policy,* vol. 25 (winter 1977), pp. 49–80; Richard P. Nathan, "Food Stamps and Welfare Reform," *Policy Analysis,* vol. 2 (winter 1976), pp. 61–70; Congressional Budget Office, "Welfare Reform: Issues, Objectives, and Approaches" (GPO, 1977); and "Comprehensive Reform vs. Incrementalism: An Exchange of Views between Richard P. Nathan and John L. Palmer," *Journal of the Institute for Socioeconomic Studies,"* vol. 2 (spring 1977), pp. 1–9.

19. For a discussion of fiscal policy and prospects for achieving the administration's economic projections, see chapters 2 and 10.

sures on wage rates and inflation will be difficult, perhaps impossible, unless the unemployment differentials faced by the groups that currently have high unemployment are reduced substantially in the process. Clearly, selective measures promoting this goal should be a top priority for employment and training policy.[20]

Current Policies and New Proposals

Current and proposed federal employment and training policies are embodied in several different legislative vehicles and initiatives.[21]

THE COMPREHENSIVE EMPLOYMENT AND TRAINING ACT. Since its enactment in 1973, CETA has been the major budgetary vehicle for federal employment and training policies. The act brought about a major consolidation and considerable decategorization and decentralization of most of the previous efforts in this area. Originally it had four program titles: a basic allocation to local prime sponsors—agents of state and local governments—for use as their priorities dictated (title I); a small permanent public service employment program for areas with high unemployment, also administered by local prime sponsors (title II); and a set of categorical programs administered primarily from the national level and aimed at small target groups, such as migrant workers and native Americans (title III) and disadvantaged youth (the Jobs Corps—title IV).[22] The real level of services under these titles was held roughly constant from 1975 through the initially planned outlays for 1977.

In late December 1974, in response to the recession, a $1 billion annual temporary, countercyclical public service employment program for all local areas was added through a new CETA title VI.[23] When title VI was renewed for 1977, the program was expanded; and a set of restrictions was imposed to improve targeting on the long-term, low-income unemployed and to reduce the flexibility of state and local governments to use the federal funds to underwrite

20. Other factors are likely to be equally or more important over the long run in reducing these differentials. Some of these are the dramatic reduction in youth's share of the labor force, which will occur in the late 1980s, and industrial location and urban policy initiatives taken at the federal, state, and local levels.

21. For more detail on previous and current federal employment and training policies, including the expansion under the economic stimulus package of 1977, see John L. Palmer, "Employment and Training Assistance," in Pechman, ed., *Setting National Priorities: The 1978 Budget*, pp. 143–75.

22. In addition, title V authorizes the National Commission for Manpower Policy.

23. The former title VI was redesignated as title VII.

employment they otherwise would have supported with their own tax revenues.

When President Carter took office, one of his first undertakings—and his major departure from the 1978 current services budget—was to propose an economic-stimulus package relying on a mixture of tax cuts and expenditure increases in employment-related programs. Congress passed it with only minor modifications. As shown in table 3-4, this nearly doubled CETA outlays from the initially estimated $5.6 billion in fiscal year 1977 to $9.6 billion for fiscal year 1978. Most of this expansion was in the public service employment programs, from 310,000 to over 750,000 job slots; however, a youth employment initiative also instituted several new programs that will approach an annual level of $1 billion by the end of fiscal 1979, and Job Corps outlays will double. Other major components of the package were an expansion of emergency public works from a one-time expenditure of $2 billion to a one-time expenditure of $6 billion and the initiation of a tax credit for private employers based on their expansion of employment.

In his 1979 budget the President has requested an expansion of outlays of just over $400 million or about 4 percent above the current services level for CETA programs. More specifically, he proposes to maintain through 1979 the CETA program levels reached by the end of 1978; increase slightly the slots funded under the new youth programs; launch pilot projects of the employment component of his welfare reform proposal; and undertake a new initiative designed to increase private sector job opportunities for CETA target groups, particularly disadvantaged youth. (Authorization for $400 million was requested for this private sector initiative, but only $250 million would be spent in 1979.)

Subsequent to his budget proposal, the President announced two additional initiatives which affect employment and training policy. First, in late February 1978 he transmitted a four-year reauthorization bill for CETA, since the current version is due to expire at the end of 1978. In conjunction with this proposal, Secretary of Labor Ray Marshall indicated that tentative administration plans call for total outlays on employment and training to rise from $12.8 billion in fiscal year 1979 to $18.2 billion in fiscal year 1982. (These figures include the small portion of employment and training funds not

Table 3-4. Budget Outlays under the Comprehensive Employment and Training Act, by Program, Fiscal Years 1977–79

Millions of dollars

		Outlays, by year		
			1979	
Program and title in act[a]	1977 Ford budget[b]	1978	Current services	President Carter's budget[c]
Basic grants to prime sponsors (I)[d]	1,780	1,891	1,942	1,942
Public service employment (II, VI)	2,758	5,735	6,203	6,203
National categorical (III)	826	1,572	2,109	2,280
Summer employment for youth	595	672	740	740
Other youth[e]	...	476	833	880
Grants to migrants and Indians	114	149	172	172
Welfare reform demonstration projects	...	...	...	125
Other	117	276	363	363
Job Corps (IV)	206	274	376	376
Private sector initiative (VII)	...	...	...	250
Young Adult Conservation Corps (VIII)[f]	...	144	307	307
All programs	5,570	9,617	10,935	11,356

Source: Office of Management and Budget. Figures are rounded.

a. The programs are described in *Special Analyses, Budget of the United States Government, Fiscal Year 1979*, special analysis K.

b. As estimated in President Ford's 1978 budget proposal.

c. Under President Carter's proposal for reauthorization of CETA, the present title I would become title II and the present titles II and VI would be merged into a single public service employment title VI; the summer youth and other youth categories under title III would be combined with the Job Corps in a new youth title IV; the private sector initiative would be a new title VII; and the remainder of the current title VIII would be unchanged.

d. Contains a small amount of other outlays.

e. These are programs authorized by the Youth Employment and Demonstration Projects Act (YEDPA) of 1977: Youth employment and training program, the youth community conservation and improvement projects, and the youth incentive entitlement pilot projects. They primarily provide work experience for disadvantaged youth. The first two are administered by local prime sponsors on a formula allocation basis. The other program consists of a series of demonstration projects in selected sites to test the effect of employment on the education of disadvantaged youth.

f. This program is administered under agreements with the Department of Agriculture and the Department of the Interior. Funds are allocated at agency discretion to develop employment opportunities for youth in general.

authorized under CETA and the implementation of the jobs component of the administration's welfare reform proposal.) The significant departures of the new bill from the current act as identified by the administration are: (1) simplified procedural requirements for local prime sponsors; (2) narrower targeting upon the disadvantaged and structurally unemployed; (3) the merging of the two public service employment titles (II and VI), which presently encompass four different programs, into a single title and program in which the number of jobs would automatically vary with the aggregate unemployment rate;[24] and (4) a shift in the overall emphasis of CETA from the provision of short-term employment and income to the promotion of long-term earnings prospects.

Because of the impending expiration of the current CETA, favorable congressional action to reauthorize the act is expected in 1978. Although Congress probably will provide authorization levels quite similar to those sought by the administration, there is likely to be controversy about the specific design of both public service employment and the private sector initiative, and possibly the nature of the general targeting requirements.

URBAN POLICY. The second initiative relating to employment and training is the urban policy proposal of March 1978. Although the President proposed elimination of the temporary employment tax credit and no expansion of authority for local public works in his 1979 budget, his urban policy includes a retargeting and extension of the tax credit and an additional $3 billion for a new local public works program.[25] The tax credit is for employers in private business who hire and retain, for at least three months of full-time employment, unemployed youth (aged eighteen to twenty-four) certified as disadvantaged by CETA prime sponsors. The maximum amount of credit will be $2,000 for the first year of employment and $1,000 for the second.[26] The administration estimates that the tax credit will result in a loss of revenues of $1.5 billion a year starting in 1979. The public works program will be a labor-intensive effort to rehabilitate and renovate public facilities in a limited number of particularly needy local jurisdictions. Half of the jobs would be for long-term unemployed and disadvantaged workers referred through the CETA system. Authorization is being sought for $1 billion a year for fiscal 1979 through fiscal 1981, but outlays would be only $100 million in 1979.[27]

24. The new title VI would provide for a base level of 100,000 slots for high unemployment areas, with 100,000 more to be provided when unemployment reaches 4.75 percent. An additional 100,000 would be provided on a more general formula allocation basis for each one-half percent of the excess of the unemployment rate over 4.75. The welfare reform jobs program has different design features and would be contained in a new, separate CETA title IX.

25. See chapter 6 for a description and discussion of the urban policy initiative.

26. The credit will be expressed as a percent of the unemployment insurance wage base and prorated over the year.

27. The administration's urban policy initiative was announced just before this volume was published. Few details beyond those reported here were known at the time and the likely congressional reception could not be gauged.

THE HUMPHREY-HAWKINS BILL. The other noteworthy initiative is the administration's endorsement in November 1977 of the latest version of the Humphrey-Hawkins full employment and balanced growth bill. This is a compromise designed jointly by the administration and congressional supporters of the bill. Among other things, it would set a target for unemployment of 4 percent within five years of its passage and require that the President specify the programs and policies he intends to pursue to achieve this goal as well as reasonable price stability.[28] Attention is directed to the need for selective and targeted policies to complement macroeconomic measures, with an emphasis on employment in the private sector. However, if the President determines that there is no other way to reduce unemployment to meet the stated goals and timetables, he is expected to utilize public service employment to the extent necessary.[29] Congressional passage of the bill appears likely in 1978.

Major Issues and Alternatives

In sum, there are five major initiatives being considered by Congress this year whose outcomes will be crucial in determining the course of federal employment and training policy over at least the next five years: the jobs component of welfare reform, the Humphrey-Hawkins bill, the 1979 CETA budget, the reauthorization of CETA, and components of the administration's urban policy initiative. Clearly this has been an active area of policy development for the new administration, but it has yet to articulate a coherent, long-term strategy into which these various pieces fit. Many important issues are raised by those proposals. Three general and crosscutting ones are discussed below, with alternative approaches to those proposed by the administration to meet similar objectives.

REGULAR JOBS VERSUS PUBLIC SERVICE EMPLOYMENT. As already noted, the administration has argued that it wishes to redirect CETA to promote long-term earnings prospects (a training and private sector focus) rather than short-term employment and income (the public service employment and work experience ap-

---

28. The administration's long-term budget, fiscal policy, and employment and training policies are intended to be consistent with the goals of the bill.
29. No new spending is authorized in the bill. Additional legislation would be required for any measures not previously authorized under CETA. After two years the President may recommend modifications of the goals and timetables, and Congress can accept or reject them.

Table 3-5. Budget Outlays under the Comprehensive Employment and Training Act, by Program and Approach, Fiscal Year 1979
Outlays in millions of dollars

	Program approach[a]				
Program and title of act	On-the-job training	Institutional training	Work experience	Public service employment	Other
Basic grants to prime sponsors (I)	224.8	793.9	780.6	128.1	14.1
Public service employment (II, VI)	5.6	3.7	152.0	6,035.5	6.2
National categorical (III)	93.6	227.7	1,641.1	147.6	170.1
Summer employment for youth	...	...	740.2	...	...
Other youth	...	...	879.8	...	...
Grants to migrants and and Indians	18.6	52.7	21.1	22.6	57.0
Welfare reform demonstration projects	...	...	...	125.0	...
Other	75.0	175.0	...	...	113.1
Job Corps (IV)	...	375.5	...	...	...
Private sector initiative (VII)	250.0	...	...	...	...
Young Adult Conservation Corps (VIII)	...	...	306.5	...	...
All programs	574.0	1,400.8	2,880.2	6,311.2	190.4
Percent of total	5.1	12.3	25.4	55.6	1.7

Source: Office of Management and Budget. Figures are rounded.
a. The program approaches are described in *Special Analyses, Budget of the United States Government, Fiscal Year 1979*, special analysis K.

proach).[30] The fact sheet supporting the CETA reauthorization states "the [private sector initiative] program represents an attempt to achieve a balance in employment and training programs between public and private sector jobs. . . . approximately 80 percent of all jobs in our economy are found in the private sector."

In fact, however, 80 percent of the outlays in the President's 1979 CETA budget is devoted to public service employment and work experience and less than 20 percent to on-the-job and institutional training (see table 3-5). Under the administration's policies the percentage of CETA outlays devoted to public service employment and work experience is likely to be even higher by 1982. Although the current titles II and VI—public service employment programs—will

30. Work experience is generally in specially created public sector slots, although a sizable minority of the job slots are in the private, nonprofit sector.

be reduced to 100,000 slots (assuming the unemployment rate is below 4.75 as in the administration's projections), the public service jobs program under welfare reform will be nearly twice as large as the current programs and account for nearly two-thirds of the projected outlays under CETA.[31] The new private sector initiative could increase substantially the outlays focused on training and the private sector, but this would be a concomitant of a much larger increase for public service employment.

Another phenomenon further reinforces this relatively strong emphasis on special public sector employment. The evidence suggests that as the unemployment rate declines, public service employment programs with the characteristics proposed by the administration are increasingly likely to substitute for the regular public and private sector employment that program participants otherwise would have had. For example, the administration estimates that at 5.6 percent unemployment, over one-half of the time spent by participants in public service employment under welfare reform may be at the expense of regular employment.[32] Recall that this is for a public service employment program that is limited to primary earners of families, pays a wage no higher than 10 percent above the minimum, and whose wages are not eligible for supplementation through the earned income tax credit. As any of these restrictions are relaxed, the extent of substitution for regular employment will increase.

Two factors should be noted in defense of this emphasis of CETA on specially created public sector jobs and work experience rather than training for regular jobs. First, the subsidized employment is not necessarily an end itself. The steadiness of the work, the skills learned on the job, and any assistance provided in making the transition to regular employment may enhance the quality of regular employment opportunities subsequently available to program participants. To date, however, there is little evidence on the longer-term effects of these public service employment programs. The large rapid expan-

31. Although the CETA slots proposed under welfare reform could be used by local prime sponsors for either training or public service employment, the administration has emphasized the latter.

32. This occurs because the participants would prefer the subsidized public service employment job, which might offer higher wages, better job security, fringe benefits, and so forth, to alternative opportunities in the private sector. It is a separate phenomenon from the fiscal substitution effect, whereby CETA local prime sponsors use some portion of the public service employment grant to underwrite employment they otherwise would have provided.

sion of such programs from the summer of 1977 to the spring of 1978 was a notable achievement, particularly because it appears that the majority of the holders of new jobs are performing useful functions. However, the jobs have not been well targeted on the disadvantaged and most of the slots have not involved the type of training, job content, and other types of assistance usually assumed to be important for increasing future regular employment opportunities.

Second, alternative program approaches for CETA target groups, more directly focused on regular jobs, have not been so successful that one can be optimistic about a rapid and multifold expansion of outlays for such purposes. On the other hand, there is no evidence that such approaches are any less effective than the public service employment, work experience approach; thus, it can be argued that they merit at least equal, if not greater, emphasis. (The urban policy public works and employment tax credit proposals, although formulated independently after the CETA initiatives, do increase the relative emphasis on regular employment of the entire spectrum of employment and training programs.)

THE DESIGN OF PUBLIC SERVICE EMPLOYMENT. It is important to distinguish between the use of public service employment for countercyclical and structural purposes.[33] In the former case, public service employment is primarily a tool of fiscal policy, to be phased in and out as the need for more or less stimulus dictates. Most of the unemployed can be eligible, and the relevance of the job content for future regular employment is less crucial than the provision of short-term employment and income. In the latter case, the program needs to be narrowly targeted on those with poor long-term employment prospects. A steady level of funding is necessary because structural unemployment is a continual problem, and the program needs to provide a type of work experience, training, and transitional assistance that will enhance participants' regular employment opportunities.

The administration appears to have this distinction generally in mind in its future plans for CETA. The proposed 1.5 million annual job slots, comprised of the 100,000 persons from the base level of the proposed title VI and the 1.4 million welfare reform slots, are in-

33. For a more detailed discussion of this and other issues related to the use and design of public service employment programs, see John L. Palmer, ed., *Creating Jobs: Public Employment Programs and Wage Subsidies* (Brookings Institution, forthcoming).

tended for those who are structurally unemployed in a relatively high employment economy. And as many as 1.5 million additional annual slots could be funded under CETA on a temporary basis in a recession of comparable magnitude to the recent one.[34] But the designs of these two public service employment titles, both separately and considered together, raise several issues.

One is that the base levels of both titles do not appear to be well targeted on the disadvantaged and structurally unemployed. Each title requires that eligible workers must be unemployed for at least five weeks. This has not proved to be an effective targeting device in the current CETA public service employment programs.[35] The proposed new title VI limits eligibility to those whose family income is less than 120 percent of the poverty level, but because this requirement is to be applied only to the previous three months, it would be met by many workers satisfying the requirement of five weeks of unemployment. And the public service jobs under the proposed welfare reform program would have no restrictions on family income. Even the new eligibility criteria for most of the recent public service employment of CETA (fifteen prior weeks of unemployment and family income below the aforementioned standard), which would be diluted under these new programs, have not been notable for reaching the intended target group.[36] Retention of this previous unemployment criterion, in combination with the restriction on family income measured over a period of six months or longer, should be considered for programs oriented to the disadvantaged and structurally unemployed.

The wage rate structure raises a second issue with particularly difficult problems for a large public service employment program. A low wage rate, along with the requirement of a relatively long period

34. About 800,000 public service slots would be triggered automatically at the peak of the recession under the new proposed title VI. Nearly the same number also might be necessary to meet the increased demand for public service jobs under the welfare reform title.

35. The characteristics of those participating under this eligibility criteria do not differ markedly from those of the general labor force. This is not surprising because, even in a high employment economy, about 15 percent of the labor force experiences at least one period of unemployment within a year, and most CETA employers can be expected to select the most qualified workers from among those eligible.

36. The new eligibility criteria do appear to be an improvement because the percentage of new participants who are AFDC recipients, black, or economically disadvantaged rose in the latter half of 1977. The education levels of new participants, however, are still above the average of those unemployed.

of previous unemployment, is crucial for restricting participants to those with poor long-term regular employment prospects and for minimizing the substitution of public service employment for regular employment.[37] This, in turn, is central to the goals of reducing unemployment differentials and achieving higher levels of employment with minimal inflationary pressures. However, wage rates at or very near the minimum are often below those of regular entry-level jobs in the public sector. In such cases, there is a concern that public service employment jobs at minimum wages either would become dead-end jobs with no relevance to regular employment or would undermine existing public sector employment standards. In any event, the creation of one and a half million or more subsidized minimum-wage jobs raises the spectre of a stigmatized second-class work force that is permanently housed in the public sector.[38]

In response to this dilemma of large public service employment programs, the administration has opted for restricting wage rates to 10 percent above the minimum in the proposed welfare reform public service employment program. Even at such low levels, as was noted earlier, the jobs would not be limited to those with the poorest long-term employment prospects and would result in a considerable substitution for regular employment. Congress, on the other hand, appears more inclined to vote for higher wage rates, placing emphasis on job quality and uniform public sector wage structures.

One way to resolve the dilemma would be to have a structurally oriented public service program of the modest size (about half a million jobs) characteristic of many incremental welfare reform proposals. In such a case, a higher wage structure would have less adverse effects, and other criteria could be introduced to ensure narrow targeting on the hard-to-employ. If the total number of jobs provided were smaller, it would also be easier to ensure that those jobs were providing useful services and developing skills relevant to either regular public sector or private sector employment. To achieve the desired shift toward a greater private sector emphasis in CETA, additional funds could then be devoted to the direct promotion of regular long-term employment.

37. See David H. Greenberg, "Participation in Public Employment Programs," in Palmer, ed., *Creating Jobs*.
38. See James W. Singer, "The Welfare Package—1.4 Million Jobs, 1.4 Million Questions," *National Journal*, vol. 9 (November 12, 1977), pp. 1764–68.

A final issue is the lack of consistency and integration between the administration's two separate public service employment initiatives under CETA. Both the base level of the proposed title VI and the proposed welfare reform title have avowedly structural objectives, serve overlapping target populations, and use the same delivery mechanism. Yet the former would have a family-income requirement and allow wages well in excess of the minimum, and the latter would have no income requirement, be limited to primary earners of families with children, and restrict wages to 10 percent above the minimum. The same person could be eligible for both programs yet receive a different wage rate depending on the program in which he or she participated.

It is difficult to perceive any rationale for such an outcome. It would seem more logical and equitable to have a common structurally oriented program, perhaps with the condition that primary earners of families with children receive a particular portion of the jobs. It is important to establish separate public service employment titles or program characteristics to distinguish between countercyclical and structural objectives, rather than to artificially segment structurally unemployed workers into welfare and nonwelfare populations.

INCREASING OPPORTUNITIES FOR REGULAR EMPLOYMENT. The administration's new private sector initiative is its primary attempt to promote the involvement of the private sector in CETA and increase private sector job opportunities for young and economically disadvantaged workers. It has been indicated that funds would be allocated to prime sponsors who establish private industry councils that approve the plans for their use if private employers have committed themselves to hire those trained. What is envisioned appears to be a new, categorical activity with strong similarities to the earlier job opportunities in the business sector (JOBS) program under which the federal government subsidized private employers' extraordinary costs for hiring and providing on-the-job training to members of disadvantaged target groups. The JOBS program met with limited success; employers were reluctant to participate because the financial incentive was too small relative to the perceived burdens of dealing with the bureaucracy and the necessity to deal with highly problematic groups of workers. (The higher rates of unemployment that prevailed in the early 1970s also contributed to an unfavorable climate.)

There is a general belief that too little of the prime sponsors' basic grants has been devoted to the promotion of private sector job opportunities. In light of this and the difficulties of the JOBS approach, an alternative design to the private sector initiative might prove more fruitful. Such an approach could involve using the new funds as seed and incentive money to sponsor promising activities for prime sponsors involving the private sector. A major intent would be to affect the use of existing discretionary funds of prime sponsors, not just create a new specific, categorical program—thereby even further increasing the linkage of CETA to the private sector. Those prime sponsors who were more responsive to this redirection and proposed innovative ideas would receive greater shares of the new money.

As a supplement to this approach, a wage subsidy program of the general type proposed as part of the administration's urban policy initiative deserves consideration. The basic objective of such a program would be to provide a substantial financial incentive for employers to hire and retain members of designated broad target groups. The subsidy should be administered with little bureaucratic difficulty. This leads many to propose a tax credit rather than a direct payment program run by the Department of Labor. If a high priority is to be placed on narrowing unemployment rate differentials sufficiently to have an effect on the inflationary consequences of low rates of aggregate unemployment, two primary target groups should be teenagers and the long-term unemployed. The former could be equally well served by a lower minimum-wage structure, but if that is not feasible, a subsidy that declines with age might be considered.[39] For the latter, the subsidy could be designed to increase with the duration of unemployment.[40]

Depending on how a wage-subsidy scheme was structured, the costs could vary considerably. In any event, the program would be a multibillion dollar one. To the extent it exceeded the $1.5 billion estimated cost of the proposed employment tax credit, it could be considered as an alternative to some portion of the more than $10

39. The administration's proposal presumably would have the subsidy end abruptly at the age of twenty-five. Given the likely high degree of substitutability of twenty-four-year-olds for twenty-five-year-olds, this could work to the severe disadvantage of the latter.

40. For example, the subsidy might be equivalent to 3 percent of the hourly wage (up to, say, 150 percent of the minimum wage) for each week of unemployment in excess of ten (up to a maximum of, say, a 50 percent subsidy) and apply to the subsequent six months or year of employment.

billion in annual expenditures for public service employment that the administration envisions for the foreseeable future.

Such a policy is not without its problems.[41] Prominent among these is the concern that it either will not lead to much additional employment for target groups (and possibly will subsidize a large amount of workers who would have been hired anyway) or that, if it does provide employment, in the case of youth it will be at the expense of jobs for adults whose earnings may be crucial to families' welfare. On the first point, it was noted earlier that the evidence strongly suggests that a lower minimum wage for teen-agers (which is conceptually equivalent to an employer subsidy except that it would have negligible budget effects) would have a major positive impact on their employment. The effect of a wage subsidy for other workers is more uncertain, but the available evidence suggests that the net budget cost per job created can compare favorably with that of public service employment.[42]

While an effective wage subsidy would result in relatively greater employment of eligible workers within any given level of employment, this would permit a lower level of unemployment consistent with inflation constraints by narrowing unemployment rate differentials. Thus, assuming accommodating macroeconomic policies, the level of employment of nontarget group members might be maintainable, while the overall distribution of employment and unemployment would be more equitable.

It should not be expected that even well-designed employer wage subsidies or tax credits for hiring disadvantaged and structurally unemployed workers will be a panacea. But such subsidies or credits may prove sufficiently effective to warrant inclusion in a broad arsenal of relevant tools, particularly as an alternative to continued expansion of specially created public service jobs. At a minimum, they might be tested on a sufficiently large basis to improve our understanding of their consequences under favorable circumstances.

41. For a discussion of a wide range of issues and some empirical estimates of the costs and effects of wage subsidy schemes, see Daniel S. Hamermesh, "Subsidies for Jobs in the Private Sector," and comments by Edward M. Gramlich and Robert I. Lerman in Palmer, ed., *Creating Jobs*.

42. A wage subsidy also could apply to regular employment in the public sector. A potential advantage of it over current approaches is that the hired workers would be integrated immediately into the regular public sector labor force and not be dependent on the transition from a public service employment or a work experience program.

Direction of the Carter Program

What generally can be said about the Carter administration's policies in the employment and income security areas? What appears to be the overall direction? With little more than a quarter of the four-year term completed it may be premature to attempt answers to such questions; however, the administration has introduced many proposals and has had the opportunity to submit its own budget as well as influence the one it inherited from the Ford administration. Thus, there is some basis for speculation.

The Long-term Budget

The new initiatives of the Carter administration to promote employment and income security would add about $20 billion to annual federal outlays by 1982 relative to the current services budget. This is a sizable expansion in dollar terms, but not relative to the economy. The result would be to maintain federal outlays devoted to employment and income security programs as a roughly constant percentage of gross national product over the five-year period from 1978 to 1982, in contrast to an approximate 75 percent increase of those outlays as a percentage of GNP over the previous decade. In large part, this outcome is a necessary result of other policies of the Carter administration. The previous growth in the GNP share of income security and employment programs was facilitated by a large decrease in the federal budget share of the national defense expenditures, coupled with a modest increase in the GNP share of the federal budget. Both of those trends are being reversed by the announced policies of the Carter administration (see chapter 10).

Administrative Efficiency

A modest amount of simplification and streamlining of administrative procedures would result. This has already been accomplished in the revision of the food stamp program. The welfare reform proposal would go much further by consolidating several existing programs and incorporating some new design features to promote this goal. And some minor changes are proposed for CETA that would reduce the reporting requirements of local prime sponsors.

Federal, State, and Local Roles

A stronger federal role vis-à-vis state and local governments is generally implicit in administration policies. The welfare reform proposal would increase substantially the federal government's financial, administrative, and standard-setting functions in this area. A similar result would be likely under any national health insurance proposal.

There has been a steady increase in the relative importance of the federal government in income security programs beginning with the Social Security Act of 1935. While it is still a controversial issue, there seems to be growing public acceptance of the proposition that the provision of basic levels of income assistance, whether through income-tested or social insurance programs, ought to be on a relatively uniform national basis. The welfare reform proposal and, presumably, any national health insurance proposal would further rationalize and clarify what are considered appropriate federal versus state and local roles.

When the Comprehensive Employment and Training Act was passed in 1973, congressional intent was to place most of the federally financed employment and training activities under one umbrella, then move toward their decentralization and decategorization and, thereby, create a greatly enhanced role for state and local governments. The Carter administration clearly is committed to CETA as the primary legislative vehicle in this area. However, its policies reflect considerable ambiguity about the degree of desirable decentralization and greatly increase the categorical nature of CETA. The administrative role of local prime sponsors has been expanded and strengthened, but both the nature of the activities and the target groups are being prescribed to a much greater degree by the federal government.

Targeting and Income Redistribution

The administration's employment and income security proposals, including the proposed income tax cut, would redistribute income toward the lower half of the population. All the increased benefits under welfare reform and much of the CETA expansion are concentrated there. The proposed income tax cut favors those below the median level of income, and the burden of the administration's social security tax increase would have fallen far more heavily upon high income earners. Although the administration's policies would establish a floor for the income of all households at about two-thirds of the poverty level, the overall income redistribution would favor low middle-income more than low-income families. This is primarily because none of the tax cut and only a small portion of the expansion of the earned income tax credit would assist the poor. Also, eligibility for the public service employment programs is quite broad, and they cannot be expected to be heavily targeted on those with low annual incomes.

Employment Emphases

There is a major emphasis on employment, which has several facets. First, endorsement of the Humphrey-Hawkins bill implies a commitment to an ambitious goal of full employment, without a clearly effective policy to contain inflation. Second, for those in the low-income population expected to work, there is a shift toward greater reliance on increased employment and training opportunities, even though they may cost more than direct income supplementation to ensure an equivalent level of family income. (Under the welfare reform proposal there actually would be a net reduction in transfer payments to low-income families.) Finally, there is the focus on subsidized public service employment and work experience, even under conditions of relatively full employment.

Conclusion

This overview of the administration's employment and income security policies suggest several general conclusions. The stronger federal role, income redistribution, and emphasis on employment are generally consistent with what one would expect of a Democratic administration. The degree of budget stringency and emphasis on efficiency flow directly from two of President Carter's most prominent campaign promises—stabilizing the relative size of the federal budget and improving government performance. Perhaps the greatest surprise is the welfare reform program, whose net cost is far in excess of President Carter's initial goal of zero, and which, together with other commitments, would greatly restrict his freedom to undertake other social policy initiatives such as national health insurance (see chapter 10). Moreover, the focus of employment policy on subsidized public sector employment is at considerable odds with the President's expressed goal of emphasizing private sector employment, although the most recent decisions made in connection with the urban policy initiative may portend a shift in the direction of the latter.

CHAPTER FOUR

Education

DAVID W. BRENEMAN

THE PRESIDENT'S 1979 education budget, in marked contrast to its recent predecessors, proposes substantial spending increases and several new initiatives. Although it may be premature to talk with certainty about the new administration's education policy, the budget is, in fact, the single most important policy statement. In addition, several events of the last year contributed to the accumulation of decisions and actions that collectively constitute policy: (1) expiring legislation provided an opportunity for the administration to develop reauthorization proposals for most elementary and secondary education programs; (2) congressional interest in tuition tax credits forced a review of existing student aid policy in a search for alternatives; and (3) President Carter's decision to create a department of education gave rise to active investigation of reorganization options. This chapter examines each of these topics together with the 1979 budget request in order to form a tentative judgment on the nature and direction of the Carter administration's education policy.

Elementary and Secondary Education

Table 4-1 presents federal outlays for elementary and secondary education programs. Most of the programs are administered by the

Many individuals in federal agencies provided the author with information and assistance in preparing this chapter; special thanks are due Mary Moore, Michael O'Keefe, Elizabeth Reisner, and Marshall Smith. Mara O'Neill provided research assistance for all budget tables, and Joseph Minarik, James McClave, and Laurent Ross prepared the tuition tax credit estimates from the Brookings MERGE file.

Table 4-1. Federal Outlays for Elementary and Secondary Education, by Program, Selected Fiscal Years, 1965–79

Millions of dollars

Program	1965	1969	1973	1975	1977	1978[a]	1979[a]
Office of Education	548	2,195	3,044	3,924	4,087	4,533	5,243
Compensatory education (title I)[b]	...	1,073	1,820	1,960	1,930	2,129	2,580
Education for the handicapped	...	54	106	151	247	366	560
Emergency school aid	...	...	41	216	241	281	305
Bilingual education[c]	...	...	30	63	89	109	130
Impact aid	349	398	580	619	765	810	781
Vocational education	95[d]	154	355	375	393	417	458
Other	104	516	112	540	422	421	429
Head Start[e]	5	350	373	426	458	536	566
Other[f]	320	374	487	667	741	839	956
Total except food	**873**	**2,919**	**3,904**	**5,017**	**5,286**	**5,908**	**6,765**
School milk and child nutrition[g]	263	336	1,298	1,832	2,792	2,811	2,699
Total	**1,136**	**3,255**	**5,202**	**6,849**	**8,078**	**8,719**	**9,464**

Sources: *Special Analyses, Budget of the United States Government, Fiscal Year 1979*, and preceding issues, except as indicated in notes.

a. Estimates by Office of Management and Budget as reported in *Special Analyses . . . 1979*.

b. Authorized by the Elementary and Secondary Education Act of 1965 (ESEA), title I.

c. Data from the Office of Bilingual Education.

d. Author's estimate, based on data from the Office of Education.

e. Head Start was first administered by the Office of Economic Opportunity. In July 1969, it was delegated to the Department of Health, Education, and Welfare, Office of Child Development. Until 1975 the money was still appropriated to the OEO before going to HEW. In 1975 and 1976 it was funded through HEW. In mid-1977, Head Start became a separate bureau in the newly formed Administration for Children, Youth, and Families under HEW's Office of Human Development Services.

f. Includes overseas dependents' education administered by the Department of Defense; Indian education administered by the Bureau of Indian Affairs, Department of the Interior; science education administered by the National Science Foundation; and other HEW programs.

g. Administered by the Department of Agriculture.

Office of Education, Department of Health, Education, and Welfare (HEW). The exceptions are the Head Start program, under the Administration for Children, Youth, and Families, and child nutrition programs (school breakfast and lunch), administered by the Department of Agriculture. The school breakfast and lunch programs are not strictly education programs; a strong case can be made for classifying them as welfare programs or even as aid to agriculture. Because of their size (nearly $2.8 billion in 1977), their inclusion as education programs would seriously affect total costs; in what follows, spending on these programs is reported separately.

Before 1965, federal support for elementary and secondary education was primarily impact aid to school districts burdened by the presence of federal installations (enacted in 1950), vocational education (authorized by legislation in 1917, and by the Vocational Education Act of 1963), Defense Department support of overseas schools for dependents, and National Science Foundation support for science education. The Elementary and Secondary Education Act of 1965 (ESEA) marked the beginning of a larger federal role in elementary and secondary education, and this act, with its numerous titles, is the principal charter of Office of Education programs. Other important legislation is the Emergency School Aid Act (1972) and the Education for All Handicapped Children Act of 1975. Since 1965 the federal share of public school revenues (including child nutrition) has been roughly 8 percent.[1] State and local governments provide the balance of support; in the 1975–76 school year, states paid 44 percent and local governments 48 percent.[2]

Federal Goals

Nearly two-thirds of federal educational appropriations provide supplemental or compensatory education services for youngsters who are educationally disadvantaged. The largest single program, title I of the Elementary and Secondary Education Act, provides money to states and to school districts based on the number of students from low-income families. The schools use the money for compensatory education services (specialized reading classes, individu-

1. W. Vance Grant and C. George Lind, *Digest of Education Statistics, 1976 Edition* (Government Printing Office, 1977), p. 71.
2. Federal general-revenue sharing funds to public schools are included in these figures as state funds. The Congressional Budget Office estimates that the federal share is between 9 and 10 percent when these funds are counted as federal dollars.

alized instruction, paraprofessional teacher aides) for youngsters who are well below the grade level in their work. Bilingual education (ESEA title VII) is aimed at children for whom English is a second language and is intended to help them develop proficiency in English. In the programs for the handicapped, federal dollars supplement state and local outlays to help ensure that all handicapped children have available to them a free appropriate public education. Emergency school aid money helps cover costs associated with school desegregation and is intended to aid those children who must overcome the educational disadvantages of minority-group isolation. Head Start is a preschool program that provides a wide range of social services—including education—to children from low-income families. The principle underlying all of these programs is the provision of additional or different educational resources to help equalize educational opportunities.

Although pressed by groups such as the National Education Association, the federal government provides no general-purpose support for school district operating expenses. Impact aid comes closest, but its purpose is to assist districts that have lost property tax revenue or have suffered extra expenditures because of the presence of federal installations or activities. Nearly 4,000 school districts are eligible for impact aid payments in the 1979 fiscal year. Federal dollars also underwrite the purchase of curricular materials and services, strengthen state and local education agencies, underwrite demonstration projects and other forms of educational innovation, and support educational research. The National Institute of Education, created in 1972, supports and coordinates federal educational research and development.

In sum, the federal government has focused primarily on the special educational needs of disadvantaged groups not well served by ordinary school programs. Existing programs cover these purposes rather comprehensively, and costly new programs are unlikely to be developed until a new—or broader—federal role in elementary and secondary education has been articulated and accepted.

The 1979 Budget

Table 4-2 presents the administration's budget proposal for elementary and secondary education for fiscal 1979, together with four benchmarks: 1977 appropriations, the Ford administration's 1978

budget, the Carter administration's 1978 budget, and 1978 appropriations.[3] President Ford's 1978 budget called for a cut of nearly
11 percent in Office of Education programs. President Carter requested approximately the 1977 appropriation, primarily by adding $350 million to title I funds. Ford's proposed cut of nearly $400
million in impact aid was left in the Carter budget, however, with
the large increase in ESEA title I offered as a quid pro quo. Congress raised the title I increase another $100 million and restored even
more than the $400 million to impact aid. In addition, Congress in-
creased funds for education for the handicapped by $100 million and
made numerous smaller increases in other programs, producing a
1978 Office of Education appropriation of $5.8 billion, a 16 percent
increase over Carter's revised budget. Combined with other agency
programs, total federal appropriations for elementary and secondary
education (excluding child nutrition) in 1978 were $7 billion, 16
percent above the 1977 level.

Perhaps chastened by this initial experience with congressional independence, the administration has requested a 15 percent increase
in current dollars for Office of Education programs in 1979. Impact
aid is still slated for a reduction (the budget requests $780 million),
but this time the administration seeks to reform the program selectively (in ways discussed later in this chapter).

The budget includes $804 million for state grants under the Educa-
tion for All Handicapped Children Act (Public Law 94-142), an
increase of $269 million, or 50 percent, over the 1978 appropriation
but substantially less than the estimated $1.3 billion authorized for
1979. The law provides for federal payments based on the number of
handicapped[4] children receiving special services in each state (up to a
maximum of 12 percent of the school-age population), multiplied by
a percentage of the national average per-pupil expenditure. This percentage increases from 5 percent in 1977 to 10 percent in 1978, 20
percent in 1979, 30 percent in 1980, and 40 percent in 1981 and be-

3. Data in tables 4-1 and 4-2 are not comparable because the first records outlays
while the second records appropriations (budget authority). Apart from administrative problems that can cause the two to differ, forward funding accounts for the main
discrepancies. Forward funding (one year's appropriation spent in the following
year) allows school administrators to plan on a certain amount of federal dollars.
Most of the large elementary and secondary education programs, with the exception
of impact aid and emergency school aid, are forward-funded.
4. The term covers seven categories of disability, and each category includes
conditions ranging from mild to severe.

Table 4-2. Federal Budget Authority for Elementary and Secondary Education, by Program, Fiscal Years 1977–79

Millions of dollars

Program	1977 appropria- tions	1978 Ford budget	1978 Carter budget	1978 Appropria- tions	1979 budget
Office of Education	4,986	4,449	4,966	5,771	6,643
Compensatory education (title I)[a]	2,285	2,285	2,635	2,735	3,379[b]
Education for the handicapped	469	470	520	693	972
State grants	315	315	365	535[c]	804
Other	154	155	155	158	168
Emergency school aid	292	275	295	310	333
National and state grants	257	240	260	275	290
Training and advisory services[d]	35	35	35	35	43
Bilingual education	115	90	135	135	150
Follow Through	59	45	59	59	35
Indian education	57	45	45	60	76
Vocational education[e]	393	385	385	418	414
Impact aid	793	395	395	839	780
A children[f]	272	292	296	298	...
B children[f]	342	0	0	345	...
Total	614	292	296	643	655[g]
Disaster assistance	...	...	...	39	12
Other	154	78	74	127	80
Construction	25	25	25	30	33
School libraries and institutional resources[h]	157	154	154	168	168
Support and innovation grants[i]	194	194	194	198	197
Special projects and training	93	90	99	101	105
Other	79	21	50	55	34
Other federal support	1,048	1,124	1,160	1,244	1,384
Head Start	475	475	485	625	680
National Institute of Education	70	109	109	90	100
Special institutions[j]	21	25	25	23	26
Indian education[k]	237	245	271	249	271
Overseas dependents' education[m]	245	270	270	257	307
Total except food	**6,034**	**5,573**	**6,126**	**7,015**	**8,027**
School milk and child nutrition[n]	2,986	2,391	2,621	2,932[p]	2,835
Total	**9,020**	**7,964**	**8,747**	**9,947**	**10,862**

Sources: Department of Health, Education, and Welfare, Office of Education, "FY 1979 Preliminary Request," unpublished data; *The Budget of the United States Government, Fiscal Year 1979—Appendix*, and preceding issue; and staffs of respective agencies.

a. Authorized by ESEA, title I.

b. This figure includes $400 million that proposed new legislation would direct to areas with high concentrations of title I children.

c. Includes $70 million carried forward from fiscal year 1977.

d. Authorized by the Civil Rights Act of 1964, title IV.

e. Author's calculations based on estimate that the elementary and secondary share of federal occu-

yond. Total federal outlays authorized under this program depend, therefore, on these percentages, on average per-pupil expenditures, and on the number of handicapped children identified and served. The $1.3 billion figure cited is based on $334 per child (20 percent of an estimated 1977–78 national average per-pupil expenditure of $1,670) for an estimated 4 million handicapped children.

Of all existing federal education programs, education for handicapped children has the most potential for explosive growth; an estimate of authorized outlays for school year 1982–83 under the existing formula is $3.9 billion.[5] The administration's 1979 request is less than authorized because the program is not a fixed entitlement but is subject to annual appropriation; $804 million is equivalent to $201 per child (assuming 4 million is an accurate estimate), or roughly 12 percent of estimated national average per-pupil expenditure.

Consistent with the administration's expressed interest in providing aid for the disadvantaged, the existing title I program is budgeted at nearly $3 billion and Head Start at $680 million, both 9 percent increases in current dollars over 1978 appropriations. In addition, the budget includes a $400 million targeting provision (a new part C of ESEA title I) to provide extra resources for high-poverty urban and rural districts. Under this provision, districts would receive support based on the number of enrolled students counted under the title I formula in excess of (1) 20 percent of district enrollment or (2) 5,000 students.[6] The 20 percent threshold will tend to channel

5. Congressional Budget Office, unpublished estimate. All estimates relating to this act are subject to considerable uncertainty, for reasons discussed in the next section.

6. Discussion of this provision within the Department of Health, Education, and Welfare predates President Carter's search for an "urban initiative," so it would be wrong to describe the $400 million as a recently developed education component of that initiative.

Table 4-2 notes (*continued*)

pational and vocational education budget is 57 percent.

f. An A child is a school child with a parent who works *and* lives on federal property. A B child is a school child with a parent who works *or* lives on federal property.

g. The 1979 budget does not disaggregate A and B children. However, data from the staff of the Assistant Secretary for Planning and Evaluation, HEW, show that $80 million is for the hold-harmless provision (for introducing formula changes gradually), and $85 million is determined by the number of children whose parents work or live in public housing.

h. Authorized by ESEA, title IV-B.

i. Authorized by ESEA, title IV-C.

j. Author's estimates.

k. Administered by Bureau of Indian Affairs.

m. Administered by Department of Defense.

n. Administered by Department of Agriculture.

p. Includes $274 million available from a special fund created to strengthen agricultural markets.

money to poor, rural districts, while the 5,000 student threshold will favor large, urban districts with high poverty levels. The rationale for providing high-poverty rural districts with extra dollars is that such districts are often located in states with low average per-pupil expenditures, meaning that fewer dollars per eligible student go to those areas under the title I formula. The arguments for spending additional dollars in large, high-poverty, urban districts are based on the high cost of educating large numbers of disadvantaged students (costs are said to rise disproportionately because of educational and behavioral problems that accompany large numbers), and on the general financial problems facing many central cities and their school districts. Since the amounts appropriated have never been sufficient to fund the program fully, many eligible children have not been helped.[7] The likely effect of the targeting provision, therefore, will be to serve more children rather than to increase resources per child.

Legislative Reauthorization

The Elementary and Secondary Education Act of 1965, as amended, expires on September 30, 1978, as do the Indian Education Act and legislation authorizing impact aid. As a consequence, the administration last year thoroughly reviewed and analyzed virtually all federal elementary and secondary education programs to prepare its reauthorization proposals. With the exception of the title I targeting provision and the reform of impact aid, the effects of the administration's reauthorization proposals will first be seen in the 1980 budget.[8]

ESEA TITLE I. The potentially most divisive issue in reauthorization is the title I allocation formula, which determines how funds are distributed among and within the states.[9] Currently, the dollars are allocated through successive jurisdictions to the schools on the basis of economic data, such as poverty counts and average per-pupil expenditure in the state; within schools, however, the children with the

7. The Committee for Full Funding of Education Programs estimates that 58 percent of eligible children received title I services in 1977. See *EFFORT: Education Full Funding Organization Report*, vol. 5 (November 15, 1977), pp. 4–5.

8. This chapter's emphasis on the budget explains the absence in this discussion of the administration's much-publicized efforts to improve basic skills. This shift in educational policy is embedded in several legislative proposals (particularly for ESEA titles II, III, and IV), but is largely one of changed program focus, administrative procedure, and targeting of existing funds. From the standpoint of educational philosophy and administration, these proposals are of considerable interest; however, virtually no new budget authority is involved.

9. For a concise description of the current formula, see National Institute of Education, *Title I Funds Allocation: The Current Formula* (NIE, 1977), pp. 103–11.

greatest educational need, regardless of family income, receive the services. These dual criteria (poverty and educational need) have caused much debate and confusion about the purpose of title I, for although low income and low achievement often coincide, they are by no means the same. Prompted by this apparent ambiguity, Congressman Albert H. Quie (Republican, Minnesota) has again introduced a bill that would drop the economic indicators from the formula and would base allocation solely on educational need. If enacted, the distributional consequences of this proposal cannot be determined accurately because the necessary student achievement data are not available; however, as many as twenty-three states might experience changes of over 15 percent in their share of funds.[10]

Assuming that economic indicators will continue to be used (as seems likely), a second issue is whether to update the poverty data by supplementing the 1970 census information with data from the 1976 Survey of Income and Education (SIE).[11] This survey produced evidence that a substantial geographic redistribution of poor children occurred between 1969 and 1975. If the 1970 census data were thus updated, southern states (with the exception of Florida) would lose title I funds to the industrial states in the Northeast, Middle Atlantic, and Great Lakes regions.[12]

Neither the administration nor the Congress want to precipitate a formula fight as part of the reauthorization. Consequently, alleged shortcomings of the SIE data are being given as reasons for not updating the formula. It seems unlikely, however, that representatives from states that would benefit from the use of more recent data (particularly those in the Northeast) will miss this opportunity to try to capture more federal dollars for their states. Furthermore, assuming that the new data are broadly accurate, not to use them would be irresponsible. As a practical matter, it is sensible to begin adjusting now to the changing distribution of poverty, rather than wait for the

10. "Statement of Paul T. Hill, Director, Compensatory Education Study, National Institute of Education" (testimony before the Subcommittee on Elementary, Secondary, and Vocational Education of the House Committee on Education and Labor, November 1, 1977; processed), p. 17.

11. A description of SIE can be found in U.S. Bureau of the Census, *Current Population Reports*, series P-60, no. 108, "Household Money Income in 1975, by Housing Tenure and Residence, for the United States, Regions, Divisions, and States (Spring 1976 Survey of Income and Education)" (GPO, 1977), pp. 1–3.

12. For example, an HEW simulation using SIE data for 1978 title I allocation yielded the following percentage changes: Illinois,+ 29; Michigan, +13; New Jersey, +23; Pennsylvania, +10; Florida, +31; Louisiana, −24; Mississippi, −20; Virginia, −20; and South Carolina, −18.

1980 census and a probably much larger and more difficult redistribution.

In theory, changing the formula through either of these alternatives would have no effect on the level of appropriations, but in practice—under a fixed budget—a change in formula would create losers, violating that informal rule of the American political system, "Do no direct harm."[13] For this reason, Congress seems to be moving toward a two-tiered formula that would not change the allocation of the first $2.8 billion (the size of the 1978 appropriation) but would change the distribution of funds in excess of that amount. This approach is appealing politically because no state would lose money compared to 1978, while the incremental funds would be allocated to reflect the shifting concentration of poverty.

Other title I reauthorization issues with potential budget impact are the part C targeting provision and a proposed part B for incentive grants to encourage the creation and expansion of state compensatory education programs. In the 1976 fiscal year, seventeen states spent a total of $364 million of their own funds on compensatory education, nearly 40 percent of the title I funds received by those states. To encourage growth of these programs, the administration proposes to match every two state dollars spent on compensatory education with one federal dollar.[14] Although administrative and conceptual problems remain, this proposal exemplifies the administration's policy of using matching funds to encourage states and localities to help achieve federal education goals.

IMPACT AID. In recent years, evaluations of impact aid have identified several features of the program that need reform:[15]

1. Payments are made for children who are not a federal burden.

2. Payments are made to wealthy districts minimally affected by federal activity.

13. Charles L. Schultze, *The Public Use of Private Interest* (Brookings Institution, 1977), p. 23.

14. Under this proposal, only state dollars spent on title I eligible schools and children would be counted for matching federal dollars. Federal payments would also be limited to a percentage of each state's title I, part A entitlement. Thus only $88 million is estimated to be eligible for matching federal funds in the 1979 fiscal year. Recent congressional action indicates that these limitations may be rejected.

15. See Harold A. Hovey and others, *School Assistance in Federally Affected Areas*, House Committee on Education and Labor, 91:2 (GPO, 1970); and Comptroller General of the United States, *Assessment of the Impact Aid Program* (General Accounting Office, 1976).

3. Payments are based on methods (particularly the use of comparable districts) that are imprecise and subject to abuse.

4. Payments sometimes increase rather than reduce financial inequities among school districts.

Successive administrations have tried to reform the program by eliminating from budget requests certain payments, such as that for B children (those whose parents live or work on federal property). Both the Ford and Carter administrations used this approach in their 1978 budgets. As always, Congress appropriated far more for impact aid than was proposed.

The Carter administration's reauthorization proposal is more finely tuned. Its major provisions are listed below.[16]

1. Payments for children whose parents are employed on federal property outside the county in which the school district is located would be eliminated. (These children clearly do not represent a loss to their districts, since their parents pay local property taxes.)[17]

2. The school district must absorb the full educational cost of federally connected children if they constitute less than 3 percent of the district's nonfederal enrollment. (Three percent is the national average of federally connected children in school districts. The purpose of this absorption provision is to end the many small payments that go to minimally affected districts, a change that would eliminate an estimated 2,400 districts from the program.)

3. Payments for children in public housing remain at the 1978 level of $85 million. (HEW wanted to end these payments on the ground that these children do not represent a federal burden of the type that impact aid was designed to ease. That proposal was rejected within the White House, and instead payments for students were to be kept at this level for two years and then phased out.)

4. The program would be shifted to forward funding.

These reforms would save an estimated $76.4 million in 1979 and, by 1983, depending on payments for public-housing students, more than $300 million a year. Early indications suggest that the proposals will not survive congressional review; the absorption provision is particularly vulnerable, since it is an assault on the principal pork-

16. Other provisions change the method of calculating the local contribution rate, modify the hold-harmless provisions, and eliminate the tier system of payments.
17. 1974 legislation eliminated payments for children whose parents work on federal property in another state and reduced payments for those out of the county.

barrel feature of the program. Nonetheless, the administration has offered a serious and well-reasoned reform package, and its fate will be a good test of congressional responsiveness.

EDUCATION FOR HANDICAPPED CHILDREN. Although the authority for grants to states for educating handicapped children is not expiring, it has figured prominently in the administration's review of education programs. First, it is enmeshed in significant ways with legislation that is expiring. Second, its potentially explosive growth could easily dominate the education budget in future years, and the administration has been forced to consider alternatives to the funding levels currently authorized.

Before the enactment of Public Law 94-142, set-asides and other provisions for handicapped children were incorporated in existing programs, including ESEA titles I and IV, impact aid, vocational education, and Head Start. Recent annual outlays under these set-asides and special provisions have been over $200 million. There is an opportunity now to rationalize and consolidate the old programs with the new law and to eliminate overlap. However, until appropriations under the new law grow substantially, consolidation may not be politically possible. For example, the administration considered proposing the transfer of ESEA title I state-operated programs for handicapped children into the new program but backed away when the political opposition became evident.[18]

For a program of such high potential cost ($3 billion to $4 billion by the early 1980s), remarkably little is known with certainty about the number of handicapped children by type and severity of handicap or about the costs of providing each with an appropriate public education. The U.S. Office of Education's Bureau of Education for the Handicapped has estimated that as many as 8 million children under the age of twenty-one are handicapped, 6 million of them school age. However, during school year 1976–77, only about 3.5 million children received aid through the new program, and, counter to expectations, very few more were reported in October 1977. An important part of the rationale for large federal payments is the assumption that many thousands of handicapped children are not being served,

---

18. Constituent groups argue, probably correctly, that education for the handicapped receives more money from the two discrete programs than it would from a consolidation, particularly since the ESEA program is fully funded "off the top" of the title I appropriation.

and that the new law will result in their being identified and provided with costly new programs. If the number of additional handicapped children turns out to be substantially less than predicted, appropriations will almost surely remain well below authorized levels, for not only will the number of eligible children be smaller than predicted, but the sizable new burden that the law was thought to place on school districts will not have materialized.

Complicating predictions further are the uncertain incentive effects of the law. The federal government pays what amounts to a bounty for each handicapped child identified and provided with the requisite educational program. Since the payment is not related to the actual cost of the education, some have feared that school districts would concentrate primarily on identifying children with very mild or questionable handicaps, whose educational needs the federal payment would cover in full. Uncertainty over funding levels in the program may offset this tendency, however, for once a student is identified as handicapped, the necessary supplemental services must be provided, regardless of the size of the federal payment.[19] Since the provision of a free, appropriate public education for all handicapped children becomes a requirement of law after September 30, 1978, the reports filed by states in October 1978 should be better indicators of the eventual size of the eligible population.

Another curious feature of the law deserves mention. Although it imposes its heaviest costs on state and local governments now, the federal share of the costs begins low and continues growing until 1982, when outlays are authorized at 40 percent of average per-pupil expenditures. Prompted by this incongruity, some administration officials during 1977 briefly considered reversing the payment schedule, providing as much as 40 percent of per-pupil expenditure in fiscal year 1979 (or even 1978), and scaling the payment down year by year. Estimation of the 1978 cost—$2.2 billion—ended serious consideration of this "front-loading" strategy. The result, however, is a payment schedule curiously out of synchronization with costs, which may lead to some questioning of the need for escalating payments after 1978.

A further problem with the legislation is that the entitlement formula does not reflect the large differences in costs associated with the various types and severity of handicap. Not being grounded in any

19. In this respect, Public Law 94-142 is also a civil rights law.

rational fashion on the actual educational costs, the formula is certain to be questioned as the size of entitlements grows. In particular, if the majority of newly identified children are minimally handicapped (as seems likely), questions are bound to be raised about why federal payments per eligible student should exceed (or even equal) ESEA title I payments.

These factors combine to make forecasts of future outlays for the education of handicapped children subject to great uncertainty. There is clearly a need to develop a better rationale for the level of federal assistance to the states, but it is difficult even to discuss that subject intelligently in the face of so much uncertainty about the basic facts. As experience with the program grows, Congress and the administration will have to reach a more rational policy for federal payments. In the meantime, appropriations will surely increase, though they will probably fall ever more behind the large sums authorized.

Future Initiatives

The Congressional Budget Office has identified three areas for possible expansion of the federal role in elementary and secondary education:[20] (1) school finance reform, (2) universal preschool, and (3) general aid to education (for example, the National Education Association's proposal to increase the federal share of school expenditures from 8 to 33 percent). Within the administration, there is discussion of a career incentives act and a community school act. Of these various possibilities, school-finance reform is most likely to be considered soon. Congressman Carl D. Perkins (Democrat, Kentucky), chairman of the House Committee on Education and Labor, introduced a bill authorizing federal incentive payments to states working to equalize school financial resources. Hearings on this bill served to stimulate interest in the topic; the 1979 budget includes $2 million to study the potential federal role in school finance reform. Possible results might be (1) modification of categorical programs so that they help, rather than hinder, state attempts at reform, and (2) a new federal program to encourage more equitable financing of elementary and secondary education both within and among states. It seems highly unlikely that

20. Congressional Budget Office, *Elementary, Secondary, and Vocational Education: An Examination of Alternative Federal Roles* (GPO, 1977), pp. 40–46. In addition, the Senate Finance Committee recently approved a bill that would provide tuition tax credits for families that send children to private elementary and secondary schools. The bill is discussed later in this chapter.

substantial new federal expenditures for this purpose will be made in the next three to five years, however, unless the Supreme Court reconsiders *San Antonio* v. *Rodriguez* (1973), in which it held (by a five to four decision) that interdistrict expenditure disparities did not violate the Constitution.

Postsecondary Education

The federal role in postsecondary education is in many ways more complex and difficult to analyze than it is at the elementary and secondary level. Over 400 separate legislative provisions govern the flow of federal dollars to postsecondary students and institutions, and virtually every federal agency provides some form of support. While HEW provides more money than any other agency, its programs do not dominate the federal connection with higher education as they do at the elementary and secondary level. The education division shares the limelight with the Social Security Administration (which dispenses over $1 billion annually in student benefits) and with the Public Health Service, which underwrites health professionals' education, biomedical research, graduate training in biological and behavioral sciences, and numerous related educational activities.

Because postsecondary programs are so widely dispersed throughout the government, it makes little sense to talk of a comprehensive higher-education policy. It is at the level of the component elements —undergraduate student aid, research, veterans' education benefits —that decisions are made. The cumulative effect of these decisions on the nation's colleges, universities, and other postsecondary institutions is largely unplanned, since the institutions and the higher education system are rarely the subject of policy analysis and debate.

Table 4-3 presents federal expenditures for postsecondary education for selected years since 1965, organized under three categories: payments to students, payments to institutions, and tax expenditures. By the 1977 fiscal year (the most recent year for which outlays are reasonably definite), expenditures under these three groupings totaled almost $14 billion, with over $7 billion spent as aid to students, over $4 billion as payments to institutions (largely for research), and $2 billion dispensed indirectly as education-related tax expenditures. In comparison with federal outlays for elementary and secondary education (table 4-1), federal expenditures for postsecon-

Table 4-3. Federal Outlays and Tax Expenditures for Postsecondary Education, by Program, Selected Fiscal Years, 1965–79
Millions of dollars

Program	1965	1969	1973	1975	1977	1978[a]	1979[a]
Payments to students	**502**	**1,687**	**4,195**	**6,913**	**7,321**	**7,522**	**8,097**
Basic educational opportunity grants	...	...	...	342	1,387	1,534	2,094
Campus-based aid[b]	131	373	829	844	865	1,033	1,099
Guaranteed loans	27	44	206	335	344	559	628
Health training and other HEW aid	206	219	283	440	303	303	309
Social security student benefits	...	366	638	840	1,181	1,338	1,505
Veterans' education benefits	43	590	2,016	3,479	2,802	2,316	2,009
Reserve Officer Training Corps and other military training[c]	42	27	113	532	330	333	349
Other	53	68	110	101	109	106	104
Payments to institutions	**1,467**	**2,750**	**3,493**	**3,613**	**4,421**	**4,719**	**5,106**
Research and development conducted at colleges and universities	934	1,426	1,888	2,228	2,702	3,061	3,339
Programs for disadvantaged students and aid to developing institutions	...	...	85	230	130	184	226
Vocational education[d]	57	121	160	137	166	176	193
Special institutions	20	38	79	89	99	112	126
Grants and loans for facilities (except health)[e]	225	597	159	73	13	56	54

Health facilities and resources and other HEW aid						
58	405	554	682	874	672	683
Service academies and other defense education[f]						
117	59	289	71	326	338	366
Other[g]						
57	104	279	103	111	120	119
Total outlays						
1,969	4,437	7,688	10,526	11,742	12,241	13,203
Tax expenditures						
n.a.	n.a.	n.a.	1,770	2,015	2,105	2,220
Exclusion of scholarships and fellowships						
n.a.	n.a.	n.a.	200	245	295	330
Parental personal exemptions for students aged 19 and over						
n.a.	n.a.	n.a.	670	750	770	790
Deductible personal contributions						
n.a.	n.a.	n.a.	440	525	585	645
Deductible corporate contributions						
n.a.	n.a.	n.a.	205	235	255	285
Exclusion of veterans' benefits						
n.a.	n.a.	n.a.	255	260	200	170

Sources: *Special Analyses, Budget of the United States Government, Fiscal Year 1979*, and preceding issues; 1979 figures updated by HEW.

n.a. Not available.

a. Estimated by Office of Management and Budget as reported in *Special Analyses . . . 1979*.

b. Components vary over the years but include educational opportunity grants, national defense student loans (supplemental educational opportunity grants and national direct student loans, respectively, after 1972), work-study program, and incentive grants for state scholarships (after 1974).

c. Administered by the Department of Defense.

d. 1965 and 1969 outlays estimated from data provided by the staff of the Office of Education.

e. 1979 amount includes $10 million for renovation grants to institutions for removing architectural barriers to handicapped students.

f. 1969 amount is not comparable to 1965 because the reporting format of the *Special Analyses* changed between those years; in 1975 a larger share of Defense Department education outlays were counted as student assistance. However, total outlays are comparable.

g. In 1973, other Office of Education and HEW programs were lumped into a general category; hence the large size of this figure relative to other years.

dary programs are large; this is, in part, attributable to the higher per-capita costs of postsecondary education and to the broader purposes served (for example, research support). While the federal share of total public outlays for elementary and secondary education hovers around 8 percent, the comparable figure for postsecondary education is over 45 percent.[21] Because federal support for higher education is provided by many agencies and is a relatively more important part of higher education than of elementary and secondary education budgets, the higher-education community has generally been ambivalent, if not opposed, to versions of the proposed department of education that would be limited essentially to HEW's education division.

Federal Goals

Before World War II, federal involvement in higher education was virtually nonexistent. After that war, the Servicemen's Readjustment Act of 1944—the GI bill of rights—made a college education possible for many thousands of veterans, and the creation of the National Science Foundation in 1950 stimulated federal support for university-based research. In the years immediately following the Soviet Union's 1957 launching of Sputnik, Washington concentrated its efforts in higher education on graduate education and research, particularly in the sciences and engineering; the National Defense Education Act of 1958 was one manifestation of this interest. These defense- and space-related education activities declined in priority as the 1960s waned and were replaced by civil rights, antipoverty, and equal educational opportunity issues. These concerns led to an emphasis on undergraduate student aid, awarded on the basis of financial need rather than academic merit and designed to ensure access to some form of postsecondary education for all who sought it.[22] These early student aid programs (educational opportunity grants, college work-

21. Calculated from data reported by the National Center for Education Statistics; Joseph D. Boyd, *National Association of State Scholarship and Grant Programs, 1976–77 Academic Year* (Deerfield, Ill.: NASSGP, n.d.); and *Special Analyses, Budget of the United States Government, Fiscal Year 1978.* The $2 billion in tax expenditures (see table 4-3) were not included. Some of the money does not accrue to the institutions; for example, a significant portion of GI bill and social security benefits are used for living expenses.

22. The Higher Education Act of 1965 created undergraduate educational opportunity grants; this act as amended provides the framework for most postsecondary education programs administered by HEW's education division.

study) provided grants to campuses for distribution to eligible students; these programs, together with direct student loans, still exist as campus-based aid programs. After tumultuous debate, Congress passed amendments in 1972 providing for direct aid to low-income undergraduates—basic educational opportunity grants. With appropriations of more than $2 billion for the 1978 fiscal year, basic grants have become the foundation of government student aid.[23]

In 1965, Congress amended the social security legislation to continue payments past the age of eighteen, up to the twenty-second birthday, for recipients' children who were full-time students and unmarried. This amendment was understandable for the time; other student aid programs were few and the problems of financing social security were less pressing. A decade later, the Ford administration questioned the need for these payments in light of expanded student aid programs and proposed (unsuccessfully) to phase them out. As other student aid programs grow, the rationale for social security education benefits will become less compelling. Nonetheless, the program's future seems politically secure.

The GI bill, managed by the Veterans Administration, is one of the largest student aid programs, with outlays of almost $3 billion in the 1977 fiscal year. When it was reinstated in 1966, it served as a type of deferred compensation and recruiting lure, but the advent of the more highly paid volunteer army largely undermined that rationale. For that and other reasons, the Ninety-fourth Congress changed the program for those enlisting after December 31, 1976, into one that requires each veteran to set aside money from salary for educational purposes, to be matched by federal dollars on a two-to-one basis. It is too early to know what effect this new legislation will have; in the meantime, the older program remains in effect until 1989, since those who enlisted before the change retain their eligibility for ten years after discharge. The number of eligible veterans has already begun to decline, however, and payments under the old GI bill will drop substantially over the next decade.

Two loan programs—national direct student loans and guaranteed student loans—round out the major federal student aid programs.

---

23. The former educational opportunity grants were renamed supplemental educational opportunity grants. The amendments also created the much smaller state student incentive grant program, which provides federal matching funds for states that establish or expand direct student aid programs.

The first dates from the National Defense Education Act of 1958 and the second from the Higher Education Act of 1965. Direct student loans are administered by the campuses, with 90 percent of the loan capital provided each year by the federal government. Loans are allocated on the basis of student financial need, with interest fully subsidized while the student is enrolled and heavily subsidized during repayment (the student pays 3 percent interest). The guaranteed loan program was legislated as an alternative to a tuition tax credit under serious consideration in the Senate in 1964. The Treasury Department, worried then as now by the enormous drain on revenues a tax credit would mean, took the lead in formulating a loan program to help middle-income families finance college costs. Financial need is not a criterion for eligibility, although interest subsidy is linked to income; students from families with less than $31,000 in adjusted gross income receive full interest subsidy while enrolled and pay 7 percent interest during repayment. Unlike direct loans, there is no federal capital contribution, for banks and other commercial lenders make the loans; federal outlays are necessary for interest subsidies and to reimburse lenders for loan defaults. In the 1977 fiscal year, $310.5 million in capital was provided for direct loans, and $367 million was appropriated for interest subsidies and loan defaults for guaranteed loans.

As is true of its role in elementary and secondary education, the federal government does not provide general-purpose institutional support for colleges and universities, for the financial health of institutions has never been accepted as an explicit federal obligation. Outlays listed in table 4-3 under "payments to institutions" are mainly for research. The federal government relies heavily on universities for basic research; in recent years, roughly half of federal basic research outlays have been spent on university research. Since most research grants and contracts are awarded competitively, guided by peer review, federal research money is concentrated in the leading institutions; the top one hundred recipients consistently garner about 85 percent of the funds.

The remaining federal payments to institutions are for specialized purposes, such as payments to medical schools for support of health manpower training and related activities, Defense Department support for military academies and reserve officer training, and Office of Education support for developing institutions. The latter program, financed at $120 million in 1978, provides direct support for small, struggling colleges, with over half of the money allocated to predominantly black private colleges, located mostly in the South.

Finally, through a variety of provisions in the tax code, the Treasury forgoes an estimated $2 billion in revenue to support activities that directly and indirectly benefit colleges and universities or their students and faculty. Various forms of income (scholarships, fellowships, GI benefits) are not taxed; parents are allowed to claim the dependent's exemption for college students, even if the student's earnings exceed the amount that would normally disqualify him or her for the exemption; and personal and corporate gifts to colleges and universities are treated as charitable deductions. The Congress is currently considering a tuition tax credit, whose lost revenues could easily surpass existing education-related credits and deductions.[24]

The 1979 Budget

Table 4-4 displays recent appropriations and presidential budgets. In a sense, there are two 1979 budgets, since the President requested additional budget authority of $1.2 billion for student aid in February, less than three weeks after the budget was released. To avoid confusion, I refer to the original as the January budget and to the enlarged version as the February budget. Since the additional $1.2 billion request was prompted by the administration's desire to head off congressional enactment of a tuition tax credit, discussion of the credit and the administration's counterproposal is deferred to the next section.

As was true of elementary and secondary education, Ford's 1978 budget request was well below 1977 appropriations, Carter raised budgets of selected programs, and Congress appropriated still more. The 1979 February budget calls for $14.4 billion for expenditure programs, up from Carter's 1978 request of $12.4 billion and congressional 1978 appropriations of $12.9 billion. The February budget is best understood when the prior year's transition budget and the momentum for middle-income aid (which prompted the additional $1.2 billion request) are recalled.

24. For a thorough discussion of tax provisions aiding education, see Emil M. Sunley, Jr., "Federal and State Tax Policies," in David W. Breneman and Chester E. Finn, Jr., eds., *Public Policy and Private Higher Education* (Brookings Institution, 1978).

Table 4-4. Federal Budget Authority for Postsecondary Education, by Program, Fiscal Years 1977–79
Millions of dollars

Program	1977 appropriations	1978 Ford budget	1978 Carter budget	1978 Appropriations	1979 January budget	1979 February budget
Payments to students	**7,857**	**6,616**	**7,743**	**8,078**	**8,159**	**9,369**
Office of Education	3,294	2,434	3,044	3,788	4,043	5,253
Basic opportunity grants	1,904[a]	1,844	2,070	2,160	2,177	3,167
Supplemental opportunity grants	250	0	240	270	270	270
Work-study	390	250	390	435	450	600
Direct student loans[b]	323	15	15	326	304	304
State student incentive grants	60	44	44	64	77	77
Student loan insurance fund and guaranteed loans[c]	367	281	281	530[d]	751	821
Graduate and professional opportunity grants	...	...	4	3	8	8
Health professions graduate student loan insurance	...	...	...	...	6	6
Health training[e]	249	214	231	300	251	251
Social security student benefits[f]	1,181	1,078	1,238	1,338	1,505	1,505
Veterans' benefits[f]	2,802	2,573	2,913	2,316	2,009	2,009
Reserve Officer Training Corps and other military training[g]	331	317	317	336	351	351
Payments to institutions	**4,401**	**4,420**	**4,634**	**4,832**	**5,043**	**5,043**
Office of Education	464	378	463	538	539	539
Programs for disadvantaged students	85	73	70	115	115	115
Aid to developing institutions	110	110	120	120	120	120

Language training and area studies	18	10	16	18	18	18
Construction[h]	3	7	7	12	82	82
Renovation grants	...	...	...	...	50	50
Interest subsidy and other loans	3	7	7	12	32	32
Strengthening research libraries	...	...	...	5	5	5
Other library resources	20	10	19	20	0	0
Vocational education[i]	161	158	158	171	170	170
Other	67	10	73	77	29	29
Special institutions[j]	94	109	109	111	122	122
Health facilities and resources[e]	539	251	380	507	401	401
Improvement of postsecondary education	12	14	14	12	14	14
Lifelong learning	...	...	...	...	5	5
Other HEW	22	27	27	24	27	27
Service academies and other defense education[g]	328	346	346	341	369	369
Research and development conducted at colleges and universities	2,942	3,295	3,295	3,299	3,566	3,566
Total	**12,258**	**11,036**	**12,377**	**12,910**	**13,202**	**14,412**

Sources: *Higher Education Daily, Supplement*, vol. 6 (January 24, 1978), and vol. 5 (January 21, 1977); *The Budget of the United States Government, Fiscal Year 1979—Appendix*, and preceding issue; *Special Analyses, Budget of the United States Government, Fiscal Year 1979*, and preceding issue; Office of Management and Budget, *Fiscal Year 1978 Budget Revisions, February 1977* (GPO, 1977); unpublished data from Social Security Administration, Veterans Administration, American Association for the Advancement of Science, and HEW, Division of Education Budget Analysis; and author's estimates as noted. Figures are rounded.

a. Includes a supplemental grant of $211 million used in 1976 but carried over into the 1977 accounts.
b. Primarily capital contributions; for example, the 1979 figure of $304 million includes $286 million in capital contributions. The $15 million in 1978 was for prior year's loans that were forgiven because of special service.
c. In 1978 the guaranteed student loan program was absorbed into and replaced by the student loan insurance fund.
d. Includes a proposed supplemental grant of $239 million as a result of cost increases.
e. Author's estimates, based on data from the Office of Management and Budget.
f. Outlays rather than budget authority most accurately reflect administration and congressional intent for these entitlement programs.
g. Administered by the Department of Defense. Author's estimates based on data from OMB.
h. Authorized by Higher Education Act, title VII.
i. Author's estimates. Assumes that the higher-education share of federal occupational and vocational education budget is about 23 percent.
j. Author's estimates.

Ford's 1978 budget called for $1.844 billion for basic opportunity grants, an amount that would have limited the maximum award to $1,400, even though Congress had authorized grants up to $1,800 in the 1976 amendments. In addition, Ford requested no money for either supplemental opportunity grants or direct student loans, arguing that basic grants, college work-study, and guaranteed student loans provided sufficient coverage. Carter raised the basic grant request to $2.07 billion (an amount estimated to allow full funding with a $1,600 maximum grant), requested $240 million for supplemental opportunity grants, and raised college work-study from $250 million to $390 million, but left direct loans unchanged on the ground that they were redundant. This heavy-handed approach to student-loan reform was no more effective than the comparable attempt with impact aid, for Congress promptly appropriated $311 million for direct loans.

The January 1979 budget raised the maximum basic grant to $1,800 but kept the total request virtually unchanged at $2.18 billion. That was possible because, even though the higher maximum grant would have raised the average award from roughly $900 to $990, it was estimated that the number of recipients would drop by nearly 200,000, from 2.4 million to 2.2 million students. Increases in nominal family incomes were projected to rise faster than the cost of living, thereby reducing the number of eligible students. The program's inflation adjustment is not sufficient to offset the annual growth in family incomes.

Although touted as expanding aid to middle-income families, the two changes proposed for basic grants in the January budget (raising the ceiling to $1,800 and increasing the asset exclusion in the family contribution formula from $17,000 to $25,000) would do little in that regard. Of the $2.18 billion requested, it was estimated that less than $140 million (approximately 6 percent) would go to recipients from families with incomes over $16,000, a minimal change from the preceding year. To use the basic grant program to help large numbers of middle-income families, the government would need to reduce the expected family contribution by changing either the income assessment rates or the family-size offset schedule, and neither change was proposed in the January budget.[25]

25. See footnote 35 for an explanation of these terms.

The three campus-based student aid programs and the state student-incentive grant program were budgeted in January at essentially 1978 appropriation levels, meaning a cut in real terms roughly equal to the inflation rate. Having learned from last year's experience that to try to restrict funding of direct student loans is futile, the President requested a $286 million capital contribution (the first time in seven years that a President has requested money for that program). The one new student aid program of 1977, graduate and professional opportunity fellowships for minorities and women, increased from $3 million to $8 million, an amount more than offset, however, by the proposed termination of fellowships for public service and mining.

Interest subsidies and loan defaults under the guaranteed loan program are paid from the recently established student loan insurance fund. Although only $281 million was initially requested for the 1978 fiscal year—because more than $230 million of unobligated funds were carried over from the previous year—$239 million more was eventually appropriated to meet the estimated $737 million required. Rising interest rates had raised the special allowance paid to lenders by roughly 1.5 percentage points, and 1976 legislative changes increased the federal government's share of the costs incurred by state guarantee agencies. The January budget anticipates expenditures at the 1978 level, including $530 million in interest subsidies and nearly $220 million in net default payments. That outlays on guaranteed loans are now second in size only to basic grants among Office of Education student aid programs is particularly ironic, since the program's original appeal was that federal outlays would be minimal.

The budget includes $1.5 billion in outlays for social security education benefits, an increase of nearly $170 million over the 1978 expenditure level. As mentioned earlier, the Ford administration had sought to phase out these benefits over four years, a decision that the Carter administration reversed but, instead, proposed to limit to amounts no larger than the maximum basic grant. Congress rejected this proposal for 1978, but the administration has advanced it again, expecting it to reduce outlays by $131 million.

Although the GI bill is an entitlement for those enrolled in eligible programs, the Ford administration found a way to cut its 1978 budget by proposing that eligibility be reduced from ten to eight years after discharge, a change that would have saved over $300 million in 1978 alone. The Carter administration rejected that proposal and projected outlays of $3.8 billion for 1978 education benefits, of which an estimated $2.9 billion were for postsecondary education. Actual 1978 expenditures are nearly $600 million lower, for reasons that are not clear. One possible explanation is that the Veterans Administration's closer monitoring of the satisfactory progress rule and similar administrative changes reduced the incentive for institutions to recruit veterans. The projected decline in 1979 payments to $2.0 billion reflects the steady drop in eligible Vietnam-era veterans, as well as the proposal to eliminate payments for general flight training and correspondence schools, which is estimated to save $100 million.

Most of the relatively small programs of institutional assistance in the Office of Education are budgeted at the 1978 appropriation level. The major breakthrough from the higher education community's standpoint is a $50 million request to help colleges and universities offset the cost of removing architectural barriers in complying with regulations governing nondiscrimination against handicapped persons. The President's budget refers to this initiative as a loan program under the higher education facilities loan and insurance fund, while HEW's budget-briefing materials claim it as a grant program under title VII of the Higher Education Act as amended. This confusion apparently reflects last-minute debates between HEW and the Office of Management and Budget (OMB), with HEW favoring the grant, OMB the loan approach. Arguments favoring grants stress the absence of an investment objective in complying with the regulations, while loan proponents argue that grants might encourage unduly zealous (and expensive) forms of compliance, which loans would discourage. The indecision apparent within the executive branch and the last-minute nature of the request suggest a need for Congress to examine this item closely. The potential costs of this program are enormous, not to mention those associated with making college buildings both energy-efficient and in compliance with federal health and safety laws.[26]

The administration's budget for basic research (the part of the R&D budget of greatest concern to universities) continues the real

26. HEW also plans a 1978 supplemental appropriation of $30 million for loans under the higher education facilities and loan insurance fund for assistance in complying with federally mandated programs.

growth that began again in the 1976 fiscal year, following nearly a decade of decline. Between 1967 and 1975, budget authority for basic research dropped by more than 20 percent in constant dollars,[27] and the real growth that began again under President Ford and continues under President Carter will only manage to regain 1967 levels (in constant dollars) by the 1979 fiscal year.[28] Specifically, the 1979 budget requests $3.6 billion for basic research, an increase of nearly 11 percent over 1978. Basic research is given favored treatment over applied research and development, for the total R&D budget of $27.9 billion is up by just 6.1 percent, barely keeping pace with inflation. The budget provides roughly an 8 percent increase in research and development at colleges and universities, rising from $3.30 million to $3.57 billion.

Tuition Tax Credits and the Middle-Income "Squeeze"

One issue dominated higher-education discussion last year—the financial squeeze facing middle-income families with children in college. Political pressure for some type of aid for middle-income families reached a near-fever pitch during late 1977 and early 1978, expressing itself initially in a congressional push for education tax allowances. Over one hundred bills for tax credits, deductions, or deferrals were introduced in the Ninety-fifth Congress,[29] and one (S. 311), sponsored by Senator William V. Roth, Jr. (Republican, Delaware), was tacked onto the Senate's social security bill and was removed by the conference committee only after steadfast resistance by several House conferees. Treasury and HEW officials testified against the tax expenditure approach to aiding middle-income families, and an HEW task force began work in late 1977 to develop

27. Willis H. Shapley, Don I. Phillips, and Herbert Roback, *Research and Development in the Federal Budget, FY 1978* (American Association for the Advancement of Science, 1977), pp. 30–36. These annual reports sponsored by AAAS provide thorough analyses of each year's R&D budget, including its impact on colleges and universities.

28. President Ford's final budget message stressed basic research and development as one of two areas where he had requested real growth in expenditures, but even those increased requests left the 1978 level more than $100 million below 1967 in 1972 dollars. Ibid., p. 33.

29. *Report on Hearings before the Task Force on Tax Expenditures, Government Organization, and Regulation on College Tuition Tax Credits,* prepared for the House Committee on the Budget (GPO, 1977), pp. 35–37.

an alternative. The administration argued that extending and modifying current student aid programs would be more efficient and more equitable than a tax credit in directing aid to families with the greatest relative need. Although the January budget did not contain specific aid for middle-income families, HEW officials claimed that $700 million in the allowance for contingencies was for additional student aid.

By early February, members of Congress opposed to tax credits began to doubt that the administration would produce its counterproposal in time. Senator Claiborne Pell (Democrat, Rhode Island), chairman of the education subcommittee of the Human Resources Committee, introduced a bill—the college opportunity act—to extend basic grants (at a cost of $1.2 billion) to an estimated 1.5 million students whose families earn up to $25,000. Congressman William D. Ford (Democrat, Michigan), chairman of the postsecondary education subcommittee of the Education and Labor Committee, consulted with representatives of the higher education associations and developed a bill for middle-income student assistance that he was prepared to introduce with or without administration support.[30] Suddenly, all assumptions about student aid expenditures (and purposes) were shattered, as members of the authorizing committees sought to derail tuition tax credits with vast (and hastily developed) increases in direct-aid programs.[31] The administration's sluggishness had nearly removed it from participation, and the opportunity to review student aid legislation with care before the 1980 reauthorization was being jeopardized by the middle-income backlash.

As the February budget shows, the administration managed to assert its role by requesting $1.2 billion for student aid programs, most of it for basic grants. Tax credit proposals still have many supporters in Congress, however, and the outcome will not be known until later this year when budget realities have been considered and

30. Budget amounts considered by Congressman Ford ranged between $1.2 billion and $2.0 billion. It was assumed that direct outlays would have to be roughly the same as the revenue loss under tax credits for the bill to be seriously considered. The administration's promised $700 million was dismissed as too small to be a serious alternative.

31. Apart from the merits of direct expenditures over tax credits, competition between committees was also involved, since tax legislation is the province of the Senate Finance Committee and the House Ways and Means Committee, while most student aid programs are governed by the Senate Human Resources Committee and the House Education and Labor Committee.

final tallies taken. Tax credits may be defeated, but the cost of that defeat will be far more expensive than the administration had originally hoped. Furthermore, until the outcome is known, it will be virtually impossible for HEW to develop legislative proposals for postsecondary reauthorizations since the shape—and purpose—of existing student aid programs will be in flux.

What are the issues and arguments that underly this emotion-laden debate? As is true of costs for virtually all goods and services in the last decade, college costs have risen sharply; for some campuses, tuition, room, and board for a year's schooling exceed $7,000, and families with more than one child in college face a particular burden. Often overlooked is the fact that median family incomes have also risen sharply during these years, generally outpacing the growth of college costs.[32] But even if the absolute burden of financing a college education has not changed dramatically, the *relative* burden has shifted against families whose incomes are too high to qualify for need-based student aid. For such families, college is no easier to finance now than it was ten years ago, while the large increases in need-based student aid have helped many low-income families finance an education that would have been totally out of reach before.

Much of the political pressure arises from this relative deterioration in the position of middle-income families, and Congress and the administration have clearly responded to this newfound student-aid constituency. The debate centers on the form such aid should take. Tax credits can be designed in endless variations, and it is impossible to analyze all of their features here; however, most versions provide a flat amount (say $250) to be subtracted from tax liability if net tuition charges of at least that amount have been incurred.[33] Table 4-5 presents an estimate of the cost and distribution of a $250 credit, similar to that proposed by Senator Roth. If the credit were nonrefundable, families with adjusted gross incomes below $10,000 would receive only 8.6 percent of the benefits, while those with adjusted gross incomes above $25,000 (representing roughly 14 percent of all families) would receive nearly 45 percent of the total. Less

32. See Breneman and Finn, eds., *Public Policy and Private Higher Education:* chapter 1 for data on family income and college costs; chapter 3 for a detailed analysis of the middle-income squeeze.

33. Low-income families that do not have $250 in tax liability would not receive the benefit of the credit unless it was refundable; that is, paid as a negative income tax.

Table 4-5. Distribution of Annual Costs of $250 Tuition Tax Credit for Undergraduate Students, Nonrefundable and Refundable Versions, by Adjusted Gross Income of Family[a]

Income class (dollars)	Distribution of population (percent)	Nonrefundable tax credit			Refundable tax credit		
		Cost (millions of dollars)	Distribution (percent)	Cumulative distribution (percent)	Cost (millions of dollars)	Distribution (percent)	Cumulative distribution (percent)
0–4,999	27.1	34.9	2.5	2.5	432.6	22.8	22.8
5,000–9,999	16.6	85.9	6.1	8.6	151.8	8.0	30.9
10,000–14,999	17.8	166.1	11.8	20.4	185.1	9.8	40.6
15,000–19,999	15.2	257.9	18.3	38.7	262.0	13.8	54.5
20,000–24,999	9.5	230.3	16.4	55.1	230.4	12.2	66.6
25,000–34,999	8.7	342.6	24.4	79.5	342.7	18.1	84.8
35,000–49,999	3.2	182.5	13.0	92.5	182.6	9.6	94.4
50,000 and above	1.8	106.2	7.5	100.0	106.2	5.6	100.0
Total	100.0	1,406.4	100.0	...	1,893.4	100.0	...

Sources: Brookings 1970 MERGE file projected to 1977; and estimates from the Congressional Budget Office of the family income distribution of the undergraduate population, based on the Survey of Income and Education.

a. No attempt was made to net out student aid in determining eligibility for the credit. Estimates allow full credits for all full-time students and one-third credits to all part-time students.

than half (46.5 percent) of total benefits would go to families in the middle-income range of $10,000–$25,000. Cost to the Treasury is estimated at $1.4 billion; it would rise sharply if the size of the credit were increased.

A refundable credit would be less regressive, reducing the proportion of the total benefit going to families with incomes over $25,000 from 45 to 33 percent. The price tag for this improvement in equity would be roughly $500 million, raising the total cost to nearly $1.9 billion.

Although a tax credit has little to commend it on equity grounds, would it offset that flaw by encouraging increased investment in education or by altering the choice between low-priced public and high-priced private institutions? Unfortunately, research supports neither of these possibilities. Although the college enrollment decision is responsive to price changes, most estimates indicate that the tuition elasticity is substantially less than 1.0, meaning that a given percentage fall in price does not produce a comparable percentage increase in demand. In particular, the price responsiveness of higher-income families (the group that receives the bulk of benefits under most tax credit schemes) has been estimated to be highly inelastic. Consequently, a $250 nonrefundable tax credit would induce very little increased college enrollment and instead would simply be pure tax relief to most families.[34]

Nor would such a credit help struggling private colleges by reducing their costs relative to state-supported institutions, since it applies to the *first* $250 in tuition paid. With the exception of the California community colleges, virtually every public institution in the land charges at least $250 in tuition, and thus most families would receive the full value of the credit regardless of the college attended; the tuition gap between public and private colleges would not be reduced. If that were the public purpose, one could devise an effective tax credit by excluding the first $500 or $1,000 of tuition, so that only those attending high-priced institutions would benefit. That type of credit would influence choice, since the benefit would depend on the price of the college attended, but the very features that make it

34. Of course, there would be no tax relief if the credit led to offsetting tuition increases. See Michael S. McPherson, "The Demand for Higher Education," in Breneman and Finn, eds., *Public Policy and Private Higher Education*, for a thorough review of the demand literature, and Emil M. Sunley, Jr., "Federal and State Tax Policies," ibid., for further analysis of tax credits.

Figure 4-1. Basic Grants[a] for College Students by Annual Family Income, under 1978 Program and Carter and Senate proposals[b]

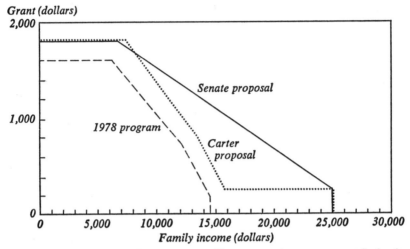

a. Assumes a family of four with one parent working, no unusual expenses, no contribution from assets, no unreimbursed tuition offset, filing a joint income-tax return, and with one child in college at a cost of at least $3,600.
b. See text for details of Carter and Senate proposals.

effective reduce its attractiveness politically, and proposals of this ilk are not likely to be enacted.

The main features of the administration's counterproposal and the Senate's college opportunity bill are illustrated in figure 4-1. Of the $1.2 billion added in the administration's budget, $1.0 billion is for basic grants. The January budget raised the maximum award from $1,600 to $1,800 and liberalized the treatment of assets. The February budget added $750 to the family-size offset (the amount of income from which no contribution to college costs is assessed) which, in combination with the larger maximum grant, increased awards for those with incomes between $8,000 and $16,000 by as much as $200; it also added a flat $250 grant for students from families with incomes from $16,000 to $25,000 and liberalized the program's treatment of independent students.[35]

35. Eligibility for basic grants is calculated as follows: applicants fill out a financial statement listing family income and assets. Adjustments for federal tax payments and living costs (the family-size offset) produce a figure called discretionary net income. Income assessment rates of 20 percent on the first $5,000 of discretionary net income and 30 percent on amounts above $5,000 are applied to determine the family contribution to education costs. This amount is subtracted from the maximum grant to determine the actual award. A similar procedure is applied to assets. Thus, basic grants can be given to higher-income families by raising the family-size offset, by lowering income assessment rates, or by liberalizing asset treatment.

If the administration's February budget for basic grants were enacted, more than $300 million of the additional money would go to
those with incomes below $16,000, and nearly $700 million would
go to families in the $16,000–$25,000 range, largely through the
$250 flat grants. Approximately 250,000 additional students would
be added to the program through changes in the family-size offset
and the liberalized treatment of independent students,[36] while as
many as 2.8 million additional students would be covered by the
$250 grants. The bulk of the benefits, therefore, would go to the
higher-income families added to the program. (The February proposal also extends the interest subsidy on guaranteed student loans
to families with adjusted gross incomes up to roughly $47,000.)

How does the administration's February proposal compare with
a nonrefundable $250 tax credit? First, it is less regressive, in that
grant benefits stop at incomes of $25,000. On the other hand, it does
little for dependent students from the lowest income families (under
$8,000). Their principal gain in 1979 is the $200 increase in the
maximum grant, an increase authorized by Congress in 1976 and
proposed in Carter's January budget. Thus, for the lowest income
levels, the February proposal confers little benefit, except for liberalizing treatment of independent students and increasing work-study
funds (see table 4-4). The flat $250 payment for students from fam-
ilies making $16,000–$25,000 a year violates the income-related
principle on which the program was founded, for surely if a family
earning $25,000 needs a $250 grant, a family earning $16,000 needs
even more. In short, the administration's proposal is essentially equivalent to a nonrefundable $250 tax credit with a cap on eligibility at
$25,000 income. Seen in this light, the proposal is not "the greatest
higher education initiative since the G.I. bill enacted 30 years ago."[37]
If it were politically possible to cap a $250 tax credit at the $25,000
income level and prevent the credit from being steadily increased,
one might even prefer the credit on grounds of administrative efficiency.

The Senate's college opportunity proposal (see figure 4-1) remedies one of the obvious deficiencies in the administration's proposal
by maintaining the link between grant size and family income. This

36. The change in the family offset schedule increases the amount of the grants
to students already in the program but receiving less than the maximum grant. It
also adds new students in higher income brackets.
37. Attributed to HEW Secretary Joseph A. Califano, Jr., *Higher Education
Daily*, vol. 6 (February 10, 1978), p. 1.

is achieved by lowering the assessment rate levied against discretionary net income to 10.5 percent, thereby producing a steadily declining grant up to the $25,000 income level. Thus, a family with $15,000 income would receive a grant of roughly $1,075, while a family with $23,000 income would receive approximately $435 in grant assistance. Assuming that the middle-income squeeze is a real problem, the Senate's bill has the merit of concentrating aid at the lower end of the middle-income range, at a cost of roughly $200 million more in basic grant expenditures than under the administration's proposal. The companion bill in the House was modified in late February to be similar to the Senate's proposal, meaning that the administration's version has been effectively rejected.

Although the details of the various direct assistance programs are important, there are much greater stakes involved in heading off a tax credit for college tuition, for a successful counterproposal should ensure the defeat of the Packwood-Moynihan tuition tax credit bill. Sponsored by Senators Robert Packwood (Republican, Oregon) and Daniel P. Moynihan (Democrat, New York) and introduced with forty-one cosponsors, this bill would provide a refundable tax credit (up to $500) equal to 50 percent of tuition paid for any individual paying tuition for higher education (including graduate study), vocational education, or accredited and tax-exempt elementary and secondary education. When fully implemented it would cost an estimated $4 billion to $4.7 billion. Senator Moynihan's goal is to prevent a state monopoly in education, particularly elementary and secondary education, by providing aid to parents sending children to private (including parochial) elementary and secondary schools. The sponsors believe that the courts will not rule this form of aid to church-related schools unconstitutional, since such schools are only a small part of all eligible institutions.

The stakes riding on this legislation are much more than the billions of dollars in cost—far more significant is the challenge to the system of public elementary and secondary schools. Unlike the $250 college tuition tax credit, which would have little effect on the choice of college, the Packwood-Moynihan credit could be expected to influence choice between public and private school. Not only is the credit larger, but it would cover a significant fraction of the cost of private elementary or secondary schooling. Its enactment might well prompt the more concerned and more affluent parents to abandon the public schools, helping to further the separation of public and private schools along economic class lines. (Since the credit covers only 50 percent of tuition, private schools would still be out of the reach of most poor parents.) Having left the public schools, many parents would be less likely to support bond issues and property tax increases earmarked for them, thereby hastening their decline.

Some supporters of the Packwood-Moynihan bill have likened tax credits to educational vouchers, arguing that increased competition from private schools will help to improve public schools. The counterargument is that tax credits would simply subsidize the withdrawal of the most vocal and concerned parents, thereby removing the strongest source of pressure for improvement in the public schools.[38] Regardless of one's view on the relative merits of competition versus working from within to maintain the vitality of institutions, the Packwood-Moynihan tax credit is not as equitable as a pure voucher system, since the benefits of the credit would be limited to those families able to pay 50 percent of tuition costs. By contrast, a voucher system would provide each student with an amount of money to spend on education equal, for example, to existing public expenditures per pupil.[39] One of the principal failings of the Packwood-Moynihan tax credit as social policy is that it would preserve an effective state monopoly in education for one group of citizens (the poor) while helping to undermine the one benefit that a state monopoly would have— the participation and involvement of all citizens, rich and poor alike. Those who believe in the value of educational diversity and competition at the elementary-secondary level should, on grounds of equity, advocate educational vouchers rather than tuition tax credits.[40]

A Department of Education?

During the election campaign, Jimmy Carter endorsed a department of education at the cabinet level, which the politically active National Education Association wants. During 1977, a reorganiza-

38. For an analysis, see Albert O. Hirschman, *Exit, Voice, and Loyalty: Responses to Decline in Firms, Organizations, and States* (Harvard University Press, 1970).

39. Some versions of the voucher proposal would provide larger payments to students from low-income families.

40. In February 1978, the Senate Finance Committee passed a phased-in version of the Packwood-Moynihan proposal.

tion task force within the Office of Management and Budget studied the issue and presented three options to the President. The most far-reaching called for a department of education and human development, embracing not only most of the programs discussed in this chapter but others such as the Labor Department's youth-oriented training programs. The second option described a more modest department, limited largely to the current education division of HEW plus activities such as the National Science Foundation's science education programs and Housing and Urban Development's college housing program. The final option, advocated by HEW Secretary Joseph Califano, would have upgraded HEW's education division, making its head an undersecretary and increasing the number of assistant secretary positions. Although the President did not endorse any option then, he reaffirmed his commitment in the State of the Union address on January 19, 1978, and instructed the task force to work on the details with congressional staff members (Senator Abraham A. Ribicoff, Democrat, Connecticut, had independently introduced a bill to create a department of education).

The dilemma is that only a comprehensive department will draw together the many education functions scattered throughout the government, but such a department may be politically impossible to create.[41] A broad department might include, in addition to the education division, such HEW programs as Head Start, vocational rehabilitation, and the Administration for Native Americans (all from the Office of Human Development Services), and health professionals' education (from the Health Resources Administration); the Veterans Administration's GI bill;[42] the Interior Department's Indian education program (from the Bureau of Indian Affairs); Labor Department's Job Corps and other youth training programs; the Defense Department's overseas dependents education program; the National Science Foundation's science education programs; and the entire National Foundation for the Arts and Humanities. However, the active constituencies of most of these programs will resist their transfer into an education department. The changes would also play havoc with the cognizant congressional committees, generating resistance

41. In addition, there are administrative obstacles. For a thorough discussion, see Rufus E. Miles, Jr., *A Cabinet Department of Education* (American Council on Education, 1976).
42. This shift was never seriously considered by the reorganization task force.

from that source as well. In the absence of a compelling reason (and few argue that an urgency exists comparable, for example, to the need for a department of energy), there is little political advantage for the President in pursuing this option—but many political pitfalls.

The second option is a modest department formed largely from Office of Education programs. But the relevant question is, Why bother? It would not provide the benefits of greater coordination or centralized control but would simply add another cabinet officer seeking the President's ear. Some argue that cabinet status is necessary to ensure larger appropriations for education programs, but the 1979 budget belies that view, for surely education was as generously treated in this year's budget as any of its supporters could hope.[43] In short, if a President wants to spend heavily on education, the structure does not stop him; if he does not want to, a secretary of education is unlikely to sway him.

A further issue is what happens to "health" and to "welfare" when "education" is removed. Is it reasonable to think that the health industry will rest content at the subcabinet level if education has gained a seat in the cabinet? And can a department of welfare (or income maintenance) be far behind a department of health? This reasoning suggests that pressure for proliferating cabinet departments is likely to result from granting cabinet status to any activity that does not absolutely require it. Although campaign pledges should not be dismissed lightly, honoring them should not take priority over clearheaded analyses of their implications.

What can be said on behalf of change is that a clear need exists to reorganize the education division of HEW. The position of assistant secretary for education (ostensibly the highest ranking education official) is simply untenable, for the commissioner of education has virtually all program and budget authority. The one resource in the assistant secretary's office is the policy development staff, but it is wasteful not to have that staff working directly for the official who has operating and budget responsibility for the programs. Whenever competent and ambitious people occupy these two positions, competition and jurisdictional disputes are sure to ensue and the result is often poor policy formulation. Clarifying lines of authority and improving the policy process within the education division would be

43. Some observers believe, however, that Secretary Califano strongly advocated the large education budget to undercut that argument for a separate department.

a sound first step in reorganization. With one official clearly in charge, less time would be spent in bureaucratic scuffles and more on program management and improvement. Elevating that person to the rank of undersecretary would enhance the status of the position and signify that a meaningful change had taken place.

In April, the administration testified in favor of a department with a heavy emphasis on elementary and secondary education. It would include all of HEW's education division plus most programs listed in table 4-1 but no other major postsecondary programs. Congressional failure to enact this limited version would be more damaging to the President than to education.

A Glance Ahead

Based on the preceding discussion, it is possible to make rough estimates of future federal education outlays and to compare them with OMB's projections. Table 4-6 presents aggregate federal education outlays, actual or estimated, for 1965–83. Education outlays as a percent of the budget hit a high of 4.8 percent in 1971 and stayed near that level through 1976. That figure dropped sharply in 1977 and 1978, to a low of 3.9 percent, largely reflecting President Ford's lean education budgets.[44] Because of forward funding, the effect of President Carter's 1979 request (if enacted) will show up mainly in 1980 outlays, when education is estimated at 4.1 percent of the budget. Based on foreseeable trends, education's share is projected to decline steadily through 1983.

The projections are based on separate estimates for seven large programs (or areas of support): ESEA title I, education for the handicapped, impact aid, GI bill, social security education benefits, basic opportunity grants, and research and development conducted at colleges and universities. All other components of the education budget are projected to increase between 6 and 7 percent a year.

For ESEA title I, the targeting provision is assumed to remain at $400 million, while part A is assumed to grow at roughly 7 percent a year, in line with the Congressional Budget Office current-policy projections. Outlays for education for the handicapped are conservatively projected to increase to $1.6 billion in 1983, while the adminis-

44. Remember that most large education programs are forward-funded, so that outlays reflect the previous fiscal year's appropriations.

Table 4-6. Federal Outlays for Elementary and Secondary Education and Postsecondary Education, Actual and Projected, Fiscal Years 1965–83

Fiscal year	Outlays (billions of dollars)			Percent of total federal outlays[a]		
	Elementary and secondary[b]	Post-secondary[c]	Total	Elementary and secondary	Post-secondary	Total
1965	0.9	2.0	2.9	0.74	1.63	2.37
1966	2.0	2.8	4.8	1.45	2.03	3.48
1967	2.7	3.7	6.3	1.76	2.42	4.11
1968	3.0	4.4	7.4	1.68	2.46	4.14
1969	2.9	4.4	7.4	1.57	2.38	4.01
1970	3.6	5.1	8.8	1.83	2.59	4.48
1971	3.9	6.2	10.1	1.84	2.93	4.78
1972	3.8	6.6	10.3	1.64	2.85	4.44
1973	3.9	7.7	11.6	1.58	3.12	4.71
1974	4.1	8.1	12.1	1.53	3.02	4.51
1975	5.0	10.5	15.5	1.54	3.23	4.78
1976	4.8	12.6	17.3	1.31	3.44	4.72
1977	5.3	11.7	17.0	1.32	2.91	4.23
Projections[d]						
1978	5.9	12.2	18.1	1.28	2.64	3.92
1979	6.8	13.2	20.0	1.37	2.65	4.02
1980	7.9	14.2	22.1	1.46	2.63	4.09
1981	8.5	14.7	23.2	1.44	2.49	3.93
1982	9.2	15.4	24.7	1.40	2.35	3.77
1983	10.0	16.3	26.3	1.39	2.26	3.64

Sources: For 1965–78, *Special Analyses, Budget of the United States Government, Fiscal Year 1979* and relevant preceding issues; for projections, see note d. Figures are rounded.

a. Total federal outlays for 1978–80 are official budget estimates; for 1981–83, outlays are assumed to be 21 percent of projected gross national product.

b. Excludes school breakfast and lunch programs.

c. Excludes tax expenditures.

d. 1978, see source note; 1979, *Special Analyses . . . 1979* and updated figures from staff of HEW, Division of Education Budget Analysis; 1980–83, author's calculations based on data from the Congressional Budget Office and HEW staff.

tration's reform of impact aid is assumed to be unsuccessful, yielding outlays of about $1.1 billion in 1983.

Projected GI bill expenditures are somewhat firmer, since the number of eligible veterans is known; these outlays for postsecondary education fall to an estimated $1.1 billion by 1983. Social security benefits are also more predictable; they will increase to an estimated $1.9 billion for postsecondary education by 1983 on the assumption that the administration will not be successful in capping the maximum benefit to coincide with basic grants. By contrast, future outlays for

Table 4-7. Federal Outlays for Selected Elementary and Secondary and Postsecondary Programs, Estimates by Author and by Office of Management and Budget, Fiscal Years 1977–83

Millions of dollars

Program	1977	1978	1979	1980	1981	1982	1983
Author's estimates	**6,888**	**7,944**	**9,438**	**11,155**	**11,917**	**12,912**	**14,018**
Elementary and secondary education (ESEA)	2,352	2,574	3,031	3,617	3,796	3,992	4,216
Impact aid	765	810	838	903	962	1,030	1,105
Education for the handicapped	247	366	560	846	1,058	1,300	1,590
Vocational education[a]	559	593	651	692	736	787	843
Postsecondary student aid and institutional support	2,965	3,601	4,358	5,097	5,365	5,803	6,264
Office of Management and Budget estimates	**6,878**	**7,971**	**9,131**	**10,139**	**10,465**	**10,528**	**10,517**
Elementary and secondary education (ESEA)	2,352	2,574	3,031	3,550	3,719	3,771	3,787
Impact aid	765	810	780	762	786	783	783
Education for the handicapped	249	367	562	850	961	978	960
Vocational education[a]	559	593	651	599	591	588	588
Postsecondary student aid and institutional support	2,953	3,627	4,107	4,378	4,408	4,408	4,399

Sources: *Special Analyses, Budget of the United States Government, Fiscal Year 1979*; Office of Management and Budget, unpublished data.
a. Adult education is excluded.

basic grants are extremely uncertain, since the outcome of middle-income student aid versus tuition tax credits is not settled. My projections assume enactment of the student aid proposal and increases of $200 million in subsequent years.[45]

Grants for research and development at colleges and universities are estimated to increase at 7 percent a year. This figure allows for modest growth but not at recent rates.

Table 4-7 compares my estimates with OMB current-service projections for several programs where large discrepancies exist between the two. In elementary and secondary education, projections for title I (including the targeting provision) differ by more than $400 million in 1983, primarily because the Office of Management and Budget projects virtually no growth after 1981. Impact-aid figures differ by more than $300 million in 1983, largely because my estimate assumes that the reform proposals are not adopted. The 1983 figures for education for the handicapped differ by $630 million, again because OMB projects no growth after 1981.

The Office of Management and Budget combines occupational, vocational, and adult education in a single category, while my figures exclude adult education. When the adult education component is subtracted from OMB figures as in table 4-7, the projections for 1983 differ by over $250 million, again because OMB projects virtually no growth for this program.

For higher education, OMB projects student aid and institutional support as a single category composed largely of Office of Education programs.[46] My estimates are grouped in table 4-7 to be consistent with the OMB category. The main reason my 1983 estimate is $1.9 billion above the OMB estimate is that the OMB projections were made before the middle-income student initiative was announced in February.

In the programs in table 4-7 alone, the difference between the two projections for 1983 is $3.5 billion. Of course, the OMB figures are not meant to be forecasts; mine are. In that sense, the two are not comparable. My estimates incorporate assumptions about congres-

45. Although HEW officials and several congressmen have reportedly discussed an additional $800 million in middle-income relief for the 1980 fiscal year, that increase is not included in these projections.

46. This category should not be confused with payments to institutions, table 4-3, which is largely R&D outlays; OMB does not project total federal R&D outlays as a separate category.

sional appropriations which, if roughly accurate, reduce discretionary space in the 1983 budget by at least $3.5 billion.

Even though projections must be taken with a grain of salt (for example, few observers could have forecast in mid-1977 that the middle-income squeeze would produce a request for $1.2 billion in additional budget authority for 1979), the figures in table 4-6 describe two seemingly robust trends: (1) the greater growth potential in elementary and secondary education programs than in postsecondary programs (that is, by 1983, their ratio is projected to be 1:1.6, while it was closer to 1:2 during much of the 1970s); and (2) the virtual certainty that education will not regain the 4.8 percent share of the budget that it enjoyed briefly during the early 1970s. In future years, education seems destined to yield budget space to other outlays or to tax cuts.

CHAPTER FIVE

Taxation

JOSEPH J. MINARIK

TAX POLICY is a major element of the President's fiscal and economic program for 1979. This chapter focuses on President Carter's tax proposals and the more extensive reform alternatives suggested by the Treasury. The 1977 social security payroll tax increases and President Carter's tax cuts are examined to show how taxpayers will be affected by the combination of the two programs. An analysis is also provided of the potential of the proposed business tax cuts to increase capital investment and combat inflation.

The Individual Income Tax

Federal tax policy is a major contributor to the current administration's reputation for vacillation and indecision. President Carter's 1977 economic stimulus proposal was cut more than half by the withdrawal of the $50 rebate. The remaining tax component of the 1977 stimulus program—an increased and simplified standard deduction—was publicized as a first installment of the thorough tax reform the President promised during his campaign. From the beginning, however, the reform package met with tough opposition. Busi-

Robert W. Hartman, Arthur M. Okun, John L. Palmer, and Emil M. Sunley, Jr., read drafts of this chapter and made many helpful comments. James G. McClave, Jr., and Laurent R. Ross performed the computer programming. The computation of taxes was performed under a grant from the RANN program of the National Science Foundation.

ness and congressional leaders voiced their skepticism throughout the development of the program, even though it was known that substantial net tax cuts were envisaged; and, surprisingly, some congressional liberals argued that there was insufficient support for comprehensive reform. Moreover, a set of option papers prepared by the Treasury appeared in the press during this period, which helped to erode public support. Opposition became intense, and in late 1977 the administration announced that the most far-reaching tax reform provisions had been dropped. Only the less ambitious changes in the law and sizable tax cuts for individuals and corporations remained.

What Is Tax Reform?

The U.S. individual income tax is widely considered the most effective and fairest income tax in the world, and it is reasonable to ask why it should be changed. Most tax experts respond that the many exclusions and deductions from the tax base make the tax less equitable, less efficient, and more complex than it could be.[1]

Equity is threatened by deductions and exclusions that are available to only a few taxpayers. An extreme example is the use of tax shelters (such as investments in coal mines, Christmas tree acreage, lithographic plates, or master sound recordings). Tax-shelter investments provide a taxpayer with tax losses (including interest and depreciation charges) greater than the amount of his investment; for taxpayers subject to high marginal rates, the resultant tax savings can exceed the amount of the investment by a substantial margin. Thereafter the investment can be liquidated as a capital gain or simply written off as a total loss, with little or no pretax income to declare but significant tax savings. Some tax shelters, such as investments in low- and moderate-income housing, were explicitly designed to achieve certain public objectives; but many taxpayers use shelters as opportunities to avoid paying taxes.

1. This sentiment was shared by William E. Simon in his address to the Tax Foundation's national conference, December 3, 1975, and by Michael Blumenthal in his speech to the Financial Analysts Federation, June 29, 1977—the immediate past and current Treasury secretaries under administrations of different political parties (*Department of the Treasury News*, WS-507 and B-318, respectively). A detailed discussion of this issue is available in Joseph A. Pechman, ed., *Comprehensive Income Taxation* (Brookings Institution, 1977). See also Department of the Treasury, *Blueprints for Basic Tax Reform* (Government Printing Office, 1977), for a similar analysis prepared by the Ford administration.

Other tax law provisions raise less obvious equity questions. The exclusion of one-half of long-term capital gains, for example, has been justified as an offset for the additional tax resulting from "bunching"[2] in order to compensate for inflation and to encourage saving and investment; in fact, however, the exclusion is poorly suited to these tasks.[3] The exclusion does provide tax savings to those who can receive their income in the form of gains but not to the majority, who cannot. Employer-financed fringe benefits are available only to some workers; those who receive them benefit without paying tax, and the higher their income from other sources, the greater the tax saving. State and local tax-free bonds are another avenue of tax saving that is profitable only for taxpayers with high marginal tax rates, and again the saving is greater as income increases. Even government transfers, which are received mainly by persons with low incomes, pose an equity problem; if one household receives a modest income and a second receives transfers in the same amount, the former pays taxes but the latter does not.

As a result of these and other features, there is considerable variation in tax liabilities at any given income level. A measure of this variation is the percent of taxpayers who paid less than one-half, two-thirds, and three-fourths the average effective tax rate in their income classes (table 5-1).[4] For example, about 22 percent of household units have tax liabilities that are at least one-third lower than the average in the $5,000–$10,000 class; the percentage decreases to 7 percent between $20,000 and $30,000, and then rises to almost 14

2. Bunching is the concentration of a gain that has accrued over several years into a lump sum in the single tax year in which it is realized. A large gain that has accrued over many years could push a taxpayer with an otherwise low income into a high-income tax bracket in the year it was realized; if it were taxed in part each year as it accrued, lower rates would apply.

3. The exclusion of gains is an inexact compensation for bunching and inflation. Bunching can best be remedied by long-term income averaging; inflation effects could be more accurately compensated by explicit indexing. Indexing raises many more questions, which are discussed below; also addressed are targeted saving and investment incentives such as the investment credit and accelerated depreciation. It should be remembered that holders of appreciated property now benefit from the deferral of tax until the realization of the gain, and from the opportunity to realize offsetting capital losses at the same time.

4. The higher figures at low income levels reflect the facts that when liabilities are small, a difference of only a few dollars can make one taxpayer's effective rate less than one-half of the average, and that transfer payments are not taxable; the lower numbers at higher income levels are the result of personal deductions and other exclusions.

Table 5-1. Percent of Tax Returns with Tax Less Than One-Half, Two-Thirds, and Three-Fourths of the Average, by Income Class, 1978[a]

Expanded income class[b] (dollars)	Taxes as proportion of average		
	Less than one-half	Less than two-thirds	Less than three-fourths
0–2,500	[c]	[c]	[c]
2,500–5,000	24.4	28.8	30.4
5,000–7,500	17.1	21.8	24.4
7,500–10,000	17.5	22.4	25.8
10,000–15,000	10.3	16.0	19.5
15,000–20,000	4.7	10.6	15.2
20,000–25,000	3.2	7.1	11.2
25,000–30,000	2.7	7.3	11.2
30,000–50,000	3.3	7.9	12.8
50,000–100,000	5.3	11.2	16.0
100,000–200,000	6.0	11.8	16.0
200,000–500,000	5.6	13.4	19.4
500,000–1,000,000	5.9	13.7	20.4
1,000,000–100,000,000	4.7	10.5	17.0
All classes[d]	9.3	14.4	18.1

Source: Brookings 1970 MERGE file projected to 1978. Figures are rounded.
a. Average effective tax rates were computed separately for 105 income classes and for joint and single tax returns, allowing for varying numbers of personal exemptions. Omitted from the analysis are returns of heads of households and married people filing separately, returns with negative income, and returns with negative or zero tax while claiming the standard deduction. The tax law in effect at the beginning of 1978 is assumed to continue for the full year.
b. Expanded income is adjusted gross income, plus excluded moving expenses, sick pay, and one-half of long-term capital gains.
c. Not calculated because of insufficient sample size.
d. Includes negative incomes not shown separately.

percent for incomes of $500,000 to $1,000,000. Some of this variation results from the use of tax preferences—income items not fully taxed or expenditures that reduce taxes—enacted to encourage certain forms of behavior, but some can be attributed to tax minimization that promotes no social purpose. Most experts hold that only tax incentives that effectively encourage desired activities should be retained and that other variations in tax liabilities should be reduced or eliminated so that people with equal economic incomes pay roughly equal taxes.

These same exclusions and preferences reduce the efficiency of the economy in two ways. First, the broader the exclusions, the higher the tax rates must be to raise the needed revenue; the higher the tax rates, the less the taxpayer can keep of his or her marginal income after taxes, the less incentive to increase work effort and savings, and the greater the incentive to expend effort to avoid taxes. Virtually every itemized tax return claims a deduction for state sales taxes, for example, and the amount of the deduction is closely related to income. If this deduction were eliminated and tax rates reduced, average taxes would be virtually unchanged but incentives for work and saving would be increased. The deduction for medical expenses has a similar effect; it was originally designed to lessen the impact of extraordinary medical expenses, but now 75 percent of all itemized returns claim a deduction for medical expenses.[5] Again, tax rates could be lower with a more restricted deduction.

The second way in which the efficiency of the economy is reduced is through the many exclusions that enter the market system of allocating resources. Because preferred investments can yield more posttax income than fully taxed investments even when pretax return is lower, resources are diverted from activities that are more profitable before taxes, and output is reduced. This is most notably true for tax-shelter investments, but tax-free interest on state and local bonds has the same effect. The growing complexity of the federal tax law, which is largely a result of the many exclusions and preferences, is felt perhaps even more widely than its equity and efficiency defects.

Virtually every recent change in the tax law, proposed or enacted, has been described as "tax reform" by its advocates. Most experts identify a proposed change as tax reform if it narrows the gap between an economic definition of income and the definition used for tax purposes.[6] Examples of tax reform under this interpretation would be the taxation of transfer payments; the elimination of the exclusion of one-half of long-term capital gains; the elimination of deductions for state and local taxes, mortgage interest, and average medical expenses; the elimination of the exclusion of the first $100 of dividends;[7] and taxation of interest on state and local securities.[8] A new tax preference that would increase the variation of tax liabilities and would not constitute reform would be a tax credit for parents paying tuition for their children's schooling (see chapter 4). A general tax reduction through higher exemptions or lower rates has no effect on the variation. Increased standard deductions are reform in a limited sense, inasmuch as they induce taxpayers to refrain from

5. This is largely because one-half of medical insurance premiums (up to $150) can be deducted without the usual income restriction.
6. See the references cited in note 1.
7. The exclusion is $200 for married couples filing joint returns.
8. For a more complete list, see note 9.

itemizing, thus indirectly reducing excessively generous deductions for personal expenditures.

A combination of broadening the income base on which the tax is levied and narrowing the exclusions and deductions permitted from that base would substantially increase taxable income and therefore tax revenue. Assuming a reduction of $11 billion in net revenue, a $3,200 standard deduction for joint returns, and a $1,000 personal exemption, tax rates under a comprehensive income tax[9] could range from 1 percent at the bottom of the income scale to 48 percent at the top, compared to the present 14 to 70 percent. (This rate schedule

9. The comprehensive tax base would include all adjusted gross income as currently defined in addition to the following:

(1) Long-term capital gains would be taxed in full.

(2) The dividend exclusion would be abolished.

(3) State and local securities could be issued in taxable form at the option of the state or locality, with a 40 percent federal subsidy.

(4) Interest on life insurance reserves would be taxed as it accrues.

(5) Capital gains on home sales would be taxed as ordinary income.

(6) Capital appreciation on property would be taxed when transferred by gift or at death.

(7) The rental value of homes, net of depreciation, repairs, interest, and property taxes, would be taxed.

(8) Employers' payments for employees' life, health, and legal insurance premiums and pension funds would be taxed; pension benefits in excess of previously taxed contributions would also be taxed.

(9) Employer's social security contributions for old-age, survivors, and Medicare coverage would be taxed currently. Old-age benefits in excess of previously taxed contributions would be taxed upon receipt. Survivors and Medicare benefits would not be taxed.

(10) Social security disability insurance, unemployment compensation, workmen's compensation, and veterans' compensation benefits would be taxed.

(11) Government transfer payments such as aid to families with dependent children, supplemental security income, general assistance, and the bonus value of food stamps would be taxed.

Most personal deductions now available would be reduced or eliminated:

(1) Deductions for mortgage interest and property taxes would be continued, but only as expenses to be deducted from taxable imputed rent.

(2) Deductibility of nonbusiness, nonmortgage interest would be limited to the amount of investment income received plus $5,000.

(3) Deductibility of state and local income, sales, gasoline, personal property, and miscellaneous taxes would be eliminated.

(4) Deductibility of medical and dental expenses would be restricted to the amount exceeding 10 percent of income, rather than the present 3 percent. The deductibility of one-half of medical insurance premiums would be treated in the same way as all other medical expenses. Unreimbursed casualty losses in excess of $100 would be added to medical expenses and subject to the same ceiling.

(5) Charitable contributions would be deductible only to the extent that they exceed 3 percent of income.

Table 5-2. Tax under Current Income Tax Law and Effects of a Comprehensive
Income Tax, by Income Class, 1978[a]

Expanded income class[b] (dollars)	Tax (billions of dollars)		Effects of comprehensive tax (percent)		
	Current law	Compre-hensive	Increase or decrease in tax	Returns with sig-nificant tax increase[c]	Returns with tax under 2/3 of average[d]
0–2,500	−0.2	2.1[e]	*	14.8	[f]
2,500–5,000	−0.1	0.5[e]	*	14.5	5.1
5,000–7,500	2.0	1.6	−18.9	15.8	2.5
7,500–10,000	4.8	3.7	−21.8	15.7	6.4
10,000–15,000	17.8	14.8	−17.0	19.7	3.7
15,000–20,000	25.3	21.4	−15.3	19.2	0.2
20,000–25,000	24.4	21.4	−12.1	20.1	0.1
25,000–30,000	21.5	19.2	−10.4	22.5	0.1
30,000–50,000	36.3	33.9	−6.7	27.7	0.2
50,000–100,000	21.0	22.0	5.0	43.0	0.4
100,000–200,000	13.9	14.9	7.1	44.6	0.8
200,000–500,000	9.4	9.5	0.7	40.7	1.1
500,000–1,000,000	3.2	3.2	2.2	48.2	1.9
1,000,000–1,000,000,000	5.5	5.5	0.2	38.6	1.8
All classes[g]	184.8	173.7	−6.0	18.2	3.1

Source: Brookings 1970 MERGE file, projected to 1978. Figures are rounded.
* 0.05 or less.
a. Comprehensive income tax is defined in text note 9.
b. Expanded income is defined in table 5-1, note b.
c. Significant tax increases are defined in text note 10.
d. Average tax computations are explained in table 5-1, note a.
e. Shifts from negative to positive aggregate tax liabilities at low income levels under a comprehensive scheme are due to broadening of the tax base and therefore of the phaseouts of the earned income credit. Continued net negative tax payments in the aggregate would require larger benefits or restricted phase-outs not included in this simulation.
f. Not calculated because of insufficient sample size.
g. Includes negative incomes not shown separately.

was drawn to distribute tax reductions by income levels in approximately the same pattern as the President's final proposal.)

The distribution of tax liabilities under a comprehensive income tax is compared with that under 1977 law in table 5-2 for estimated 1978 incomes. The tax cut is a sizable fraction of expected liabilities, and comparison with table 5-1 shows that the number of taxpayers paying much less than the average tax burden is substantially reduced. What is less obvious from the aggregate figures is that the reform portions of such a program would adversely affect certain taxpayers who make heavy use of preferences in the existing law. About 18 percent of all taxpayers, roughly 19 million returns, would face significant tax increases in 1978 even with the sizable tax cuts assumed here; the frequency increases from about 15 percent at low income levels to about 43 percent above $50,000.[10]

The Treasury's Options

Reforms to broaden the income tax base are extremely controversial. Some of the reforms are generally assumed to have virtually no chance of becoming law within the foreseeable future. The administration's reform agenda, as revealed in a set of option papers prepared by the Treasury and dated September 2, 1977, was accordingly more modest than full comprehensive reform.[11] The major features of the option papers, like the comprehensive tax, were full taxation of capital gains and substantial reductions of marginal tax rates. Restrictions on homeowner tax preferences and charitable deductions were conspicuously absent; taxation of transfer payments was approached cautiously.[12]

A source of revenue loss in the package was a new deduction for married couples in cases when both spouses worked. The spouse with

10. A tax increase is "significant" if it is $100 or more and at least 5 percent of 1977 law liability. Therefore, a 100 percent increase in tax from $1 to $2 would not be significant, but an increase from $1 to $101 would; a $100 increase from $100,000 to $100,100 would not, but one from $100,000 to $105,000 would.

11. These papers were never officially sent to the President but were leaked to the press and widely distributed; thus they do not represent the precise state of the administration's thinking at any time but are merely indicative of the range of alternatives considered. The contents of the option papers appeared in several newspapers and journals. See, for example, *Tax Notes,* vol. 5 (October 10, 1977), p. 16.

12. The Treasury options would broaden the tax base as follows:
    (1) Long-term capital gains would be taxed in full.
    (2) The taxable state and local bond option would be phased in.
    (3) Life insurance interest would be taxed as it accrued.
    (4) Accrued capital gains would be taxed upon death or when transferred by gift.
    (5) Employers' legal and group term life insurance contributions in excess of $25,000 of insurance per employee would be taxed.
    (6) Social security benefits, veterans' benefits, and unemployment compensation would be taxed in part if the beneficiaries' income exceeded $20,000.
    Personal deductions would be restricted as follows:
    (1) Deductibility of nonbusiness, noninvestment interest would be limited to $10,000.
    (2) Deductibility of sales, gasoline, personal property, and miscellaneous taxes would be terminated.
    (3) The sum of medical and dental expenses and insurance premiums and the excess of unreimbursed casualty losses over $100 would be deductible to the extent that the amount exceeded 10 percent of adjusted gross income.
    The proposals also included restrictions on tax shelters and a withholding of tax on interest income similar to the current withholding on wages.

the lower earnings could exclude from taxable income 10 percent of earnings up to a maximum $600 deduction. This was designed to reduce the so-called marriage tax, which is the increase in tax of most married couples with two wage earners over the tax they would have to pay if they were single. The increase for such couples results from the lower rate schedule given to single people in 1969 to answer their complaints about overtaxation, a standard deduction for married couples that is less than twice as large as that for single people ($3,200 versus $2,200), and a tax credit of 2 percent of taxable income (with a maximum credit of $180) available to both single people and married couples. In practice, what constitutes "fairness" for single people and married couples and for married couples with one earner and couples with two earners is by no means obvious. The solution proposed in the Treasury package would have helped to balance the claims of taxpayers in some circumstances, but it would not have resolved all the issues.[13] The package also gave single taxpayers another tax rate cut relative to married couples.

Because the Treasury reforms were less ambitious than the comprehensive tax described above, the proposed reduction in the tax rates was much smaller. Using a $250 personal credit and the same standard deductions, the rates in the Treasury's option papers ran from 10 to 50 percent. This package was never formally proposed, and so many details (including tax rates) could have been changed to alter the final effect; but as originally planned, the options would have cut taxes almost across the board. Table 5-3 shows that on a percentage basis the largest tax cuts would have applied to those in the lowest income classes. With fewer of the preferences in the current law removed, there would have been less reduction in the variation of taxes paid at given income levels. Thus, for example, 13 percent of all taxpayers would pay less than two-thirds of the average effective tax rate in their income classes; this is lower than the 14.4 percent under present law, but much more than the 3.1 percent under the comprehensive tax. There are fewer significant tax increases than under the comprehensive tax, but the percentage increases more rapidly with income.

13. It would not have eliminated the marriage tax entirely, and single people would have continued to pay more tax than married people with the same taxable income. For a discussion of these issues, see Joseph A. Pechman, *Federal Tax Policy*, 3d ed. (Brookings Institution, 1977), pp. 92–97.

Table 5-3. Tax under Current Income Tax Law and Effects of Treasury Options, by Income Class, 1978[a]

	Tax (billions of dollars)		Effects of Treasury options (percent)		
Expanded income class[b] (dollars)	Current law	Treasury options	Increase or decrease in tax	Returns with significant tax increase[c]	Returns with tax under 2/3 of average[d]
0–2,500	−0.2	0.4	*	0.8	e
2,500–5,000	−0.1	−0.1	*	4.5	34.7
5,000–7,500	2.0	1.6	−16.3	5.8	20.2
7,500–10,000	4.8	4.3	−9.0	9.9	17.1
10,000–15,000	17.8	15.6	−12.4	9.4	17.9
15,000–20,000	25.3	22.8	−10.0	11.8	11.8
20,000–25,000	24.4	22.7	−6.7	13.4	5.6
25,000–30,000	21.5	20.5	−4.7	15.6	4.1
30,000–50,000	36.3	34.9	−4.0	17.0	3.8
50,000–100,000	21.0	21.2	0.9	26.5	6.0
100,000–200,000	13.9	13.7	−1.5	24.9	5.5
200,000–500,000	9.4	9.0	−4.9	28.4	5.9
500,000–1,000,000	3.2	3.1	−3.2	39.4	7.8
1,000,000–100,000,000	5.5	5.3	−3.7	33.7	5.9
All classes[f]	184.7	174.9	−5.3	8.3	13.0

Source: Brookings 1970 MERGE file, projected to 1978. Figures are rounded.
* 0.05 or less.
a. Treasury options are defined in the text; the shareholder credit for dividends is not included. Full-year effects are estimated even though some of the proposals would be in effect for only part of 1978.
b. Expanded income is defined in table 5-1, note b.
c. Significant tax increases are defined in text note 10.
d. Average tax computations are explained in table 5-1, note a.
e. Not calculated because of insufficient sample size.
f. Includes negative incomes not shown separately.

As mentioned briefly at the beginning of this chapter, what reform there was in the Treasury tax package, however, was sufficient to arouse strong opposition. Perhaps the strongest voice came from business and financial groups, which opposed full taxation of capital gains. Their major argument against full taxation was that it would discourage risk-taking and investment in new and expanding firms. If taxes on capital gains were increased to be the same as those on fixed income investments (such as bonds of an existing firm or a government), capital might shift to uses that were freer of risk and deprive the economy of much valuable innovation. Equity would become less attractive relative to debt in the financial markets, further tilting the debt–equity ratio toward bond financing and increasing the danger of corporate bankruptcies in cyclical downturns. All these factors might combine to discourage capital investment and contribute to a growing capital shortage over the coming years.

On the other hand, proponents of the Treasury package argued that tax policy should not alter choices between more and less risky investments; the market should set relative rates of return to obtain the optimal amount of each. Even beyond this, the administration added general and targeted tax cuts to offset any negative effects of elimination of the capital gains exclusion. The large reductions in marginal tax rates and the substantial cut in taxes due might have stimulated sufficient additional saving and investment to outweigh any ill effect from equalizing the relative burden on capital gains and ordinary income. A further offset would have been provided by reductions in taxes on corporate earnings, including a credit for dividends received by individual taxpayers and a broadened investment credit; the total projected revenue cost of these provisions would be approximately $13 billion in 1981.[14]

Full taxation of gains would also bring subsidiary benefits. The substantial reduction in marginal tax rates made possible by full taxation would encourage work as well as saving. The elimination of the capital gains tax preference would greatly simplify the tax law, which now contains many complicated sections whose sole purpose is to distinguish between capital gains and ordinary income. Without the preference, the potential of tax-shelter schemes would be dramatically reduced, and the enormous amount of effort now going into the conversion of ordinary income into capital gains could be redirected into more productive channels.

The President's Proposals

The initial reaction of the opponents of full taxation of capital gains was, of course, made in the context of the Treasury options. The critics did not consider the tax cuts on corporate earnings to be adequate compensation for the heavier relative taxation of gains and feared that full taxation might be enacted without the corporate tax cuts. The administration saw this pressure as a preview of a legislative battle and drastically reduced the reforms in its final proposal of January 1978.[15] Full taxation of capital gains was abandoned. The

14. These proposals are discussed in the section entitled "Business Taxes."
15. Department of the Treasury, *The President's 1978 Tax Program* (GPO, 1978).

only reforms remaining in the proposal were the repeal of the alternative tax on capital gains,[16] taxation of part of unemployment insurance benefits for taxpayers with incomes above $20,000 if single, $25,000 if married; the tightening of deductions for state taxes and medical and casualty expenses; slightly modified tax shelter reforms; and a slight tightening of the minimum tax, which would offset part of the loss of full taxation of capital gains.[17] The exclusion for married couples with two wage earners was dropped, and the additional rate cuts for single taxpayers were reduced.

With this less ambitious reform program in which the capital gains exclusion was retained, the amount of rate reduction possible through reform alone was severely limited. However, the administration proposed a large net revenue reduction for stabilization purposes that would cut the tax rates from the present 14–70 percent to 12–68 percent and replace the present $750 exemption and credit of $35 with a credit of $240.[18]

The President's proposal substantially reduces tax liabilities on the average (table 5-4). The distribution of the cuts is more progressive than the original Treasury options and is weighted toward the lower- and middle-income brackets; households with adjusted gross income above $100,000 have modest tax increases on average. Because the base-broadening elements of the program are cut, the dispersion of

16. This is a provision that allows recipients of long-term gains who face a marginal tax rate of more than 50 percent to pay tax on the first $50,000 of their gains at only 25 percent. Repeal of the alternative tax would thus affect only taxpayers with the highest income, would still allow them the usual preferential tax on gains, and would raise $151 million of revenue a year by 1980.

17. The present deduction from the minimum tax base of one-half of ordinary tax paid would be abolished, making the minimum tax a tax on preferences (above a basic exemption of $10,000), regardless of the amount of ordinary tax due.

18. The alternative to the personal credit of $35 is a credit of 2 percent of taxable income (with a maximum $180 of credit per return); it would be eliminated at the same time. The usual argument for the personal credit is that it is more progressive than an exemption, because its value is the same for all taxpayers regardless of their marginal tax bracket. This argument is flawed, however, because the same distributional effects could be achieved with a personal exemption and slight changes in the rates. The real difference between the credit and the exemption is in their effects on the tax liabilities of families of different sizes. When compared with an exemption, a credit is much more generous to large, low-income families, and much less generous to large families with high incomes. Under present law, a family of two people with an income of $5,200 or less will have no tax liability; nor will a family of four with $7,200 or less, six with $9,167 or less, or eight with $11,133 or less (based on the assumptions that the families choose the standard deduction and that the earned income credit is not used). Under the President's proposal, those amounts would be raised to $6,553, $9,256, $11,884, and $14,411. The proposal thus increases the tax-free income level more for very large families.

Table 5-4. Tax under Current Income Tax Law and Effects of the President's Proposal, by Income Class, 1978[a]

Expanded income class[b] (dollars)	Tax (billions of dollars)		Effects of President's proposal (percent)		
	Current law	President's proposal	Increase or decrease in tax	Returns with significant tax increase[c]	Returns with tax under 2/3 of average[d]
0–2,500	−0.2	−0.2	*	0.0	e
2,500–5,000	−0.1	−0.4	*	0.0	31.1
5,000–7,500	2.0	1.4	−30.4	*	20.4
7,500–10,000	4.8	3.9	−18.5	1.5	22.5
10,000–15,000	17.8	15.2	−14.5	2.6	18.4
15,000–20,000	25.3	22.4	−11.3	4.4	11.8
20,000–25,000	24.4	22.0	−9.7	4.9	6.9
25,000–30,000	21.5	19.8	−7.8	5.2	6.5
30,000–50,000	36.3	34.8	−4.3	6.8	7.3
50,000–100,000	21.0	20.8	−0.6	9.9	11.2
100,000–200,000	13.9	14.0	1.2	14.1	10.8
200,000–500,000	9.4	9.6	1.5	23.5	11.6
500,000–1,000,000	3.2	3.2	1.9	32.0	11.6
1,000,000–100,000,000	5.5	5.5	0.9	18.0	9.3
All classes[f]	184.8	172.2	−6.8	2.3	14.2

Source: Brookings 1970 MERGE file, projected to 1978. Figures are rounded.
* 0.05 or less.
a. President Carter's proposal is defined in the text. Full-year effects are estimated even though some of the proposals would be in effect for only part of 1978.
b. Expanded income is defined in table 5-1, note b.
c. Significant tax increases are defined in the text.
d. Average tax computations are explained in table 5-1, note a.
e. Not calculated because of insufficient sample size.
f. Includes negative incomes not shown separately.

tax burdens is not reduced for the population as a whole. Another result of the narrowing of the scope of reform, however, is the lower frequency of tax increases; again, that frequency generally increases with income. The administration opted for a less controversial program with fewer major changes from the present tax system.

The course of the current tax legislative process is not unlike past experience. A president pledged to reform the income tax and ordered his administration to develop proposals; as proposals became known, those who enjoyed preferences that were now threatened made every effort to keep them; those efforts were largely successful, even before the proposals reached Congress for formal public debate. How Congress will alter the Carter administration bill is difficult to predict, but it is clear that the few remaining reform elements are in serious jeopardy. If the past is any guide, the final bill will have less reform and the same or more net tax reduction.

The Social Security Payroll Tax

It has been apparent for several years that the social security system has entered a period of financial difficulty, in sharp contrast to the 1950s and 1960s.[19] The system faces several serious financial problems: the recent recession and high unemployment drained the trust funds and caused operating deficits; continuing large deficits developed in the disability insurance program; demographic trends resulted in the number of retired persons increasing faster than the working population; and a faulty adjustment formula overcompensated for inflation. Congress tackled each of these problems. The final product, the social security amendments of 1977, provided for substantially increased payroll taxes to cover projected deficits and rebuild the trust funds. One alternative to increased payroll taxes proposed by President Carter—transfers from the Treasury into social security trust funds in periods of high unemployment—was rejected, and the Congress also dropped a proposed offset to some of the increase in employee taxes through the elimination of the ceiling for calculating the employers' portion.[20]

Once Congress had decided to increase the payroll tax revenues, it had to choose how to do it. Increasing the payroll tax rate would increase revenue for every dollar of taxable wages. It has the disadvantage of putting a heavier burden on the workers receiving the lowest wages but the advantage of not increasing obligations for future benefits. Raising the maximum amount of earned income subject to tax would increase taxes only for workers receiving the highest wages, hitting hardest those just above the former ceiling. But because benefits are a function of covered earnings, this approach has the disadvantage of increasing the future benefits of those whose taxes are

19. See Joseph A. Pechman, Henry J. Aaron, and Michael K. Taussig, *Social Security: Perspectives for Reform* (Brookings Institution, 1968); John L. Palmer and Joseph J. Minarik, "Income Security Policy," in Henry Owen and Charles L. Schultze, eds., *Setting National Priorities: The Next Ten Years* (Brookings Institution, 1976), pp. 539–55; and Alicia H. Munnell, *The Future of Social Security* (Brookings Institution, 1977).

20. See the section titled "Social Security" in chapter 3 for a more detailed discussion of the administration's proposals and the final legislation.

Table 5-5. Social Security Payroll Tax Rates and Contribution and Benefit Base
under Previous Law and under 1977 Social Security Amendments, 1979–2011

	Tax rate (percent)				Contribution and benefit base (dollars)	
	Employer and employee, each		Self-employed people			
Year	Previous law	1977 law	Previous law	1977 law	Previous law[a]	1977 law[a]
1979	6.05	6.13	8.10	8.10	18,900	22,900
1980	6.05	6.13	8.10	8.10	20,400	25,900
1981	6.30	6.65	8.35	9.30	21,900	29,700
1982	6.30	6.70	8.35	9.35	23,400	31,800
1983	6.30	6.70	8.35	9.35	24,900	33,900
1984	6.30	6.70	8.35	9.35	26,400	36,000
1985	6.30	7.05	8.35	9.90	27,900	38,100
1986	6.45	7.15	8.50	10.00	29,400	40,200
1987	6.45	7.15	8.50	10.00	31,200	42,600
1988–89	6.45	7.15	8.50	10.00	b	b
1990–2010	6.45	7.65	8.50	10.75	b	b
2011 and later	7.45	7.65	8.50	10.75	b	b

Source: *Summary of the Conference Agreement on H.R. 9346, The Social Security Amendments of 1977,*
prepared for the House Committee on Ways and Means, 95:1 (Government Printing Office, 1977), pp. 2, 3.
   a. Figures under "previous law" for 1979–87 and under the 1977 law for 1982–87 are based on automatic wage growth adjustment and forecast inflation.
   b. Based on automatic wage growth adjustment and inflation beyond forecast period, and thus not
calculated.

increased. Further, each time the taxable ceiling is raised it adds less
additional earnings to the tax base (because the number of earners
decreases at successively higher levels of earnings) and raises less revenue. The revenue potential of increasing the wage ceiling is therefore
limited. Beyond these problems, any increase in the payroll taxes on
employers would add to costs and therefore to inflation.[21]

   The final legislation significantly increased both the tax rate and
the wage base, as shown in table 5-5. The total payroll tax rate was
previously scheduled to be increased four times between 1978 and
2011, but will rise even more under the new law. The tax rate for the
self-employed will increase still more, to come closer to a long-
standing relationship whereby it is one and one-half times the employee's rate. The portion of the tax earmarked for the troubled
disability insurance program was increased substantially in the final

21. See chapter 2.

Table 5-6. Social Security Payroll Tax under Previous Law and under 1977 Social Security Amendments, by Income Class, 1979[a]

	Tax[c] (billions of dollars)		Effects of 1977 law	
Expanded income class[b] (dollars)	Previous law	1977 law	Increase in tax (percent)	Increase as percent of income
0–2,500	0.7	0.7	0.9	0.06
2,500–5,000	1.5	1.6	2.1	0.17
5,000–7,500	2.5	2.6	2.2	0.18
7,500–10,000	3.7	3.7	2.0	0.17
10,000–15,000	10.7	10.9	1.8	0.14
15,000–20,000	14.1	14.4	2.3	0.17
20,000–25,000	12.7	13.6	7.1	0.35
25,000–30,000	9.5	10.4	9.8	0.33
30,000–50,000	15.1	16.8	11.3	0.19
50,000–100,000	3.6	4.1	15.0	0.09
100,000–200,000	0.4	0.5	18.0	0.05
200,000–500,000	*	*	19.0	0 01
500,000–1,000,000	*	*	12.6	0.01
1,000,000–100,000,000	*	*	21.8	†
All classes[d]	74.4	79.2	6.5	0.18

Source: Brookings 1970 MERGE file projected to 1979. Figures are rounded.
* 0.05 or less.
† 0.005 or less.
a. The rates and bases for the tax laws are shown in table 5-5.
b. Expanded income is defined in table 5-1, note b.
c. Tax shown is total payroll tax for each household, distributed by the total expanded income of all tax returns of the household (and all nonfilers as if they had filed tax returns).
d. Includes negative incomes not shown separately.

legislation. At the same time, the tax base will be substantially increased between 1979 and 1981, with automatic proportional increases for growth in money wages thereafter. These steps, combined with correcting the inflation adjustment system for benefits, largely eliminate the expected long-term deficit of the system.

One of the most important considerations in the formulation of the President's income tax proposal was to offset, in the aggregate, the additional burden introduced by the payroll tax law. This objective would be accomplished for the next few years, but at the same time, the payroll tax increases would absorb most or all of the seemingly large income tax cut for most taxpayers.

Table 5-6 compares the increased payroll tax liabilities in 1979 with the liabilities under previous law.[22] While taxes are increased

22. The first year for which the 1977 law changed tax liabilities is 1979; the increases in 1978 were in the law passed in 1972.

across the board, the largest percentage increases occur for the upper-income classes, which are affected by both the higher tax rate and the larger tax base; when measured as a percentage of income, however, the increases for both the lower- and the upper-middle income groups are greater. The effect also varies according to the composition of the labor force. Government employees, who are not covered by the program, are of course unaffected by the tax increase. Households with two earners just at or under the former taxable ceiling can have a sizable total income but might be affected by only the increase in the rate, while a household with one earner whose wages are at the new ceiling (or with two earners at that ceiling) will face substantial tax increases from both the higher ceiling and the higher rate.

Table 5-7 compares the combined income and payroll tax liabilities estimated in 1979 under the current income tax and previous payroll tax with taxes under President Carter's income tax proposal and the recently enacted payroll taxes. Except at the top and bottom of the income scale, aggregate tax liabilities are lower in all income classes, but there are many cases even at comparatively modest levels where total taxes are significantly increased. This reflects the many different patterns of household earnings—whether there are one or two workers and whether they are employed or self-employed (or not covered by the system). Such patterns should have been expected; the income tax, which is a tax on all *household income,* is necessarily an inexact instrument to offset the payroll tax, which is a tax on *personal earnings.*

In only a few years further payroll tax increases (and inflation) would increase tax liabilities under the President's proposal beyond those that would be due under the previous payroll and current income tax laws, unless new compensating reductions were made. By 1985, for example, total liabilities under the new proposal would be $656 billion, compared to $639 billion under the tax laws in effect in 1977.[23] This is perhaps a major reason why President Carter suggested in his tax message that further tax cuts may be necessary in just a few years.

Inflation makes the need for such tax cuts more immediate. It is fairly well known that inflation tends to increase real tax burdens under the income tax, although it may not be understood how per-

23. Derived from simulations using the 1979 Brookings MERGE file projected to 1985.

Table 5-7. Combined Tax under Current Income Tax Law and Previous Social Security Tax Law and under President Carter's Income Tax Proposal and 1977 Social Security Amendments, by Income Class, 1979[a]

Expanded income class[b] (dollars)	Tax[c] (billions of dollars)		Effects of proposal and 1977 law	
	Current income tax law and previous payroll tax law	President Carter's income tax proposal and 1977 payroll tax law	Increase or decrease in tax (percent)	Households with significant increase (percent)[d]
0–2,500	0.5	0.5	1.1	*
2,500–5,000	1.3	1.2	−7.5	1.2
5,000–7,500	3.5	3.1	−10.4	1.6
7,500–10,000	7.0	6.3	−10.8	1.5
10,000–15,000	25.8	23.4	−9.1	2.0
15,000–20,000	40.0	36.9	−7.9	2.4
20,000–25,000	42.4	39.7	−6.4	2.1
25,000–30,000	37.2	35.2	−5.4	3.4
30,000–50,000	76.6	73.7	−3.7	3.8
50,000–100,000	39.0	38.3	−1.9	5.8
100,000–200,000	18.5	18.4	−0.3	9.7
200,000–500,000	11.0	11.0	−0.1	11.8
500,000–1,000,000	3.5	3.5	−0.3	11.2
1,000,000–100,000,000	3.5	3.6	0.3	8.0
All classes[e]	309.9	294.8	−4.9	2.0

Source: Brookings 1970 MERGE file, projected to 1979. Figures are rounded.
* 0.05 or less.
a. President Carter's income tax proposal is defined in the text. Data for the applicable payroll tax laws are shown in table 5-5.
b. Expanded income is defined in table 5-1, note b.
c. Tax shown is total payroll tax for each household, distributed by the total expanded income of all tax returns of the household (and all nonfilers as if they had filed tax returns).
d. Significant tax increases are defined in text note 10.
e. Includes negative incomes not shown separately.

vasive this phenomenon is.[24] The question is whether the President's tax cuts are sufficient to offset both the higher payroll taxes and inflation. To answer this question, table 5-8 compares what taxes would

24. Most commentators speak of inflation "pushing people into higher tax brackets" and thereby raising taxes, but inflation can raise taxes without pushing people into higher brackets. If gross income and deductions inflate at the same rate, taxable income will also grow at that rate, but the added dollars will be taxed at the taxpayer's highest marginal rate (which is higher than the average unless the taxpayer is in the lowest tax rate bracket) and so taxes will grow faster. In fact, deductions may not grow as fast as income for the individual taxpayer because some are fixed by statute (personal exemptions, the standard deduction) and others are set by long-term contract (mortgage interest, installment interest); therefore taxable income might grow faster than gross income, and taxes would grow still faster. If the taxpayer is pushed into a higher tax rate bracket, these other effects are compounded.

Table 5-8. Combined Tax under Current Income Tax Law Adjusted for Inflation and Previous Social Security Tax Law and under President Carter's Income Tax Proposal and 1977 Social Security Amendments, by Income Class, 1979[a]

	Tax[c] (billions of dollars)		Effects of proposal and 1977 law	
Expanded income class[b] (dollars)	Current income tax law and previous payroll tax law	President Carter's income tax proposal and 1977 payroll tax law	Increase or decrease in tax (percent)	Households with significant increase (percent)[d]
0–2,500	0.6	0.5	−2.2	*
2,500–5,000	1.2	1.2	−1.4	1.2
5,000–7,500	3.2	3.1	−2.0	2.4
7,500–10,000	6.4	6.3	−2.7	4.4
10,000–15,000	23.7	23.4	−1.4	9.6
15,000–20,000	36.8	36.9	0.1	16.7
20,000–25,000	39.2	39.7	1.2	20.2
25,000–30,000	34.4	35.2	2.5	25.8
30,000–50,000	70.4	73.7	4.8	40.6
50,000–100,000	35.6	38.3	7.3	61.2
100,000–200,000	17.1	18.4	7.4	62.3
200,000–500,000	10.4	11.0	5.5	46.2
500,000–1,000,000	3.4	3.5	3.8	45.1
1,000,000–100,000,000	3.5	3.6	2.8	28.8
All classes[e]	286.0	294.8	3.1	14.5

Source: Brookings 1970 MERGE file, projected to 1979. Figures are rounded.
* 0.05 or less.
a. President Carter's income tax proposal is defined in the text. Data for the applicable payroll tax laws are shown in table 5-5. Inflation adjustment includes computation of 1977 tax law at 1979 real-income levels in 1977 dollars, and then reflation of tax amounts to 1979 dollars.
b. Expanded income is defined in table 5-1, note b.
c. Tax shown is total payroll tax for each household, distributed by the total expanded income of all tax returns of the household (and all nonfilers as if they had filed tax returns).
d. Significant tax increases are defined in text note 10.
e. Includes negative incomes not shown separately.

have been in 1979 under the 1977 laws and without inflation with the taxes under the new social security law and the President's proposed income tax cuts, assuming 6 percent inflation in both 1978 and 1979. The table shows the additional taxes due to inflation and the recent payroll tax increases, less President Carter's proposed tax cut. The key finding is that, even as early as 1979, the proposed cuts will not compensate for the 1977 payroll tax increase and the 1977–78 inflation for the population as a whole. Households below $15,000 receive modest real tax cuts, but those above $15,000 face real tax increases of up to 7 percent. While only 15 percent of all households face significant tax increases, above $25,000 of adjusted gross income the fraction is in excess of 25 percent, and from $50,000 to $500,000 it is about 60 percent. The increase in the real tax bill is about 3 percent on average.

Whether or not the income tax should be automatically indexed for inflation, with the additional cost and complexity that indexing would entail, depends upon one's views about the equity of the distribution of the tax burden.[25] Those who believe that the automatic growth in tax receipts should be restrained favor indexing; those who are dissatisfied with the present distribution and oppose automatic restrictions on federal receipts favor the type of ad hoc adjustments made in recent years.

In the final analysis the voters and their elected representatives must decide what the level and distribution of the tax burden should be, with or without inflation. Another question to be decided is whether the social security system should be funded entirely through payroll taxes, or whether the recent increase should be rolled back. With a relatively far-reaching tax bill now being considered and a lively debate in progress, the President and the Congress will make these decisions, by design or by default.

Business Taxes

Business investment has been lagging in the recovery from the 1974–75 recession. As of the final quarter of 1977, real expenditures on plant and equipment were still below the 1973 prerecession peak. More investment would generate additional jobs and income. Further, without more investment soon, plant capacity in key industries could fall behind demand within the next two or three years and cause inflationary pressures (see chapter 2).

Some analysts have been concerned about investment in a longer term context.[26] They maintain that the nation's capital stock is growing at a much slower rate than it could, and that future income is therefore reduced.

Critics of investment performance in both the long and the short run often cite tax policy as one of the problems. The Carter administration was sympathetic to this concern; capital formation was

25. See Henry J. Aaron, ed., *Inflation and the Income Tax* (Brookings Institution, 1976), chapter 5.
26. This question is examined by Barry Bosworth, James S. Duesenberry, and Andrew S. Carron, *Capital Needs in the Seventies* (Brookings Institution, 1975).

made one of the chief objectives of its tax reform effort, and a multi-pronged business tax program was developed to achieve it. In this section, the investment potential and implications for economic efficiency of these proposals are analyzed.

Business Tax Reduction Alternatives

A basic tax deterrent to both investment and saving may be the high tax rates that are applied to income from property. With a corporate rate of 48 percent and the highest personal tax rate for dividends of 70 percent,[27] dividends received by people with the highest incomes are ultimately taxed at 84.4 percent. With that prospect, a potential stockowner might well prefer to spend his ready cash. Advocates of using tax policy to encourage investment seek a reduction of the 84.4 percent to encourage sales of equity and spending on plant and equipment that can follow. Four general approaches are considered below.

A more generous depreciation allowance for plant and equipment is especially favored during rapid inflation. Depreciation based on historical cost does not provide sufficient funds to replace an asset at inflated prices at the end of its useful life. As firms find depreciation allowances insufficient to procure replacement capital and foresee allowances on new investments similarly falling short, they might be less likely to purchase new plant and equipment. This situation could be altered in two ways. Depreciation allowances could be explicitly indexed to the price level;[28] this would precisely solve the problem but might open the floodgates to indexing the entire tax system, which would be exceptionally costly and complex and have the unfortunate side effect of making inflation more palatable.[29] An alternative is to liberalize depreciation generally, perhaps through a broadening of the asset depreciation range system.[30] Such a path was one alternative in the Treasury options but was not included in the final proposal.

27. The marginal tax rate on earned income has been limited to 50 percent since 1971.

28. A general price index is preferred to the cost of a particular investment good. The tax system should not subsidize a production process that has become relatively more costly.

29. Aaron, ed., Inflation and the Income Tax, chaps. 2, 3.

30. Under present law, firms are allowed to depreciate a capital asset 20 percent faster or slower than the usual expected lifetime. This tolerance is referred to as the asset depreciation range. The Council of Economic Advisers recommended extending the depreciation range from 20 percent to 40 percent.

One argument against liberalizing depreciation allowances is that the investment tax credit already provides such an extra incentive for investment; if still more stimulus is needed, a second option would be to broaden the credit by (1) extending it to plant (rather than merely equipment), (2) making it available as a cash payment to nontaxable entities (universities, for example), (3) permitting it to cover more of the tax otherwise due (rather than the present limit of $25,000 plus one-half of the remaining tax liability), or (4) liberalizing treatment of short-lived assets. (The credit is available in full only to investments with an expected life of seven years or longer, is phased down for investments with lives of three to six years, and is not available for investments with lifetimes of less than three years.) The credit could also be enlarged by simply raising the rate from the present 10 percent.

A choice between higher depreciation allowances and larger investment credits requires a judgment on a second criticism of tax policy and its effect on investment: that it alters incentives and therefore "distorts" investment choices and reduces economic efficiency. Because the credit is now available for equipment only, firms are encouraged to invest more heavily in equipment than in plant.[31] Further, the constant investment credit rate for equipment with an expected lifetime of seven years or more reduces the attractiveness of machines with potentially long lives. On the other hand, the credit costs less per dollar of additional investment.[32] The credit can also be modified or eliminated as economic conditions require, whereas accelerated depreciation tends to become embedded in the tax system and is virtually impossible to alter for past investments because its tax effects extend over several years.

A third set of policy options arises from the taxation of corporations at both the firm and the individual level, whereas unincorporated business is taxed only at the individual level (the owners). This differing tax treatment tends to encourage investment in unincorporated enterprises. Some argue that the existence of corporations

31. This is true to the extent that such a choice is possible; if plant and equipment must be purchased together, the effect is like a general credit at a lower rate. Another view would describe the restriction of the credit to equipment as an offset for excessively generous plant depreciation allowances.

32. The credit costs less because benefits are concentrated in the first year of the asset's life and are therefore worth more to the firm than the future benefits of faster depreciation. Of course, this also means that the revenue loss to the government is concentrated in the first year, while part of the loss resulting from accelerated depreciation is deferred.

and the advantages of the corporate form disprove this argument;[33] a more subtle interpretation is that, while the corporate form has advantages for some industries, the *marginal* investment dollar is more easily attracted to unincorporated business, where a lower pre-tax return could yield a higher posttax return. This would mean that industries characterized by unincorporated firms (such as real estate) would be overdeveloped relative to largely incorporated industries, resulting in efficiency losses.

A counteracting distortion arises when corporations try to mini-mize the "double tax" effect by retaining as much of their profits as possible. Stockholders encourage corporations to retain earnings because retentions, unlike dividends, are not currently taxable; the resulting increase in the value of the firm is taxable at the lower capi-tal gains rate only when the stock is sold. For that reason firms will sometimes reinvest their retained earnings even when the return on that new investment is quite low. Another factor is that retentions are free to the firm, while borrowing or equity finance incurs future interest or dividend liabilities.

The most commonly proposed remedy for double taxation is inte-gration of the corporation and personal income taxes.[34] Integration of the two taxes would reduce or eliminate the tax difference between incorporated and unincorporated business, between debt and equity capital, and between retained earnings and dividends of corporations, thus mitigating the distortions described above. Several different forms of integration have been suggested. Full integration would treat corporations like partnerships, with all profits (whether dis-tributed or not) taxed at the individual shareholder level. Partial in-tegration schemes are almost infinite in variety; the most commonly favored one would treat the corporation tax paid on profits distributed as dividends as withholding against the tax ultimately due at the in-dividual level.[35]

All these integration schemes share an extreme complexity beneath

33. These advantages are primarily limited liability and the ability to raise capital from a large number of investors. Corporations increased their share of the national income produced by all business enterprise from 58.1 percent in 1929 to 74.6 percent in 1976.

34. George F. Break and Joseph A. Pechman, *Federal Tax Reform: The Impos-sible Dream?* (Brookings Institution, 1975), chap. 4.

35. For example, if a firm that earned $100 and paid a $50 corporation tax then distributed the $50 remaining after tax, the shareholder would include the entire $100 in income when calculating individual income tax and take a credit for the $50 corporate tax against personal liability.

a veneer of simplicity. Details such as treatment of corporation tax preferences, treatment of foreign and nontaxable shareholders, delays in determination of final corporate income and taxes, attribution of profits and taxes among part-year shareholders, and trafficking in shares of corporations with losses can have dramatic effects on the tax system; many of these details pose difficult and costly administrative burdens. Depending upon the final decisions on these details, the investment impact of integration is uncertain.

An additional problem is that many integration schemes would dramatically reshuffle tax burdens among corporations, depending on their use of tax preferences and their dividend payment practices. This redistributive effect within the corporate sector, combined with the uneasiness of corporate managers over increased pressure to distribute earnings as dividends, may explain why the administration's early interest in a partial integration scheme waned. Integration was not included in the final package.

The fourth tax option is a simple reduction in the corporation tax rate. A rate cut would provide greater cash flow to all taxpaying firms, regardless of their behavior; thus it could not be expected to increase investment more than an equivalent increase in posttax profit from another source. The absence of such preconditions makes the rate cut more attractive to corporate managers; it also provides a more visible benefit on corporate financial statements than accelerated depreciation or tax credits and therefore more encouragement to the stock market.

The President's Business Tax Proposals

The corporation tax that was finally proposed was relatively simple. It was designed both to stimulate investment and improve its allocation. Part of the investment stimulation comes from a straightforward reduction in corporation tax rates; the surtax rate would be reduced from 48 to 45 percent on October 1, 1978 (the other lower rates would be comparably reduced)[36] and to 44 percent in 1980. The revenue loss is expected to be $8.5 billion in 1980. This rate cut would also contribute modestly to a more efficient allocation of capital between the incorporated and unincorporated sectors.

To encourage investment and remove some distortions of alloca-

36. The rates would be reduced from 20 to 18 percent on the first $25,000 of taxable income, and from 22 to 20 percent on the next $25,000.

tion, the President would broaden the investment credit while maintaining its 10 percent rate.[37] Investment in industrial plant, as well as in equipment, would be covered; investment in pollution control equipment would be eligible for both the full credit and rapid amortization; and the maximum amount of credit available in any one year would be increased to 90 percent of tax liability. These changes would reduce revenues by $2.2 billion in 1980.

The lower corporation tax rates and higher investment credit would increase investment in three ways. First, corporate cash flow would increase, and at least part of that increase would probably be added to investment. Second, the greater posttax return to all corporate activity (because of the tax rate cut) and the reduced posttax price of plant and equipment (because of the increased credit) would encourage greater investment with any level of cash flow. Finally, additional posttax corporate income, whether invested or distributed, would stimulate higher expenditures and encourage investment through the need for greater production capacity. More efficient allocation of investment would result from the elimination of the credit distinction between plant and equipment.

It must be recognized, however, that the same investment objectives might have been achieved with less revenue loss if a more focused approach had been adopted. The corporation tax rate cut provides a general benefit to all corporations, whether or not they are expanding; greater emphasis on the investment credit (perhaps through a higher rate) or on accelerated depreciation (for example, through a wider asset depreciation range) would have increased the investment payoff. One independent estimate indicates that the increment to investment that would result from the administration's proposal—$4.5 billion in 1980—could be increased by about two-thirds through conversion of the corporate rate cuts to a higher investment credit and more liberal depreciation.[38]

The sum of the investment-inducing elements in the business tax proposal, $10.8 billion in 1980, is partially offset and then reinforced by other features. Almost $4 billion of additional revenue would be raised through reforms, including restriction of numerous

37. The rate is scheduled by law to *decrease* to 7 percent in 1981; the President proposed a permanent 10 percent rate.
38. Allen Sinai and Terry Glomski, "The Carter Tax Proposal: Impact on Business Spending," *Data Resources Review*, vol. 7 (January 1978), pp. 1.11–1.16.

deductions for business entertainment, tighter tax treatment of large corporate farms and banks, and elimination of benefits to exporting firms (through the domestic international sales corporation, or DISC) and to firms operating in other countries (through deferral of tax liabilities on foreign operations until earnings are repatriated). The net business tax cuts average about one-third of the individual income tax cuts for the next five years, which is roughly the amount that might be expected on the basis of historical precedent.

Anti-Inflation Tax Cuts

Some additional revenue loss would arise through reductions aimed at cutting business costs and thus exercise a desirable downward pressure on prices. Elimination of the telephone excise tax would cost the Treasury $0.9 billion, and reduction of the employer's payroll tax for unemployment compensation another $0.9 billion in 1980. The aggregate price level would be reduced by less than 0.1 percent.

A more vigorous anti-inflation tax program was a real alternative to the entire administration package.[39] The theory is to provide the tax cuts needed to stimulate the economy in a way that would encourage anti-inflationary behavior on the part of business, labor, and state governments, thereby making progress in both growth and price stability. Firms and workers would receive tax cuts if they agreed to smaller wage and price increases. State governments would be reimbursed for part of the revenue lost if they reduced sales taxes (which add to the price level) and would be encouraged to recover the difference through income taxes (which do not). The mechanics of such schemes—including verification, paperwork, and exceptions—are clearly complex. Even with perfect efficiency, more than $20 billion revenue loss would be needed to budge the price level by one percentage point, thus preempting any additional reductions (and probably reform) through normal channels. Business and labor both opposed the "government interference" involved in such a plan, and the administration apparently heeded this viewpoint and rejected all but the most minor anti-inflation tax cuts.

While the anti-inflationary tax policies appear to be weak, the inflationary bias of the payroll tax increase appears strong. The em-

39. Arthur M. Okun, "The Great Stagflation Swamp," *Challenge*, vol. 20 (November/December), pp. 6–13.

ployers' share of the social security payroll tax will be higher by $4.8 billion in 1979 and $12.0 billion in 1983. In the short run, firms can be expected to raise prices to recoup the increase to the greatest degree possible. A full recovery of these costs would add almost 0.3 percent to the price level in 1979 and 0.4 percent in 1983.

The Prospects

President Carter's tax message was greeted with hostility in many quarters almost immediately upon its release. For the individual income tax, complaints were voiced about reducing the deductibility of medical expenses and taxing unemployment insurance. The inevitable worst-case imbalances between payroll tax increases and income tax cuts were widely aired. No aspect of the plan appeared to be immune to criticism.

The reactions to the President's business tax reform proposals were also largely negative. Business leaders were concerned that the tax cuts would fail in many cases to compensate fully for increased social security payroll taxes (even though the employers' share of the taxes may be expected to be promptly passed on in the form of higher prices). Resentment also was expressed concerning what was seen as a punitive and capricious attack on ordinary business operations— the elimination of deductions for hunting lodge and country club fees, theater and sporting event tickets, first-class air fare, and the "three-martini lunch." The entertainment and restaurant industries pressed hard against this threat to their businesses. Firms doing business overseas were outspoken in their criticism of the deferral and the DISC reforms, claiming that such reforms would limit the ability of the United States to compete around the world. The tax cuts were generally viewed as helpful but insufficient compensation for the reforms and additional payroll taxes.

There was no conspicuous congressional support for the plan; on the contrary, several members immediately pronounced the cause of tax reform hopeless. The theme of their opposition was almost exclusively political: there was no constituency for reform; the affected parties would fight long and hard; and in the end the votes for reform would disappear. Their prediction was that few elements of reform in the President's package would survive, but there was little argument that significant cuts are in the offing.

President Carter's ability to influence the Congress is uncertain. In his tax message, the President said that he chose the net tax cut, including the revenue-raising reforms, with an eye on the overall economy. He held that defeat for the reforms would require smaller tax reductions to maintain the overall net figure. However, there is no consensus in the Congress that a net reduction of $25 billion should be regarded as sacred. Some conservative members have advocated $50 billion or more in cuts at the end of three years, to be accompanied by equal spending reductions; and some liberals have spoken of a $35 billion countercyclical tax cut with no restriction on spending for the additional reductions. (Significantly, this figure is close to the revenue loss of the President's package without the reforms in 1980.)[40] Another possible approach with strong support is to cut the payroll tax rather than the income tax. Variations on this theme include funding all or part of hospital insurance (and possibly disability insurance) from general revenue or suspending the new legislation while providing general revenues to the trust funds for several years. The administration will doubtless attempt to hold the tax cut to $25 billion, but if a bill with larger reductions and little or no reform (not an unlikely outcome) is passed, the President must accept it or must veto a large fiscal stimulus, which could bring an economic slowdown in an election year.

Even after the 1978 battle is over, many signs indicate that the tax war will go on. The income tax cuts will reimburse the public for the additional social security payroll taxes only through 1979 (although omission of the reforms could extend this offset by perhaps a year). If inflation does not slow significantly, real tax bills will continue to increase; a sluggish economy that does not respond to the present program might need further real stimulus. Beyond all this, the administration has suggested that the President's campaign promise of fundamental tax reform has been postponed rather than renounced. All these factors suggest that taxation will remain near the top of the public agenda for years to come.

40. A few have argued for fixed taxes and increased government spending to provide fiscal stimulus, but this position seems to have virtually no support.

CHAPTER SIX

Urban Policy

ANTHONY DOWNS

FOR MANY YEARS, big-city politicians and other urban leaders have been urging the federal government to formulate an effective national urban policy. Up to now, no administration has been serious enough about such a policy to create one. However, the Carter administration drew much of its political strength from city voters, especially blacks in inner-city neighborhoods, and it has proposed a national urban policy of unprecedented scope. This chapter examines the basic trends that provide the context for urban policy, presents a possible approach for developing alternative urban strategies, and examines the urban programs in the 1979 budget and the administration's recent policy proposals.[1]

Trends Affecting Urban Areas

Population

Six population trends crucially affect American urban areas. The first is a dramatic slowdown in the nation's overall population growth rate. In the 1950s, the U.S. residential population grew an average of

1. Richard P. Nathan and Paul R. Dommel, "The Cities," in Joseph A. Pechman, ed., *Setting National Priorities: the 1978 Budget* (Brookings Institution, 1977), gave a detailed analysis of specific urban-oriented federal programs and alternatives to them. Much of their analysis is still applicable. However, in view of the comprehensive scope of the recently proposed national urban policy, this chapter emphasizes the broader context within which specific urban programs must operate.

Table 6-1. Metropolitan Population Changes, 1970–75

Characteristic of metropolitan area	Number of areas	1970–75 population change		Percent of total 1975 metropolitan area population	Share of change in total population, 1970–75 (percent)
		Number (thousands)	Percent		
Lost population	37	−914	−2.2	26.7	−14.6
Gained less than 1 percent	15	49	0.3	11.5	0.8
Gained 50,000– 99,999	25	1,630	7.4	15.2	26.0
Gained 100,000 or more	14	2,760	14.7	13.8	44.0
Other	168	2,745	5.7	32.8	43.8
Total	259	6,270	4.2	100.0	100.0

Source: U.S. Bureau of the Census, *Current Population Reports*, series P-25, no. 709, "Estimates of the Population of Counties and Metropolitan Areas: July 1, 1974 and 1975" (Government Printing Office, 1977). Figures are rounded.

2.8 million people a year, or 1.71 percent; from 1970 through 1976, it rose an average of only 1.8 million people a year, or 0.87 percent. This slowdown results from a nearly 50 percent fall in fertility rates.

Slower growth has accentuated differential population growth rates. Table 6-1 groups all 259 metropolitan areas (as of 1975) into various categories based upon their population growth from 1970 to 1975. In the 1960s, all but five gained population. But from 1970 to 1975, thirty-seven such areas lost population, and another fifteen were almost stagnant. In contrast, the fourteen fastest growing areas captured 44 percent of all population growth, and another twenty-five captured 26 percent.

The drop in the birthrate affects cities because young people aged fourteen to twenty-four account for a high proportion of urban crime and unemployment. From 1960 to 1970, this age group exploded in size, growing by 48 percent, or 13.3 million. It grew another 4.5 million from 1970 to 1976. But from 1976 to 1980, this group will increase by only 409,000, and from 1980 to 1990, it will decline by 7.3 million, or 16 percent. This dramatic turnaround will be true of both white and black youths, though the latter group will not decrease as rapidly in relative terms. This shift should lead to declining rates of urban crime and urban unemployment in the 1980s.

The second population trend is migration from the Northeast and Midwest to parts of the South and West. From 1970 to 1975, the nation's total population rose 4.5 percent. However, the Northeast gained only 0.6 percent and the Midwest gained 1.7 percent, whereas the South grew 7.9 percent and the West, 8.4 percent. Similar Sunbelt dominance occurred concerning new jobs. From 1970 to August 1977, total employment in the nation's nonagricultural establishments grew only 2.8 percent in the Northeast and 12.7 percent in the Midwest, but it grew 25.5 percent in the South and 27.8 percent in the West. Moreover, in mid-1977, there were 669,000 fewer manufacturing jobs in the Northeast and 54,000 fewer in the Midwest than there had been in 1970, in contrast to gains of 588,000 such jobs in the South and 347,000 in the West.

Why have so many people been moving to the South and West? The South still has the nation's lowest level of real incomes—hence the lowest wages—and also a low fraction of unionized workers. Therefore, it attracts "footloose" private firms. Living costs are significantly lower in much of the South because of lower taxes, lower wages, and lower heating and housing costs. This attracts retired people and others living on fixed incomes. Weather and recreational conditions are widely regarded as more attractive in the South and much of the West than in other regions.

The third major population trend is a decline in the growth of all metropolitan areas compared to nonmetropolitan areas. From 1970 to 1975, for the first time in the twentieth century, counties outside metropolitan areas grew faster than metropolitan areas (6.9 percent to 4.0 percent). One cause is a spillover of growth from metropolitan areas to surrounding counties. Another cause is the fading of the century-old migration of people from farms to cities. A third cause is the recent increase in people moving into small communities in nonmetropolitan counties.

A trend of longer duration is the movement of people out of large cities and close-in suburbs into surrounding suburbs. There are 153 cities in the United States with 1970 populations of 100,000 or more. In the 1950s, 42 of them lost population; in the 1960s, 56 did so; and from 1970 through 1975, 94 fell in population. In the last period, 95 percent of the large cities in the Northeast lost population, as did 86 percent of those in the Midwest, 45 percent of those in the West, and 33 percent of those in the South. Furthermore, many cities that did not fall in total population nevertheless lost people from their older, inner-core neighborhoods.

The households moving out of cities into suburbs have higher incomes, on the average, than those remaining. As a result, the portion of people in all central cities with incomes below the official poverty level in 1975 was 15.0 percent, just about double the 7.6 percent in all suburbs.[2] Much of the impetus for creating a national urban policy comes from this decline in the size and relative affluence of city populations.

The fifth population trend is the rapid increase in number of households since 1970. In the 1960s, the number of households in the entire nation rose an average of 1,060,000 a year; but in the 1970s, it has risen 1,543,000 a year—up 46 percent. Moreover, from 1970 to 1975, 84 percent of new households consisted of one or two people. These small households now account for over half of all U.S. households, partly because the babies of the postwar baby boom are reaching the age to form households, partly because the divorce rate is increasing, and partly because more elderly people live alone. Average household size declined from 3.33 people in 1960 to 2.94 in 1975. The growing number of households somewhat offsets declining total population in many large cities and even in whole metropolitan areas, thereby keeping the demand for housing at a higher level than population losses would indicate.

The sixth population trend important to a national urban policy is continuing racial segregation in nearly all metropolitan areas. This keeps minority populations concentrated in the cities and the housing market split in two. In 1970, 58.2 percent of all blacks in the nation lived in central cities; by 1976, this fraction had declined only slightly, to 57.4 percent. The proportion of blacks living in suburbs rose from 16.1 percent in 1970 to 17.8 percent in 1976. At the same time, however, blacks in central cities rose from 20.4 percent of the total population in 1970 to 22.9 percent in 1976. In the suburbs the proportion of blacks increased slightly, from 4.8 percent to 5.3 percent. Studies of racial settlement patterns reveal that most minority-group households still live in clusters separate from predominantly white

2. The largest city in each standard metropolitan statistical area (SMSA) is always classified as a central city. Other cities are classified as central cities if their populations exceed 250,000 or are at least one-third that of the largest city. The term "central cities" refers herein to all central cities in all SMSAs considered as a group.

areas, both in cities and suburbs. This separation far exceeds what would be expected to occur purely because of income differentiation among neighborhoods.

Urban Growth

Trends in urban development are also central to national urban policy. One is the pattern of housing construction in most metropolitan areas since World War II: most new housing is built on vacant land around the edges of built-up areas and according to very high standards of quality legally required by local zoning and building codes. Therefore, it is too expensive for most households. This legal exclusion of the poor and near-poor from new-growth areas results in spatial separation of most middle- and upper-income households from most poorer ones. The former are concentrated in newer neighborhoods in the periphery of the metropolitan area (and in a few close-in neighborhoods). The poor are concentrated in neighborhoods with the oldest and most deteriorated housing, generally in the center of the metropolitan area. Such segregation of the poor benefits a majority of metropolitan-area residents by allowing them to reside in neighborhoods free from the problems of extreme poverty. But it severely injures the poorest households by forcing them to live in areas dominated by poverty and by such social maladies as high levels of unemployment, crime, drug addiction, and physical deterioration. It also penalizes central cities, which must bear the costs of poverty that most surrounding suburbs escape.

In 1975, 21 percent of all central-city residents lived in poverty areas, defined as all census tracts in which 20 percent or more of the 1970 population had incomes below the official poverty level. (In suburbs, only 5.3 percent of the population lived in such areas.) The poverty areas in central cities contained 12.7 million people, 35 percent of whom had incomes below the poverty level. About 56 percent of them (and 64 percent of the poor) were black. Moreover, 44 percent of *nonpoor* blacks (but only 9 percent of nonpoor whites) in central cities lived in poverty areas. Thus, the black community in central cities is more affected by concentration of poverty than the white community.

Provision of adequate housing for low-income households depends heavily on the rate at which new housing is added in each metropolitan area. When the rate of new construction exceeds that of new household formation, a surplus of housing is created. This causes many chains of moves: every time a newly built housing unit is occupied—usually by a middle-income or upper-income household—another household moves into the unit vacated by the first, a third household occupies the unit vacated by the second, and so on. This is the heart of the trickle-down process. Studies show that with each new unit occupied 2.0–3.5 households (about 10 percent poor) improve their housing.

From 1970 through 1973, housing starts (including mobile-home shipments) were 10.03 million, a record for any four-year period. They exceeded new household formation by about 900,000 units a year. Population migration absorbed some of the surplus, but large local surpluses remained in most metropolitan areas, stimulating millions of households to filter up through the inventory. Consequently, vacancies filtered down and became concentrated in the oldest, most deteriorated neighborhoods. Thus, accelerating abandonment of housing in inner-city neighborhoods was caused in part by high production of new housing in the suburbs. The concomitant drop in population in central cities and the rise in population in the suburbs add credence to the relationship: out-migration from all central cities increased from 345,000 a year in the 1960s to 1,404,000 a year in the early 1970s. Clearly, suburban growth and inner-city deterioration are closely linked by the operation of housing markets.

The effect of this linkage may change in the future with the adoption of more stringent growth controls by suburban communities alarmed by an influx of new residents, greater congestion, and higher property taxes. A variety of new regulations slow the reaction time of the housing industry to increases in demand and raise new housing prices. This restriction on housing supply will deflect a larger portion of demand to the existing inventory. However, the long-established process of population decentralization within U.S. metropolitan areas is far from over.

Another ingredient in decentralization is the astounding increase in the ownership and use of automotive vehicles. From 1950 to 1975, the number of cars, trucks, and buses in use soared from 43.8 million to 120.5 million—an enormous rise of 76.7 million, or 175 percent, while the human population increased by only 61.1 million, or 40 percent. The average annual increase in vehicle population was 2.4 million during the 1950s, 3.0 million during the 1960s, and shot up to 4.4 million in the years 1970–76. In fact, the vehicle population is now rising 2.5 times as fast as the human population in absolute terms, and 5.0 times as fast in percentage terms. By 1977, about half of all American households owned two or more cars or trucks.

Vehicle ownership and use reduce the relative locational advantages of older cities. First, the cities suffer more from traffic congestion and shortages of parking space than most suburbs. Second, public transportation becomes less necessary. And third, centralized locations are not as important.

Changing Neighborhoods

Within each city, diverse forces cause opposite kinds of neighborhood development. The trickle-down process generates a decline of many older neighborhoods, especially in cities losing population. When high-cost new suburban housing production reduces the demand for central-city housing, the oldest areas with the lowest socioeconomic status and the greatest physical deterioration are hardest hit. These areas often go through several stages of decline involving deterioration in physical condition, declining socioeconomic status of their residents, worsening psychological expectations, and decreased levels of economic investment. Property values in such areas may fall to almost zero. These phenomena are often mixed with racial segregation and intense poverty among minority-group residents, thus concentrating the greatest abandonment in minority-group areas. Many cities—especially newer ones in the South and West—do not have any neighborhoods in the most serious stages of decline. But where those stages have appeared it is difficult to reverse the process of decline, because few households or business firms with enough resources to choose among locations will voluntarily locate there.

Paradoxically, at the same time that many neighborhoods are sinking into decay, other neighborhoods in the same cities are undergoing a striking renewal. Thousands of young households, mainly those with good incomes and without children, are buying older houses in city neighborhoods, sometimes in slum areas. By renovating the houses themselves or with nonunion workers, they enjoy roomy, aesthetically interesting houses that cost less than most new suburban units. In a few cities, this phenomenon has caused worries about large-scale displacement of poor residents by middle-income and upper-income newcomers.

The coexistence of revival and decline within a single city suggests that the city as a whole is not always the most appropriate geographic unit for either analyzing urban trends or designing policy responses to them. Neighborhoods or specific business or industrial districts are often more relevant targets for remedial action. Although some tactics, like fiscal assistance, must operate at a citywide level, many could be applied at lower levels. This would allow the use of several different strategies simultaneously within one city.

Economic Development

Just as a city may contain, simultaneously, physical decay and revitalization, it also may experience opposite economic trends. Manufacturing jobs continue to move out of most cities and into suburban and rural areas. These job losses once were offset by growth in government employment; from 1960 to 1976, local government employment rose at a compound rate of 3.8 percent a year (compared to 1.8 percent a year for all civilian employment). However, from 1974 to 1976, governments in cities of over 50,000 people reduced employment by 6 percent. Though part of the cause was undoubtedly the 1974–75 recession, it is unlikely that most cities, especially those losing population, will again expand public employment (unless subsidized by federal funds).

Moreover, the skills of many unemployed urban residents and the skills required by the types of jobs available in cities are mismatched. Both factors exacerbate unemployment among the unskilled workers living in low-income neighborhoods, especially racial minority areas. In all metropolitan areas in 1976, the unemployment rate was 13.5 percent in all poverty areas but 7.4 percent in nonpoverty areas. In 1977, the unemployment rate among black and other nonwhite teenagers (most of whom live in cities) was 38.3 percent, compared to 15.4 percent among white teenagers—and it was much higher in low-income inner-city neighborhoods. At the same time, many "downtowns" are enjoying a renaissance of investment by both private firms and public agencies, and many big-city service facilities, like medical centers, are flourishing (although others, like universities, are experiencing financial strains). Thus, cities often have islands of prosperity in a sea of economic decline. The result of these events has been a net loss of employment in most large cities in the 1970s.

Conclusions

The trends described above lead to three conclusions crucial to the formulation of a national urban policy. The first is that living standards of most residents of metropolitan areas have improved during the past three decades. Although rising real incomes are part of the cause, the massive growth of relatively low-density suburbs played a key part by upgrading housing, neighborhoods, and other facilities in both suburbs and central cities. The suburban population doubled absolutely from 1950 to 1976 and rose from 43 percent of the metropolitan-area total to 57 percent.[3] From 1970 to 1976, all central cities combined lost 2.2 million residents; hence suburbs captured *all* metropolitan-area growth.

Suburban residents are significantly more satisfied with their neighborhoods than city residents. In 1975, 72.8 percent of all central-city residents but 86.8 percent of all suburban residents rated their neighborhoods as good or excellent. Ratings for both areas were slightly higher than in 1973, when such ratings began. This difference favoring suburbs existed in both years for owner-occupants and renters at all income levels. Thus, suburban living has raised the overall level of satisfaction people feel with their neighborhoods. Moreover, suburban growth lowered the density in large cities, improving housing and neighborhood conditions there (at least until around 1965, when abandonment began). Black households in particular benefited by spreading out within cities from the slums where they had been bottled up before racially restrictive housing covenants were ruled unconstitutional in 1948.

In fact, housing quality has risen markedly since 1950. About 57 percent of all metropolitan housing units in 1975 had been built since 1949; 33 percent of those in cities and 77 percent of those in suburbs. For a majority of American households, the percentage of household income devoted to housing costs has declined almost con-

---

3. The suburban share would have been much higher in 1976 if many southern and western cities had not expanded their boundaries through annexation. For example, from 1960 to 1970, 98 percent of the 4.4 million gain in total central-city population resulted from annexation. See Everett S. Lee, "How Cities Grow," in Oak Ridge National Laboratory, Urban Research Section of the Health Physics Division, *Civil Defense Research Project—Annual Progress Report, March 1971– March 1972*, p. 21, as reported in Thomas Muller and Grace Dawson, *The Impact of Annexation on City Finances: A Case Study in Richmond, Virginia* (Urban Institute, 1973), p. 1. If no annexation had occurred, the suburban share of total urban population in 1970 would have been 57 percent instead of 53.9 percent.

tinuously since 1950, in spite of soaring home prices since 1970.[4] Automobile ownership and use have expanded enormously. Thus, contrary to widespread belief, urban trends and urban policies have improved the quality of life for the majority.

At the same time, however, they imposed social and economic costs on the minority of people who live in areas of concentrated poverty. These people have more unemployment, more crime, more inadequate housing, lower-quality public schools, and far less desirable neighborhoods than most urban Americans. Thus, the same arrangements (low-density zoning, strict building codes) that benefit a majority of urban Americans unfairly penalize a numerical minority, many of whom are also ethnic minorities. The main political difficulty of carrying out effective urban policies is persuading the majority to change arrangements that benefit them or to adopt compensatory arrangements to offset costs they unjustly—and often unknowingly—force upon the poorest households in urban society.

The second conclusion is that concentration of low-income households helps cause the fiscal strain many cities are now experiencing. Such concentration not only raises public service costs but encourages affluent households and businesses to move out. (High wages for municipal employees and higher-than-average services to citizens also contribute to the fiscal strain; obsolete housing and other facilities contribute to the emigration of the affluent.)

The third conclusion is that the decline in population densities in American cities is probably going to continue. Americans have been moving from cities to suburbs for decades. Recently, they have also been migrating from relatively high-density places in the Northeast and Midwest to low-density places in the South and West. Density is surely not the only factor in these movements; yet the momentum generated by American mobility and preference for low-density living cannot easily be reversed or even slowed down by public policy.

Formulating a National Urban Policy

A workable national urban policy must recognize the trends described above and be realistic about the great diversity of urban conditions. For one thing, no policy should apply uniform programs and

4. See Anthony Downs, "Public Policy and the Rising Cost of Housing," *Real Estate Review*, vol. 8 (Spring 1978), pp. 27–38.

actions to all urban areas—conditions in New York, Phoenix, Green Bay, Seattle, and Atlanta differ too much. Therefore, policies should be general or should recognize multiple categories of communities; block grants and broadly defined funds are preferable to categorical programs; and program selection should be decided at regional and local levels.

A realistic approach also would recognize the lack of consensus—in fact, the sharply conflicting views—on what cities should be like and what the federal government should do about them. Therefore, the administration cannot simply announce goals and programs and expect them to work. The federal government is only one of the actors in the nation's urban affairs; there are also thousands of state government agencies, local governments, private firms, community organizations, labor unions, and consumer groups whose decisions affect cities. If an urban policy is to work, it must be partly followed by these nonfederal actors. In our democratic system, that means they must have a voice in formulating that policy. Therefore, the administration should regard its national urban policy announced in March 1978 as the opening statement in a long dialogue with other participants. The aim should be a relatively comprehensive consensus on the way urban areas should develop. Complete consensus is of course impossible, but public discussion focused on a specific set of policies and programs can lessen existing differences and ambiguities in viewpoints.

Determining Goals

Which urban problems are most pressing? It seems reasonable to select those that inflict the greatest harm, that injure people least capable of enduring injury, that are least likely to be remedied without outside assistance, that arose because of forces beyond the control of those injured, and that are likely to become worse.

By these criteria, two kinds of problems are the most pressing: the human needs of the poor, the unemployed, and the low-skilled who are concentrated in the deteriorated parts of cities; and the fiscal problems of some cities, mostly in the Northeast and Midwest. These strains cause cutbacks in service, layoffs of municipal employees, and poor maintenance. These problems are more pressing than the problem of rapid growth, which many communities face, because growth brings with it additional resources, expands the tax base, and thereby helps solve problems. In contrast, decline and decay involve the loss of resources. Furthermore, since the development that causes inner-city decline benefits a majority of metropolitan-area residents, justice is best served by concentrating additional federal resources on those most injured by that development.

Designing Strategies

After goals are chosen, a strategy must be designed to reach them. The federal government has a choice of letting declining cities adjust to decentralization (either with or without added federal aid) or opposing further decentralization to stimulate their revival. In the following discussion, these are referred to as the *adjustment* and *revival* strategies, respectively.

The aim of an adjustment strategy is to enable distressed cities to adjust to their less significant roles by (1) helping them cope with their most pressing problems (such as high unemployment), (2) providing transitional aid as they reduce services and municipal work forces, and (3) increasing the mobility of unemployed workers so they can move to places with greater economic opportunity. An adjustment strategy would limit federal long-term capital investment to repairing existing infrastructures or coping with immediate needs. Such a strategy operates on the principle that restoring every deteriorated neighborhood to its former population and vitality is impossible; it concentrates resources on revitalizing certain areas while avoiding major investment in others. A major objective is to create a new middle class by helping existing residents rather than attracting middle-class residents back from the suburbs.

Although dozens of adjustment strategies are conceivable, just three are discussed here: (1) adjustment based on raising the level of federal spending, (2) adjustment based on encouraging self-help by reducing federal spending, and (3) adjustment based on encouraging state governments to assume a greater role.

1. *Increased spending.* An amply funded adjustment strategy would have the money to provide more jobs and moving assistance to unemployed urban residents, emphasizing wage subsidies or training aimed at getting workers into the private sector, rather than jobs tied to local governments (hence geographically immobile). Temporary federal funding would help to wind down some services and help municipal workers find jobs elsewhere. Physical improvement

assistance would focus on maintaining existing structures rather than building new ones.

2. *Reduced spending.* A strategy based on reduced federal spending would force cities to rely more on themselves to cope with decentralization. Norton Long and Bennett Harrison advocate such a self-help strategy.[5] They contend that cities themselves should maximize employment opportunities for indigenous low-skilled, unemployed workers, particularly young minority-group members. This would require extraordinary wage-demand restraint by municipal workers, whose rising salaries and fringe benefits are a major cause of local fiscal strain. It would also require reorienting public schools toward providing job training for the needs of local employers. Efforts to attract private firms would focus on those that provide low-skilled jobs, since that is the type of labor force such cities have in abundance. Neighborhood cooperatives could generate jobs by mutually providing goods and services for each other.

The idea that local residents should assume more direct responsibility for conditions in their own neighborhoods could be adapted to other strategies, too. It could also take the form of neighborhood anticrime surveillance teams, improved cleanliness efforts to cut down on municipal costs, and mutual assistance with property repairs and improvements.

3. *Incentives to states.* The federal government could pressure state governments into accepting more responsibility for dealing with urban problems. The rigid boundaries that block central cities from gaining fiscal access to the tax-base growth of the surrounding suburbs (including growth in real estate values, retail sales, and household incomes) could be broken by state governments, which have legal control over access to metropolitan-area tax bases. Hence states could ease the fiscal pressure on distressed cities by creating fairer arrangements for tax-base sharing. This would allow the federal government to switch its focus from places to people—the unemployed and the poor. The federal government could encourage such action by the states by providing incentives such as giving extra general revenue sharing funds, withholding existing general revenue sharing funds, or assuming more welfare costs if states gave more

5. Norton E. Long, *The Unwalled City: Reconstituting the Urban Community* (Basic Books, 1972), and Bennett Harrison, *Urban Economic Development* (Urban Institute, 1974).

local fiscal assistance (as suggested by the Advisory Commission on Intergovernmental Relations).

A revival strategy seeks to restore large cities to the roles they had in the past, though with perhaps not precisely the same activities. This includes attracting back both economic activities and households that have moved elsewhere. This strategy emphasizes permanent capital investments to make cities more competitive with suburban locations, and forms of aid that geographically tie their recipients to the community. Since 1974, when urban renewal was absorbed into the annually funded community development block grant program, there has been no feasible way for city governments to use federal money for large-scale, long-term capital improvements that require land value write-downs or other subsidies. (The recently adopted urban development action grant program—UDAG—and the proposed national development bank may close this gap.) A revival strategy would not reduce levels of service or municipal work forces.

Every revival strategy is counter to the dominant forces that decentralize cities, so it must include some means of reducing the relative power of those forces. One tactic would be to offer incentives to firms and households for locating within declining cities: federal tax credits for investing in declining areas, wage subsidies for hiring unemployed city workers, low-interest public financing for buying sites and building or renovating factories or offices, funds to enrich public school education, and federal contracting advantages for firms located in declining areas. However, it would take very large added federal expenditures to make these incentives strong enough to reverse the outflow of jobs and households from most declining cities (unless freedom of movement for firms and households were curtailed, a move not politically possible in our decentralized democratic system).

Although the adjustment and revival strategies prescribe conflicting long-run remedies, their short-run tactics overlap. Because both strategies would give immediate aid to those most injured by decentralization, both could include tax credits for hiring unemployed workers, expanded public service employment, stronger affirmative action programs among both city and suburban employers, transportation assistance for inner-city workers seeking or working in suburban jobs, and transitional fiscal aid to city governments. Both could encourage states to take more responsibility for urban problems, and emphasize voluntary and self-help activities at the neighborhood level.

One difference between these two strategies is that the revival strategy would use heavy capital investment in declining cities to make them competitive with suburban growth areas, whereas the adjustment strategy would minimize investment and stress increased mobility for unemployed workers. In addition, an adjustment strategy accepts the continuance of decentralizing forces, trying only to soften their adverse effects, whereas a revival strategy tries to reduce the strength of those forces. If large-scale suburban expansion continues unabated, it would offset the cities' efforts to revive their economies. Devices for limiting suburban sprawl have been developed in other nations and similar limitations were recently proposed in the state land-use plans of California and Massachusetts. Such an attack on suburban sprawl is the principal antidecentralization tactic in the administration's national urban policy. But what weakens cities is not low-density sprawl itself but the total amount and speed of suburban growth.

Should suburban growth be restricted in order to strengthen housing and commercial demand within declining cities? There have been several proposals for removing anticity biases from federal policies and programs (such as tax incentives favoring new construction over rehabilitation, and greater subsidies for highway construction than for transit operation). But even the strongest advocates of city revival do not espouse deliberate federal action to slow down suburban growth. That would outrage the huge homebuilding industry and many suburban communities benefiting fiscally from new growth. Furthermore, national or regional interference in local control over land use would antagonize millions of suburbanites. And slowing suburban growth might create housing shortages, raising prices and rents. This situation reveals a fundamental conflict between local governments and property owners within cities on the one hand and renters (including most poor households) and the building industry on the other hand. A strong housing demand in cities raises property values and, consequently, taxes and rents. But high rents injure renters, and less building harms the construction industry. Coping with this political dilemma is one of the toughest tasks for any urban policy.

Applying the above strategies at the neighborhood level rather than at the city or metropolitan levels would allow policymakers to choose preservation for neighborhoods in excellent condition, revival for those that have partly deteriorated, and adjustment to low populations and levels of investment for badly deteriorated neighborhoods. Massive suburban building has generated a housing surplus in most metropolitan areas that expresses itself as falling demand somewhere, usually in the oldest, most deteriorated neighborhoods. Yet these areas do not completely empty out. Further focusing this declining demand by assisting remaining residents to move elsewhere is politically difficult because it requires local elected officials to designate which areas will be, in effect, written off so far as physical upgrading in the near future is concerned. Yet the residents who stay argue that they are in the most dire need, that their neighborhoods are in the worst condition, and that they should get the most public assistance.

Poor residents of deteriorating areas should certainly receive more direct transfer payments and other personal aid than nonpoor residents of more affluent areas, as well as their fair share of normal city services. But the extent to which public resources for physical upgrading should be focused upon such areas is debatable. In some cities, the cost of adequately upgrading the most deteriorated areas exceeds all public resources available. In other cities, public resources could be effectively spent in such areas to demolish the worst structures, maintain vacant lots, and stabilize the environment. In still other places, the worst areas could be substantially improved. One variable is the extent to which public funds can be *leveraged*—that is, used to attract private capital. Leverage is easier to achieve in areas that are not terribly deteriorated. In short, effective use of public funds for physical upgrading varies from city to city.

Choosing a Strategy

Whether the administration uses a revival strategy or an adjustment strategy depends in part upon whether decentralization can be successfully opposed. That in turn depends upon its causes. Some urban experts believe that it is abetted, if not caused, by federal policies that favor suburban development. If these policies were altered, the federal bias against older cities would be erased, and they might blossom again. Also, high energy costs will encourage urban revival by restricting housing construction in the suburbs and the use of automobiles and trucks. According to this view, changes in federal urban and energy policies could dramatically improve the chances for revival of declining cities.

However, most evidence indicates that the main cause of urban decentralization is the strong preference of Americans for living and working in low-density areas—combined with rising real incomes that allow them to realize this preference. Consequently, when energy costs rise, Americans will probably switch to smaller cars and better-insulated homes rather than sacrifice personal transportation or low-density living. Furthermore, full employment in the politically powerful automotive and homebuilding industries requires further decentralization of large cities. And even the most conservative population forecasts predict about 25 million more people between 1980 and 2000. Where will they all live if the suburbs stop growing? Finally, the federal government does not now have the tools to reverse decentralization. All these factors make it unlikely that decentralization can be significantly turned around in the near future.

Coordinating Policy and Programs

Currently, dozens of federal departments and agencies carry out urban programs, raising the problem of coordination within a national urban policy. There are three kinds of coordination involved. One is coordinating the "menu" of programs the federal government offers to state and local governments. This requires continuous federal review of all programs to determine how effectively they work, how they might be more fruitfully related to each other, whether any conflict, what new programs are needed, and what existing programs should be modified or terminated. (This review is similar to what the President's urban and regional policy group has been doing, but it must be permanent and ongoing if a national urban policy is to have any real impact over time.) Those who conduct this review should ideally (1) be attached to the White House or the Office of Management and Budget, (2) have no program-operating responsibilities, (3) work full time on this task, and (4) have a sufficiently large and skilled staff to perform this complex task well.

Another level of coordination concerns deciding the specific activities needed in each community and how to interrelate them. One way to achieve such coordination is to merge all federal urban funds into one giant block grant, distribute it by some formula, and let each local government decide how to use the money. However, Congress will never adopt such all-encompassing general revenue sharing. Federal funds would then not be focused on the purposes lying within the purview of each congressional committee—and committee members and interested constituents believe their programs are vital to the nation's interests. At the other extreme, categorical programs, such as the United States had in the 1960s, meant that parts of specific federal agencies funded activities of parts of city governments (sometimes through state governments). No effective coordination existed at any level.

The nation has already moved away from that chaotic approach toward specialized block grants. Such grants allow significant local discretion concerning related activities, within federal guidelines. The community development block grant program of the Department of Housing and Urban Development (HUD) and the Comprehensive Employment and Training Act (CETA) program in the Department of Labor are examples of this approach. The Department of Transportation has proposed consolidation of several categorical highway programs in its fiscal 1979 budget. But experience proves that both Congress and the administration tend to make those guidelines ever more restrictive as time passes. This gradually shifts specialized block grant funding back toward categorical funding. That in turn reduces local governments' ability to coordinate programs. The federal government has two conflicting goals: focusing federal funds on national goals, and allowing local officials autonomy in using those funds. Since there is no clearly superior way to reconcile these goals, arrangements will continue to swing back and forth, favoring one goal, then the other, and always trying to achieve both.

There are two ways to improve coordination in each city. One is for federal agencies to concentrate on creating a "balanced menu" of offerings and let state and local governments choose among them. That means folding categorical programs into broad (but specialized) block grants and adopting relatively unrestrictive guidelines for them. Coordination would be accomplished by each local government. Its effectiveness could be increased by (1) encouraging local chief executives to establish federal assistance coordinators within their own offices to help obtain and interrelate all local federal grants, and (2) providing more federal managerial and technical assistance to local governments.

Another approach is for the federal government to assign a generalist to confer with each community as the latter makes a selection among programs. The community could get its package of federal aid only with this person's approval; its choice would be heavily influenced by him or her. In theory, this official would expedite the approval of each program application by the federal agency concerned. However, prospects for achieving such cooperation among myriad federal agencies are not bright. Moreover, this approach injects another layer of personnel into the process. And such officials would develop ambivalent loyalties—to the federal government and to the localities to which they were assigned.

All things considered, the most feasible approach seems to be providing individual communities with maximum choice among federal programs. The federal government could then concentrate on improving the quality of its programs, ensuring that there was a balanced array of programs, and following up to see whether they had the desired effects.

The third level of coordination concerns relations among federal, state, and local agencies and governments. To what extent should the federal government deal directly with local governments in carrying out its national urban policy, and to what extent should it work through state governments? Existing arrangements are so complex and confusing they have come to be called marble-cake (rather than layer-cake) federalism. This perplexing coordination problem is beyond the scope of this analysis.

Translating Policy into Action

Merely announcing goals, strategies, and programs does not make them work—permanent procedures must be institutionalized to translate them into realities. Among the institutional arrangements required for an effective urban policy are the following:

1. A much stronger urban analysis and coordination capability within the White House or OMB. The White House is woefully understaffed compared to the agencies it supposedly oversees and coordinates. A specific urban policy office should be created to perform ongoing program review, described earlier. Without such a central group, one outside the major programmatic agencies, no attempt to create a meaningful national urban policy can succeed.

2. Estimates from federal agencies of the likely urban impact of

major legislation and regulations at the time they are proposed. To avoid excessive red tape, this requirement should definitely not be applied at the project level.

3. More effective monitoring of major existing federal programs to determine their urban impacts.

4. Continuation of an interagency consultative process within the federal government for periodically revising national urban policies. Such a process is limited because representatives from each agency oppose anything that reduces the significance of programs in their agency. The group as a whole will thus almost never agree to reducing the activities of any of its members. Therefore, no strategies calling for lower total federal activity or major reshuffling of roles among agencies are ever recommended. Nevertheless, those federal agencies responsible for carrying out a national urban policy must have a strong voice in designing it. Otherwise, it is impossible to gain their full cooperation. The urban policy group could supervise and influence this consultative process.

5. Increased federal assistance to help local governments improve their management capabilities. Such assistance should realistically recognize that the incentives given local urban program managers are rarely related to performance. Assistance could include setting standards for the local collection of data, relating local or state personnel promotion systems to output performance through positive incentives, and direct funding of useful operational innovations without regard to their potential transferability.[6]

6. Publication of a revised national urban policy at regular intervals—at least once every two years. All interested nonfederal parties should be encouraged to express their views about what its contents should be.

The 1979 Budget

The Carter administration's fiscal 1979 budget contains an implicit national urban policy of major magnitude. In the broadest sense, federal urban policy encompasses all federally financed or influenced activities that occur anywhere within the nation's metropolitan areas and perhaps also within smaller urban communities.

6. Francine F. Rabinovitz and Edward K. Hamilton, "Coping with Urban Management: Can Washington Really Help?" working paper 226-03 (Urban Institute, 1977; processed).

Table 6-2. Budget Outlays for Central Cities, 1979, and 1977–79 Change

Program	1979 outlays		1977–79 change	
	Total (millions of dollars)	Central cities (millions of dollars)	Millions of dollars	Percent
Place-oriented	60,682.0	25,223.3	6,557.7	35.1
Jobs and economic development	14,523.0	6,847.3	3,487.0	103.8
Fiscal assistance	8,262.0	3,637.1	−179.0	−4.7
Physical development	20,808.7	9,102.0	2,472.6	37.3
Social and health services	17,088.3	5,636.9	777.1	16.0
Person-oriented	195,448.0	66,433.9	10,713.9	19.2
Total	256,130.0	91,657.2	17,271.6	23.2

Sources: *The Budget of the United States Government, Fiscal Year 1979;* ibid, *Appendix;* information provided by federal agency officials; and estimates by the author.

However, the administration's current urban concern is focused on distressed cities and people. The fiscal strength of this concern can be roughly measured by total federal spending proposed for central cities (that is, principal cities within metropolitan areas as defined by the Census Bureau). True, most of these cities are not suffering from severe fiscal distress. On the other hand, nearly all of them contain many distressed people and some distressed neighborhoods.

Table 6-2 presents an analysis of federal urban spending proposed in the 1979 budget (not counting the supplemental urban initiatives discussed later). This analysis excludes federal spending not directly related to urban affairs, such as defense expenditures and farm price supports. It also excludes tax expenditures related to urban activities, because there is no reliable way to allocate them geographically. But, it does include most forms of federal assistance that have a major effect on urban residents and their governments. Outlays for these programs are $256.1 billion—51.2 percent of the total budget and 68.4 percent of all nondefense outlays.

These programs are somewhat arbitrarily divided into place-oriented (those in which funds are directed to governments or other geographic entities) and person-oriented (those in which funds are directed to eligible people regardless of their location). This division corresponds to the two kinds of urban problems earlier identified as most pressing, although most activities included in tables 6-2 to 6-4 are not responsive to real urban distress. Specific programs included in these categories are listed in the appendix to this chapter.

For many programs, there is no reliable information about how total outlays are distributed geographically, so estimates of the central-city share are very crude. Some were made by the agencies concerned; others are based on the proportion of the nation's total population—or total elderly population or total poverty population or total unemployed population—living in the central cities. No attempts were made to measure the possible benefits derived by central city residents from federal spending elsewhere.

The increases from 1977 to 1979 provide a measure of the Carter administration's policy, since the fiscal 1977 budget was largely determined by the Ford administration.

Central-City Outlays

The Carter administration's budget proposes spending $91.7 billion in all central cities in fiscal 1979, about 18.3 percent of total federal outlays and 24.1 percent of nondefense outlays. Most of it is for assisting individuals. About 63.2 percent of these person-oriented funds are for retirement or other social security assistance, but $28.7 billion is for assistance such as income maintenance, health care, food stamps, and unemployment compensation. Another $25.2 billion—27.5 percent of all central-city spending—is for place-oriented programs. Thus, by any reckoning, the 1979 budget underwrites a large-scale urban policy.

The 1979 budget provides for a 23.2 percent increase in central-city spending over 1977 outlays, or about the same rate of increase as for the entire budget. However, place-oriented central-city spending increases by 35.1 percent in the two-year period, a much faster rate than for the budget as a whole, showing an increase in the relative emphasis on place-oriented assistance. Nevertheless, person-oriented spending is still 2.6 times greater than place-oriented spending; the administration is clearly putting much more emphasis on meeting human needs in central cities than on helping local governments meet their fiscal needs.

These current and proposed urban expenditures greatly exceed the $2.7 billion of additional spending (including forgone revenues) recommended in the administration's national urban policy statement for 1979, and even the $4.6 billion for fiscal years 1980–81. Therefore, making more effective use of federal funds already requested or allocated is more important to both those cities and the nation than spending more funds, at least in the amounts likely to be politically feasible in the near future.

The federal government estimates that its total grants to state and local governments in fiscal 1979 will be $85 billion, 26.2 percent of all state and local government expenditures—about the same fraction as in 1977 and slightly less than in 1978. However, this estimate includes many person-oriented programs, as well as nearly all place-oriented programs. Total state and local government expenditures (as measured in the national income accounts) will be about $324.4 billion in fiscal 1979. From 1970 through 1975, city government expenditures were about 26.3 percent of state and local government expenditures. So total city government expenditures in fiscal 1979 will probably be about $85 billion. Approximately 75 percent of this amount will be spent in cities of 50,000 or more, most of them central cities. A rough estimate of total central-city government spending for fiscal 1979 is therefore $64 billion.

The federal government's planned spending of $25.2 billion for place-oriented programs within central cities is thus equivalent to 39.4 percent of all central-city government expenditures. This does not mean federal spending accounts for 39.4 percent of central-city government spending, because not all federal place-oriented spending goes through central-city governments. Nevertheless, federal place-oriented spending is vital to the solvency of most central-city governments, and its importance is rising.

Central-city governments long ago ceased to be fiscally self-supporting. In 1975, all U.S. cities received 39.4 percent of their revenues from intergovernmental transfers, over two-thirds of which came from state governments. Cities of 50,000 or more people received 41.9 percent of their revenue from such transfers, and cities of 500,000 or more, 45.8 percent. In fact, intergovernmental transfers provide as much revenue to central cities as local taxation. Though most of these transfers come from state governments, the states themselves received 23.3 percent of the money they spent in 1975 from the federal government. That is almost twice the amount they transferred to all cities. So the federal government, directly and indirectly, crucially supports city governments.

Given these conditions, the idea that central-city governments can soon—or ever—become economically self-sufficient is absurd. These governments, in fact, act as mechanisms for the local delivery of

Table 6-3. Share of 1979 Urban-Oriented Budget Outlays, by Area
Percent unless otherwise stated

Program	Central cities	Suburbs	Nonmetropolitan areas
Place-oriented	41.6	29.8	28.6
Jobs and economic development	47.1	25.4	27.4
Fiscal assistance	44.0	28.5	27.5
Physical development	43.7	31.8	24.5
Social services	33.0	31.7	35.3
Person-oriented	34.0	34.0	32.0
All urban-oriented	35.8	33.0	31.2
Outlays (billions of dollars)	91.7	84.5	79.9

Sources: Same as table 6-2.

services financed by the federal government. Who decides how much to spend, and on what? Can it be left to local officials, when they do not have political responsibility for raising half of the money? These are examples of the questions an effective national urban policy must answer.[7]

The Central-City Share

Table 6-3 presents a crude estimate of the share of all urban-oriented federal spending that in fiscal 1979 will go to central cities, suburbs (all portions of metropolitan areas outside central cities), and nonmetropolitan areas. These estimates are even more approximate than those in table 6-2 because of the rougher means of estimating total federal outlays in metropolitan areas.

According to this admittedly imprecise table, central cities would receive about 41.6 percent of all place-oriented federal urban spending proposed in the 1979 budget. This share is significantly higher than the percentage of the population residing in central cities, whether the percentage is of the total, the elderly, the poor, or the unemployed. Central cities receive an especially high proportion of all spending on employment and economic development (47.1 percent), although their share may decline as public works spending is phased out. The estimated central-city shares of social and health

7. For a thoughtful discussion of the confusion of roles, power, and funding in American federalism, see Edward K. Hamilton, "On Nonconstitutional Management of a Constitutional Problem," *Daedalus*, vol. 107 (Winter 1978), pp. 111–28.

Table 6-4. Place-Oriented 1979 Budget Outlays for Cities and 1977–79 Change, by Federal Funding Agency

	1979 outlay		1977–79 change	
Federal agency	Millions of dollars	Percent	Millions of dollars	Percent
Labor	5,681.6	22.5	2,779.4	95.8
Housing and Urban Development	4,923.6	19.5	1,271.5	34.8
Health, Education, and Welfare	4,897.8	19.4	701.7	16.7
Treasury	3,637.1	14.4	−179.0	−4.7
Transportation	2,714.9	10.8	952.2	54.0
Environmental Protection	1,740.0	6.9	328.0	23.2
Commerce	1,008.8	4.0	699.8	226.0
All others	619.5	2.5	4.1	0.6
Total	25,223.3	100.0	6,557.7	35.1

Sources: Same as table 6-2.

services and of all person-oriented federal spending are heavily influenced by the simple allocation assumptions made in distributing these types of spending among areas. Nevertheless, it is noteworthy that, for every category except total person-oriented spending, central cities receive higher shares than all suburbs combined (and for person-oriented spending, their shares are almost identical), even though suburbs contain about one-third more population.

These data do not necessarily show that central cities receive more than their fair share of federal urban spending: they have higher shares of the poor, the elderly, and the unemployed, and many have lower average incomes and taxable assessed value per capita than their suburbs. An Urban Institute study of twenty-eight large metropolitan areas showed that, in nineteen of them, 1971–72 assessed property value per capita in the suburbs exceeded that in the central city by a median of 34.1 percent.[8] Moreover, since central-city residents and businesses contribute a large share of federal tax revenues, not all federal spending in central cities is a net transfer from somewhere else. It is in fact impossible to determine, unequivocally, what a fair share is.

Who Spends Place-Oriented Funds?

The federal agencies responsible for place-oriented spending are shown in table 6-4, listed in descending order of total 1979 budget

8. George E. Peterson, "Finance," in William Gorham and Nathan Glazer, eds., *The Urban Predicament* (Urban Institute, 1976), p. 76.

The Administration's Ten Key National Urban Policies

1. The federal government will administer existing and new programs in a coordinated, efficient and fair manner. All key federal activities will be evaluated to assure that they are as consistent as possible with the administration's urban policies.

2. The federal government will develop a firm partnership with state governments to respond to urban problems. Federal incentives will be provided for states to implement comprehensive urban policies and strategies.

3. The federal government will encourage and support efforts to improve local planning and management capacity. Federal programs will support local efforts to develop economic, social service, community development policies, and environmental quality policies and strategies. Local governments will play a major role in coordinating the use of federal funds within city borders.

4. The federal government will encourage and support the efforts of neighborhood and voluntary groups and citizens in revitalizing their communities.

5. The federal government will carry out strong measures to eliminate discrimination and racism from all aspects of urban life.

6. The federal government will help expand business and job opportunities for the urban poor and minority men and women. Federal programs will seek ways to increase the mobility of the growing number of men and women trapped in poverty or dead-end jobs.

7. The federal government will offer strong incentives for businesses and industries to remain, expand, or locate in economically troubled central cities. To the extent possible, federal disincentives for locating in troubled central cities will be ended.

8. The federal government will help distressed cities address their critical short-term fiscal problems. The federal government, working with states and local governments, will make efforts to strengthen the long-term fiscal condition of cities and reform the current system of intergovernmental aid.

9. The federal government will help make troubled central cities attractive places to live and work. It will help improve the range and quality of decent social services available to their residents. Federal efforts will help make decent housing available to the poor and remove barriers to their choice of neighborhoods. Federal programs will encourage the middle class to remain in or return to central cities.

10. The federal government will help cities develop efficient land settlement patterns. Federal laws and programs will be amended to discourage sprawl and encourage energy efficient and environmentally sound settlement patterns in urban areas.

outlays. The Department of Labor will spend the most, the Department of Housing and Urban Development and the Department of Health, Education, and Welfare are almost tied for second place, followed by the Treasury Department and the Department of Transportation. Considerably below them are the Environmental Protection Agency and the Department of Commerce.

National Urban Policy and the New Initiatives

In April 1977, President Carter designated the secretaries of six departments and the heads of several related agencies to form an urban and regional policy group, chaired by Patricia Harris, secretary of the Department of Housing and Urban Development. In March 1978 the group made its final report, a long statement analyzing urban conditions and recommending goals and strategies. President Carter then announced proposals for programs supplemental to the fiscal 1979 budget. The President's endorsement of the policy document has made it the administration's official policy, so it is worth examining briefly (see facing page).[9]

About fifty implementation strategies elaborate on these principles, some derived from analyses of thirty-eight existing federal programs. Of course, the real impact of these principles can be determined only as their actual application unfolds over time. However, some significant conclusions about the administration's intentions can be gleaned from them.

One striking implication is that the federal government intends to take an extremely active role in urban affairs. There are apparently no limits on "proper federal concerns"; the administration is interested in influencing all aspects, from the individual level through neighborhoods and cities to state and national levels. In fact, it promises to do just about everything good conceivable for just about everyone in all urban areas. Of course, this is impossible to achieve. What it means is that these principles are actually *desired goals,* not practical rules of operation. Nevertheless, analysis of these goals and the proposed strategies reveals they are more than just pious platitudes.

The administration clearly places high priority on aiding distressed

9. Several versions of these principles have appeared in connection with the President's announcing a national urban policy. This version is from the President's Urban and Regional Policy Group Report, *A New Partnership to Conserve America's Communities: A National Urban Policy* (HUD, March 1978), pp. III-3 and III-4.

cities. It promises short-term fiscal aid and help in strengthening their long-term fiscal condition, incentives for business growth, and help in making cities attractive places to live and work. This emphasis reflects the views of HUD's leaders, who forcefully argue for concentrating federal funds on the most distressed cities and the most distressed people and neighborhoods within the cities.

But such concentration violates the "law of political dispersion," which states that elected officials always distribute the benefits they control to all parts of their constituencies, regardless of the economic or other gains from concentrating those benefits on just a few parts. The administration has already targeted federal urban aid on distressed cities to a significant degree in the formulas it persuaded Congress to accept in 1977 for allocating community block grants, local public works funds, and some CETA funds contained in the economic stimulus package. Since then, many southern and western mayors, governors, and congressmen have expressed vehement opposition to this targeting, because it has chiefly benefited cities in the Northeast and Midwest. Undoubtedly, such targeting increases the efficiency of federal funds in achieving stated congressional goals, but that does not placate those communities with small shares. So the administration may not entirely succeed in giving high priority to the most distressed cities. The Department of Housing and Urban Development has had to retreat from its initial plan to require cities to spend 75 percent of their community development block grants in census tracts with majorities of low-income households.

Another key implication of the policy principles is that the administration favors a revival strategy for declining cities. It espouses major capital investments, incentives for business growth, improvement of social services, and encouraging the middle class to return to them. Moreover, it promises to remove anticity biases in federal policies and to discourage sprawl and encourage energy-efficient settlement patterns (a euphemism for higher density). The policies stop short of recommending a slowdown in suburban growth. Whether the administration is willing to spend enough money on revival to overcome powerful decentralizing trends remains to be seen. The modest size of the supplemental programs indicates it is not. However, these proposals must be seen in the context of urban spending proposed in the fiscal 1979 budget, discussed earlier.

A final inference from these policies is that the federal government wants to energize state governments, local governments, and neighborhood groups to help cope with urban problems. Although no mention of encouraging urban investments or planning participation by private business firms and nonprofit organizations is contained in these ten policies, the text accompanying them indicates clear awareness of the need to attract private capital. This inference may seem inconsistent with the inference of active federal involvement. Such inconsistency is not caused by an error in interpretation; rather, it illustrates the ambiguity inherent in all comprehensive lists of desired goals.

Supplements to the 1979 Budget

Two months after the 1979 budget was made public, President Carter presented his national urban policy. It consists of the policy document discussed earlier, supplements to the budget, and recommendations for changes in existing programs. The White House called the policy "a new partnership to conserve America's communities." By stressing conservation, the administration appealed to environmentalists, ecologists, and many suburbanites not usually sympathetic with the plight of distressed cities. The White House also emphasized that large-scale federal spending is already taking place in the cities and has increased under the Carter administration.

The President proposed four groups of supplemental initiatives.

1. *Improved administration.* An interagency coordination council would coordinate programs and act upon projects involving several federal agencies. Studies of the likely urban impacts of all major legislative proposals would be required. New federal facilities would be located in cities when feasible. Federal procurement would be targeted in areas with labor surpluses. Incentive grants (totaling $200 million a year) would be given to state governments that reorient resources they control toward declining or distressed communities.

2. *Fiscal assistance.* A new fiscal assistance program would replace the expiring program of countercyclical revenue sharing (using $1 billion already in the 1979 budget). The fiscal relief portions of the welfare reform program would go into effect as soon as it is adopted, rather than gradually.

3. *Jobs and economic development.* A three-year public works program, aimed at creating jobs for the long-term unemployed and disadvantaged workers, would be undertaken. At least 70 percent of

the $1 billion a year would be for labor, and half the jobs would be for these target groups. An employment tax credit of $2,000 the first year and $1,000 the second year would be given to employers hiring young workers referred by CETA. The revenue loss would be $1.5 billion a year. A national development bank would be created to encourage long-run capital investments in cities. The bank would be an interagency institution with a board of directors consisting of the secretaries of HUD, Commerce, and Treasury. It would provide up-front grants, guarantee loans, extend the limit on industrial revenue bonds in economically distressed areas, and provide a secondary market for private loans there. Economic development programs in HUD and the Commerce Department would receive $550 million more a year for use with the national development bank. A 5 percent investment tax credit would be added to the 10 percent tax credit for projects in distressed communities, with a limit of $200 million a year for two years.

4. *Community and human development.* An additional $150 million would be provided for low-interest housing rehabilitation loans in 1979. A program would be created to rehabilitate and maintain urban parks and recreation facilities at a cost of $150 million a year. A fund of $200 million a year would be earmarked for development of intermodal transit facilities (such as pedestrian transit malls) within cities. An additional $150 million a year would go toward improving the delivery of social services in areas of concentrated poverty. Smaller projects at the neighborhood level and voluntary local improvements, including an urban volunteer corps, would be encouraged.

Total budget authority for all these initiatives would be $4.4 billion in 1979, $6.1 billion in 1980, and $5.6 billion in 1981. Outlays would rise from $742 million in 1979 to about $2.9 billion in both 1980 and 1981. Revenue losses would raise these costs by about another $1.7 billion a year.

On paper, these supplemental initiatives, plus the programs in the fiscal 1979 budget, form a national urban policy that, at first glance, is remarkably similar to the "ideal" version described earlier in this chapter. (That version was written before any of the supplemental initiatives had been selected by the administration.) However, the following crucial details of these initiatives had not been worked out at the time this chapter was written:

1. The formulas for distributing the funds for the public works program, the new revenue sharing program, and the tax credit program will determine whether the programs spend their funds efficiently, targeting them on cities, people, and neighborhoods in distress, or spend inefficiently, spreading the funds out to less distressed areas, too.

2. The initiatives must be meshed with the congressional budgetary process—and be shepherded through Congress. The administration estimates that these programs will increase spending by about $2.4 billion in 1979 and $4.6 billion in 1980 (including revenue losses from tax credits). If all these expenditures went to central cities (which will not occur), they would represent 9 percent and 18 percent increases, respectively, in place-oriented federal spending in those cities. But if passage of the required legislation is delayed, some parts of these increases may not occur until later, if at all. Moreover, the added spending that goes to suburban and nonmetropolitan areas will lessen the impact on central cities.

3. The administration, wisely recognizing the need to convert policy announcements into an ongoing decision-and-action process, created a new interagency coordinating council. The council consists of the assistant secretaries for policy planning (or equivalent officials) in all federal agencies with major urban program responsibilities. The nature and organizational location of its staff had not yet been determined. A crucial clue to the real impact of the new policy will be where the council's staff is placed (it should be attached to the office of the President), the number and caliber of people on it, the resources it has to work with, the strength of its leadership, and how much authority it is given by the White House.

4. The trade-off between continued rapid suburban growth and strengthened demand for housing and commercial facilities within declining cities is politically sensitive. A HUD press release says, "Energy inefficient, resource wasteful sprawl will be reduced." If sprawl is a euphemism for all low-density suburban growth, then perhaps the administration means to brake suburban expansion in order to bolster the revival strategy it now espouses. However, it has included no effective means of accomplishing this in its policies and programs. Without such means, suburban growth will undermine many of the administration's efforts to make older cities economically and socially more vibrant. In fact, failure to deal with this issue will

transform the administration's revival strategy into an adjustment strategy.

5. Also unresolved are the roles that federal, state, and local governments will take in deciding what programs are needed in each community. The administration's "new partnership" rhetoric is empty without a strategy for implementation. There is no simple course; the funding and administrative arrangements already linking these levels of government are a bewildering labyrinth. However, urban policy will probably be most effective in the long run if it leaves the greatest discretion to local officials—but helps them improve their management capabilities.

Conclusion

The national urban policy announced by President Carter in March 1978 has the potential to substantially improve the way governments cope with urban problems. Without any large or elaborate new coordinating institutions, and without reorganizing existing agencies, the functions of federal agencies can be better coordinated, and many gaps in the programs identified and filled. In addition, a policy statement can be the focus of a nationwide dialogue on urban problems, which might lead to a greater consensus on urban goals and on the means to reach them. Such a consensus should modestly improve the effectiveness of the key actors in urban areas. Expecting more than this from a national urban policy is wishful thinking, given the tremendous decentralization of decisionmaking in our pluralistic society.

Appendix

The programs summarized in table 6-2 and the text discussion are listed below.

Place-Oriented Programs for Jobs and Economic Development
   1. Comprehensive Employment and Training Act assistance
   2. Youth employment assistance
   3. Private sector initiative
   4. Work incentive program

5. Urban economic development
6. Local public works grants
7. Small business loans

Place-Oriented Programs for Fiscal Assistance

1. General revenue sharing
2. Countercyclical revenue sharing
3. District of Columbia and Pennsylvania Avenue project

Place-Oriented Programs for Physical Development

1. Housing subsidies (including public housing operating subsidies)
2. Housing for the elderly
3. Rehabilitation loans
4. Mortgage credit insurance support
5. Mortgage purchases by Government National Mortgage Administration
6. Urban development action grants
7. Community development block grants
8. Former categorical HUD programs
9. Urban development research and planning
10. Urban highway support
11. Interstate highway system
12. Construction safety aids
13. Urban mass transportation grants, technical studies, and interstate transfers
14. Airport development assistance
15. Waste water and sewage treatment assistance

Place-Oriented Programs for Social and Health Services

1. Elementary and secondary school assistance
2. Impacted area school assistance
3. Emergency school aid
4. Education for the handicapped
5. Occupational, vocational, and adult education
6. Library resources
7. Social and child welfare grants
8. Services to the disabled, elderly, and others
9. Child development grants

10. Health services and alcohol, drug abuse, and mental health assistance
11. Health resources
12. Community services
13. Domestic volunteers
14. Law Enforcement Assistance Agency grants

Person-Oriented Programs

1. Social security
2. Railroad retirement
3. Federal retirement and disability
4. Supplemental security income
5. Aid to families with dependent children
6. Children's nutrition and school lunches
7. Food stamps
8. Medicare
9. Medicaid
10. Unemployment compensation
11. Crude-oil equalization fund

CHAPTER SEVEN

Farm Commodity Programs

MARTIN E. ABEL

THE FEDERAL GOVERNMENT'S agricultural commodity programs were designed to (a) prevent sharp declines in commodity
prices and farm incomes below minimal levels; (b) assure an adequate supply of food to U.S. consumers and world markets through
grain reserves; (c) expand U.S. agricultural exports; and (d) assure
food supplies to developing countries through food aid.

The budgetary costs of agricultural commodity programs are of
particular interest not only because they may be unpredictable and
unstable, but because they are, at times, quite large. They are large
now. In the 1960s and early 1970s, when low commodity prices and
surplus production capacity in agriculture prevailed, costs were
relatively large. They fell during 1974–76 as a result of worldwide
tight food supplies and high prices. Recent increases in food production have lowered prices significantly and have raised the levels of
price and income support.

The costs of other Department of Agriculture programs—domestic food assistance and those involving research, information, regulation, economic development, and human and natural resources—are
not examined in this chapter. While outlays for domestic food assistance are a large part of the agricultural budget, they are relatively
predictable. Furthermore, these programs are designed to improve
the welfare of various groups in society and their costs, therefore, are
not specific to agriculture. The other programs are not a large part of
the agricultural budget and their outlays, also, are not highly variable.

195

Similarly, the Food for Peace Program (Public Law 480) is not counted here as a commodity program. While this program affects the commodity outlook, its current purpose is foreign aid and its costs should be counted in that portion of the total budget.[1] In the 1950s and 1960s, the Food for Peace Program was used to get rid of surplus agricultural commodities and thus played a significant role in supporting farm prices and incomes. In more recent times, however, partly by policy design and partly because there were no food surpluses, the program has been directed at foreign aid.

Recent Developments

Outlays for agricultural commodity programs during the last ten years and their relation to other expenditures on food and agriculture are shown in table 7-1. The table illustrates the magnitude and variability of commodity program costs as represented by Commodity Credit Corporation (CCC) outlays.[2] The costs of income security programs (mostly domestic food programs) have risen steadily since 1969 and since 1974 have been larger than the cost of commodity programs. All other outlays account for less than a fifth of total outlays by the Department of Agriculture.

Prices and production of agricultural commodities and associated government policies and programs have changed dramatically in recent years. In the 1960s and the first few years of the 1970s, agricultural prices were low, farm incomes were low, and there were large surpluses of many agricultural products. Therefore, government expenditures for containing production and disposing of food surpluses were high. The government guaranteed prices and restricted production of major crops to prevent the accumulation of more surpluses. At the same time, it disposed of existing surpluses through food aid programs for developing countries. Between 1961 and 1973, the annual net budgetary costs of agricultural commodity programs ranged from $1.4 billion to nearly $4.2 billion.

In 1973, the situation changed quickly from one of food surpluses and low prices to one of food scarcity and high prices. Four factors

1. If this assumption does not hold and the Department of Agriculture again uses P.L. 480 as a surplus-disposal mechanism, the future costs of commodity programs would be raised, but the trend in outlays would not be altered.
2. Donated commodities are included under income security programs in table 7-1. Later in the chapter these commodities are included in the costs of commodity programs. Thus the figures are not identical.

Table 7-1. Department of Agriculture Outlays, Fiscal Years 1969–79[a]

Billions of dollars

			Program				
Year	Commodity Credit Corporation[b]	Other commodity support	Income security[c]	International affairs	Natural resources	All other	Total
1969	4.0	0.9	1.3	0.9	0.6	0.2	7.9
1970	3.6	1.0	1.7	1.0	0.5	0.2	8.0
1971	2.8	1.0	2.6	1.0	0.9	0.2	8.5
1972	3.9	1.1	3.3	1.0	0.8	0.3	10.4
1973	3.4	1.1	3.8	0.7	0.6	0.5	10.1
1974	0.8	1.2	4.7	0.7	0.6	0.2	8.2
1975	0.7	1.2	6.9	0.7	1.1	0.3	10.9
1976	1.0	1.2	8.0	0.7	1.1	0.4	12.4
1977	3.8	1.5	8.5	0.9	0.9	0.5	16.1
1978[d]	7.0	1.5	9.2	1.0	1.2	1.1	21.0
1979[d]	4.3	1.5	9.3	1.1	0.9	1.0	18.1

Source: Department of Agriculture, Office of Budget, Planning, and Evaluation.
a. Excluding revolving loan funds.
b. Excludes donated commodities.
c. Includes commodities donated by CCC.
d. Estimates.

accounted for this reversal. One was the entry of the Soviet Union into world grain markets as a relatively large-scale and recurring buyer. The Russians, as a consequence of a change in food policy, began to rely heavily on world markets to meet shortfalls in their food production. Their initial grain purchases from the United States were large and unexpected.

The second factor was the desire of the United States to reduce its grain stocks. It welcomed Soviet purchases. Rebuilding grain stocks to levels that would ensure a modicum of price stability proved difficult, however, and was not accomplished until 1977.

A third and important factor was that the rate of growth of grain production worldwide began to slow down in the 1970s. Yet demand has continued to grow at about the same rate.

Finally, the devaluations of the dollar in 1971 and 1973 led to more agricultural exports and higher domestic prices. While the magnitude of the effect is debated, it is agreed that the effect is significant.[3]

3. For contrasting views on the importance of devaluation see G. Edward Schuh, "The Exchange Rate and U.S. Agriculture," *American Journal of Agricultural Economics*, vol. 56 (February 1974), pp. 1–13, and Paul R. Johnson, Thomas Grennes, and Marie Thursby, "Devaluation, Foreign Trade Controls, and Domestic Wheat Prices," *American Journal of Agricultural Economics*, vol. 59 (November 1977), pp. 619–27.

198   Martin E. Abel

Table 7-2. Agricultural Exports by Commodity Group, 1970, 1975–77[a]
Millions of dollars

Commodity group	1970	1975	1976	1977[b]
Grains and feeds	2,531	11,561	11,920	9,900
Oilseeds and products	1,885	4,753	4,692	6,350
Livestock and products	829	1,666	2,207	2,620
Cotton and linters	328	1,055	919	1,540
Fruits, nuts, and vegetables	632	1,373	1,532	1,690
Tobacco (unmanufactured)	537	897	929	1,040
Other	215	549	560	710
Total	6,957	21,854	22,759	23,850

Source: Department of Agriculture, *1977 Handbook of Agricultural Charts*, Agricultural Handbook 524 (USDA, November 1977).
a. Year measured from October of the previous year to September of year.
b. Preliminary.

The tight food situation in other parts of the world in the past five years has brought great demand for U.S. farm products and a surge in U.S. agricultural exports, as shown in table 7-2. In 1970, total agricultural exports were nearly $7 billion. By 1977, they had risen to nearly $24 billion. The largest increases were in grains and oilseeds (primarily soybeans). These exports rose from $4.4 billion to $16.3 billion between 1970 and 1977.

Two developments which will influence the budgetary cost of farm programs for several years occurred in the United States in 1977. One was the return of grain surpluses. The other was enactment of the Food and Agriculture Act of 1977. This act sets out the basic legislation through 1981 for major agricultural commodities, domestic food programs, and foreign food aid. For the immediate future, these two developments signal an increase in government expenditures on agricultural commodity programs from the low levels of recent years. The longer-term effect depends on whether the current surpluses persist or whether a tight food situation with high and unstable prices returns.

The Food and Agriculture Act of 1977

In the 1950s and early 1960s, commodity policy was structured to support farm incomes through minimum price guarantees. These support prices were set at levels above free market equilibrium prices, and large stocks of commodities were accumulated by the Commodity Credit Corporation, the agency responsible for implementing commodity programs. Attempts were made to keep these stocks at "manageable" levels through export subsidies and food aid to developing countries. However, these measures were not enough to reduce surpluses.

In the 1960s, agricultural policy shifted to a market orientation, with farmers' incomes supported by direct government payments for the major crops. Support prices were at or slightly below world market prices and kept U.S. products competitive in world markets. The support of farm incomes relied increasingly on direct cash payments to make up the difference between market prices and those prices deemed necessary to achieve farm-income goals. Further, when surpluses existed, farmers were required to reduce production by idling land in order to be eligible for the price-support guarantees and the direct-income payments.

The implication of this policy evolution for budgetary costs in a situation of chronic excess production capacity is illustrated in table 7-3. The column labeled "net loss on commodity inventory operations" represents the costs associated with price-support and stock-accumulation programs. These dominated the agricultural commodity program budget until the early 1960s. Thereafter, payments to producers grew very rapidly and began to dominate as direct price-support costs declined. This trend continued up to 1973, after which rising prices and tight supplies drastically reduced government expenditures on both price- and income-support programs.

The Food and Agriculture Act of 1977 continues the policy of supporting farm income through producer payments and keeping support prices (loan rates) at or below world-market price levels. Authority to require producers to idle land in times of excess production in order to be eligible for government support is also provided in the act, as it was in previous legislation.

Both farmer and consumer interests in the Congress strongly supported the Food and Agriculture Act of 1977. Since its passage, farm prices have declined, and they remain low, causing discontent in some farm groups. Congress is now working to modify the act to provide greater income support to producers.

For purposes of this evaluation, it is assumed that the act will continue in its present form through 1981, but if farm prices and incomes remain depressed, changes in the act are likely. Such changes

Table 7-3. Net Cost of Agricultural Commodity Programs, Fiscal Years 1954–76
Millions of dollars

Fiscal year	Net loss on commodity inventory operations	Producer payments[a]	Export payments	Other	Interest and operating expense	Total
1954	546.1	...	...	5.9	114.1	654.3
1955	980.3	...	...	13.8	125.2	1,119.3
1956	1,138.6	...	...	60.3	214.8	1,413.7
1957	1,320.0	...	81.6	77.6	332.8	1,812.0
1958	1,086.3	...	96.0	88.8	376.5	1,647.6
1959	980.0	...	122.4	109.2	198.4	1,410.0
1960	971.2	...	301.9	133.1	478.3	1,884.5
1961	965.0	333.2	288.8	51.7	443.1	2,081.8
1962	1,235.0	868.1	244.2	78.6	373.5	2,799.4
1963	970.1	945.9	178.0	94.0	466.9	2,654.9
1964	1,147.1	1,284.9	212.0	112.9	469.9	3,226.8
1965	871.1	1,608.3	98.7	90.6	560.5	3,048.0
1966	684.6	1,656.5	208.2	105.7	329.9	2,984.9
1967	763.5	2,457.8	167.7	95.9	328.7	3,813.6
1968	710.1	2,033.1	73.5	88.9	292.6	3,198.2
1969	410.7	2,145.6	33.0	155.0	368.9	3,113.2
1970	398.3	2,944.9	100.7	178.4	591.0	4,213.3
1971	316.3	2,909.3	176.1	175.3	481.0	4,058.0
1972	454.2	2,369.2	116.9	188.1	329.0	3,457.4
1973	161.3	3,122.4	349.3	201.3	259.4	4,093.9
1974	71.5	2,351.1	57.0	32.0	247.5	2,759.1
1975	113.9	560.2	3.1	3.4	29.0	709.6
1976	162.3	288.1	0.7	0.4	73.2	524.7

Source: Department of Agriculture, Agricultural Stabilization and Conservation Service, "Commodity Credit Corporation Charts Providing a Graphic Tabular Summary of Financial and Program Data through September 30, 1976" (April 1977; processed). Figures are rounded.
a. Payments through 1974 were based on land diverted from production; 1975 and 1976 payments were principally for losses caused by natural disaster or other conditions beyond the control of the producer.

would probably increase the budgetary costs of the agricultural commodity programs presented later in this chapter.[4]

The 1977 act provides for target prices for grains and cotton at levels yielding a "fair return" to producers. Target prices are to be adjusted to reflect increases in production costs. The legislation also provides for support prices—loan rates—but at lower levels than target prices. The secretary of agriculture can adjust loan rates, within limits, to changing market conditions and can thus keep loan

4. Developments during spring of 1978 suggest that modifications in the act will be made and the programs undoubtedly will cost more.

rates in line with world market prices and U.S. commodities competitive in world markets without subsidizing exports. Producers' payments are calculated on the basis of either the difference between the target price and loan rate or the target price and market price, whichever difference is smaller. The per-unit payment rates are applied to production bases, whose methods of calculation are specified in the 1977 act.

Below we provide a simple example of how the system of loan rates and target prices would have worked for wheat in the 1977–78 crop year (June 1–May 31). The loan rate for wheat was $2.25 per bushel. This was a guaranteed price to wheat producers. If the market price fell below this level, as it did for several months during the first part of the 1977–78 crop year, farmers could obtain a loan on their wheat crop from the Commodity Credit Corporation at the rate of $2.25 per bushel.[5] Then if the market price rose above the loan rate, a farmer could sell his wheat and repay the loan. If prices did not rise above the loan rate, the farmer could forfeit the loan; that is, the CCC would take title to the grain placed under loan.

The target price for wheat in 1977–78 was $2.90 per bushel. Farmers were eligible for full target-price payments in 1977–78, because the market price averaged at or below the loan rate for the relevant portion of the crop year.[6]

A farmer who harvested 500 acres of wheat with an average yield of 30 bushels per acre produced 15,000 bushels. In addition to the guaranteed loan rate of $2.25 per bushel ($33,750),[7] he received a cash payment of $0.65 per bushel ($2.90 minus $2.25), or $9,750. Total gross receipts would have been $43,000.

Actual and projected target prices and loan rates for grains and cotton from 1977 through 1982 are presented in tables 7-4 and 7-5. Target prices and loan rates through the 1978–79 crop year are specified in the Food and Agriculture Act of 1977. The target prices are adjusted upward after 1978–79 at 5 percent a year to reflect increases in production costs. While the secretary of agriculture has the authority to adjust most loan rates, it is assumed that they will be fairly constant between 1978–79 and 1981–82. There is no compelling reason to raise them if average market prices go above them.

5. Storage and interest charges for the first year are deducted from this rate.
6. For wheat it is the first five months.
7. Storage and interest charges are not subtracted.

Table 7-4. Target Prices, Crop Years 1977–78 through 1981–82
Dollars

	Actual		Projected		
Commodity	1977–78	1978–79	1979–80	1980–81	1981–82
Wheat (bushel)	2.90	3.00	3.15	3.31	3.48
Corn (bushel)	2.00	2.10	2.20	2.31	2.43
Sorghum (bushel)	2.28	2.22	2.33	2.45	2.57
Barley (bushel)	2.15	2.26	2.37	2.50	2.62
Rice					
(hundredweight)	8.25	8.45	8.87	9.32	9.78
Cotton (pound)	0.48	0.52	0.55	0.57	0.60

Sources: Food and Agriculture Act of 1977 and various Department of Agriculture regulations.

Table 7-5. Loan Rates, Crop Years 1977–78 through 1981–82
Dollars

	Actual		Projected		
Commodity	1977–78	1978–79	1979–80	1980–81	1981–82
Wheat (bushel)	2.25	2.35	2.35	2.35	2.35
Corn (bushel)	2.00	2.00	2.00	2.00	2.00
Sorghum (bushel)	1.90	1.90	1.90	1.90	1.90
Barley (bushel)	1.63	1.63	1.63	1.63	1.63
Rice					
(hundredweight)	6.19	6.31	6.31	6.31	6.31
Cotton (pound)	0.45	0.44	0.45	0.46	0.47
Sugar (pound)[a]	0.14	0.14	0.14	0.15	0.16
Peanuts (pound)[a]	0.22	0.21	0.21	0.21	0.21
Butter (pound)[a]	1.03	1.08	1.11	1.14	1.17
Cheese (pound)[a]	0.98	1.02	1.05	1.08	1.11
Dry milk (pound)[a]	0.68	0.71	0.73	0.75	0.77

Sources: Food and Agriculture Act of 1977 and various Department of Agriculture regulations.
a. Not subject to target-price payments.

And if market prices remain at the loan rates, loan rates could be adjusted downward (and in the case of cotton, they must be). However, it is assumed for this analysis that world market prices will remain at or above loan rates and that it will not be necessary to lower loan rates to keep the United States competitive in world markets.

Target-price payments—the difference between target prices and loan rates—are projected to rise over time because target prices must reflect increases in production costs. These are shown in table 7-6.

Table 7-6. Maximum Target Price Payments, Crop Years 1977–78 through 1981–82
Dollars

Commodity	Actual		Projected		
	1977–78	1978–79	1979–80	1980–81	1981–82
Wheat (bushel)	0.65	0.65	0.80	0.96	1.13
Corn (bushel)	...	0.10	0.20	0.31	0.43
Sorghum (bushel)	0.38	0.32	0.43	0.55	0.67
Barley (bushel)	0.52	0.63	0.74	0.87	0.99
Rice (hundredweight)	2.06	2.14	2.56	3.01	3.47
Cotton (pound)	0.03	0.08	0.10	0.11	0.13

Sources: Food and Agriculture Act of 1977 and various Department of Agriculture regulations.

The projected increases in payment rates between 1978–79 and 1981–82 are substantial for some commodities; for example, 74 percent for wheat, 62 percent for rice, 330 percent for corn, and 110 percent for sorghum.

The implications of the policy approach to farm prices and incomes embodied in the 1977 act are twofold. If production outpaces demand and market prices remain at about loan rates, direct payments to producers and the budgetary costs of commodity programs will increase substantially. If, on the other hand, demand grows faster than supply, market prices will be above the loan rates, budgetary costs of commodity programs will be smaller, but agricultural and food prices will be higher. Market prices at or above target prices would result in no direct payments to producers but sharply higher food prices.

The trade-off inherent in the 1977 act is between growing budgetary costs for commodity programs and stable food prices on the one hand, and low budgetary costs and rising food prices on the other. This dilemma is discussed in detail later. Suffice it to say now, it is an important consideration for the total U.S. budget. Rising food prices mean rising inflation rates, which increase the total budget, since a large part of it is directly or indirectly indexed to the overall price level. But higher inflation rates also increase tax revenues. It is not obvious, therefore, what effect a reduction in the budget for agricultural commodity programs would have on the total budget.[8]

8. The impact of inflation on the budget is discussed in Edward M. Gramlich, "The Economic and Budgetary Effects of Indexing the Tax System," in Henry J. Aaron, ed., *Inflation and the Income Tax* (Brookings Institution, 1976), pp. 271–90.

Some agricultural commodities whose prices are supported—dairy products, soybeans, sugar, and peanuts—are not subject to target-price payments. Support prices for these commodities are likely to rise as production costs increase, and the program costs of these commodities are also examined in this chapter.

The 1977 act also provides authority to establish a long-term grain reserve to ensure supplies of grain and to stabilize prices in times of short crops at home or abroad. This reserve is to be held by farmers, who would be paid for storing the grain. The secretary of agriculture has announced reserve targets of 300 million bushels of wheat and 17–19 million metric tons of feed grains. Farmers who place grain in the reserve cannot sell it without penalties until the price of wheat reaches 140 percent of the loan rate, or $3.15 a bushel, and the price of corn reaches 125 percent of the loan rate, or $2.50 a bushel. The penalties for selling grain before market prices reach these levels are rather stiff. A farmer would have to pay the Commodity Credit Corporation the storage payments received plus the difference between the release price and the price at which he sold his grain.

The long-term grain reserve is an integral part of the budget of commodity programs. There will be outlays in the form of loans to farmers on the grain that goes into the reserve. There will also be ongoing costs in the form of payments to farmers for storing the grain. (For example, storage costs are estimated to be $278 million in fiscal year 1979.) When the grain is sold and the loans are repaid to the Commodity Credit Corporation, there will be net income from long-term grain reserves.[9]

Commodity Prices

The costs of commodity programs depend both on production restraint through the use of set-aside programs and on commodity prices. Prices are a function of world demand and supply; both overall trends and fluctuations about the trends are caused principally by weather and its effect on crop production.

The experience with widely fluctuating commodity prices in the 1970s is instructive. Table 7-7 shows what happened to wheat, corn,

9. The regular loans operate the same way, but they are for a much shorter duration.

Table 7-7. Average Annual Price Received by Farmers for Wheat, Corn, and Soybeans, Crop Years 1960–77

Dollars per bushel

Year	Wheat	Corn	Soybeans
1960	1.74	1.00	2.13
1961	1.83	1.10	2.28
1962	2.04	1.12	2.34
1963	1.85	1.11	2.51
1964	1.37	1.17	2.62
1965	1.35	1.16	2.54
1966	1.63	1.24	2.75
1967	1.39	1.03	2.49
1968	1.24	1.08	2.43
1969	1.25	1.16	2.35
1970	1.33	1.33	2.85
1971	1.34	1.08	3.03
1972	1.76	1.57'	4.37
1973	3.95	2.55	5.68
1974	4.09	3.03	6.64
1975	3.56	2.54	4.92
1976	2.73	2.15	6.81
1977	2.30[a]	2.05[b]	5.50[c]

Sources: Department of Agriculture, *Agricultural Statistics 1977* (GPO, 1978), and *Agricultural Supply and Demand Estimates* (USDA, January 26, 1978).
a. Midpoint of a range of $2.25–$2.35.
b. Midpoint of a range of $2.00–$2.10.
c. Midpoint of a range of $5.25–$5.75.

and soybean prices. The average annual farm price of soybeans went from $3.03 a bushel in the 1971 crop year to $6.81 a bushel in 1976, an increase of nearly 125 percent. Between 1971 and 1974, the prices of wheat and corn increased 200 percent and 180 percent, respectively, and then fell sharply during the three subsequent years. These wild price fluctuations resulted from a combination of adverse weather conditions and changes in the import policies of the Soviet Union and Eastern Europe designed to meet their shortfalls in grain production through imports.

There is no reason to assume that weather fluctuations in the future will not influence agricultural commodity prices. However, several factors will be at work to dampen its effects. U.S. grain reserves have been rebuilt: wheat and feed-grain stocks at the end of the 1977–78 crop year are estimated to be about 75 million metric tons. In 1971–72, just before the tight food situation of the 1970s, U.S. grain stocks were 72 million metric tons, and in 1974–75, the year of lowest carryover levels, U.S. stocks equaled 27.1 million metric tons. Further, there is every indication that stocks will be managed in ways that contribute to stabilizing prices. For one, the United States is working to establish a long-term grain reserve to be used to stabilize wide price swings. Second, an international system of grain reserves is now being discussed. Even with larger reserves, there is the possibility of substantial price swings, though probably not as dramatic as those of the 1970s.

Potential price swings are all-important in estimating the future cost of commodity programs. If market prices are close to loan rates, budget expenditures will be at their maximum, since per-unit target-price payments will be at their maximum. If, however, market prices are at or above target-price levels, target-price payments to producers will be zero and the cost of commodity programs will be at minimal levels. Since the actual situation may be any place in between, both extremes are examined in this chapter.

Commodity Supplies

Low supplies and high prices of the world's food sharply reduced the cost of commodity programs from 1972 to 1976. Stocks of grains and other commodities were reduced, and government expenditures to support farm prices and incomes were at minimal levels.

In 1976 world weather and crop-growing conditions improved markedly, resulting in record grain production and large increases in reserves. Production conditions in 1977, while not as good as the previous year, were good enough to lead to further accumulation of grain stocks in the United States. Carry-over stocks of wheat rose from 665 million bushels in the 1975–76 crop year to an estimated 1,210 million bushels at the end of the 1977–78 crop year. Similarly, stocks of feed grains went from 17.2 million metric tons to an estimated 42.4 million metric tons during the same period (table 7-8). These developments for grains, and a few other commodities as well, resulted in sharply lower prices (table 7-7) and, as farmers made greater use of the price-support and income-support programs, rising commodity program costs. From $3.8 billion in 1977 they have risen to an estimated $7.3 billion in 1978 (see table 7-9).

There are several components in the high program costs. First, the Commodity Credit Corporation pays farmers target-price payments

Table 7-8. Carry-over Stocks of Grain, Crop Years 1975–76, 1976–77, and 1977–78
Millions

Commodity	1975–76	1976–77	1977–78
Wheat (bushels)	665	1,112	1,210
Feed grains (metric tons)	17.2	29.9	42.4

Source: Department of Agriculture, *Agricultural Supply and Demand Estimates* (USDA, January 26, 1978).

for wheat, sorghum, barley, rice, and cotton. Second, as more farmers use the price-support programs, greater quantities of commodities are placed under commodity credit loans, representing a net outlay. In subsequent years, if farmers redeem the loans, current program costs will be reduced by the amount of loan repayments. If farmers do not repay the loans, the Commodity Credit Corporation will take title to the commodities and pay for their storage until they are sold. Third, the cost of commodity programs includes disaster payments. These payments are made to producers when natural disasters adversely affect crop production. They are high in 1978 because of heavy crop losses during the 1977–78 crop year.

Finally, in times of low prices and large stocks, efforts are made to expand exports, and one mechanism is the Commodity Credit Corporation's short-term (up to three years) credit on exports. The program is expanding rapidly in 1978. As with loans, export credits appear as expenditures in the year they are granted and income in the year they are repaid.

Future Costs of Commodity Programs[10]

Several factors are working to reduce 1979 commodity program costs. A set-aside program for wheat requires producers to idle an area equal to 20 percent of that planted for harvest in order to be eligible for support prices, target prices, and disaster payments. The program is designed to reduce carry-over stocks at the end of the 1978–79 crop year by about 200 million bushels. Stock reduction will reduce wheat under loan, and loan repayments will be reflected as income in the year they are made. Lower wheat production will also mean that target-price payments will be made on a smaller

10. These calculations do not include the effects of the programs announced in March 1978 that will further reduce production of feed grains, wheat, and cotton.

Table 7-9. Commodity Program Costs, Fiscal Years 1977–79 and 1982
Millions of dollars

					1982[b]	
Commodity	1977	1978[a]	1979[a]	1979[b]	Maximum	Minimum
Wheat	1,899	1,922	486	900	2,300	300
Feed grains	659	2,033	1,572	1,550	2,000	300
Rice	145	−45	50	100	300	50
Cotton (upland)	104	476	455	450	800	100
Soybeans	5	412	209	300	300	10
Dairy products	469	746	495	800	850	200
Other	268	515	188	200	300	190
Export credit, storage, and interest	271	1,272	860	1,000	1,900	350
Total	3,820	7,333	4,315	5,300	8,750	1,500

Source: Department of Agriculture, "1979 Budget Summary" (USDA, n.d.; processed). This source is used for actual 1977 and estimated 1978 and 1979 program costs because of the commodity detail provided. These numbers differ slightly from those in *The Budget of the United States Government, Fiscal Year 1979*, pp. 131 and 312–13, which does not contain the desired budget detail by commodity and by relevant function.
a. Department of Agriculture estimates.
b. Author's estimates.

amount of wheat. Furthermore, the market price is likely to average above the loan rate, lowering the target-price payment per bushel to less than the maximum allowable.

A set-aside program has also been announced for feed grains (10 percent idle acreage) and will probably end accumulation of feed-grain stocks. As with wheat, net loans will probably be lower in 1979 than in 1978. However, though target-price payments on corn are not being made in fiscal year 1978 on the 1977 crop, they will be made in fiscal year 1979 on the 1978 crop (see tables 7-4 and 7-5).

Cotton is not subject to production restraints in crop year 1978, but target-price payments will be required in fiscal year 1979.

Other factors will offset some of the reduction described above. Expenditures for other commodities will probably rise as price-support levels increase, production is not restrained, and market prices show little sign of increasing. The costs of export credits, storage, and interest will probably also rise as the Commodity Credit Corporation assumes ownership of larger amounts of commodities and as aggressive export efforts continue.

Two estimates are presented in table 7-9 for the cost of commodity programs in 1979. Both are well below the 1978 estimate, but the author's estimates are significantly higher than the official estimates for wheat, soybeans, dairy products, and export credit, storage, and interest. While the official calculations have not been published, some differences between the two sets of assumptions can be inferred and deserve explanation.

In the case of wheat, the author assumes that market prices will average near loan-rate levels while government analysts appear to assume significantly higher market prices. Assumptions of production levels are about the same.

Another large soybean crop is expected in crop year 1978, based on the January 1978 survey of farmers' production intentions. Commodity Credit Corporation loans are expected to increase in 1977–78 and are reflected in the large jump in expenditures in 1978. Stocks should also increase, unless there is a large decline in oilseed production in the rest of the world, and would lead to further increases in stocks and soybeans under loan.

This writer expects dairy production to continue to be in surplus, stocks to increase, and prices to remain at support levels, continuing the trend since late 1976. The sharp decline in dairy costs indicated by the official estimates implies a reduction in surpluses.

The costs of export credit, storage, and interest are expected to decline in both estimations, but the official prediction is for a sharper decline. Three factors lead the author to a higher estimate of this category of costs. First, large supplies of commodities and strong interest in agricultural export growth will expand the use of export credits. The recent increase in export credit sales to Poland and a number of other countries supports this view.

Second, the Department of Agriculture is determined to reach the desired levels of grain reserves in the 1978 fiscal year. To make participation more attractive, the department raised the storage payment from 20 cents to 25 cents per bushel per year. The rate can be raised further to attract participation. Higher storage payments, together with other possible costs, such as subsidized interest rates, will probably increase storage costs and interest costs above the official estimates for 1979.

Third, as the regular loans on commodities mature, many farmers will not take grain out of loan. The Commodity Credit Corporation will assume ownership of these commodities and will then pay for their storage, thereby increasing storage costs.

The cost of commodity programs in 1982, the last year covered by the Food and Agriculture Act of 1977, cannot be predicted with any degree of precision. Uncertainty about future crop production in the United States and elsewhere in the world makes it impossible to estimate these costs. There are, however, limits within which costs might fall. (See table 7-9.) At one extreme, assuming a period of favorable weather in the United States and elsewhere, supplies large enough to keep market prices at loan levels, and set-aside programs to prevent unwanted increases in stocks, costs would be at their maximum. Commodity programs could then cost nearly $8.8 billion. The main reason for the rise would be the increases in target-price payments and price-support payments, as shown in tables 7-4 and 7-5.

The other extreme assumes poor weather and low crop production. If food and fiber supply-demand balance tightens progressively until 1982 and if market prices are at or above target prices (or above loan levels for those commodities for which target prices are not applicable), costs will be low. This is possible even with a long-term grain reserve program to dampen price fluctuations. Under this program, farmers are required to hold reserves until the price of wheat rises to 140 percent of the loan rate ($3.15 per bushel), the price of corn rises to 125 percent of the loan rate ($2.50 per bushel), and similar prices prevail for other feed grains, before they can sell grain from the reserve without penalty. Projected target prices in 1982 for wheat and corn are $3.47 and $2.43 per bushel, respectively (see table 7-4). Thus, release prices are close to projected target price levels, and if the world grain supply tightens enough for the United States to use the reserve, target-price payments on grains will be negligible.

Poor weather and low production would probably affect the prices and commodity program costs of other commodities the same way it affects grains. Under these assumptions, commodity program costs in 1982 are estimated at $1.5 billion (see table 7-9).

Thus, even with efforts to stabilize commodity prices (such as a U.S. long-term grain reserve and an international agreement on wheat that requires other countries to hold stocks), the cost of commodity programs could vary by as much as $7.3 billion by 1982. Most of this variation would be caused by weather-related events, which cannot be controlled.

Food Prices and Inflation

Apparent in the Food and Agriculture Act of 1977 is an inverse relation between the federal budgetary cost of commodity programs and agricultural and food prices. If events and the operation of commodity programs lead to large production, low prices, and relatively large stocks, the cost of the programs will be high. If, on the other hand, small production, high prices, and low stocks prevail, costs will be low.

The alternative levels of budgetary costs projected for 1982 have important implications for food prices and for the general price level. High expenditures on commodity programs lead to stable commodity prices, which do not contribute to inflation. On the other hand, low expenditures on commodity programs can be achieved only with high agricultural prices, which contribute to inflation. Just as there is an inverse relation between commodity program costs and agricultural prices, there is an inverse relation between program costs and inflation. In addition, since a significant part of the federal budget is directly or indirectly linked to changes in the cost of living, reduction in the agricultural commodity budget could result in even larger increases in other components of the federal budget.[11]

To see how much is at stake, the effect on the consumer price index of the difference in agricultural prices assumed under the two 1982 commodity program budget alternatives is calculated. Under the minimum budget, with prices of grains at target-price levels, the price of wheat would be 54 percent above the loan rate and feed grains 27 percent above the loan rate. Prices for livestock and dairy products would adjust to the higher grain prices, rising to about 25 percent above what they would be with grain prices at the support level (maximum budget). The forces that raised grain prices presumably also raised oilseed prices, especially soybean prices, by about 25 percent. Prices of other agricultural products are assumed to have remained at the levels projected for 1982 (table 7-6).

These changes in grain, livestock, and oilseed prices translate into an increase in the consumer price index of 1.75 percentage points.[12]

11. As noted by Gramlich, "The Economic and Budgetary Effects of Indexing the Tax System," higher inflation rates would also increase tax revenues.

12. This calculation is based on the relation between farm and retail food prices, as discussed in Council on Wage and Price Stability, *The Responsiveness of Wholesale and Retail Food Prices to Changes in the Costs of Food Production and Distribution, Staff Report* (Executive Office of the President, November 1976).

For example, if the rate of increase in consumer prices is 6 percent in 1982 under the assumption of low prices (maximum budget), the inflation rate would be 7.75 percent under the assumption of high prices (minimum budget).

Of course, these calculations deal with extremes in costs for commodity programs and prices of agricultural commodities. Neither extreme is outside the realm of possibility. However, the most likely outcome would probably be somewhere between the two.

Summary

The costs of agricultural commodity programs are once again rising, after being relatively low for about five years. The return of surplus agricultural capacity and relatively low prices plus the price-support and income-support provisions of the Food and Agriculture Act of 1977 will raise the budgetary cost of commodity programs in 1978 to $7.3 billion. As grain and cotton production are controlled, costs will drop. Projections for 1979 are $5.3 billion (author's) and $4.3 billion (Department of Agriculture).

The long-term budget outlook is more uncertain. Much depends on commodity prices, which are a function of set-aside programs, grain reserves, and weather. The impact of weather on crop production is beyond anyone's control. However, national (and possibly international) grain reserves, if properly managed, could cushion the impact of bad weather and moderate the year-to-year swings in commodity prices, farm incomes, and budget costs. Even with the cushion, the range of budget costs can be extreme. For 1982, costs are estimated between $1.5 billion and $8.8 billion, a difference of over $7 billion.

Under the Food and Agriculture Act of 1977, budget expenditures on commodity programs and commodity prices are inversely related; they decline as commodity prices rise. (Set-aside programs, which reduce production, also reduce program costs.) Rising commodity prices are directly related to inflation—a rise that reduces budget costs from their maximum to minimum levels would add nearly 2 percent to the inflation rate during the year in which price rise occurs.

CHAPTER EIGHT

Defense Spending

HERSCHEL KANTER *and* OTHERS

THE 1979 defense budget and its five-year projection forecast a continuation of the growth in defense spending begun in the Ford administration, though at a slower pace. President Carter has proposed a budget of $126 billion in total obligational authority, an increase in real terms of 1.8 percent, or $2.3 billion, over 1978 levels. For fiscal years 1980 to 1983, a 2.7 percent annual increase is projected.[1]

The 1979 budget is $8.4 billion lower than the amount projected by President Ford. This reduction was achieved by canceling some major development and acquisition programs and by slowing down others. These decisions have given rise to concern in the Congress about the budget's adequacy, measured against the extent of the

John C. Baker, Robert P. Berman, and Heidi M. Pasichow contributed to this chapter.

1. The defense budget excludes military assistance and foreign military sales for the first time. Prior-year figures in the budget and the secretary of defense's annual report reflect these changes. Figures in this chapter are consistent with that presentation.

The budget is presented to Congress in two forms, budget authority and outlays. Budget authority is the legal limit on a federal agency to obligate the Treasury to pay for equipment, services, and personnel. Outlays are the actual payments from the Treasury and can occur many years after the year for which Congress gives budget authority. Total obligational authority (TOA), or the total cost of the fiscal year program, is used in presenting the defense budget. It differs from budget authority only in financing adjustments, such as stockpile sales and recisions and, in the past, in the military assistance program. Proposed budget authority for 1979 is $125.6 billion. Because the executive branch and congressional committees also use TOA in reviewing the defense budget and individual programs, this chapter uses TOA figures.

Soviet military buildup over the last ten years. This concern, together with the normal political interest in particular defense spending projects, makes uncertain the congressional response to the administration's proposals.

To look beyond 1979, the administration's projected defense programs for the fiscal years 1980–83, if carried through, would cost in excess of $20 billion more than the total defense budget forecast for the same years. The uncertainty is compounded by the fact that the Department of Defense, in effect, operates on two budgetary tracks: annual budget estimates for the defense program as a whole, and individual spending programs, the sum of which exceeds budget estimates by a wide margin. Either the projected programs will have to be cut or future defense budgets will grow much more than 2.7 percent a year.

This budgetary dilemma could have important implications for the nation's defense strategy. These are considered in more detail in the next chapter. This chapter examines the major modernization programs in the five-year defense plan, as well as recent and projected changes in force levels, and the implications of both for future defense budgets. It also discusses some of the more general policies that influence the cost of carrying out the modernization programs and operating the forces.

Trends and Projections

The proposed budget continues the upward trend in real spending that began in 1976 with increases in TOA. Total obligational authority will grow in 1979 dollars from $111.7 billion in 1975 to $126 billion in 1979, a 12.8 percent increase in four years, or 3.1 percent a year (table 8-1). The baseline TOA, which is arrived at by subtracting retired pay and the incremental cost of the Vietnam War from the total defense budget, will rise from $102.9 billion in 1975 to $115.8 billion in 1979, an increase of 12.5 percent, or 3 percent a year.

Outlays, which lag behind TOA, reached a low point of $107 billion in 1976. If the Congress approves the proposed TOA, then outlays, according to the administration, will be $115.2 billion in 1979, or 3.1 percent above 1978. However, in the last few years estimates of outlays for many federal agencies have been high by signifi-

Table 8-1. The Defense Budget, Selected Fiscal Years, 1964–83

Billions of 1979 dollars[a]

Category	1964	1968	1975	1976	1977	1978	1979	1983
Total obligational authority	127.8	161.3	111.7	116.6	122.6	123.7	126.0	140.3
Baseline[b]	124.5	117.1	102.9	107.6	113.1	113.9	115.8	128.8
Retired pay	3.3	5.0	8.4	8.9	9.5	9.8	10.2	11.5
Vietnam War	...	39.2	0.3	...	...	...	...	...
Outlays	125.9	164.5	110.5	107.0	108.8	111.7	115.2	129.6
Baseline[b]	122.6	119.1	101.2	98.1	99.3	101.9	105.1	118.2
Retired pay	3.3	5.0	8.4	8.9	9.4	9.8	10.1	11.4
Vietnam War	...	40.4	0.9	...	...	...	...	...
Addenda								
Outlays as a percent of federal budget	41.8	43.3	26.1	24.1	23.8	22.8	23.0	n.a.
Outlays as a percent of gross national product	8.0	9.3	5.8	5.4	5.2	5.2	5.1	n.a.

Sources: Office of the Assistant Secretary of Defense (Comptroller) computer printouts (January 27, 1978; processed), and Department of Defense, "Department of Defense Annual Report, Fiscal Year 1979" (February 2, 1978; processed), pp. 12, 14; Office of the Assistant Secretary of Defense (Comptroller), "National Defense Budget Estimates for FY 1979" (1978; processed), p. 16. Figures are rounded.

n.a. Not available.

a. The Defense Department used special price indexes for each appropriation category to convert amounts into constant dollars. These indexes have increased more since 1964 than the standard indexes used to measure inflation: the consumer price index, the wholesale price index, and the gross national product deflator.

b. Defense program costs without the costs of the Vietnam War and retired pay. This measure is more useful for period-to-period comparisons.

cant amounts, and this will doubtless hold for defense estimates for 1978 and 1979 presented in the 1979 budget. The Congressional Budget Office estimates defense outlays in 1979 dollars at $109.4 billion for 1978 and $113.4 billion for 1979—$2.3 billion and $1.8 billion lower, respectively, than the Defense Department figure shown in table 8-1.

In any case, the administration expects 1979 defense outlays to rise as a proportion of the federal budget, to 23 percent from the estimated 22.8 percent in 1978. But they are well below the 1964 level of 41.8 percent—before the Vietnam War—and the 43.3 percent level in 1968, at the height of the war. Another measure of the burden of defense is its share of gross national product. That figure was 8 percent in 1964, 9.3 percent in 1968, and has dropped steadily since then to its 1979 level of 5.1 percent. Indeed, one must go back before the Korean War to find a lower figure.

Congressional Review

Over the past eight years, Congress has reduced the President's defense budgets by an average of 5 percent a year. This year there are several considerations that may instead move Congress to vote a defense budget above the President's request: (1) its having been led to believe by administration statements that higher defense spending is needed than that proposed in the budget; (2) its own perception—and the public's—that Soviet forces have been steadily and substantially upgraded; (3) growing pressure to preserve or restore defense programs important to their states and districts; and (4) its tendency to focus on immediate outlays and to pay less attention to the long-range budget implications.

During 1977, administration officials stated both publicly and for background that a 1979 budget of around $130 billion—3 percent over President Carter's 1978 amended budget—would be necessary to support an adequate defense posture. These statements followed a pledge to NATO to increase U.S. real defense spending 3 percent a year over a five-year period. In August, President Carter reaffirmed his commitment to the 3 percent real increase in a formal decision memorandum, a decision later made known to the press by a White House official, and thus also introduced into the public debate. When presenting the 1979 budget, Secretary of Defense Harold Brown said that the 3 percent increase applied to outlays, not to total obligational authority, but outlays will grow at this rate simply from the balances left in procurement programs from the past.

Concern about the Soviet threat rests particularly on the buildup of its ground and air forces in Europe, its naval forces overall, and its strategic arm. For some congressmen, the emphasis in the 1979 budget on strengthening the NATO central front appears to be at the expense of the naval and strategic balance, and they can be expected to question reductions in the latter programs and to try to return to the earlier, more costly proposals for strategic missiles and shipbuilding.

Controversy over the regional impact of defense procurement decisions is not new, nor is congressional interest in specific military spending programs. But there is much less public support now for reductions in defense spending than there was several years ago. Many congressmen and senators who were concerned, a few years ago, about holding down the defense budget are now more concerned about supporting programs that will give employment and income to their constituents.

Finally, the large, costly development and procurement programs typically do not require large outlays in the current fiscal year. The budget resolution enables the Congress to assess the two components of the deficit: current year outlays and receipts. Most congressional proposals for additional defense programs call for deceptively small increases in 1979 outlays. For example, the nuclear-powered aircraft carrier requires large budget authority but small first-year outlays. Full-scale development of the M-X missile carries a small price tag for both budget authority and outlays in 1979. Being concerned about the impact of defense outlays on the deficit, Congress can compromise by making relatively small increases in 1979 outlays—and thus in the 1979 deficit—but large increases in budget authority and future outlays.

Opposing these forces toward larger defense spending, the congressional budget process has built-in restraints. The first of these restraints is the deficit. The defense budget, since it represents 23 percent of the federal budget, is an important determinant of that deficit. Second, the detailed review by the Armed Services and Appropriations Committees that follows the setting of the defense target in the budget resolution usually produces more than enough reductions to offset proposed increases. Thus, the size of the 1979 defense budget is still unknown. Final figures may well disappoint both those who feel that spending is too low to meet the Soviet threat and those who feel that spending is growing too fast and that domestic programs or a balanced budget should have higher priority.

Two Five-Year Projections

The administration has explained and defended the 1979 defense budget with two sets of figures. First, the budget projects total defense spending for 1980–83. Second, the Defense Department presented to the Congress and to the public detailed projections for the same period. The latter imply much higher spending than the former.

Secretary Brown said in his prepared testimony for the Armed Services and Appropriations Committees:

The long-range projections for defense contain a real increase in TOA of about 2.7 percent a year. . . . The body of my annual report explains in detail the defense policies and programs adopted by the Carter administration. In this summary and opening statement, I will focus on the main reasons for the proposed *modest increases* in real terms in the FY 1979 defense budget and long-range projections.[2]

2. Department of Defense, "Department of Defense Annual Report, Fiscal Year 1979" (February 2, 1978; processed), p. 1. Emphasis added.

Table 8-2. Comparison of Annual Dollar Authorizations and Other Defense Programs, Fiscal Years 1979 and 1980

Amounts are total obligational authority in billions of current dollars

			1979–80 increase	
Category	1979	1980	Amount	Percent
Annual dollar authorizations	35.4	43.7	8.3	23.4
Procurement	22.9	29.5	6.6	28.8
Research and development	12.5	14.2	1.7	13.6
Other defense programs[a]	80.4	82.3[b]	1.9	2.4
Total[c]	115.8	126.0	10.2	8.8

Source: *The Budget of the United States Government, Fiscal Year 1979;* Department of Defense, "The FY 1979 Department of Defense Program for Research, Development, and Acquisition" (February 1, 1978; processed), pp. A-2 and A-8.

a. Includes military construction. Although military construction is authorized annually, it was decided that the Department of Defense need not submit a 1980 request.

b. Derived by subtracting annual dollar authorizations from administration projection of total.

c. Excluding retired pay.

However, the "detail" in the secretary's annual report—which is supplemented by other administration statements to the Congress—shows more than "modest increases." How much more than 2.7 percent can only be estimated, because the detail does not cover the whole defense budget. But because the administration is required to submit dollar authorizations for the year following the budget, 1980 figures are available for the cost of all research and development and about two-thirds of procured items, and for the number of military and civil service employees, as well. Subtracting the $43.7 billion 1980 authorization request for dollar items only (procurement and research and development) would leave $82.3 billion, or only a 2.4 percent increase for all other categories (table 8-2). This is about 3 percent below the rate of inflation forecast for defense purchases. Of course, there is no plan to reduce the remainder of the budget in real terms: military pay can be expected to at least keep pace with inflation, and the Defense Department proposes a small increase in military manpower.

Estimates for the remainder of the budget in 1980 are high by $4.7 billion. For 1980–83, the Defense Department plans will cost about $24 billion more than the President's budget projection (table 8-3). But this is a conservative estimate because it does not include the expected increase in the cost of major weapon systems already in the program. This increase has been about 3–5 percent annually, exclusive of unanticipated inflation and of changes in quantities procured.

Table 8-3. Defense Costs by Appropriation Contrasted to 1979 Budget Projections of
Total Defense Costs, Fiscal Years 1979–83

Total obligational authority in billions of dollars

Category	1979	1980	1981	1982	1983	Total
Appropriation estimates[a]	115.8	130.7	142.1	153.7	165.6	707.9
Military personnel	28.7	30.6	32.4	34.2	35.9	161.8
Operation and maintenance	38.1	41.1	44.4	48.0	51.8	223.4
Total procurement	32.0	39.5	43.6	47.4	51.4	213.9
Research and development	12.5	14.2	16.0	18.0	20.0	80.7
Military construction	2.7	3.2	3.5	3.8	4.1	17.3
Family housing	1.6	1.8	1.9	2.0	2.1	9.4
Other	0.2	0.3	0.3	0.3	0.3	1.4
1979 budget projections	115.8	126.0	136.4	147.3	158.4	683.9
Discrepancy	0.0	4.7	5.7	6.4	7.2	24.0

Source: *The Budget of the United States Government, Fiscal Year 1979;* 1979 and total 1980–83 appropriations from "Department of Defense Annual Report, Fiscal Year 1979," pp. 370, C-5. Other figures are authors' estimates (see note a). Total and administration projections are shown exclusive of retired pay.

a. Military personnel estimates for 1980–83 assume the number will remain constant; appropriate Department of Defense price index was applied. Operations and maintenance estimates for 1980–83 assume a 2 percent annual growth rate in real terms; appropriate Department of Defense index was applied. Procurement estimates for 1980 used proposed authorizations; 1981–83 used 1979 budget projection for shipbuilding appropriation and authors' estimates for other categories. Research and development estimates for 1980 from proposed authorization; 1981–83 are authors' estimates. All other categories are authors' estimates for 1980–83.

It is not surprising that such a difference exists, since the detailed policies and programs for 1980–83 are based on an internal Defense Department document, the "Five Year Defense Program" (FYDP), about which Secretary Brown had this to say:

The FYDP detail upon which we depend for mission displays is *significantly different* from the top line projections contained in President Carter's FY 1979 budget; the differences will be resolved each year during the programming and budget processes as the various programs compete for funds. The uncertainty about how we will make future choices among competing claims . . . requires us to plan each of such programs at a level whose sum exceeds what we plan as the total defense program.[3]

Thus the modernization programs presented in the remainder of this chapter for ships, aircraft, missiles, tanks, and so forth represent "competing claims . . . whose sum exceeds what we [the administration] plan as the total defense program." For reasons discussed at the end of the chapter, it is these programs that can be expected to bear the brunt of the $24 billion reduction over the years 1980–83.

3. Covering letter, February 23, 1978, "FY 1979 Department of Defense Budget: Display by Mission Category" (January 23, 1978; processed). Emphasis added.

The Defense Budget by Mission

In this section, the budget is examined according to the four major defense missions: strategic, general purpose, auxiliary missions, and support. As shown in table 8-4, the major increase in spending from 1977 is for general purpose forces—21.5 percent over the two-year period, or 7.5 percent in real terms. This increase is a result of U.S. NATO commitments (1) to modernize ground combat forces and land-based tactical air forces and (2) to increase the operational capability of these and the naval forces assigned to Europe. This increased spending is accompanied by reductions in funds for strategic forces and naval modernization.

Strategic Forces

Costs of strategic forces are expected to be about $11.6 billion, which means a drop in real spending of 11.2 percent. These figures

Table 8-4. The Defense Budget by Mission, Fiscal Years 1977 and 1979

Amounts are total obligational authority in billions of current dollars

Mission[a]	1977	1979	1977–79 change Amount	Percent	Percent real[b]
Strategic forces	**11.5**	**11.6**	**0.1**	**0.9**	**−11.2**
General purpose forces	**47.4**	**57.6**	**10.2**	**21.5**	**7.5**
Ground combat	17.3	21.9	4.6	26.6	12.0
Land-based tactical air	10.3	13.7	3.4	33.0	17.2
Naval (including air)	17.8	19.8	2.0	11.2	−1.6
Mobility	2.0	2.2	0.2	10.0	−2.7
Auxiliary missions	**13.0**	**15.0**	**2.0**	**15.4**	**2.1**
Communications and intelligence	7.7	8.8	1.1	14.3	1.2
Research and development	5.3	6.2	0.9	17.0	3.5
Support	**28.2**	**31.5**	**3.3**	**11.7**	**−1.2**
Logistics	10.6	12.1	1.5	14.2	1.1
Personnel support	14.9	16.3	1.4	9.4	−3.2
Administration	2.7	3.1	0.4	14.8	1.6
Total[c]	**100.1**	**115.6**	**15.5**	**15.5**	**2.2**

Source: Department of Defense, "FY 1979 Department of Defense Budget Display by Mission Category" (January 23, 1978; processed), pp. 13–15. Figures are rounded.

a. The major differences between display by mission and by program (as normally presented by the Department of Defense) is (1) some research and development is allocated to missions and is not confined to a single program; and (2) all reserves are allocated to missions and are not grouped in a single program.

b. Calculated using the Department of Defense price index for the average of all TOA, excluding retired pay. This index is predicted to rise by 13 percent from fiscal 1977 to 1979.

c. Excludes retired pay.

Table 8-5. Costs for Major Weapon Systems, Fiscal Years 1978–83 and to Completion
Total obligational authority in millions of current dollars

Weapon system	1978	1979	1980	1981	1982	1983	1979–83	1984 to completion
Land-based missile forces								
Improved Minuteman	104	93	85	85	30	0	293	0
M-X ICBM[a]	135	158	520	1,100	1,600	2,450	5,828	20,000
Sea-based missile forces								
Trident submarine	1,930	1,657	1,310	1,365	2,720	1,450	8,502	13,000[b]
Trident I missile	1,505	1,130	1,020	865	825	805	4,645	2,000[b]
Trident II missile[a]	5	16	205	550	800	1,150	2,721	13,500
Sea-launched cruise missile[a]	210	152	195	415	535	485	1,782	130
Strategic bomber forces								
B-1 bomber[a]	443	106	109	0	0	0	215	0
B-52 modifications	130	293	437	360	360	320	1,770	1,100
Air-launched cruise missile	389	426	455	600	600	600	2,681	50
Cruise-missile-carrier aircraft[a]	15	41	30	100	150	200	521	16,000[c]
Advanced strategic air-launched missile[a]	37	48	151	225	170	195	789	n.a.
Total	4,903	4,120	4,517	5,665	7,790	7,655	29,747	...

Sources: Department of Defense, "Department of Defense Annual Report, Fiscal Year 1979," and "Program Acquisition Costs by Weapon System" (1978; processed); 1980–83 figures are authors' estimates.

n.a. Not available.

a. No decision has been made to procure these systems.

b. Official U.S. Navy figures for the cost of the Trident SSBN program include only the number of Trident submarines and Trident I SLBMs that are found in the current five-year defense plan. Under the new Carter five-year shipbuilding program, this would be thirteen Trident submarines and associated SLBMs. Defense Department officials have stated that the United States will eventually procure at least twenty Trident SSBNs. The figures listed here project the total acquisition cost of a force of twenty Trident submarines and associated Trident I SLBMs for these submarines as well as the installation of twelve Poseidon SSBNs with Trident I SLBMs. Given the usual cost escalation of these programs, this figure is probably conservative.

c. Recent press reports indicate the United States is considering deploying 100 wide-bodied cruise-missile-carrier aircraft beginning in the late 1980s. Each of these aircraft would be capable of carrying sixty air-launched cruise missiles. This is an estimate of the procurement cost of both the aircraft and the cruise missiles that they would carry. By comparison, a smaller force of fifty aircraft and associated missiles would cost about $9.2 billion in current dollars.

reflect a $3 billion to $4 billion reduction from the Ford program attributable to two Carter administration decisions: to cancel production of the B-1 bomber and to defer full-scale development of the M-X land-based missile system.

These costs are projected to rise in 1980–83 as the United States continues to increase its strategic weapon capability. Additions and improvements include 1,300 new air-launched cruise missiles, 6 new Trident submarines, 192 Trident I missiles installed in Poseidon submarines, an increase in both accuracy and destructive power for 300 Minuteman missiles, and for the rest of the Minuteman missiles, an increase in accuracy only.

Table 8-5 lists all major weapon systems approved or under serious consideration, with estimates of their 1979–83 costs, and where possible the costs to complete them. These systems account for the major portion of the investment funds allocated to strategic forces. Projected expenditures average about $6 billion a year over the next five years. Annual expenditures will vary depending largely on the number of Trident submarines procured that year. The current program includes full funding for one Trident submarine every year except 1982, when two are planned. But the Trident program has encountered serious problems, and its ultimate costs and production schedules are in doubt.

Beyond 1983, strategic spending will continue to increase if the United States develops and deploys the M-X and Trident II missiles and continues Trident submarine production. Increases will be greater if the United States augments the strategic bomber force in the 1980s with wide-bodied aircraft to carry cruise missiles or a new penetrating bomber. By 1983 less than 20 percent of the funds required by these programs will have been requested. The largest part of the expenditures will occur over the following ten years. Because of the high fixed cost of these new systems, the United States will be forced to give up one or more of them unless there is a significant increase in defense spending or lower spending for general purpose programs during that ten-year period.

General Purpose Forces

General purpose forces are intended to deter wars or to fight wars that do not use intercontinental missiles and bombers. They are categorized as ground combat, tactical air warfare from land bases, naval warfare, and mobility or the long-distance movement of other forces. The 1979 budget for ground combat forces is 26.6 percent over the 1977 budget, and investment is up 44 percent.[4] Spending for land-based tactical air forces will also increase substantially. In contrast, the increase for naval forces is only 11.2 percent, a decrease of 1.6 percent in real terms over the two-year period.

GROUND COMBAT FORCES. The 1979 budget for ground forces calls for an increase of $4.6 billion over 1977. For the most part, it continues the modernization programs initiated during the Ford administration.

Roughly $1.1 billion of the proposed increase will go to finance

---

4. Investment here includes procurement, research and development, and construction appropriation categories.

Table 8-6. Modernization of Ground Combat Major Systems, Fiscal Years 1976–80
Total obligational authority in millions of current dollars

System	1976	1977	1978	1979	1980
Close combat[a]	150	299	515	753	1,073
Development	150	278	367	350	290
Procurement	0	21	148	403	783
Fire support[b]	14	45	104	140	401
Development	14	45	82	84	79
Procurement	0	0	22	56	322
Air defense[c]	208	295	411	724	865
Development	208	295	321	351	169
Procurement	0	0	90	372	696
Combat support[d]	94	201	242	349	385
Development	94	75	38	3	0
Procurement	0	126	204	346	385
Total	465	839	1,272	1,956	2,724
Development	465	692	808	788	538
Procurement	0	147	464	1,178	2,186

Sources: Office of the Army Comptroller, "The Army Budget, FY 1978" (March 1977; processed), pp. 28–29; ibid., "1979" (January 1978; processed), pp. 27–28.
a. XM-1 tank, advanced attack helicopter, Hellfire antitank missile, and infantry fighting vehicle.
b. Copperhead laser-guided artillery shell and general support rocket system.
c. Stinger infantry surface-to-air missile, Roland low- and medium-altitude surface-to-air missile, Patriot medium- and high-altitude missile, and Divad division air-defense gun.
d. Blackhawk utility tactical transport helicopter UH-60A.

eleven major systems in the Army pipeline. These are summarized in table 8-6. The cost of these systems is $1.96 billion in 1979, rising to $2.7 billion in 1980. In the four years from 1976 to 1980, the procurement costs of these systems will rise from zero to $2.2 billion. They account for most of the increased investment in ground force matériel and can be expected to continue to grow well into the 1980s.

The increase in U.S. strength in NATO that began with the 1975 budget has been carried forward and further emphasized by the Carter administration. Since 1974 the Army has increased by three divisions, while forces stationed in Europe have increased by two-thirds of a division. Equipment positioned in Europe for forces stationed in the United States is to be increased from enough for three divisions in 1978 to five divisions by 1983. Planned improvements in the readiness of these divisions and in airlift capabilities will allow their movement to Europe within ten days.

TACTICAL AIR FORCES. Spending for land-based tactical air

Table 8-7. Tactical Aircraft Programs, by Service, Fiscal Years 1979–83

Cost in total obligational authority in millions of current dollars

Type of aircraft	1979 Number	1979 Cost	1980 Number	1980 Cost	1981 Number	1981 Cost	1982 Number	1982 Cost	1983 Number	1983 Cost	1979–83 Number	1979–83 Cost	1984 to completion Number	1984 to completion Cost
Air Force	**385**	**3,935**	**415**	**3,947**	**323**	**3,241**	**180**	**1,708**	**180**	**1,717**	**1,283**	**14,999**	**423**	**4,066**
F-15														
Development	...	10	...	10	...	...	...	...	...	...	...	20	...	...
Procurement	78	1,406	78	1,333	73	1,146	...	...	...	...	229	3,885	...	...
F-16														
Development	...	108	...	80	...	13	...	...	...	...	...	201	...	...
Procurement	145	1,487	175	1,620	180	1,700	180	1,708	180	1,717	660	8,232	423	4,066
A-10														
Development	...	18	...	18	...	19	...	...	...	...	...	505	...	...
Procurement	162	907	162	886	70	363	...	...	...	...	394	2,156	...	...
Navy and Marine Corps	**29**	**1,623**	**39**	**1,733**	**102**	**2,642**	**180**	**3,374**	**192**	**3,405**	**542**	**12,941**	**783**	**12,418**
F-14														
Development	...	...	...	...	...	...	...	...	...	...	...	...	...	...
Procurement	24	672	24	706	24	678	24	717	24	749	120	3,522	58	1,284
F-18 and A-18														
Development	...	474	...	261	...	102	...	62	...	10	...	909	...	...
Procurement	5	391	15	643	48	1,287	96	1,645	108	1,730	272[a]	5,696	539	8,243
AV-8B														
Development	...	86	...	123	...	...	...	...	...	...	...	...	...	...
Procurement	...	...	...	...	30	575	60	950	60	916	150	2,714	186	2,891
Total	**414**	**5,558**	**454**	**5,680**	**425**	**5,883**	**360**	**5,082**	**372**	**5,122**	**1,825**	**27,940**	**1,206**	**16,484**

Sources: "Department of Defense Annual Report, Fiscal Year 1979"; "Program Acquisition Cost by Weapon System"; "National Defense Budget Estimate for 1979"; "Department of the Air Force, Fiscal Year 1979 Budget Summary" (1978; processed). Figures for 1981–83 are authors' estimates.

a. Includes 12 development aircraft.

forces will rise from $10.3 billion in 1977 to $13.7 billion in 1979, an increase of 33 percent. Part of the increase is attributable to investment ($2.8 billion, up 46.7 percent) and part is associated with the increase in NATO forces.

The Air Force's tactical aircraft modernization program for 1979 and beyond is shown in table 8-7. The cost of the program was $2.6 billion in 1977, is over $4 billion in 1978, and is expected to stay near that amount for two more years before falling sharply. Over the five-year planning period 1979–83, the Air Force is projected to buy 1,283 tactical aircraft worth $14.9 billion. By then it will have substantially completed its modernization program with the additions of an air superiority fighter (F-15), a multipurpose aircraft (F-16), and a close-air-support aircraft (A-10), to supplement its all-weather, deep interdiction, strike aircraft (F-111).

This modernization program is a significant part of the NATO buildup begun in 1974. The Air Force's tactical fighter squadrons increased from seventy-one to eighty. Fighter squadrons deployed in Europe have increased from twenty-one to twenty-four, including an increase from three to six squadrons of F-111 fighters. According to the five-year plan, the twenty-four squadrons will be completely modernized by 1983 and will consist of approximately six squadrons each of F-15s, F-16s, F-111s, and A-10s.

Between now and the mid-1980s, the Air Force will be deciding on the next generation of aircraft and whether they will be manned or piloted by remote control. Meanwhile, Air Force modernization dollars will go to technological innovations for target identification and acquisition, for increased accuracy, and for improved command, control, and communications systems.

In contrast, the Navy and Marine Corps are projected to spend $12.9 billion in 1979–83 to buy only 542 aircraft, with $12.4 billion left over to spend for 783 aircraft. The Navy and Marine Corps program includes two air defense fighters (F-14 and F-18), eventually a light attack aircraft (A-18), and possibly a second-generation, vertical or short takeoff and landing aircraft, V/STOL (AV-8B). None of these aircraft will significantly increase Navy and Marine Corps offensive air capability, although the AV-8B will provide valuable operational experience with sea-based V/STOL aircraft. The high costs of operating aircraft at sea limit the Navy's ability to operate against Soviet land forces, but Navy and Marine tactical aircraft

Table 8-8. Shipbuilding Programs in Carter and Ford Budgets, Fiscal Years 1979-83

Cost in total obligational authority in billions of current dollars

Budget	1979 Number	1979 Cost	1980 Number	1980 Cost	1981 Number	1981 Cost	1982 Number	1982 Cost	1983 Number	1983 Cost	1979-83 Number	1979-83 Cost
Ford[a]	**29**	**8.8**	**43**	**9.9**	**42**	**10.6**	**35**	**12.4**	**30**	**12.1**	**179**	**53.7**
General purpose ships	28	6.9	41	7.7	41	9.2	33	9.6	29	10.4	172	43.8
Strategic ships	1	1.1	2	2.0	1	1.2	2	2.5	1	1.3	7	8.0
Miscellaneous[b]	...	0.8	...	0.2	...	0.2	...	0.3	...	0.4	...	1.9
Carter January budget[c]	**15**	**4.7**	**21**	**7.5**	**23**	**9.0**	**28**	**10.1**	**23**	**11.3**	**109**	**42.4**
General purpose ships	14	2.8	19	5.3	22	7.4	26	7.2	21	9.6	102	32.2
Strategic ships	1	1.2	2	2.0	1	1.2	2	2.5	1	1.3	7	8.0
Miscellaneous[b]	...	0.8	...	0.2	...	0.4	...	0.4	...	0.4	...	2.1
Carter March budget[d]	**15**	**4.7**	**16**	**5.2**	**22**	**5.9**	**15**	**6.8**	**15**	**7.1**	**83**	**29.7[e]**
General purpose ships	14	2.8	15	3.8	21	4.2	13	3.7	14	5.2	77	19.7
Strategic ships	1	1.2	1	1.2	1	1.3	2	2.7	1	1.5	6	7.8
Miscellaneous[b]	...	0.8	...	0.2	...	0.4	...	0.4	...	0.4	...	2.1

Sources: See notes. Figures are rounded.

a. Figures for 1979-81 are from *Department of Defense Appropriations for 1978*, Hearings before the House Committee on Appropriations, 95:1 (1977), pt. 1, p. 356; those for 1982-83 are authors' estimates.

b. Includes service and landing craft, costs for outfitting and delivering ships to the fleet during the fiscal year, and cost overruns on ships authorized in prior years. For 1980-83 all three alternatives should probably be increased by $500 million to $1 billion a year for additional cost increases.

c. Although the administration failed to send a five-year shipbuilding program to Congress in January, the total of $42 billion appeared in *The Budget of the United States Government, Fiscal Year 1979*, p. 72. The fiscal year 1980 total appeared in Navy budget testimony. Other figures are authors' estimates.

d. 1979 figure from Navy budget; 1980-83 numbers contained in the shipbuilding plan attached to Secretary Brown's letter to Speaker of the House Thomas P. O'Neill, March 1978. Costs are authors' estimates.

e. On April 10, 1978, Secretary Brown testified that the total cost of the program would be $32 billion. "Statement by Secretary Harold Brown before the House Armed Services Committee on Shipbuilding on FY 1979-83 Navy Shipbuilding and Conversion Program" (processed). Estimates given to the press in March ranged from $28 billion to $32 billion.

will be equipped to operate in traditional ways from aircraft carriers and to support amphibious landings outside the NATO area. The Air Force, on the other hand, will have the necessary forces and associated electronics to face the sophisticated weapon systems of the Warsaw Pact countries.

NAVAL FORCES. Naval general purpose forces (416 ships and 1,178 aircraft) will cost $19.8 billion to operate in 1979—$2 billion more than in 1977 but a reduction in real terms.

The administration proposes to reduce sharply the previously planned level of naval modernization. As shown in table 8-8, the 1979 budget for general purpose ships would cut spending from the $6.9 billion proposed by President Ford to $2.8 billion. The budget also presented a five-year program that would have reduced 1979–83 spending for general purpose vessels from $44 billion to $32 billion. In March, the administration presented a new five-year program to the Congress proposing a reduction to about $20 billion.

The Ford program was for 172 general purpose ships over the five-year period, the January budget projected 102 ships, and the March budget, 77 ships. Despite the reductions, 477 general purpose ships are projected by 1983—61 more than in 1979—as ships already approved by the Congress are delivered. The operating costs of the Navy are likely to continue to climb over the next five years as the new ships are added, while older, less complex ships are retired.

The drastic changes in shipbuilding programs over short periods of time reflect the uncertainty about the appropriate role of naval forces in defense strategy and about the design and missions appropriate to particular ships, most notably large aircraft carriers and cruisers.

The Carter administration has also stressed shipbuilding problems as a reason for reductions in planned procurement. The Navy has been plagued for at least ten years with cost overruns, late deliveries, and large claims. Combat ships are the most complex weapons in the Defense Department inventory. For example, the DDG-47 guided-missile destroyer has five antiaircraft systems, three antisurface-ship systems, five antisubmarine systems, and six command and control systems. Combat ships must be designed to carry and integrate not only these systems but new systems that may be designed over the next twenty-five to forty years. The Navy has considered many of its ships as carriers of individual systems rather than carriers of integrated systems and has made costly design changes while the ships were being built. That ships are so complex and take so long to build (five to eight years) has been an excuse for changes during the building process. But their complexity should instead be a reason for more caution in designing a new ship or making a major change while a ship is being built.

Shipbuilders have signed contracts with the Navy with badly underestimated costs and unrealistic schedules. But because the Navy made design changes and is responsible for late delivery of equipment, the blame for the increased costs and late deliveries of ships is disputed, leading to an almost complete breakdown in relations between the Navy and the shipbuilders. In the short run, the administration is attempting to break the impasse and to settle the $2.7 billion claims that the shipbuilders have entered against the government. In the longer run, the administration must find a better way to design and build ships if these problems are not to recur. One solution, discussed later in the chapter, is to include the ships in the more orderly approach to acquisition called for in Office of Management and Budget Circular A-109.

MOBILITY FORCES. To complement the general purposes forces, the administration proposes to spend $2.2 billion on mobility forces in 1979, an increase of only $200 million over 1977, a real reduction of nearly 3 percent. This program includes airlift and sealift, with major improvements confined to airlift associated with the NATO buildup. The major new capability in this year's program is the advanced tanker cargo aircraft, which will be used both to move cargo and to provide aerial refueling of other airlift forces, such as the Air Force C-5A and C-141 cargo aircraft, and of tactical aircraft as well. The budget provides funds for increasing the hours that the C-141 could be used in wartime and for structural modifications to the wide-bodied civil fleet so that it can move oversized Army equipment.

Auxiliary Missions

The administration proposes to increase spending on the two remaining missions—intelligence and communications, and research and development—to $15 billion in 1979, a $2 billion, or 15.4 percent, increase over 1977. The $2 billion is about equally divided between the two missions.

An important reform in research and development (required by Office of Management and Budget Circular A-109 on major system acquisitions) began in the last administration at the instigation of the Congress. Under the reform, funds are increased for basic research and technology but decisions on the development of major weapon systems are postponed until their purposes are examined and approved by the secretary of defense, the President, and the Congress. Once the general characteristics of a system are approved, both the services and their contractors would be freed from the continual interference that now reduces accountability; progress would be reviewed by high-level authorities only at a few decision points. Project managers and contractors would define a system's specific characteristics and associated costs and schedules and would be accountable for them—and the government could then begin enforcing contracts.

Such a system requires considerable discipline on the part of everyone involved, including Congress, the executive office of the President, the office of the secretary of defense, the services, the project managers, and the contractors. If it works as hoped, five years from now the problems with shipbuilding, cited earlier, and similar problems with other major weapons systems will be greatly reduced.

The new system has two budget implications. First, it may prevent the substantial cost increases in weapon systems due to changes in plans, unrealistic cost estimates and schedules, and changes in characteristics. Second, to complement the elaborate early review of a program, the new system will raise the general level of technology by increasing funding for research and advanced technological development. Although the planned increase in this part of the research and development budget is only $400 million in 1979—from $2.3 billion to $2.7 billion—substantial increases can be expected over the next four years.

Support Activities

The Defense Department proposes to spend $31.5 billion on support activities in 1979. This consists of $16.3 billion for training, medical, and other personnel activities, $12.1 billion for logistics, and $3.1 billion for administration and associated activities. The 1979 level is an increase of $3.3 billion over 1977, but it is a decrease of 1.2 percent in real terms. (Some support costs directly associated with forces—for example, operation of bases—are included in the cost of the forces and missions previously discussed and are not counted in the $31.5 billion.)

The Carter administration has proposed to continue the initiatives of the Ford administration for increasing the efficiency of the support establishment. Attempts are being made to cut the size of the Washington headquarters, although much of the reduction already accomplished within the office of the secretary of defense was merely a rearrangement of activities, to place them outside the direct supervision of the secretary. Similar attempts and similar results can be expected in the services.

The administration's proposed reduction of 20,000 uniformed personnel—from 2,069,000 to 2,049,000—is tied largely to cuts in military training. (Recruit training has been shortened and there is less specialized skill training, so fewer instructors and training support personnel are required.) This decision, apparently taken despite the opposition of the services, is more significant than it may appear. For, although 10,000 support positions will be converted to combat positions, under the Ford administration virtually all reductions in support forces were used to increase combat forces. The services are certain to resist further reductions in military manpower. Even modest cuts will be increasingly difficult as the symbolic level of "two million strong" is approached.

The administration also proposes a reduction of some 13,000 civilian employees, roughly half of them because of anticipated transfers to private firms of functions such as laundry, vehicle maintenance, and food services. But whether the Congress will agree is uncertain—a similar proposal last year failed when Congress, under pressure from constituents and government employee unions, prohibited the contracting of a variety of support activities.

The 1979 budget also anticipates financial savings from reform of the federal blue-collar pay formula. Quirks in the formula now used to calculate pay increases for blue-collar employees have caused the pay of many of these workers to exceed the levels required to maintain comparability with their counterparts in private industry. Given the domestic political interests involved, prospects for enactment of the proposed reforms are far from bright. Similar legislation was proposed by the Ford administration, but it died in congressional committee. If it fails to pass again this year, the defense budget will be $136 million higher in 1979 and over $500 million higher in 1983.

The Carter administration, in the tradition of its recent predecessors, has proposed a base realignment package; this one involves eighty-five military installations or activities. If fully implemented (the usual congressional resistance can be anticipated), these changes are expected to eliminate 14,600 military and 8,600 civilian positions, yielding savings of up to $337 million a year. These actions are unlikely to be instituted in time to offset the 1979 budget. Moreover, since the Pentagon has indicated that the eventual savings could be used to meet higher priority defense needs, future budgets will probably not be affected.

In sum, the 1979 defense budget must be a disappointment to those who anticipated that the Carter administration would make substantial reductions in the support establishment. As the above discussion suggests, most of the proposals are carried over from previous years. Indeed, the only thing new is the apparent willingness of the administration to make modest reductions in military manpower.

Budget Prospects

By reducing strategic and naval forces, the Carter administration has held the 1979 defense budget well below the level proposed by President Ford. But to pay for the programs that the Defense Department has proposed to the Congress, the 1980–83 budgets must rise well above the President's projections.

The administration has already submitted a curtailed shipbuilding program that will reduce the gap between Defense Department programs and the President's 1980–83 projections by as much as $12.5 billion. (That program also implies great changes in the role of the Navy.) But additional reductions will be required, and they are likely to come from cuts in strategic forces. The future of the three major new strategic systems must be decided within the next few years. These systems would require increasing amounts of money not only in the five-year planning period but in the late 1980s.

Moreover, the administration has proposed large increases for the modernization of ground combat forces and land-based air forces that would be involved in the early stages of a NATO conflict. If the large real increases of the last two years continue through 1983, there would be further pressure to reduce strategic and naval force spending or to raise the projected budget. There is significant sentiment in Congress for restoring the 1979 budget cuts from the Ford program—a move that would involve large commitments for future years.

Whatever the outcome, the case for measures to increase efficiency within the Defense Department will remain. However, most of the suggestions for savings, such as closing bases, contracting to private firms for base operations, and reforming the pay system for blue-collar workers, are politically unpopular. If such savings are not made, the budget targets for 1980–83 will be even more difficult to achieve.

CHAPTER NINE

Defense Policy

CHARLES A. SORRELS *and* OTHERS

ALTHOUGH defense spending is not the largest part of the national budget, it has—in principle at least—a substantial discretionary element. Fiscal policy in any circumstances and a balanced budget objective in particular are affected by the choices that determine the size of defense outlays. At the present time, these choices are peculiarly difficult. Efforts to contain future defense budgets within the limits proposed by President Carter raise many complex issues that will provoke lengthy and often heated debate in both the executive branch and Congress.

At bottom, the reason for the present situation is the expansion of Soviet military power. That expansion has been steady over more than a decade. It has been sizable and it is continuing. There is wide agreement in the United States and among its allies that this is legitimate cause for concern. That it requires a further response on the part of the United States is not in serious question. Indeed, the increased defense budget for fiscal 1979 supports this conclusion. Nonetheless, important details about the nature of the response remain to be decided. They bring to the fore military, political, economic, and even psychological considerations that are subject to differing interpretations and opinions.

It is evident, first of all, that standard measurements of Soviet

John C. Baker, Robert P. Berman, Herschel Kanter, and Frederick W. Young contributed to this chapter.

233

military power—numbers of divisions, missiles, ships—provide only partial and rudimentary guidance. Translation of these measurements into assessments of relative capabilities demands sophisticated application of technical knowledge and also realistic definitions of the military and political settings in which such capabilities might be exercised. Inevitably some judgments must be subjective.

Second, if relative capabilities cannot be precisely appraised, estimates of Soviet intentions must be even more matters of informed guess. Too little is known about the motivations and the decision-making procedures of the Soviet leadership to make a confident forecast of Soviet courses of action. It is not even known, for example. how the Russians assess their military capabilities in relation to those of the United States and its allies, a matter having an obvious bearing on Soviet intentions.

The probable or possible reaction of third countries to military developments in the United States and the USSR is another important consideration. After all, the U.S. military establishment has been built and shaped in major part to help assure against Soviet control of areas considered crucial to American security, notably Western Europe and Japan. And if the belief were to take hold that American power was in permanent relative decline, it is conceivable that the Russians might acquire dominant influence over these peoples without firing a single gun. Here again the range for guesswork about the perceptions and likely responses of other nations is a very wide one.

This chapter focuses on three areas, in which key and perhaps critical budgetary choices are to be made: in the missions assigned to the ground forces and land-based tactical air forces, to the Navy, and to the strategic forces. The budget for fiscal 1979 emphasizes the strengthening of the ground forces and land-based tactical forces. Spending on the Navy is to fall in real terms; and plans for the longer future envision a smaller naval arm than that proposed by President Ford. Having dropped the B-1 bomber, the administration has deferred decisions about the strategic forces.

The large questions posed by these budget proposals are: (1) Should the program that began in 1974 to strengthen and improve forces for the NATO central front be continued and expanded? (2) Should the shipbuilding program assume that the Navy will continue to be built around the aircraft carrier? (3) Should the M-X intercontinental ballistic missile be developed and deployed—or, more broadly, should the strategic triad of land-based missiles, bombers, and ballistic missile submarines be preserved?

Ground and Tactical Air Forces

If President Carter's decision to withdraw the Second Army Division from the Republic of Korea is carried out, the orientation of American ground forces toward Western Europe will be more pronounced than at any time during the postwar period.

The current force structure includes 16 active and 8 reserve Army divisions, plus 3 active and 1 reserve Marine division. The Army also has a number of brigade-sized units which, when counted as the equivalent of one-third of a division each, increase the size of the Army force to the equivalent of 17⅓ active divisions and 14⅔ reserve divisions. The equivalent of 6 Army divisions (including a brigade in West Berlin) are stationed in West Germany on the NATO central front. To facilitate rapid reinforcement, the equipment for another 3 divisions will be stocked—pre-positioned—in Germany by the end of 1978. The proposed 1979–83 five-year defense plan includes funds to pre-position equipment for three more divisions and to nearly double airlift capability. Apart from the withdrawing Second Division in South Korea, the only other American ground combat forces stationed outside the United States are two regiments of the Third Marine Division in Okinawa and one Army brigade in Panama.

Of 134 squadrons of land-based tactical aircraft (Air Force, Marine, and National Guard), 24 are based in the European theater, 9 in Japan, 3 in Korea, and 2 in the Philippines. Under the Department of Defense's five-year plan, the 24 European-based squadrons would be completely modernized by 1983.

The overriding orientation of conventional land forces toward Western Europe derives, of course, from the deployment of large Soviet and other Warsaw Pact ground and air forces in Central Europe. It is the balance between the Warsaw Pact and NATO forces that continues to preoccupy American thinking about conventional war. As usually now conceived, the primary concern is that Soviet and allied forces might attack with great armored strength and on short notice in an effort to overwhelm the NATO forces in a brief, intense conflict. Thus, if recourse to nuclear weapons is to be avoided, it is necessary to confront the Warsaw Pact with sufficient strength to make the success of such an attack very doubtful—that is, to deter it.

The Current Balance in Central Europe

Discussion of the balance of forces in Central Europe often centers on the impressive buildup in Soviet offensive capabilities and neglects substantial improvements within NATO. As suggested last year in *Setting National Priorities,* it is difficult to determine whether the overall balance has changed significantly over the past decade once account is taken of the buildup in forces on both sides. Table 9-1 summarizes the current situation.

In terms of numbers of immediately available ground forces, the balance favors the Warsaw Pact armies. The margin, however, is not as wide as is sometimes believed. In manpower the Warsaw Pact advantage is about 1.2 to 1.0. The Pact has a larger portion of its manpower in divisions, which are somewhat smaller than those of NATO, and places much greater emphasis on armor. In actual numbers of divisions and tanks, therefore, the ratios favor the Pact by 2.1 to 1.0 and 2.3 to 1.0, respectively. But the non-Soviet divisions in the Warsaw Pact armies are manned at less than 75 percent of full strength in peacetime, and some have only skeletal cadres. NATO, moreover, is considered to retain a qualitative advantage in weapons. When these factors are taken into account, the Pact's superiority in immediately available ground combat power (armored division equivalents) is calculated at about 1.4 to 1.0. The NATO forces are believed to be more sustainable than those of the Pact because of a larger ratio of support to combat forces and because of better equipment. Questions have been raised, however, about the adequacy of NATO's ammunition stocks, and data on which to make a quantitative comparison with those of the Pact are not available.

The numerical balance in the air also favors the Warsaw Pact. NATO has a large advantage in offensive power owing to the greater range and payload-carrying capacity of its airplanes, while numbers of aircraft configured for air-to-air combat give the Warsaw Pact an edge in defensive capability. The Soviet air forces are being modernized, with more multipurpose aircraft such as the Flogger signaling a move away from purely defensive fighters toward a ground-attack and deep-strike capability. NATO, for its part, is bringing into service more high-performance fighters like the F-15 and F-16. Overall, the quantitative strength of the Warsaw Pact's air forces is considered to be somewhat more than offset by the superior quality of the NATO air forces, particularly the U.S. Air Force.

If each side were to reinforce its forces in the Central Region for thirty days before a conflict, numbers of men and equipment would be much greater, but the balance would not be altered significantly. The shift would favor the Pact slightly on the ground while the opposite would be the case in the air.

Other factors affect judgments about the military balance. Each side has a superpower member, but the United States has had far less influence in NATO than the Soviet Union within the Warsaw Pact. As a result, the Pact is considered to have a comparative military advantage over NATO in terms of standardized organization, equipment, and doctrine. However, individual NATO soldiers, pilots, and small-unit commanders are believed to be better trained to exploit battlefield opportunities than their putative opponents, who are under much tighter and more centralized control.

Which alliance would be more cohesive in time of conflict is uncertain. Eastern Europeans, resentful of the strong Soviet presence in their countries, could become serious liabilities to a Soviet war effort. The NATO alliance has its own question marks, notably the role to be played by France in a European conflict and the impact of the severely strained relations between Greece and Turkey.

If both sides were to begin to mobilize simultaneously, neither side would appear to have a decisive margin of superiority. The more likely case would have the Warsaw Pact begin to mobilize first. How long the NATO countries would need to reach a political consensus on mobilization after first warnings cannot be predicted, particularly because the early indications of Warsaw Pact intentions might be ambiguous. Even if the lag between mobilizations were no longer than a few days, the Warsaw Pact could increase its advantage to a point where an attack might well leave NATO with the ultimate choice between acceptance of defeat and the first use of nuclear weapons.

Further Measures for Central Europe

Given the ponderables and imponderables of the situation, it is understandable that successive administrations should concentrate on raising the immediate combat capabilities of the American forces

Table 9-1. The Balance of Forces in Central Europe, 1978

Type of force	NATO forces			Warsaw Pact forces			Ratio of Warsaw Pact forces to NATO forces
	Combined (number)	United States		Combined (number)	Soviet		
		Number	Percent		Number	Percent	
			Available immediately				
Ground							
Manpower (thousands)	804	193	22	935	475	51	1.2
Divisions[b]	28.3	6.0	21.0	58.3	27.0	47.0	2.1
Tanks	6,930	2,000	30	16,200	9,250	57	2.3
Armored division equivalents[c]	25	6	24	35	23	66	1.4
Air							
Aircraft	1,946	558	29	2,682	1,305	49	1.4
Offensive F-4D equivalents[d]	1,800	1,260	70	400	260	65	0.2
Defensive F-4D equivalents[e]	3,000	1,200	40	3,800	1,600	42	1.3
Tactical air wing equivalents[f]	28	15	53	22	11	50	0.8

Available after thirty days of reinforcement

Ground							
Manpower (thousands)	n.a.	n.a.	n.a.	n.a.	n.a.	n.a.	n.a.
Divisions[b]	40	10	25	89	58	65	2.2
Tanks	n.a.	n.a.	n.a.	n.a.	n.a.	n.a.	n.a.
Armored division equivalents[c]	38	10	26	58–65	44–45	69–76	1.5–1.7
Air							
Aircraft	3,032	1,644	54	3,546	2,169	61	1.2
Offensive F-4D equivalents[d]	2,900	2,400	82	600	470	78	0.2
Defensive F-4D equivalents[e]	4,400	2,600	59	5,000	2,800	56	1.1
Tactical air wing equivalents[f]	44	31	70	30	18	60	0.7

Sources: Authors' estimates based on information in International Institute for Strategic Studies, *The Military Balance, 1977–1978* (London: IISS, 1977); and Robert P. Berman, *Soviet Air Power in Transition* (Brookings Institution, 1978); Robert Lucas Fischer, *Defending the Central Front: The Balance of Forces* (London: IISS, 1976); Office of the Secretary of Defense, "A Report to Congress on U.S. Conventional Reinforcements for NATO" (June 1976; processed).

n.a. Not available.

a. Includes forces of France and Denmark.

b. Each brigade and regiment (including those in Berlin) is counted as a third of a division.

c. The Defense Department uses this measure of combat capability to take into account the quality and quantity of weapons and the readiness of the units composing a land force.

d. Offensive capabilities of individual aircraft, assumed to be proportional to their combat radius and payload, are expressed relative to the F-4D Phantom and then summed over all the aircraft in the force. Medium-range bombers based in western USSR are not included in these figures, although they would fly missions in central Europe.

e. Defensive capabilities of individual aircraft, assumed to be proportional to thrust-to-weight ratio and inversely proportional to wing loading, are expressed relative to the F-4D Phantom and then summed over all the aircraft in the force.

f. This is a measure of overall tactical air capability relative to a wing of F-4Ds airframe characteristics as measured by offensive and defensive F-4D equivalents plus the authors' judgment based on differences in armament and avionics.

in Central Europe and on making possible their rapid reinforcement. The Carter budget for fiscal 1979 follows the pattern of earlier budgets in this respect.

EARLIER AVAILABILITY OF COMBAT POWER. The present estimate is that the equivalent of some six U.S. divisions in West Germany could be increased to ten within thirty days (table 9-1). If equipment for an additional three devisions were pre-positioned and airlift capability nearly doubled—as proposed in the 1979–83 five-year plan—all active Army divisions in the United States could conceivably be deployed to Europe within the same thirty-day span.

Along with provision for increased mobility, the five-year plan envisages the purchase of about four hundred additional units of the most modern tank, the XM-1, over the next five years. Six hundred fewer M-60 tanks would be purchased, with the result that the 1983 tank fleet would be slightly smaller but more modern. This decision, together with the proposed pre-positioning of additional tanks in Europe, could mean that filling shortages in reserve component tank units would be delayed for as long as a year.

Any delay in reserve component modernization might be opposed in Congress, which has been traditionally sympathetic to views of state governors (who have peacetime control of National Guard forces) and such lobby groups as the National Guard and Reserve Officer Associations of the United States. While some National Guard forces are needed for such domestic contingencies as riots and natural disasters, the principal reason for maintaining most Army reserve component units is to reinforce NATO forces in Central Europe. Since the greatest imbalance of forces in a Central European conflict would exist during the period before such combat units could be deployed, a shift in resources from the reserves to active forces, as suggested by the change in the tank program, appears to have substantial justification.

The distribution of budget resources between the active forces and the reserves can affect the improvement of the forces that would bear the brunt of a conflict in Central Europe. There is the fundamental choice: to equip, train, and locate existing forces to deter— or if need be to fight—an expected short war, or to continue to fund at present levels large reserve forces, most of which would become available for combat according to a timetable more nearly resembling that of World War II. A hypothetical trade-off to illustrate this can

Table 9-2. Number of Antitank Missiles and Ten-Year Cost for a Battalion
as Currently Equipped and for a Battalion Equipped with ICVs

Type of battalion	Antitank missiles			Ten-year cost (millions of 1979 dollars)
	TOW	Dragon	Total	
As currently equipped	22	40	62	176
Equipped with ICVs[a]	67	40	107	203
Difference (percent)	205	0	73	15

Sources: Numbers of antitank missiles for currently equipped battalion from Robert Lucas Fischer, *Defending the Central Front: The Balance of Forces* (London: IISS, 1976), table 4, note i. Costs for currently equipped battalion are authors' estimates based on data published by the Office of the Comptroller of the Army, "The Army Force Planning Cost Handbook" (June 1976; processed), pp. III-241 and on unpublished data from the Department of Defense.
a. Numbers of antitank missiles are authors' estimates, assuming forty-five ICVs would replace thirty-six M113A1s. The TOW missiles are now mounted on M113A1s in the antitank and scout sections of the battalion and these are assumed not to be replaced by the ICV. The TOW has a range of 3,000 meters compared with 1,000 meters for the man-portable Dragon. Ten-year cost increase includes the cost of an additional fourteen ICVs for maintenance float and ninety days of war reserve stocks; it also assumes that operating and maintenance costs are 10 percent higher than for the currently equipped battalion.

be found in the decision, reflected in the 1979 budget, not to proceed with the Army's proposed infantry combat vehicle. The ICV was to have replaced M113A1 armored personnel carriers in infantry platoons of mechanized infantry battalions. Because it was to be armed with the precision-guided antitank weapon, TOW, it would have greatly enhanced the antitank capability of each battalion. The ICV would have cost about $390,000 per vehicle and would carry fewer men than the M113A1. Although the Army had not decided how to reorganize the mechanized infantry battalion to accommodate the new vehicle, one constant-manpower option would have been to replace the four M113A1s in each infantry platoon with five ICVs. If this were the only change, forty-five ICVs would have replaced thirty-six M113A1s, more than tripling the number of long-range antitank guided missiles per battalion. The total number of antitank guided missiles, including the much less capable man-portable Dragon, would have been increased by more than 70 percent. In sum, the antitank capability of a battalion could have been more than doubled for roughly a 15 percent increase in cost over ten years (see table 9-2).

Procurement of the ICV was canceled because of concerns about its high cost; less expensive alternative vehicles are being examined for the ICV role. Over ten years, however, the estimated costs of placing the already designed and tested ICV in the twenty-eight mechanized battalions located in West Germany could be offset by only a 3 percent reduction in spending for Army reserve component forces.

DEPLOYMENT OF THE NEUTRON BOMB. A different issue is presented by the development of enhanced radiation-reduced blast (ER-RB) weapons, better known as the neutron bomb.

Tactical nuclear weapons now in the field are designed to destroy targets with heat and blast effects. These effects, along with associated falling and blowing debris, would kill most people close to the detonation. Some people, however, would be killed by radiation, depending on their proximity to the blast and degree of protection from varying weapon effects. Tanks and other armored vehicles, for example, provide relatively good protection from heat and blast but only moderate protection from radiation.

The United States has essentially completed development of a class of nuclear weapons designed to maximize prompt radiation effects while minimizing heat, blast, and fallout. These weapons could be produced for existing aircraft, missile, and artillery delivery systems. They would be considerably more effective than currently available warheads against certain targets, such as troop concentrations and armor formations located in areas where it would be desirable to minimize collateral damage; they would be less effective against targets where the main objective was to destroy enemy matériel.

Opposition to ER-RB weapons centers on two points. One is that killing with radiation is more reprehensible than killing with blast, because death would occur after hours or even weeks of suffering. The other is that the possibility of reduced blast damage from the neutron weapon may lessen NATO's reluctance to use nuclear weapons, thus increasing the chances of an escalation from conventional to nuclear war. The first point hardly seems decisive: the use of any kind of nuclear weapon will cause casualties from radiation sickness, but a neutron weapon would have less fallout and therefore radiation hazards would be shorter in duration and more likely to be confined to the intended target. The second point is also a dubious one. An ER-RB weapon, in the end, is another piece of nuclear armament. The risk that the Russians would respond with their own nuclear weapons would far outweigh considerations of collateral damage in any NATO deliberation on whether to use nuclear weapons first.

On the premise that resort to any type of nuclear weapon by either side poses uncertain risks of escalation that neither the Warsaw Pact nor NATO can contemplate with equanimity, the new weapon would be looked upon as a marginal addition to the existing nuclear deterrent. As such, it probably should be given a lower priority than the other deterrent—the strengthening of NATO's conventional power. Yet canceling the program might mean giving up a bargaining chip in arms control negotiations. President Carter, having said that he would base his decision on the deployment of neutron weapons largely on the extent of support from the European members of NATO, has decided not to produce ER-RB weapons for the time being but to keep that option open.

RATIONALIZATION AND STANDARDIZATION. Like previous administrations, and like the governments of other NATO nations, the Carter administration recognizes the potential advantages of greater standardization of equipment within NATO. Repeated public statements calling for the rationalization of defense-related tasks and improved interoperability of forces through increased standardization of matériel and procedures have been underscored by the appointment of a single individual to coordinate such efforts, directly responsible to the secretary of defense. Within NATO, more than seventy groups, committees, subgroups, task forces, and the like have been formed to examine the issues. So far, however, real progress remains disappointing.

The choice of a NATO tank gun is an example. The United States has elected to equip the first 1,000 to 1,500 of its new XM-1 tanks with the 105-millimeter gun that now arms most of NATO's tank fleet. West Germany, meanwhile, has decided on a 120-millimeter gun for its new Leopard tank. Beginning in 1984, however, newly produced U.S. tanks are to be fitted with the 120-millimeter weapon —a decision that could cost up to $1 billion over the next ten years. This, according to the administration, will provide a hedge against unforeseen improvements in Soviet armor and will be a significant step toward the standardization of NATO weapons. In view of the large number of 105-millimeter guns that will remain in the NATO tank fleet for the next two decades, the selection of the 120-millimeter gun for the XM-1 can scarcely be viewed by itself as enhancing standardization. It could be a significant step forward, however, if it were part of a larger deal, such as one to secure West German support of a standardized airborne warning and control system (AWACS). The administration has so far denied that such a deal exists, though the Germans have in the past indicated that they would view a NATO AWACS program more favorably if the United States adopted the German tank gun.

The most efficient way to achieve standardization would be through a buy-at-lowest-cost doctrine within a free trading alliance. Since the United States would hold a comparative advantage in most areas of technology related to the development and production of military hardware, NATO forces would become predominantly equipped with American weapons. This is unacceptable to European members of the alliance, who want to maintain or develop their own defense industries. Thus real progress toward standardization will require compromises. European nations should be willing to concentrate their defense industry efforts in a few specialties while the United States, for its part, should be willing to buy European systems even if they are slightly more expensive or slightly less effective than competing U.S. systems. One way to make these compromises would be through negotiated agreements linking standardized procurement of two or more separate systems. The advantages of securing West German participation in a common AWACS program, for example, promises to outweigh the disadvantages of arming the XM-1 tank with the German 120-millimeter gun.

Conventional Forces in East Asia and the Pacific

East Asia has a distinctly secondary priority to Western Europe as a region for the deployment of American ground and air power. Unless Soviet policies and deployments undergo a major change, the trend may continue toward a reduction in the numbers of uniformed Americans stationed in the area.

MILITARY BALANCE IN KOREA. An early national security decision by the Carter administration was to direct a phased withdrawal of the Second Infantry Division from South Korea. If carried through, this will complete a redeployment that began in 1971 when the Nixon administration withdrew one of the two divisions then stationed in Korea.

The implications for stability in Northeast Asia are ambiguous. South Korea's security has been considered, in Washington and Tokyo alike, as being linked to the security of the United States' major ally in Asia, Japan. It is apparent and understandable that Japanese authorities have viewed the withdrawal with misgivings, while recognizing that the choice was one to be made by the United States. The government of South Korea has accepted the plan in similar fashion.

In assessing the military balance on the Korean peninsula, the importance attached to the removal of the Second Division depends on judgments made in other areas: on relative populations, military strength, and the like.

The Republic of Korea (ROK) has more than twice the North's population (37 million compared with 17 million) and more than three times the GNP. Its active armed forces are larger (635,000 compared with 520,000), and some of its divisions have had battle experience in Vietnam. The North, however, has a substantial advantage in firepower and mobility: nearly twice as many tanks (1,950 compared with 1,100), more armored personnel carriers, and multiple-rocket launchers suited to offensive operations. It has a force of commando regiments that could be airlifted behind South Korea's lines as part of a general attack. In combat aircraft, the North Koreans have a substantial quantitative advantage, but half of the North's combat planes are outdated MIG-15s and MIG-17s, whereas the South's air arm is in process of acquiring advanced American fighters.

Geography both handicaps and favors South Korea. Seoul, the South's political capital and economic center with over six million residents, is about twenty miles from the demilitarized zone, just north of which are fourteen of the twenty-five North Korean divisions. It is also within the range of surface-to-surface missiles and some artillery. The Republic would therefore be vulnerable to a major surprise attack. If the South's initial forward defenses to an armored attack should falter there would be little time to bring up reinforcements. On the other hand, the terrain north of Seoul provides obstacles that would channel an attack from the North into vulnerable concentration points along the two principal approaches to the city. In addition, extensive barrier systems have been emplaced by the South.

Both South and North Korea have undertaken significant improvements in their forces. In 1971, South Korea began a modernization program with $1.5 billion in U.S. military assistance. Later, in 1975, after the collapse of Vietnam, it began an ambitious and expensive ($5-billion) force improvement plan. The South Koreans intend to substantially increase their fighter aircraft with F-4Es and F-5Es, improve their air defenses, upgrade their tank fleet, acquire antitank missiles, and commence some domestic production of small arms and artillery. With foreign military sales credits, a realistic completion date of the improvement plan would be 1983. The United States has agreed to transfer to the Republic, subject to congressional assent, much of the equipment of the Second Division as it is withdrawn, including helicopters, artillery, antitank weapons, and tanks, valued in all at $800 million.

North Korea, although operating from a weaker economic base, has concentrated much more heavily upon military priorities than has the South. During the 1971 to 1977 period, North Korea also pursued an extensive modernization program emphasizing armored and artillery forces. It has developed a domestic weapons production base currently larger than that in South Korea, which enables it to be relatively independent of the Soviet Union or the People's Republic of China for small arms, armored personnel carriers, tanks, and even submarines. Even with increased stockpiles, however, North Korea is estimated still to be heavily dependent on logistical support from these two countries for sustained combat. For advanced weaponry, such as improved air defense missiles or aircraft, North Korea must continue to rely upon Soviet assistance.

In sum, the military balance between North and South Korea has not been and will not be static. Time seems clearly to be on the side of the South, with its much larger economic base and its access to Western technology, while the growth of North Korean capabilities depends in large measure on Soviet decisions. The USSR has not sent to North Korea the advanced combat aircraft and mobile surface-to-air missiles that were provided to Egypt and Syria, and at present Moscow's policy in Korea generally appears to be one of restraint.

EFFECT OF U.S. TROOP WITHDRAWAL. The relative military contribution of U.S. forces in South Korea has diminished in recent years but remains significant in command and control, tactical air support, logistics, intelligence, and ground force mobility and firepower. The three squadrons of F-4 tactical fighter aircraft in Korea and other U.S. tactical air forces in the Western Pacific supplement the South's capability in an area of diminishing advantage for the North. Even after 1983, nonetheless, a U.S. tactical air presence will be required to assure adequate direct support firepower to counter a North Korean armored attack. The contribution of the Second Infantry Division to the defense of South Korea has been in command and control, intelligence gathering, and—what is more important— mobility and antitank firepower to supplement the capabilities of the single ROK mechanized division.

A first phase of the removal of the Second Division was scheduled for 1978. But because Congress delayed in authorizing the transfer of military equipment to South Korea, President Carter has limited the 1978 withdrawal to a small contingent of combat troops. In any case, the plan had been to keep the core of the division's combat capability in Korea until the final phase in 1982 or 1983.

The Carter administration has stated that the withdrawal of ground forces will be subject to change depending upon developments on the peninsula. If the division is finally removed, there would still be several ways in which American military power and political commitment in the area could be made visible as the withdrawal proceeds. These could include transferring an F-4 squadron from the Philippines to South Korea, using the Chinhae naval support base as the home port for some Navy vessels, and conducting periodic joint military exercises with South Korean forces, in which possibilities for rapid reinforcement from the United States could be demonstrated.

Whether the Second Division should eventually be brought home rests primarily on the assessment, which remains controversial, that the risk of an automatic involvement of ground forces in a new Korean war outweighs the risk of upsetting the military balance and encouraging a North Korean attack. Budget considerations were not paramount in the decision. Indeed, for the short run the withdrawal will have a distinctly negative impact. One-time costs of rebasing the division will be in the order of $500 million, while if Congress agrees to transfer to South Korea the bulk of the division's equipment the reequipment cost will be at least another $800 million. Once based in the United States, the division's annual costs are expected to be cut by about $110 million.

If economies alone were the objective, at least two alternatives would be available. One would be to withdraw from the force structure the two Marine regiments and the Marine air wing from Japan, for savings of about $250 million a year between fiscal 1979 and 1983. The Marines, who are lightly equipped for action in the event of a Korean war, have no other evident mission in Asia to justify so large a force. Another would be to use Japan as the home port for a second Seventh Fleet carrier. If opposition in Japan could be overcome, this would allow the retirement of two carriers from the fleet, with estimated savings of $2.1 billion over the period.

GROUND AND AIR FORCES IN THE PACIFIC. Although the two Marine regiments in Okinawa (another in Hawaii rounds out the Third Division) could be deployed to Korea in an emergency, this force is not suited for a war against armored troops, and it could not get to Korea any sooner than Army or Marine units in Hawaii or in California. Other missions for these relatively large numbers of Marines—13,000—are obscure. A much smaller regional force would be sufficient for local contingencies like the often-cited *Mayaguez* incident in 1975 and even for a core capability for amphibious assault in Korea. The possible reaction in Japan would have to be taken into account, however, before a further reduction in the American military presence in the area could be proposed.

At all events, the trend surely is toward virtually exclusive reliance on air and naval power to sustain U.S. security interests in Asia and the Pacific. Large Soviet armies and air forces in the Far East are directed overwhelmingly toward China. (The Soviet Pacific Fleet and its air units, as potential threats to Japan and to U.S. naval forces, are considered in the following section.) Soviet air power, particularly if the long-range Backfire bomber is deployed to the Far East, could be given a variety of missions, including attacks on Japan's sea lines of communication, but its primary assignment is China.

At present, U.S. land-based air power in East Asia appears to be sufficient for likely contingencies. Besides the Air Force wing in South Korea, there are two wings, one Marine and one Air Force, in Japan and two squadrons at Clark Field in the Philippines. These forces can be reinforced rapidly from Hawaii or the continental United States; in 1976, after an incident in the demilitarized zone in Korea, a squadron of F-111s from Idaho was in Korea and in operational status within fifteen hours after being alerted. Presumably, prudence would argue against any significant reduction in the Asian-based air forces until the impact, political or otherwise, of the withdrawal of the Second Infantry Division from Korea has been fully absorbed.

General Purpose Naval Forces

The Navy differs from the Army and the Air Force in the relatively long time needed to change the character of its forces. Shipbuilding commitments made during the next five years will not have an appreciable effect on the naval force structure until the late 1980s or early 1990s. Many of the ships built now can be expected to be in service after the turn of the century. Today's decisions about shipbuilding programs relate less to the kind of Navy that is desired for the next decade than to the requirements and thus the capabilities anticipated for the 1990s and beyond.

The Carrier Navy

In its present configuration, the U.S. general purpose Navy is centered on the thirteen aircraft carriers in the fleet.[1] This reflects judgments made in the past about the defense needs for naval power. Given the expected service life of the existing carriers, these ships, with their expensive escorts, support vessels, and complex aircraft built especially for the carrier missions will continue to dominate the Navy's structure through the rest of the century—unless, that is, major and seemingly unlikely changes are made in the Navy's programs. A carrier and the ships and aircraft associated with it cost $4 billion to $6 billion to buy and about as much again to operate over fifteen years. Although change appears somewhat remote today, the place of these costly ships in the American defense structure of the future is open to serious question.

AIR ATTACK MISSION. One of the wartime missions that has been assigned to the carrier task force Navy has been air attack against Soviet naval and air facilities and support of possible amphibious operations on the flanks of the NATO region in Norway, Turkey, and

---

1. Although there are thirteen carriers in service, one—the *Coral Sea*—is not capable of handling the most advanced naval aircraft under combat conditions. In 1980 the carrier *Saratoga* is scheduled for a major overhaul to extend its service life. If the carrier force is to be kept at twelve during that overhaul, it will be necessary to assign aircraft to the *Coral Sea*.

Greece. The carrier missions might include destruction of naval facilities in the Soviet Union, bombing of airfields that would be supporting an attack on the northern and southern flanks, and protection of allied territory. Amphibious operations on the flanks might be for the purpose of recapturing bases seized by the Russians in the early stages of a war.

The Soviet response to the U.S. carrier task force has been to devote large resources to creating a defense capability emphasizing cruise missiles to be fired from submarines, surface ships, and land-based aircraft, coordinated if possible in saturation attacks.

In turn, the United States has had to buy defensive aircraft (F-14 fighters) and escorts with antisubmarine and anti-air systems. But despite these protective systems, the surface fleet's offensive capability, concentrated in a few carriers, has become—at least pending the development of more effective defenses—notably vulnerable when deployed within range of Soviet defensive power, as in the eastern Mediterranean and the Norwegian Sea.

Given the carrier's vulnerability, a reasonably ready alternative for the defense of the NATO flank would be to station, or deploy on warning, land-based aircraft and mobile air defense units to defend against Soviet attempts to seize or neutralize bases. In a later stage of conflict, after Soviet defenses had suffered some attrition, carriers might be deployed at more acceptable levels of risk.

PROTECTION OF SEA LANES. The traditional and still primary naval mission is to protect sea lines of communication. If Soviet forces were able to mount a sustained attack on these communications—which is by no means certain—then protection would be needed both to enable carriers and amphibious forces to perform missions, such as those cited above, and to assure the flow of supplies when NATO forces would have to be reprovisioned by sea, probably after thirty days of fighting. If the Russians could effectively interrupt the resupply operation, NATO might be unable to maintain a nonnuclear defense. In the Far East, similarly, a sufficient threat to sea lanes could cut Japan off from food and raw materials, including fuel. Unless Japan's stockpile position were to be made much more comfortable than it is at present, a threat to merchant shipping might force Japan to abandon its alliance with the United States and to accept Soviet terms.

If the Russians were to mount a naval threat to military and merchant ship movements in a nonnuclear conflict, the submarine would be its principal vehicle. The carrier would not be a normal choice to counter that threat against convoys. This duty in the first instance would fall on U.S. attack submarines, antisubmarine surface vessels, and land-based aircraft, all relying on advanced detection and destruction devices. Although the carrier carries some antisubmarine aircraft, it must itself depend on the other systems for underwater protection. Carrier aircraft, to be sure, would be the main counter to hostile surface ships in the rather improbable event that the Soviet command would risk its combatant vessels in ocean areas outside the range of land-based air cover. In due course, the deployment of the short-range (60-nautical-mile) Harpoon and the longer-range (300-nautical-mile) Tomahawk cruise missile on surface vessels will reduce the importance of the carrier for this limited role. In the sectors where Soviet land-based aircraft might be more effectively used against merchant convoys—in the Atlantic along the line and above the line from the United Kingdom through Iceland and Greenland—it will be possible to detect and intercept hostile forces from air bases on land.

In short, there seems to be little doubt that existing naval forces, other than carriers, and land-based aircraft are now adequate to protect essential movements by sea against the kind of attacks that appear at all likely. Planned improvement should preserve this capability in the face of increased and improved Soviet forces. Thus the need for the carrier in this role is questionable.

POLITICAL PRESENCE. If neither offensive action against Soviet or nearby areas, such as the Mediterranean, nor sea control are in fact going to be the missions primarily of the aircraft carrier, there still will be the tasks of protecting or advancing American interests where local upheavals or conflicts may occur or simply of demonstrating in distant places the reality of U.S. naval and air power. Under current circumstances, the carrier certainly can discharge these responsibilities. Carrier task forces have the unique and important advantage of being able to use air power in a local crisis without having to secure approval for, depend upon, or defend, land bases. The ability to conduct essentially self-sustained operations offshore is an attractive option to retain for a variety of contingencies short of a major U.S.-

USSR war. Even as new ships like the five large (40,000-ton) helicopter assault vessels (LHAs) come into service, the carrier undoubtedly will continue to provide a valuable crisis response force.

But in a total accounting, the principal functions of the carrier may be less and less directly related to the most crucial defense contingency—a war engaging the United States and the USSR. The question then is whether the general purpose Navy of the longer-run future should not be different from the one inherited from an earlier era.

The Soviet Naval Missions

The missions of the Soviet Navy are dictated by geographical limitations, by the perceived threat from abroad, and by the particular kinds of forces that have been produced to meet that threat.

Geography is a ma;or constraint. Soviet naval vessels must traverse straits and narrow seas to and from their home bases. This is true for three of the fleets: the Northern Fleet based in the Barents Sea, the Baltic Fleet, and the Black Sea Fleet. Except for a remote submarine base on the Kamchatka Peninsula, it is also true of the Pacific Fleet. The risk of being denied ready access to their secure bases means that Soviet ships are limited in their ability to operate outside home waters or to attempt to control broad areas of the oceans.

The Soviet Union sees a twofold threat from abroad to be countered with naval forces: the U.S. ballistic missile and bomber forces that can target on the Soviet Union from the United States and naval forces—aircraft carriers and ballistic missile submarines—that can mount nuclear or conventional weapon attacks against the Soviet Union. The missions assigned to the Soviet Navy are "fleet against shore" and "fleet against fleet."

THE "FLEET AGAINST SHORE" MISSION. Ballistic missile submarines are assigned the task of attacking enemy land areas. They require extensive protection against advanced U.S. antisubmarine warfare systems and that, in turn, becomes a major mission for Soviet nuclear attack submarines, for large antisubmarine surface ships, such as the *Kiev* aircraft carrier, and for some aircraft.

THE "FLEET AGAINST FLEET" MISSION. There are two objectives: defense of the homeland against seaborne attack, mainly by carriers, and antisubmarine warfare against U.S. ballistic submarines.

Attack submarines, surface ships equipped with cruise missiles, and land-based aircraft, supported by surveillance systems, which include ships, aircraft, satellites, and land-based electronics, are charged with this mission.

In recent years the Soviet Navy has shown an active interest in obtaining overseas bases for ships and aircraft and for peacetime surveillance. Soviet naval ships have been regularly deployed in the Pacific and Indian Oceans, as well as in the Atlantic and the Mediterranean Sea. These displays of force undoubtedly are in part for political effect, in part for more definitive military and intelligence purposes. But Soviet ships away from their home bases would be extremely vulnerable in wartime; and the Soviet fleet has not been developed for the purpose of control over distant seas.

The Surface Navy in the 1980s

In 1976 the Ford administration set out a five-year program for what it regarded as a balanced Navy with a long-term goal of about 550 general purpose ships, compared with the 1979 fleet of 416 ships. All aspects of naval power were to be enhanced, including the addition of two medium-sized (40,000- to 50,000-ton) carriers to be used outside the areas where defenses are strongest. The Ford administration, like the Carter administration later, rejected proposals for a new, fifth, large-deck (90,000-ton) nuclear aircraft carrier because of concerns over cost and vulnerability. The growing vulnerability of the existing carrier force was not overlooked but was to be remedied by providing each carrier with cruiser or destroyer escorts equipped with the AEGIS air defense system.[2] Research and development was to be accelerated on the advanced vertical or short take-off and landing (V/STOL) aircraft that would operate from medium-sized carriers and other "air capable" ships so as to disperse air power throughout the fleet in many vessels.

The Carter administration's current proposals amount to a considerable write-down from the Ford program but they would not alter the basic carrier-centered structure of the Navy during the next decade. One new 60,000-ton conventionally powered carrier would

2. The AEGIS system combines with a radar and computer, which can track a large number of targets, surface-to-air missiles, which need not be controlled until they approach close to their target. It can engage a number of targets simultaneously, as in a saturation attack of cruise missiles.

be added to the fleet, and a program to extend the service lives of existing carriers (from thirty to fifty-five years) would be carried forward—in effect, assuring that the fleet would have a total of thirteen in 1990, as in 1979. The requisite large investment would be made in AEGIS-equipped escorts—probably all destroyers—needed to protect the carriers from hostile forces. These destroyers are expected to cost $500 million, and one or two will be bought to protect each carrier. AEGIS would be the only major capability in the 1990 Navy that has not yet been introduced into the fleet.

Under the Carter plans, the general purpose Navy of 1990 would have ninety fewer ships than under the Ford administration proposals (see table 9-3), and shipbuilding costs would be down by about $24 billion over the five-year period of 1979 to 1983. But the 1990 fleet would be much like the present one, with fifty more ships, mostly escorts, than are projected for 1979. By implication, planning would continue to call for deploying four carrier task forces forward, two in the Mediterranean and two in the Western Pacific. This forward deployment requires at least twelve carriers, assuming the continuation of current policy of rotating forces overseas every six months and using Japan as the home port for one carrier. To the extent that forward deployment policy is the major factor influencing the carrier force level, two carriers could be retired if an additional carrier also used an overseas home port.

There will be further decisions for this administration and its successor to make, but the commitment to the aircraft carrier for the next decade, as represented by the destroyer building and carrier service life extension programs, appears to be firm. Misgivings about the vulnerability of these large and costly ships either have been set aside or have been reduced in the light of the potential of the AEGIS and other protective systems.

The prospect for large-scale retirements of older ships in the 1990s (see table 9-3) means that those deciding building programs in 1983 and 1984 will have to face more squarely the question of the kind of fleet that will be needed in the last years of the century. For the present, it seems, decisions for change are being deferred.

A number of considerations may have contributed to the choices now being made. One is that the existing Navy is built around the carrier, with its known qualities and capabilities. Since advanced defensive weapon systems may make the carrier less vulnerable within

Table 9-3. Projections of Numbers of General Purpose Ships in Use in 1979, 1983, and 1990, and Retirements between 1990 and 2000

Type of ship	1979	1983	1990 Ford	1990 Carter	Retirements, 1990–2000
Aircraft carriers	13	13	15	13	1
Cruisers and destroyers	102	108	106	99	48
Escorts	65	96	156	115	45
Attack submarines[a]	80	90	87	84	44
Amphibious	65	65	65	60	47
Minesweeper and patrol	6	10	27	17	2
Support	85	95	92	70	31
Total	416	477	548	458	218

Sources: 1979 and 1983 figures are derived from a Navy computer printout (February 3, 1978; processed) identifying ships in the fleet by age, ships approved from prior years but not yet delivered, and projected deliveries by 1983. The 1990 Ford force is derived from the program shown in *Department of Defense Appropriations for 1978*, Hearings before the House Appropriations Committee, 95:1 (GPO, 1977), p. 356. The 1990 Carter force is derived from Secretary of Defense Harold Brown's proposed five-year shipbuilding program under cover of a letter to Speaker of the House Thomas P. O'Neill, March 1978. Both 1990 forces include building programs through 1985. Retirements are estimated using the Navy computer printouts and recent Navy experience.

a. Nuclear, except for six in 1979 and two in 1983.

the next few years, the argument for staying with an existing force, which still has important advantages, could be persuasive. Moreover, the carriers have elicited a substantial buildup of Soviet forces over the years. In the absence of the carriers, these forces would be available to disrupt sea communications or to further challenge the U.S. ballistic missile submarines.

Finally, the forward-deployed carrier task force has long been the symbol of American military power in the Mediterranean and the Far East. What the political reactions would be in Italy, Greece, Turkey, Egypt, and Israel—or Japan—if smaller ships were to be substituted for carriers is uncertain, but the hazard is that they would be unfavorable. At home, the carrier has powerful advocates in Congress and the Navy. So it is by no means assured that the proposed slowdown in new ship construction will be accepted. Any proposal for more fundamental change would encounter serious resistance.

Naval Aviation

The carriers operating through the 1980s will either have to add a substantial number of new fighter and attack aircraft or have to extend the life of existing aircraft through extensive maintenance overhauls and the procurement of new engines. The Marines will also require new planes for their fighter and attack aircraft inventory to replace aging aircraft.

Under the Ford administration's plans, nine carriers would have been fully equipped with the advanced and expensive F-14 fighter by 1981, giving them the maximum available ability to carry out missions against Soviet defenses. A new fighter, the F-18, and its attack version, the A-18, was to be bought for the other carriers and the Marine air force. Development of the vertical and short take-off aircraft, the AV-8B, would have been pressed forward.

The Carter administration has made two modifications in these proposals. Completion of the F-14 program would be slowed, so that the target of eighteen squadrons would be reached in 1985 rather than in 1981. And the V/STOL development program would be put on a slower schedule. The somewhat controversial F-18–A-18 program, costing an estimated $8 billion over the next twelve years, would be carried through.

Proponents of the F-18–A-18 proposal make a number of points: the new fighter will provide the Navy with a more appropriate and less costly plane than the F-14 for use in lower-threat (that is, non-Soviet) environments. At the same time it will replace the Marines' inventory of F-4s. The A-18 will replace the Navy's A-7 attack aircraft with a plane sharing common features with the F-18 fighter, thus promising savings in operating costs. It will also give the Marine air arm a new aircraft without waiting for the—uncertain—development of V/STOL technology.

There are counterarguments to each of these points. First, the value of the F-18's dogfight capability is in question at a time when more advanced aircraft, such as the Russian MIG-23, are likely to be available to a number of countries. The F-14 fighter with the Phoenix missile could shoot down such aircraft at a distance. Second, the Navy's A-7 can be upgraded by adding a new engine, while the life of the Marines' F-4 can be extended by replacing and strengthening the wings. A relatively low-cost attack plane, the A-4, is available to the Marine Corps instead of the F-18. Third, the anticipated savings in operating costs may be illusory. It could be cheaper to continue with current aircraft models with which the Navy and Marine Corps will have had twenty years' experience by the late 1980s, than to switch to a few new, relatively untried models. Finally, although

V/STOL technology is indeed uncertain, and will in any case cost more per unit to attain the capability of a conventional aircraft, a successful V/STOL aircraft would greatly increase the number of ships capable of handling sea-based aviation missions. The AV-8B aircraft could provide a bridge between the operational sea-based V/STOL aircraft and a new generation of such aircraft for the 1990s.

Congress undoubtedly will wish to consider alternatives to or modifications of the administration's proposals, the more so because important domestic and regional economic interests are involved. With the commitment to the big carrier having been confirmed, however, there is no possibility of a radical change in the naval aircraft program, any more than in the basic configuration of the Navy itself.

Submarines

One of the most versatile of naval systems is the nuclear-powered attack submarine. This boat can be used to conduct barrier patrols in the straits and narrow seas surrounding the Soviet Union, to trail and destroy Soviet submarines, and to act as escort for aircraft carriers.

The U.S. attack submarine force will be subject to "block obsolescence" in the 1990s when over forty of the ships can be expected to be retired (see table 9-3), so that unless a construction program of four to five new boats a year is undertaken no later than the mid-1980s the force level will fall significantly. While U.S. submarines have a marked qualitative advantage over Soviet boats, the numbers in the Soviet Navy are larger, a difference that will continue to grow unless the high unit costs of the U.S. vessels can be reduced. A new class of cheaper submarines, now under consideration, will need to be pursued intensively if the fleet is to be maintained at levels consistent with the expected growth and improvement of the Soviet undersea navy.

The Russians have taken seriously the vulnerability of their ballistic missile submarines to U.S. attack submarines. Both Soviet attack submarines and most surface ships (including the *Kiev* aircraft carrier) now act as antisubmarine escorts for Soviet ballistic missile submarines. Further, the Russians have developed and deployed longer-range missiles that can be fired from home waters in the Barents Sea and the Pacific.

Soviet antisubmarine warfare capabilities—in particular, detection—may also eventually be sufficient to threaten the U.S. ballistic missile submarine force. If such a Soviet capability is developed, the U.S. attack submarines, in addition to protecting general purpose ships like the aircraft carrier, would also be used to protect strategic ballistic missile submarines.

In the long run, the U.S. attack submarine combined with other antisubmarine forces could, by threatening the Soviet ballistic missile submarines and their protective forces, provide a substitute for aircraft carriers in diverting Soviet naval resources from offensive operations against sea lines of communication and the U.S. ballistic missile submarines.

The Navy beyond 1990

If the Carter program is adopted, the Navy of 1990 will look much like the Navy of 1979, with the same number of aircraft carriers, almost the same number of cruisers and destroyers for protecting carriers, but with fifty more escorts for assuring sea lines of communication. Other major ship types will be at about the same level as in 1979, with only smaller ship types and support vessels at significantly lower levels. The next five years, however, will provide the opportunity to reexamine the appropriate missions for the Navy of the future, to guide the development and design of the ships that will be bought between 1985 and 1995 for the Navy of the following century, and to make greater use of land-based aircraft. It seems inevitable that the direction of change will have to be away from a carrier-centered fleet to a Navy with much more widely dispersed offensive power and an enhanced ability to protect both merchant shipping and the strategic submarine force.

Strategic Nuclear Forces

The Carter budget for fiscal 1979, as noted in chapter 8, sets the direct costs of strategic nuclear forces at $11.6 billion, about the same figure as in fiscal 1977. Congressional approval of the administration's proposal would mean a real reduction of 11.2 percent from the 1977 level. The highly controversial decision to cancel the B-1 bomber was the principal factor influencing this course of strategic force spending. Other strategic force decisions are still pending, however. They promise to be equally controversial and will have a similarly large impact on the strategic sector of future defense budgets.

The Carter administration has reaffirmed the main premises of strategic doctrine as these have evolved under earlier presidencies. Accepted without question is the requirement for a credible deterrent, which is to say the assured ability to retaliate after absorbing a Soviet nuclear attack. Nuclear stability—a situation in which neither superpower has, or sees the other as acquiring, a first-strike advantage—is also considered an important objective. As a corollary, "essential equivalence" with the USSR in nuclear weapons is considered necessary, particularly to insure against any perception by its allies that the United States may be falling behind the Soviet Union in strategic nuclear power. The ability to respond to a Soviet attack in a controlled and selective fashion has also been endorsed.

Secretary of Defense Brown has made it clear that the United States would prefer to maintain nuclear balance by way of arms control agreements but that the option of taking unilateral action to preserve equivalence and stability must remain open.

The elements of strategic doctrine, of course, can be interpreted and applied in different ways. Statements of the current administration suggest other departures from the views of the Ford administration besides the obvious disagreement about the requirement for producing the B-1 bomber. Thus the Ford administration tended to define essential equivalence as meaning that the United States should offset Soviet superiority in certain static indicators of strategic power, such as throw-weight of missiles or numbers of delivery vehicles, by maintaining a lead in other specific measures of nuclear strength. Secretary Brown contends that equivalence can better be calculated in terms of the target destruction potential of the two nations under reasonable assumptions about the character of a possible conflict. He has stressed mutual deterrence based on capacity for assured destruction and appears skeptical about strategic planning based on limited nuclear war scenarios. A limited nuclear exchange is unlikely, he believes, since "any use of nuclear weapons would run the risk of rapid escalation."[3] Nonetheless, the administration has approved funds for

3. *Department of Defense Authorization for Appropriations for Fiscal Year 1978, Hearings on Military Posture and H.R. 5068 [H.R. 5960] and H.R. 1755,* Hearings before the House Armed Services Committee, 95:1 (GPO, 1977), pt. 1, p. 96.

improving the effectiveness and targeting flexibility of the Minuteman missiles so as to improve the strategic force's ability to respond selectively to a possible Soviet limited nuclear attack.

In general, the Carter administration's warnings about the Soviet strategic buildup appear to be more restrained than those of the Ford administration. This can be attributed to at least two considerations. While concerned over the continued strengthening of Soviet forces, it has also been worried about the exaggeration of Soviet strategic capabilities. Secretary Brown has suggested that "alarmist" statements about relative U.S. and Soviet nuclear positions could have the effect of eroding the confidence of U.S. allies, leading to a political advantage for the USSR. Second, the administration's more skeptical outlook on the political and military utility of strategic nuclear weapons is coupled with its concern over the conventional balance between NATO and the Warsaw Pact. As a consequence, it has accorded relatively higher priority and greater attention to what it considers a more immediate danger, an unstable military situation in Europe; Secretary Brown has noted that preoccupation with implausible Soviet strategic threats could divert attention and resources from the pressing need to strengthen conventional military capabilities.

The differences of strategic view between the Carter and Ford administrations will probably find expression in decisionmaking about the intercontinental ballistic missile (ICBM) portions of the present strategic nuclear triad of land-based missiles, ballistic missile submarines, and bombers.

Intercontinental Ballistic Missiles

The American ICBM force consists of 1,000 Minutemen and 54 older Titan II missiles in silos located principally in the western United States. Of the total, 550 Minuteman IIIs have been fitted with multiple, independently targetable reentry vehicles (MIRVs), which make possible attacks on widely separated targets with warheads released from a single missile. In addition, Minuteman warheads have been improved in accuracy and yield, targeting has been made more flexible, and silos have been strengthened (hardened). This ICBM force has been considered to combine characteristics of accuracy, destructive potential, and selective responsiveness to command and control, which together make it a distinctive and valuable part of the triad.

Now, however, the momentum of Soviet ICBM programs has raised serious doubts about the ability of the Minuteman missiles to survive a counterforce strike in the years just ahead. As the estimated accuracy of some of the new-generation, MIRVed Soviet missiles has improved faster than expected, the prospect has grown that in the early to mid-1980s a relatively small part of the Soviet ICBM force would be able to destroy most of the Minutemen in a single strike. That threat was judged to be sufficiently serious by the Ford administration to warrant a fiscal 1978 budget request for the accelerated development of a new ICBM, the M-X, that would be deployed in a fashion calculated to reduce the vulnerability of the U.S. ICBM force. The Carter budget for fiscal 1979 provides funds for continued but slower M-X development, while the decision about eventual procurement and deployment has been deferred.

SOVIET STRATEGY. The question of ICBM vulnerability involves estimates of Soviet strategy and risk assessment as well as Soviet capabilities. It seems evident, on the one hand, that a decision to strike at the Minuteman force would require that a rational Soviet leadership resolve a number of crucial uncertainties. Some would be technical. It is not known, for example, how missiles would perform in a large-scale attack; one warhead's nuclear detonation could destroy or disable others, the so-called fratricide problem. But even if all the Minutemen could be destroyed, strategic bombers on alert and ballistic missile submarines at sea could deliver a devastating response (more than 2,000 sea-launched warheads alone) against Soviet population centers and industries and also against military targets. Since even an attack limited to the ICBM silos could result in an enormous loss of American lives—estimates range from 5 million to 20 million—it would represent an extraordinary view of things on the Soviet part to discount the likelihood of an American retaliatory strike. Indeed, Moscow could not be sure that the United States would not elect to launch the Minutemen themselves in the very short interval between warning of a Soviet attack and the arrival of Soviet warheads.

On the other side of the case, some of the uncertainties about reliability and accuracy of the Soviet ICBMs will be reduced as modernization and test programs are continued. Beyond that, the Soviet leaders could proceed from an estimate that developing a large counterforce capability would give them major advantages. For one thing, the confidence of U.S. allies could be shaken, once the imbalance in ICBM forces was fully grasped. For another, the Soviet position in some future crisis might be strengthened if an American administration knew that its ICBM force—its principal means for flexible, limited response—was at risk; for, by hypothesis, to order a retaliatory response to a Soviet attack would then expose the country to a Soviet second strike, this time against population centers.

Whether Soviet politicians and planners draw up scenarios along these lines is not known. Nor can it be known, of course, whether the leaders of the USSR would act in the way presupposed. Soviet military writings continue to focus on the actual fighting of a nuclear war and on developing the capability to wage it; the proposition that a nuclear war might be fought and in some sense won can be found in these doctrinal pronouncements. The political leadership, however, echo American presidents in expressing the belief that a nuclear exchange could only be a catastrophe for both sides.[4] What is not in doubt is that the USSR has been largely indifferent to proposals for mutual restraint on an ICBM buildup that could be considered to give first-strike advantages and to warnings that the United States would have to react to the prospect of a serious imbalance in ICBM counterforce capabilities. Since 1972, four new fourth-generation Soviet ICBM systems have been flight-tested and at least three of them are being deployed. A fifth generation of at least four other ICBM systems is known to be under development. This modernization was allowed under the SALT I agreement freezing the levels of ICBM launchers, but it has gone forward on an unexpectedly broad scale.

U.S. RESPONSE. The M-X missile has been under development since 1974 as a potential counter to the strengthened Soviet land-based missile force. As envisaged by Ford's planners, it would be much more powerful—with about three times the throw-weight—and considerably more accurate than the Minuteman III. While it could be deployed in a variety of ways, including installing it in existing Minuteman silos, in a large constellation of shelters (some of which would be empty), or in new silos, a much-discussed proposal has been to put the M-X in concrete-covered trenches where it could

4. Leonid Brezhnev, speaking at Vladivostok on April 7, 1978, said: ". . . there is no more important task in present conditions, one touching the destiny of every person on earth, to ensure progress toward reducing and eventually removing the threat of a thermo-nuclear disaster" (Foreign Broadcast Information Service, *Daily Report: Soviet Union*, vol. 3, no. 68 (April 7, 1978), p. R-1).

be shuttled from place to place so as to minimize its vulnerability to Soviet ICBM targeting. Estimates are that the deployment of 200 M-X missiles in trenches would cost about.

A number of nonbudgetary questions about the M-X remain. In the design proposed by the Ford administration it would be itself a major counterforce weapon. Deployed in numbers beyond two hundred it would pose a severe threat to the Soviet ICBM force, which is a much larger part of Soviet strategic nuclear capability than the Minuteman's part in the U.S. triad.

Unless the United States restricted the force level of an M-X system, the Soviet Union might become as concerned with the vulnerability of its ICBM system as the United States is becoming about the Minuteman. And, again, if the M-X missiles were housed in the fairly vulnerable Minuteman III silos, they might pose a real threat to nuclear stability, since the Soviet Union could regard them as more accessible and more valuable targets than their predecessors. On the other hand, if the M-X could be made secure against any likely Soviet strike, the United States would not be under pressure to "use or lose" its ICBMs in a crisis.

A semimobile deployment of M-X missiles also would have problems associated with it. Concealment would contribute to survivability, but it might also preclude or seriously limit the assured verification of force levels important to nuclear stability. While agreed rules for verification might be negotiated, it is at least equally conceivable that the Russians would themselves move to a form of concealed deployment. Indirect verification of force levels would be more difficult for the United States than for the USSR, given the lack of open sources on Soviet nuclear programs.

There are some important uncertainties, moreover, about the effectiveness of M-X deployment in covered concrete trenches. The possible effect on the missiles of shock waves set off by a Soviet nuclear hit on a trench is still to be determined. A concentrated location for deployment of the M-X compared with the widely dispersed deployment of the Minuteman force might be another source of vulnerability. And it is predictable that the M-X program would encounter resistance and delays because of concerns over the environmental impact of the trench or other new basing modes using large areas of federal land.

Given the problems associated with the M-X, a basically different option, which would be less expensive and possibly lead to greater nuclear stability, would be to phase down or eliminate the Minuteman force and to rely upon an upgraded and expanded submarine-launched ballistic missile force, along with the currently planned air-launched cruise missile and an upgraded B-52.

Submarine-Launched Ballistic Missiles

The Navy's current force of ten Polaris and thirty-one Poseidon nuclear-powered ballistic missile submarines (SSBNs) was built between 1959 and 1967. These submarines are considered by the Navy to have useful service lives of twenty and twenty-five years, respectively, so that "block obsolescence" is a near-term prospect. A replacement SSBN, the Trident, is now in production; it is designed to be faster and quieter than existing submarines and it will carry a longer-range (4,000-nautical-mile) missile, the Trident I, and in larger numbers (twenty-four as against sixteen) than the current force.

Present programming calls for thirteen Tridents, with the first scheduled to come into service in 1981 (if all the launchers were to be replaced, it would require twice this number). The cost of the scheduled Trident program, which includes the installation of Trident I missiles in twelve Poseidon submarines, is now estimated at $30 billion in current dollars. Unanticipated problems have plagued production. The schedule on the first boat has slipped one year and its cost has increased 50 percent, from $0.8 billion to $1.2 billion. It is questionable whether sufficient numbers of Tridents will be available to offset a significant (from 656 to about 500) decline in the number of missiles that could be deployed in the early 1990s.

One solution would be to extend the expected service life of the thirty-one Poseidon submarines from twenty-five to thirty years. The life span of these boats is not known with certainty, and it is possible that they could be maintained for a few additional years at a reasonable cost.[5] Extending their lives another five years would postpone a "drop-off" in force levels until about 1996. They could also be made more effective by being fitted with the Trident I missile.

An alternative or complementary approach would be to develop

---

5. According to the Navy's testimony before Congress, extending the service life of this force would cost about $2 billion in current dollars.

and deploy a smaller, lower-cost follow-on submarine to the Trident. The new submarine could be about half the size of the Trident, use a smaller nuclear reactor or some other type of advanced propulsion, and carry about sixteen Trident I missiles. Although a similar concept, known as the SSBN-X, was examined and rejected by the Navy in 1975 on the ground that it would not be as cost-effective as the larger Trident submarine, the continuing difficulties with the latter suggest that the matter should be reconsidered.

Deployment of a smaller, less expensive ballistic missile submarine ten years from now, as a supplement to the dozen or so Tridents that would then be operational, could offer several advantages. A smaller submarine might avoid many of the construction delays incurred by the Trident, which the Navy has attributed to its large size and complexity. This advantage, combined with the new boat's relatively lower cost, would allow an eventual increase in submarine production that would insure against a fall in future launcher force levels. The new small submarine would also increase the number of submarines on station that the USSR would have to locate and destroy, and its smaller size would be a hedge against the possible development of a Soviet antisubmarine warfare (ASW) detection system based on size or mass. In view of the ten-year lead time required, designs for this new submarine would have to be on the boards in the near future to meet the objectives described.

A further issue related to the sea-based ballistic missile force is the development of a Trident II missile. Deployment of this missile, which would have a greater range (6,000 nautical miles) and throw-weight than the Trident I, could begin in the late 1980s. Its range would further increase the operating area of the Trident submarine force and thereby its survivability.

The increased throw-weight of the Trident II, coupled with prospective improvements in missile accuracy during the next decade, could for the first time give the U.S. SLBM force a significant counterforce capability against hardened Soviet targets. Decisions about its production, which is expected to cost about $16 billion in current dollars, will involve questions both of need—will prospective ASW improvements require a hedge beyond that to be afforded by Trident I?—and of strategy—what will be the effect on nuclear stability of a presumptively invulnerable American counterforce?

All of the possible SLBM alternatives will need the long lead times that mark naval construction programs. While the ballistic missile submarine will continue to give the United States a highly survivable strategic capability, it will not substitute for the Minuteman's combination of accuracy and destructive power until perhaps the late 1980s. In earlier prospect are improvements in the third element of the triad, air-launched nuclear weapons.

Bombers and Cruise Missiles

President Ford's 1978 budget request would have begun production of 241 B-1 aircraft, with total research, development, and procurement costs of $24.8 billion. The first production aircraft was scheduled to be operational in 1980. President Carter canceled B-1 production in favor of a much less expensive but equally effective force, making more extensive use of newly developed, highly accurate cruise missiles (ALCMs), which can be launched from stand-off aircraft (outside Soviet air defenses). By 1985 roughly one-half of the weapons of the U.S. strategic bomber force will be long-range cruise missiles to be launched from B-52s. Of the 349 B-52s currently in the bomber force, 173 B-52 G-class aircraft will be converted to carry up to twenty long-range, air-launched cruise missiles each. The remaining B-52 D and H aircraft as well as 66 FB-111As will be retained as penetrating bombers that will be expected to attack targets at close range with gravity bombs or short-range attack missiles (SRAMs). The Department of Defense believes that these bombers can effectively penetrate existing Soviet air defenses and that they are likely to be able to do so at least until 1985.

During the early 1980s the mixed force of stand-off cruise missile carriers and penetrating bombers will greatly complicate the task of Soviet air defenses, which will have to be prepared to cope with two systems of attack. After 1985 the ability of the upgraded B-52s to conduct attacks on the USSR probably will come increasingly into question. By the mid-1980s, the Soviet Union could have begun to upgrade its air defenses with three new systems—a warning and control aircraft with the ability to track objects flying near the ground, an advanced interceptor with a "look down, shoot down" capability, and surface-to-air-missiles effective at low altitudes.

The 1979 budget contains substantial funding for research and development for hedges against such improved Soviet air defenses. They include reduced detectability and increased speed for the air-launched cruise missile and studies of wide-bodied aircraft (such as 747s carrying about sixty ALCMs) as cruise missile carriers for the mid- to late 1980s. Testing of three B-1 prototypes will continue and studies will be conducted of less costly ways, such as stretching the FB-111 aircraft, to keep alive the option to produce a new penetrating bomber for use after the mid-1980s.

Adherents of the mixed-force concept warn that a force made up only of cruise missile carriers would enable the USSR to maximize defenses against this one type of potential attack. This might be done by extending barrier defenses of airborne warning aircraft and long-range interceptors far beyond the Soviet borders in an effort to intercept and destroy U.S. cruise missile carriers while still out of range of their targets. It is also argued that even a small force of penetrating bombers would ensure that the U.S. bomber force would be able to cover much of the Soviet target base as well as to strike targets with large gravity bombs that would otherwise require a disproportionate number of cruise missiles.

Funds have been requested in the fiscal 1979 budget to study the requirement for a penetrating bomber beyond 1985. One possibility would be to convert 65 existing FB-111A medium bombers at an estimated cost of $2.3 billion and to procure 100 new FB-111Hs for about $4.2 billion. The FB-111H would probably be less effective than the canceled B-1 bomber, but it could be maintained as a production option much longer than the B-1.

Critics of a new penetrating bomber argue that there is no compelling reason to consider its early deployment. Soviet air defenses against the present U.S. B-52 and FB-111A bombers are ineffective at low altitudes and will remain so at least through the early 1980s. The advanced air defense systems that could seriously threaten both the current penetrating bombers and the initial U.S. cruise missile do not exist today. Furthermore, the United States would have two to three years of warning before any substantial deployment of new systems could occur. In consequence, the case goes, the United States probably will not need to undertake advanced development of a new bomber until the character and extent of probable Soviet air defense improvements have become more evident. Existing bombers should be adequate to maintain a mixed force until that time and possibly even longer, given prospective advances in weapon systems for these aircraft.

The Future of the Nuclear Deterrent

As the foregoing discussion suggests, decisions must be made relatively soon both about the individual parts of the triad of nuclear deterrents and perhaps about the future of the triad concept itself. The issues center on the land-based ICBM force. It will be possible to begin to replace the capabilities of the increasingly vulnerable Minuteman with either the M-X system in the mid-1980s or the Trident II submarine-launched missile in the late 1980s. Cost is likely to rule out the development and deployment of both systems.

Choice of Trident II, with its long-range capability, would go far toward providing a maximum survivability to the U.S. nuclear deterrent. Armed with this missile, the submarine would have a very wide area of the oceans for its habitat, so wide as to make its detection and destruction an exceedingly formidable task. Moreover, if the Trident II is equipped with highly accurate (terminal-guidance) warheads, the ballistic missile submarine could be a close substitute for the M-X.

To put aside development of the M-X, however, could mean that as the Minuteman's vulnerability increases the land-based missile force might eventually have to be scrapped. The land-based ICBM has been regarded as a deterrent to a limited nuclear strike against the United States and as an important hedge against an unanticipated failure or vulnerability in other parts of the triad. It is also an element in essential equivalence.

As table 9-4 shows, the specific elements of the strategic nuclear situation have changed since the 1972 SALT agreements were concluded. By 1985, a still different constellation of nuclear forces will exist, with its details dependent on decisions yet to be made in Washington and Moscow. Although definitions of essential equivalence differ, static measures—numbers of launchers, missiles, warheads, and throw-weights—are customarily used as indicators. It is observed in table 9-4 that removal of the ICBMs from the U.S. armory would greatly alter the launcher ratio—and by extension other elements—in the nuclear relationship. In consequence, there will be strong pressure to keep the Minuteman force, despite its vulnerability. Unless substitute or replacement weapons—which could be the M-X or the Trident II and additional cruise missile carriers—become available, essential equivalence, at least as measured in static terms, may not be maintained past the mid-1980s.

Table 9-4. U.S. and Soviet Strategic Forces, 1972, 1977, and 1985

Index of strength	May 1972		October 1977		October 1985 with SALT II[a]		
	U.S.	USSR	U.S.	USSR	Ford	Carter	USSR
Force levels							
(launchers)	2,241	2,097	2,127	2,475	2,200	2,105	2,200
ICBMs	1,054	1,527	1,054	1,490	908	992	1,232
SLBMs	656	430	656	845	712	712	908
Heavy bombers	531	140	417	140	580	401	60
Throw-weight (millions							
of pounds)[b]	9.6	8.3	9.3	10.8	14.9	9.5	14.1
Missiles only	3.9	7.2	4.5	9.7	5.0	4.7	11.1
Targetable warheads							
(missile warheads							
and bombs)[c]	5,812	2,237	8,543	3,641	15,249	11,660	8,737
Missiles only	3,090	1,957	6,007	3,361	8,011	7,420	8,497
Equivalent mega-							
tonnage[d]	4,490	3,971	3,396	4,905	6,824	4,197	8,733
Missiles only	1,605	3,516	1,613	4,450	2,420	2,122	8,495

Sources: Authors' estimates derived from International Institute for Strategic Studies, *The Military Balance, 1977–78* (London: IISS, 1977), pp. 4–7; ibid, *1969–70* (London: IISS, 1969), pp. 1 and 2; *Aviation Week and Space Technology*, vol. 103 (October 13, 1975), pp. 15–19; ibid., vol. 107 (October 17, 1977), pp. 14 and 15; Admiral Thomas H. Moorer, "United States Military Posture for FY 1975" (statement before the House Armed Services Committee, February 7, 1974; processed), pp. 12–18; *Department of Defense Authorization for Appropriations for Fiscal Year 1978, Hearings on Military Posture and H.R. 5068 [H.R. 5960] and H.R. 1755*, 95:1 (GPO, 1977), pt. 4, p. 57; *Annual Defense Department Report*, fiscal years 1969 through 1979 (GPO, 1968–78); and the declassified posture statements of the secretaries of defense to Congress for fiscal years 1963 through 1973; processed.

a. These projections assume that both superpowers will abide by limits on strategic forces. Although a final SALT accord has not been concluded, it is assumed that both sides will be limited to 2,200 strategic delivery vehicles, with a subceiling of 1,320 on launchers capable of delivering MIRV warheads or long-range cruise missiles. Further subceilings would restrict both sides to no more than 820 MIRVed ICBMs and to a limit of 1,200 on MIRVed ICBMs and SLBMs together.

The Ford administration's 1978 budget request included 241 B-1 bombers and aimed at an initial deployment of the M-X ICBM in late 1983. The Carter administration's 1979 budget calls for an increase in air-launched cruise missile procurement but a slowdown of M-X development (and thus in its deployment) until after 1985. To stay within the total and MIRVed limits of a putative SALT II, some sixty Minuteman ICBMs would be dismantled by 1984 as additional numbers of Trident I SLBMs become operational. The USSR position is based on a projection of the current deployment rates of the present Soviet ICBMs and SLBMs. It assumes that by 1983 a new generation of Soviet ICBMs and a new, larger ballistic missile submarine will become operational.

b. The weight-carrying capacity of missiles and bombers is not directly comparable. This index includes the payload of each system that could be used to carry nuclear weapons, its protective structure, and associated guidance system.

c. Includes only weapons associated with operational forces.

d. A measure of the destruction capacity of a nuclear arsenal based on the number and explosive yields of its various component weapons but taking into account the fact that the ground area that would be destroyed by a nuclear explosion does not increase constantly with increases in the yield of the nuclear warhead.

Most generally, the argument for trying to keep an effective triad in being is the very high degree of deterrence it provides. Its deliberate redundancy insures against a disarming first strike and should make Soviet resort to nuclear war an option of intolerably high risk.

A key point in favor of the triad—as a guarantee against the risk of a Soviet technological breakthrough—undoubtedly is stronger now than five years ago. Because of the extensive Soviet research and development related to strategic forces, the technical options available to the Russians are wider; the reduced technological leads of the United States in some areas gives it less of a basis in experience for anticipating with confidence what step the Russians might take or what breakthroughs they might make. For example, the United States currently has a substantial lead over the Soviet Union in antisubmarine warfare technology and systems. However, the Russians are making a major effort in this area, and Secretary Brown has cautioned against placing even more reliance upon the U.S. submarine-launched ballistic missile force.

In principle, both the United States and the USSR have an interest in reaching arms control agreements that would enhance stability in the nuclear relationship and restrain the costs of strategic competition. The negotiation for a second SALT agreement have these as their proclaimed objectives.

SALT II

A first nuclear arms agreement, SALT I, was concluded in 1972, in two parts. One, a treaty of unlimited duration, sharply limited the deployment of antiballistic missiles (initially to two sites of 100 launchers each, later by protocol to one site) and put restrictions on qualitative improvements in the antiballistic missile. The other was an interim agreement (which expired in 1977 but which both sides continue to observe) that froze the level of strategic ballistic missile launchers at 1,710 for the United States and 2,358 for the USSR—a disparity acceptable to the United States because strategic bombers were not included and because the United States had a qualitative lead in accuracy and the possession of MIRVed missiles.

These agreements were intended to accomplish two U.S. aims: to reduce or remove the ABM defensive system as a destabilizing factor in mutual deterrence and to check the development of a Soviet first-strike capability and the potentially costly and dangerous competition it might engender. The ABM agreement is generally conceded to have met its objective and to have saved both countries sizable budgetary expenditures. The USSR, however, has taken advantage of the possibilities for modernizing its ICBM force below the interim agreement ceilings; as has been seen, this modernization may be bringing it within sight of being able to overwhelm the American land-based ICBM force.

A tentative accord on SALT II was reached at Vladivostok in 1974. The interim agreement would have been succeeded by a treaty, extending through 1985, setting equal aggregate ceilings of 2,400 launchers (including heavy bombers), of which 1,320 could be fitted with MIRVs. This accord has failed to come to the ratification stage because of disagreements within the U.S. government and between the United States and the USSR. Under the Soviet interpretation, the American long-range cruise missile would have been included but not the Backfire bomber. The U.S. position was that the cruise missile was not included; the Department of Defense argued that if cruise missiles were to be covered, then the Backfire, which has the range to reach the United States, should be, also.

In an attempt to break the deadlock, the Carter administration last March offered two options to the Russians. One would have been to settle for the time being on the Vladivostok launcher ceilings and to defer other issues. A second was a comprehensive proposal that would have reduced the ceilings from 2,400 to a range of from 1,800 to 2,000, cut back heavy Soviet ICBMs (such as the SS-9 and its successor, the SS-18) from 308 to 150, prohibited new (such as mobile) types of ICBMs, limited ballistic missile testing, and restricted the range of cruise missiles to about 1,500 miles. Moscow rejected both options.

Subsequent discussions established a three-part framework for SALT II: a treaty setting overall launcher ceilings; a protocol that would prohibit the deployment of some new systems, such as cruise missiles and mobile ICBMs, for three years; and a statement of objectives for a prospective SALT III. The Vladivostok ceiling of 2,400 launchers would be reduced by about 10 percent, retaining the MIRV subceiling of 1,320. The sublimit of 308 heavy Soviet ICBMs would be continued as in the 1972 interim agreement. A new subceiling of 820 MIRVed ICBMs (compared with 550 in the March 1977 comprehensive proposal) would give the USSR room to continue to develop its threat to the Minuteman.

The proposed three-year protocol has particularly controversial features. On the U.S. part, it would provide a limit on the range of the air-launched cruise missile and would count bombers carrying them against the subceiling for launchers fitted with MIRVs; there would also be constraints during the protocol period on the deployment and range of ground and sea-based cruise missiles. The Soviet Backfire bomber would not be counted against aggregate launcher ceilings but would be covered by a separate pledge to restrain Back-fire production, basing, training, and refueling.

Because the cruise missile types to be covered by the protocol could be medium-range weapons suitable to the European theater, there is uneasiness in NATO that the United States may be giving away a basis for bargaining for restrictions on Soviet ballistic missiles deployed against Europe, especially the new mobile, MIRVed SS-20 medium-range weapon. Until now, it has been American policy to refuse to negotiate about "theater" nuclear weapons in SALT without NATO allies being involved and as long as the Russians insist on the exclusion of their medium-range systems.

To these concerns the administration has replied that the three-year prohibition on cruise missile deployment is no more than a recognition of the fact that missile development schedules, which are in no way circumscribed, would preclude deployment anyway. It disagrees that the protocol is a precedent for SALT III and it points to language in the protocol that would permit the United States to test long-range cruise missiles launched not only from aircraft, as originally insisted upon by the Russians, but also from ground and sea platforms. The administration also says that the protocol's ban on the deployment of new ballistic missiles would put a brake on Soviet mobile ICBM deployment, which appears to be a near-term prospect, whereas the U.S. development schedule would not permit any deployment until well after the three-year period.

Since the talks are still under way, any definitive and overall judgment on a SALT II treaty that might be offered for ratification would be premature. What does seem clear from the frame of reference agreed for the treaty is that the outlook is dim for a satisfactory resolution through SALT II of the triad problem. SALT II, itself, will not assure stability in the nuclear balance. Its direct effect on the budget, moreover, will be small. The proposed modest reductions in aggregate launcher ceilings, although they could be a beginning toward a winding down of the nuclear arms race, will hardly relieve the expected Soviet threat to the Minuteman ICBM. Nor will the Soviet Union—or the United States—be prevented from modernizing and strengthening other offensive and defensive nuclear systems. Unless a subsequent SALT goes considerably beyond the goals set for SALT II, nuclear arms will continue to confront U.S. defense planners with difficult strategic issues and major budgetary questions.

A failure of SALT II could make all problems worse, signaling the end of hopes for détente and setting off a round of heightened nuclear competition. Whether it would actually do so is not certain. For the USSR to undertake a significantly greater strategic nuclear effort would require a further diversion of scarce resources from other military and civilian needs to a technological race in which the United States continues to have important advantages. Nonetheless, the experience of more than two decades argues that a breakdown or rejection of SALT II would require a renewed effort to negotiate limits on nuclear arms. Neither side of the U.S.-USSR confrontation can say with confidence that its security has been assured by all the huge sums already invested in strategic weapons. The prospect that the competition might go on unchecked cannot be a desirable one for the leadership in either country.

CHAPTER TEN

The Budget Outlook

JOSEPH A. PECHMAN

WHEN HE CAME INTO OFFICE, President Carter had a number of impressive budget and economic objectives, which still govern his decisions on federal tax and expenditure policies. The major objectives are (1) to reduce federal expenditures to 21 percent of the gross national product (they were 22.5 percent in the fiscal year before he came into office); (2) to bring the budget into balance by 1981; and (3) to reduce unemployment from almost 8 percent of the labor force in late 1976 to below 5 percent by 1981. In the 1979 budget, the President reaffirms the first and third of these goals, but acknowledges that achievement of a balanced budget must be deferred, unless there is unusually strong growth of nonfederal demands.

Federal spending is difficult to alter in the short run, because many expenditures are determined by existing laws. Social security payments, welfare payments, and federal employee pensions automatically rise as population, prices, and national output increase. In addition, about a fifth of spending in fiscal years 1978 and 1979 consists of outlays for contracts and obligations made in prior years. However, many of these built-in increases can be reduced by modifications in formulas or by substitution of new programs for old ones. Thus, while any president is hampered in his efforts to change the budget totals in the short run, he has more flexibility in the long run because some of the so-called uncontrollable programs are controllable and because

The author is grateful for the suggestions of Robert W. Hartman, Darwin Johnson, and Arthur M. Okun on an early draft of this chapter.

receipts increase rapidly as incomes rise in response to economic growth and inflation.

Budget documents in recent years provide increasingly more information for years beyond the budget year. The Congressional Budget Office is required by law to provide expenditure and revenue estimates for a five-year period on a current service basis (that is, on the basis of present laws), and the Office of Management and Budget prepares such estimates as well. The President's 1979 budget provides considerably more detail on prospective developments than any budget in the past. It is thus possible to project the effect of current budgetary decisions with more precision and to consider the implications of alternative policies for the budget five years hence. Because of the President's commitment to multiyear budgeting (see appendix B), even more long-range detail can be expected in future budgets.

In this chapter, budget estimates for the next five years are examined in relation to the President's objectives. First, the expenditure and revenue projections for fiscal years 1979–83 based on current programs and proposed legislative changes are reviewed. Second, the effects of possible changes in the basic assumptions underlying the budget are evaluated. Third, the five-year figures are projected on the basis of other possible budget policies. These calculations suggest the extremes between which the budget might vary and the implications of alternative policies for the balance between revenues and expenditures.

The Official Budget Projections

Projections of expenditures and revenues depend heavily on assumptions regarding economic developments. On the expenditure side of the budget, federal retirement and social security benefits are adjusted to keep pace with the cost of living, procurement costs reflect market prices, interest payments reflect interest rates, unemployment compensation and other transfer benefits go up and down with the rise and fall in the rate of unemployment, and federal pay is adjusted to compare to pay in similar jobs in the private sector. On the receipt side, collections of most taxes (but particularly individual and corporate income taxes and payroll taxes) depend on personal and corporate incomes, which in turn respond to economic growth and inflation.

Table 10-1. Official and Alternative Economic Assumptions, Calendar Years 1977–83
Percent

Indicator	1977[a]	1978	1979	1980	1981	1982	1983
	Official assumptions						
Gross national product, current dollars[b]	10.8	11.0	11.2	10.8	10.5	9.6	8.5
Gross national product, 1972 dollars[b]	4.9	4.7	4.8	4.8	5.0	4.7	4.2
Consumer prices[b]	6.5	5.9	6.1	5.7	5.2	4.7	4.2
Unemployment[c]	7.0	6.3	5.9	5.4	5.0	4.5	4.1
	Alternative assumptions						
Gross national product, current dollars[b]	10.8	11.0	11.2	11.1	11.3	10.7	10.1
Gross national product, 1972 dollars[b]	4.9	4.7	4.8	4.8	5.0	4.4	3.9
Consumer prices[b]	6.5	5.9	6.1	6.0	6.0	6.0	6.0
Unemployment[c]	7.0	6.3	5.9	5.4	5.0	4.8	4.7

Sources: Official assumptions, *The Budget of the United States Government, Fiscal Year 1979*, pp. 31 and 33; alternative assumptions, 1978–79, ibid, 1980–83 are the author's.
a. Actual.
b. Year to year change.
c. Average rate for the year.

In preparing the budget for fiscal year 1979, President Carter was clearly sensitive to the probable effects of his current decisions on the state of the budget in the future. The official budget estimates for fiscal years 1979–83 assume that national output will continue to grow at a rate of about 4.75 percent a year after adjusting for inflation. (See table 10-1 for the administration's assumptions.) At this rate, unemployment would decline from an average rate of 7 percent in calendar year 1977 to 5 percent in 1981 and 4.1 percent in 1983. Consumer prices are assumed to rise by about 6 percent in 1978 and 1979 and then to taper off by half a percentage point a year, declining to 5.2 percent in 1981 and 4.2 percent in 1983. (The administration emphasizes that only the economic assumptions for 1978–79 are forecasts; those for 1980–83 are projections consistent with employment and price targets.)

It is helpful to begin the budget outlook before the social security amendments of 1977 were enacted on December 20, 1977.[1] This

1. The figures in this chapter are not corrected for a possible shortfall in actual outlays. On March 13, 1978, the Office of Management and Budget reduced outlays for fiscal year 1978 from the $462.2 billion estimated in the budget to $453.5 billion, but modified the 1979 estimate only slightly (down from $500.2 billion to $499.4 billion). Even if the shortfall continues, it is likely to be only a small fraction of total outlays for fiscal years 1981–83. For a discussion of the shortfall, see appendix A.

legislation raises payroll taxes significantly beginning January 1, 1979, and reduces social security outlays by smaller amounts, thus increasing the fiscal drag, which had to be offset by tax reductions in 1978 and later years (see chapter 2). From a budgetary standpoint, however, the higher payroll taxes and lower social security outlays reduce (and ultimately will eliminate) the deficit in the social security account and thus remove a large potential claim on the general funds of the budget.

Outlays for the federal programs authorized for fiscal year 1978 (and not including the changes made by the 1977 social security amendments) are estimated to be $461.8 billion (see table 10-2). If the programs continue into the future, outlays would rise to $500.1 billion in 1979, $570.8 billion in 1981, and $645 billion in 1983.[2] In percentage terms, the increase in outlays falls from 8.3 in 1979 to 6.3 in 1983—considerably lower than the projected annual increase in gross national product.

The federal tax system in effect before the 1977 social security amendments would have generated receipts of $400.7 billion in fiscal year 1978, with increases averaging almost 13 percent a year for the succeeding five years—a much faster rate than the rate of increase in gross national product. As a result, given the economic conditions assumed in the Carter budget, receipts could be expected to rise to $591.1 billion in 1981 and $732.6 billion in 1983, thus generating budget margins—the excess of receipts over outlays—of $20.3 billion in 1981 and $87.6 billion in 1983 (table 10-2, line 15).

The social security amendments of 1977 changed the budget picture quite a bit. By raising taxes and lowering outlays, these amendments lifted the original budget margin in 1981 from $20.3 billion to $38.6 billion and in 1983 from $87.6 billion to $117.2 billion (table 10-2, line 16).

With this much elbow room in the long-run budget, one might have expected proposals for significant increases in outlays as well as for tax reductions. In fact, while there were some discretionary increases in outlays, there were also some reductions; on balance, the President's budget allows for a small net increase in outlays over the five-

2. These estimates assume that outlays for individual programs remain the same in dollar terms, except where projected beneficiary levels change or where the legislation explicitly calls for an increase or decrease in program levels over time. Included in the estimates are mandated cost-of-living adjustments, pay raises, inflation, adjustments for defense procurement, and other built-in cost increases (such as interest).

Table 10-2. Budget Projections under Various Assumptions, Fiscal Years 1978–83

Billions of dollars

Assumption	1978	1979	1980	1981	1982	1983
			Outlays			
1. Current programs without 1977 social security amendments	461.8	500.1	541.9	570.8	606.6	645.0
2. Effect of 1977 social security amendments	−0.3	−0.5	−0.9	−1.7	−2.4	−3.5
3. Current programs with 1977 social security amendments	461.5	499.6	541.0	569.1	604.2	641.5
4. Effect of Carter's legislative proposals[a]	*	−2.1	−2.2	1.6	2.1	2.6
5. Proposed programs under official economic assumptions	461.5	497.5	538.8	570.7	606.3	644.1
6. Effect of alternative economic assumptions[a]	...	...	1.2	4.1	10.9	21.1
7. Proposed programs under alternative economic assumptions	461.5	497.5	540.0	574.8	617.2	665.2
			Receipts			
8. Current law without 1977 social security amendments[b]	400.7	460.6	519.9	591.1	661.7	732.6
9. Effect of 1977 social security amendments	*	3.2	8.8	16.6	23.8	26.1
10. Current law with 1977 social security amendments	400.7	463.8	528.7	607.7	685.5	758.7
11. Effect of Carter's legislative proposals[a]	−0.2	−25.4	−26.2	−28.0	−33.4	−40.4
12. Proposed law under official economic assumptions	400.5	438.5	502.5	579.6	652.1	718.3
13. Effect of alternative economic assumptions[a]	...	...	1.3	6.2	14.7	28.9
14. Proposed law under alternative economic assumptions	400.5	438.5	503.8	585.8	666.8	747.2
			Margins			
15. Without 1977 social security amendments	−61.1	−39.5	−22.0	20.3	55.1	87.6
16. With 1977 social security amendments	−60.8	−35.8	−12.3	38.6	81.3	117.2
17. After Carter's proposals, official economic assumptions	−61.0	−59.0	−36.3	8.9	45.8	74.2
18. After Carter's proposals, alternative economic assumptions	−61.0	−59.0	−36.2	11.0	49.6	82.0

Sources: *The Budget of the United States Government, Fiscal Year 1979*, pp. 11, 33–35; Office of Management and Budget; and author's estimates. Figures are rounded.
* Less than $50 million change.
a. See table 10-1 for economic assumptions. The effect of the energy proposals are not included.
b. Assuming extension of temporary tax provisions of the Tax Reduction Act of 1975.

year period. All told, his legislative proposals other than the energy program would reduce outlays by $2.1 billion in fiscal year 1979 and raise them by only $2.6 billion in 1983 (table 10-2, line 4).[3]

In contrast to the modest changes in outlays, changes in receipts are large. The tax cuts proposed by the President reduce receipts by $25.4 billion in fiscal year 1979 and $40.4 billion in 1983 below what they would be under current law with the social security changes.

3. The energy program is excluded from these figures because it is already clear that the President's proposals will be substantially modified by Congress. In fiscal year 1983, the administration's energy proposals would raise outlays by $5.8 billion and receipts by $7.9 billion. Moreover, these projections incorporate certain increases not requiring legislative authority, which account for the difference between the discretionary outlays shown in chapter 2 and in line 4 of table 10-2.

But the margin for 1983 is still $74.2 billion because economic growth and inflation will continue to generate large increases in receipts (table 10-2, line 17).

In brief, unlike last year when expenditure increases provided about half of the fiscal stimulus for economic expansion, this year President Carter increased outlays only enough to keep federal programs at about current levels and used tax cuts to stimulate the economy. If the economy were to grow by 4.75 percent in the next five years, the President could limit outlays to 21 percent or less of the gross national product (outlays projected from his 1979 budget proposals would be 20.4 percent of the gross national product in fiscal year 1981 and 19.3 percent in 1983), provide for additional tax cuts, and still balance the budget. But the economic assumptions underlying these projections are not likely to be attained. First, the price and unemployment assumptions are optimistic; second, the economy may not be able to expand at the assumed rates without continuing budget deficits. The budget message itself warns that the proper fiscal policy for 1981–83 "depends both on economic conditions too far in the future to forecast, and on the need for new or expanded programs or for further tax cuts."

Economic Prospects

It is virtually impossible to predict economic developments five years hence. The economy is subject to frequent unexpected shocks that may accelerate inflation, generate unsustainable expansion or deep recession, and interfere with the growth in productivity. The economic policies of other countries affect the balance between U.S. exports and imports and the value of the dollar, which in turn influence domestic prices and output. Military and diplomatic considerations can cause large swings in defense expenditures. For these and other reasons, instability in the economy cannot be avoided, and the precise economic and budget projections shown in tables 10-1 and 10-2 are not likely to be realized.

The Price and Unemployment Assumptions

The official budget projections assume continued reductions in the rates of inflation and unemployment, assumptions that seem optimistic from the present vantage point. Few people believe that the policy of wage and price deceleration will work (see chapter 2). Recent history suggests that prices will probably continue to rise by at least 6 percent a year rather than taper off to 5 percent in 1981 and 4 percent in 1983, as assumed in the budget.

The unemployment rates now widely used to measure the economy's potential output take into account changes in the demographic composition of the labor force.[4] (These revised rates have been accepted by the Council of Economic Advisers of both the Ford and Carter administrations.) The benchmark unemployment rate that was 4 percent in 1952–58 is 4.9 percent for the years 1976–79, 4.8 percent for 1980–81, and 4.7 percent for 1982–83.[5] Thus, the official budget assumption that the unemployment rate will decline to 4 percent in 1983 as inflation tapers off to 4 percent a year is also open to serious question. A rate of unemployment this low would require an unprecedentedly successful jobs and training program to dramatically reduce structural unemployment and increase the effective labor supply.

Substitution of more realistic figures for inflation and unemployment in the economic assumptions for the 1980–83 budget projections (see alternative assumptions, table 10-1) raises the annual rate of inflation for the period 1980–83 and the rate of unemployment in 1982–83. The higher price assumptions would increase money incomes and therefore budget receipts, but budget outlays would also rise because at least three-quarters of budget outlays are tied directly or indirectly to prices. The higher unemployment rate would reduce the growth of incomes and budget receipts and raise outlays for unemployment compensation. On balance, because of the progressivity of the federal tax system, the additional receipts generated by inflation would exceed the additional outlays resulting from both inflation and the higher rate of unemployment, but the budget picture for fiscal years 1981–83 is essentially the same as that projected by the administration (see table 10-3). The budget margins are raised a bit, while the shares of projected federal outlays in the gross national product are not affected.

4. For a discussion of the effect of demographic changes on potential gross national product, see Joseph A. Pechman, ed., *Setting National Priorities: The 1978 Budget* (Brookings Institution, 1977), app. A, pp. 419–24.

5. *Economic Report of the President, January 1977*, pp. 48–51, and *Economic Report of the President, January 1978*, pp. 83–84, 93–95.

Table 10-3. Relation of Budget Projections to the Gross National Product,
Fiscal Years 1977–83

| Fiscal year | Amounts (billions of dollars) | | | | Percent of GNP | | |
	Gross national product	Receipts[a]	Outlays[a]	Margin	Receipts[a]	Out-lays[a]	Margin
			Official assumptions				
1977[b]	1,838	356.9	401.9	−45.0	19.4	21.9	−2.4
1978	2,043	400.5	461.5	−61.0	19.6	22.6	−3.0
1979	2,275	438.5	497.5	−59.0	19.3	21.9	−2.6
1980	2,524	502.5	538.8	−36.3	19.9	21.3	−1.4
1981	2,790	579.6	570.7	8.9	20.8	20.4	0.3
1982	3,064	652.1	606.3	45.8	21.3	19.8	1.5
1983	3,333	718.3	644.1	74.2	21.6	19.3	2.2
			Alternative assumptions				
1977[b]	1,838	356.9	401.9	−45.0	19.4	21.9	−2.4
1978	2,043	400.5	461.5	−61.0	19.6	22.6	−3.0
1979	2,275	438.5	497.5	−59.0	19.3	21.9	−2.6
1980	2,529	503.8	540.0	−36.2	19.9	21.4	−1.4
1981	2,814	585.8	574.8	11.0	20.8	20.4	0.4
1982	3,118	666.8	617.2	49.6	21.4	19.8	1.6
1983	3,437	747.2	665.2	82.0	21.7	19.4	2.4

Sources: *The Budget of the United States Government, Fiscal Year 1979*, pp. 31, 33, 486, 488; and tables 10-1 and 10-2. Figures are rounded.
a. Not including energy proposals.
b. Actual.

The Growth Assumptions

The budget shows a fast-rising margin for fiscal years 1981–83 (table 10-2), because receipts increase more than proportionately as money incomes rise, whereas outlays rise less than proportionately. However, the economy will not grow at the rates projected in the budget unless the budget margins are drastically reduced or entirely eliminated. To understand why this is so, it is necessary to briefly review recent economic history.

The recovery from the 1974–75 contraction, which turned out to be the deepest recession experienced in the United States since the end of the Second World War, has been relatively slow by past standards. Unemployment in early 1978 was still above 6 percent of the labor force and the rate of capacity utilization in industry was only about 83 percent. Although residential construction has recovered nicely, the rate of business investment is disappointing. State and local governments, as a result of fiscal difficulties during the period of double-digit inflation and deep recession, are cautious about spending and are accumulating large surpluses. To add to these depressing elements, the nation's merchandise trade deficit jumped from $6 billion in 1976 to $27 billion in 1977, thus siphoning off considerable purchasing power from domestic markets.

Expansion continues, however, because federal fiscal and monetary policies have provided an offsetting stimulus. The federal budget ran deficits of $45 billion, $66 billion, and $45 billion in fiscal years 1975, 1976, and 1977, respectively, and interest rates declined sharply in 1975 and 1976. The deficits (generated by discretionary tax cuts and expenditure increases, as well as by the stabilizers built into the budget) increased the disposable income of consumers and business and thus helped sustain private spending. Although business investment is still lagging, consumption expenditures have been rising at a healthy rate and have made a major contribution to the economy. The decline in interest rates helped stimulate home-buying; and the growth in money and credit contributed to the availability of funds for business borrowing as well as for residential construction.

The question facing the budget planner is whether the private sector will generate enough demand to keep the expansion going without continued substantial fiscal stimulus from the federal government. Clearly, the growth targets of the administration will not be realized with a swing in the budget from a $59.0 billion deficit in fiscal year 1979 to surpluses of $11.0 billion in 1981 and $82.0 billion in 1983 (see table 10-2). While a resurgence of nonfederal demand is conceivable, most economists inside and outside the government believe that such a swift and sizable reversal of the deficit would quickly lead to a recession; in fact, many doubt that a recession can be averted without continuing deficits. For example, the Congressional Budget Office estimates that a federal deficit of at least $40 billion would be needed in fiscal year 1981 to keep the economy growing at the rate projected by the administration.[6] In its annual report, the Council of Economic Advisers points out that, in recent years, the federal deficit has been needed to offset the large surpluses of state and local governments and the nation's current account deficit with the rest of the world.[7] The council acknowledges that "marked shifts in net saving

6. *An Analysis of the President's Budgetary Proposals for Fiscal Year 1979* (Congressional Budget Office, January 1978), pp. 170–71.

7. For a discussion of the relationship between nonfederal saving and the federal deficit, see chap. 2.

by the non-Federal sectors would be required to reach high employment with a balanced budget in 1981" and suggests that additional tax reductions (over and above the proposed 1978 cut) may be needed to keep the recovery going.[8]

It can be concluded that the President will probably be forced to give up his balanced budget objective if he wishes to come close to his unemployment target of 5 percent in 1981. But there is no reason to change policies now to meet the 1981 target. Assuming that the monetary authorities maintain a satisfactory growth of money and credit, the fiscal policies proposed by the administration should achieve the 4.75 percent average growth rates it predicts for 1978 and 1979. Late 1979 or early 1980 should be time enough to decide whether to prolong the fiscal stimulus and by how much, and what particular combination of expenditure increases and tax cuts will best serve the national interest.

Budget Options

The discussion thus far assumes that, except for his energy proposals, the President's expenditure and tax programs will be enacted in toto. However, the President's budget is always modified—sometimes to a major degree—before it is enacted. The administration itself may propose changes, in response to pressure it did not fully anticipate when the original budget plan was prepared. And Congress often substitutes its own judgment for that of the President in key areas of the budget. In this section, the major alternatives are priced out (see tables 10-4 and 10-5) and the budget prospects for 1981 and 1983 are reevaluated in light of these modifications.

Outlays

Major changes will be made in the administration's legislative proposals affecting expenditures in fiscal year 1979 and later years. The President has been criticized for restraining the growth of defense spending in the face of the continuing rapid buildup of Soviet military capability; but he has also been criticized for not living up to his campaign pledge to cut defense outlays. The budget incorporates in full the President's 1977 energy plan, even though it was clear at the time the budget was prepared that the energy plan would not be approved

8. *Economic Report of the President, January 1978,* p. 90.

by Congress in anything approaching its original form. The limit on hospital cost increases proposed last year is languishing in the congressional committees, but national health insurance is still on the administration's agenda. There are persistent demands for new and improved urban programs to provide more federal assistance for the large cities. The administration has proposed additional grants and subsidized loans for college students to head off a $250 per capita income tax credit. Congress may not accept a proposed curtailment of impact aid, a program that overcompensates communities for lost property taxes on federal facilities by paying for the costs of educating the children of federal employees. Expenditures for agricultural price and income supports will exceed the budget estimates if there is a succession of good harvests.

To reduce outlays below those projected in the President's budget, it is necessary not only to withstand the pressure to increase them but to actually make cuts, even though they might reverse important administration policies and eliminate or sharply curtail programs dear to Congress. For example, the growth in real defense outlays could be cut; the administration's welfare program could be rejected by Congress; the jobs and training program could be phased down as the economy approaches full employment; and the impact aid program could be eliminated.

DEFENSE. The Carter budget proposes to increase defense outlays by 3 percent a year in real terms over the next five years. If the real growth of defense expenditures were raised another 2 percentage points a year (to an annual rate of about 5 percent), projected budget outlays would be increased by $8.1 billion in fiscal year 1981 and $16.4 billion in 1983. If the real growth of these expenditures were reduced by 2 percentage points a year (to an annual rate of less than 1 percent), outlays would be cut by $7.9 billion in 1981 and $15.3 billion in 1983.

WELFARE. Last year the President proposed a comprehensive revision of the nation's welfare system, which would replace several state and federal programs with a uniform cash assistance program, create 1.4 million public service jobs in 1981, and expand the earned income credit. According to the official budget estimate, the net cost of the program would be $12.9 billion in fiscal year 1983, but the Congressional Budget Office estimate is $9.2 billion higher. The high cost has caused opposition among influential members of Congress

Table 10-4. Possible Changes in Budget Outlays, Fiscal Years 1979–83
Billions of dollars

Program and assumption[a]	1979	1980	1981	1982	1983
Defense					
1. Real outlay growth increased by 2 percentage points a year	2.2	4.9	8.1	12.0	16.4
2. Real outlay growth reduced by 2 percentage points a year	−2.3	−4.9	−7.9	−11.3	−15.3
Welfare					
3. Comprehensive reform enacted	...	...	3.0	8.8	9.2
4. Incremental reform enacted	...	...	...	−3.2	−6.8
Energy					
5. President's energy program adopted	2.6	4.1	4.7	6.1	5.8
6. Strategic petroleum reserve enlarged	0.3	0.4	0.8	2.4	2.7
Urban aid					
7. National urban policy enacted	0.7	2.9	2.9	3.1	3.3
Health					
8. 9 percent limit on annual hospital cost increases not enacted	0.4	1.6	2.7	3.9	5.1
9. Catastrophic health insurance enacted	...	...	9.1	11.5	13.1
10. Federalized Medicaid enacted	...	...	10.5	12.0	13.6
Education and training					
11. President's education program costs as estimated in chapter 4	0.3	1.0	1.5	2.4	3.5
12. Impact aid eliminated	−0.8	−0.9	−0.9	−0.9	−0.9
13. CETA phased down and public jobs eliminated	...	−1.0	−2.1	−3.2	−4.5
Agriculture					
14. Higher price and income supports enacted	3.1	3.9	5.2	5.0	4.0
Fiscal assistance to state and local governments					
15. Other grants adjusted for inflation	...	...	1.8	4.2	6.5
16. Authorization for revenue sharing increased	...	...	1.0	1.0	1.0

Sources: Author's estimates based on data from the Office of Management and Budget and the Congressional Budget Office.
a. See text for details.

to the expanded cash assistance program and the jobs program, so there is a distinct possibility that the administration's program will be replaced by less costly incremental welfare changes. One possibility is to federalize the present program for aid to families with dependent children and raise the combined value of food stamps and cash assistance to a uniform 75 percent of the poverty line. These changes would not affect the 1979–81 outlays, but they would reduce the administration's projections by $3.2 billion in 1982 and $6.8 billion in 1983.[9] In addition, the elimination of the proposed liberalization of the earned income credit would raise tax receipts by $4.8 billion in 1983.

ENERGY. The President's energy program would add $4.7 billion to outlays in fiscal year 1981 and $5.8 billion in 1983; receipts would be increased by $4.3 billion in 1981 and $7.9 billion in 1983. Although the program will be substantially altered before it is enacted, a proposal to increase the strategic petroleum reserve from 500 million barrels in 1982 to 1 billion barrels in 1985 is likely to be approved by Congress. Approval of the larger reserve would raise budget outlays by $0.8 billion in fiscal year 1981 and $2.7 billion in 1983.

URBAN AID. On March 27, 1978, President Carter announced a new national urban policy to increase investment in the cities and create jobs for long-term unemployed city workers. The proposal would overhaul federal programs and give financial assistance to state and local governments and private industry, adding $0.7 billion to outlays in fiscal year 1979, $2.9 billion in 1981, and $3.3 billion in 1983. In addition, a new employment tax credit and an additional 5 percent credit for investment in distressed areas would reduce receipts by $1.7 billion in fiscal years 1979–80 and $1.5 billion thereafter.

HEALTH. The budget assumes congressional approval of the administration's proposal to limit the increases in hospital costs under Medicare and Medicaid to 9 percent a year. Congress has not acted on this proposal, however. Instead, the hospitals themselves have proposed a voluntary cost containment program to head off federal regulation, and Congress is considering standby legislation in case the voluntary program should fail. The outcome is not predictable, but it is hardly likely that the voluntary program would reduce costs by as much as the original administration proposal. Under the circumstances, only a portion of the saving estimated in the budget would be realized. If the cost saving is only half, health outlays would

9. Savings of state and local governments are not included in these figures. Comprehensive reform would save state and local governments $3.4 billion in 1982 and $3.6 billion in 1983. Incremental reform would reduce state and local spending by amounts ranging from $3 billion in 1979 to $4.2 billion in 1983.

be higher than those projected in the budget by $2.7 billion in fiscal year 1981 and $5.1 billion in 1983.

National health insurance is on the administration's agenda, but details of the program have not been announced. As a beginning, any nationwide plan would have to provide payments for catastrophic illness and coverage of the health costs of all the poor under Medicaid (rather than, as now, those covered by welfare and, under some state programs, those defined as medically indigent). Catastrophic health insurance and a federalized Medicaid (with continuation of state funding responsibility) would increase outlays by a total of $19.6 billion in fiscal year 1981 and $26.7 billion in 1983.

EDUCATION AND TRAINING. As indicated in chapter 4, the official budget projections do not allow fully for increases in federal education grants to state and local governments and for the administration's recent student aid proposal. And they optimistically assume that the impact aid program will be reformed to assist only those school districts where federal activities actually reduce tax revenues. Thus, all told, education outlays are underestimated by $1.5 billion in 1981 and $3.5 billion in 1983.

The education budget could be cut by eliminating the much-criticized impact aid program; the budget estimate for this program is $900 million in 1983. In addition, if the economy reaches full employment, the employment and training program (which would cost $6.9 billion in 1983) could eliminate all the categorical programs under the Comprehensive Employment and Training Act, leaving only general grants to state and local governments that support the discretionary activities of local prime sponsors. This would reduce outlays by $2.1 billion in 1981 and $4.5 billion in 1983.

AGRICULTURE. The administration's estimates assume that expenditures for programs to support farm prices and income will decline from $7.2 billion in 1978 to $1.9 billion in 1981 and that they will rise again in 1983, to $3.1 billion. The costs of these programs under present legislation will vary from year to year; while lower outlays are possible, so too are higher ones. The costs will depend almost entirely on weather conditions; if there are good harvests throughout most of the period, outlays for these programs will certainly not go down and may even rise (see chapter 7). Moreover, Congress is considering additional legislation that would further increase these outlays. Under the circumstances, it is best to assume that weather and crop conditions will be relatively favorable and the cost of the price and income support programs will remain at the 1978 level through 1983.

FISCAL ASSISTANCE. The official budget projections assume that federal grants will remain at fixed dollar levels except when beneficiary levels change or when legislation or a presidential proposal alters the budget authorizations. Since federal grants have become a major prop to spending by state and local governments—they now amount to 27.5 percent of state and local outlays—budget authorizations for many of these programs are likely to be raised as prices continue to increase. Inflation adjustment alone will increase outlays by $1.8 billion in 1981 and $6.5 billion in 1983. (These figures exclude grants for education, training, welfare, and health, which have already been adjusted.)

The general revenue sharing program distributes $6.9 billion a year to state and local governments. It is scheduled to terminate at the end of fiscal year 1980, but the official budget projections assume that the program will be extended, at the same rate of expenditure. Given the continuation of inflation, an increase in the budget authorization for this program of $1 billion a year is possible.

Receipts

Although a major tax bill will probably be enacted this year, it may be only a prelude to further tax action in the years ahead. As people are pushed into higher tax brackets by inflation, the effective rate of the individual income tax will rise, which Congress, if it follows past practice, will offset. Corporate taxes are also likely to be reduced, partly to compensate for inflation[10] and partly to balance the individual income tax cuts. The social security amendments of 1977, together with previous legislation, would raise payroll taxes sharply over the next decade, but Congress is having second thoughts about these tax increases (see chapter 3). Tax changes along these lines would significantly reduce the budget margin in the next four years.

TAX REFORM. The President's tax program includes reforms that would increase revenues by $13.2 billion in 1981 and $17.5 billion

10. Since the corporate tax is levied virtually at a flat rate, there is no inflation penalty from the rate structure. However, profits are overstated during inflation, and in the past Congress adjusted for this effect through changes in depreciation methods, the investment credit, and corporate tax rate reductions.

Table 10-5. Possible Changes in Budget Receipts, Fiscal Years 1979–83
Billions of dollars

Source and assumption[a]	1979	1980	1981	1982	1983
Individual income tax					
1. Earned income credit held at present level	...	...	...	1.9	4.8
2. Two-thirds of proposed tax reforms rejected	−2.8	−4.9	−5.9	−7.1	−8.2
3. Ratio of individual income tax to personal income held at 10.7 percent[b]	...	...	−16.0	−32.8	−50.1
Corporate income tax					
4. Two-thirds of proposed tax reforms rejected	−0.7	−2.0	−2.9	−3.3	−3.5
5. Tax cut by one-third of individual income tax cuts (line 3)	...	...	−5.3	−10.9	−16.7
Payroll tax					
6. 1977 payroll tax increases eliminated	−3.2	−8.8	−16.6	−23.8	−26.1
7. Hospital insurance financed through general revenues	−19.9	−23.2	−30.6	−36.1	−39.5
Energy taxes					
8. President's program enacted	1.1	2.9	4.3	5.5	7.9
Urban aid					
9. President's program enacted	−1.7	−1.7	−1.5	−1.5	−1.5

Sources: Author's estimates based on data from the Office of Management and Budget and the Congressional Budget Office.
a. See text for details.
b. Assumes also that Congress rejects two-thirds of the tax reforms proposed by the President.

in 1983. The reforms, which are intended to reduce tax preferences and simplify the tax law, have provoked considerable opposition (see chapter 5). Observers believe that most of the reforms will not be enacted in this year's tax-cutting atmosphere. If only a third of the President's tax reform program is approved, receipts would be reduced by $8.8 billion in fiscal year 1981 and $11.7 billion in 1983.

INDIVIDUAL INCOME TAX. This tax is the mainstay of the federal revenue system. In recent years it has accounted for about 45 percent of total federal receipts. It will amount to 10.7 percent of personal income in fiscal year 1978 and would rise to 11.4 percent in 1979 if rates and exemptions remained unchanged. The President's tax program would reduce the burden to 10.3 percent in 1978 and 10.5

percent in 1979, but then it would rise to 12.5 percent in 1983. Historically, Congress has kept the individual income tax from rising above 11 percent. If the individual income tax ratio were kept at 10.7 percent throughout the period 1980–83, receipts would be reduced by $16.0 billion in fiscal year 1981 and $50.1 billion in 1983.[11]

CORPORATE INCOME TAX. In fiscal year 1978, corporate income tax receipts will amount to less than 3 percent of the gross national product, but the tax will account for 31.5 percent of corporate profits before taxes and thus will have a major effect on the rate of return to investment and on the disposable income of corporations. The President's proposals would reduce the effective tax rate on corporate profits to 28.9 percent in 1981 (when the proposed cut in the corporate rate becomes fully effective).

Traditionally, Congress has coupled individual tax cuts with business tax cuts; the Carter proposals would reduce the two taxes by a ratio of approximately three to one. Depreciation allowances and, to a lesser extent, inventory costs are understated during inflation and there is considerable agreement that business investment needs to be stimulated to raise productivity and promote economic growth. For these reasons, corporate taxes might be cut by about one-third of the amount of the cuts for individuals; this would reduce receipts by $5.3 billion in 1981 and $16.7 billion in 1983.

PAYROLL TAX. The adverse public reaction to the higher payroll taxes scheduled for the coming decade has precipitated considerable congressional discussion of alternatives. Suggestions range from substituting general revenues for part or all of the new increases to the enactment of an income tax credit to compensate for these increases. At question is the basic rationale for the use of the payroll tax to finance social security[12] and the perceived fairness of last year's tax increases, so the outcome of the debate is uncertain. General revenues could be used to replace some of the 1977 payroll tax increases, which

11. This would adjust for the increase in effective rates resulting from real growth as well as from inflation. An alternative would be to adjust the personal exemptions and the tax brackets for inflation annually, but Republican and Democratic administrations and the Congress have preferred to make ad hoc adjustments. In his last budget, President Ford's long-term projections were based on the assumption that the adjustments would hold the individual income-tax ratio to the 1979 level. For a detailed analysis of the problems of correcting the tax system for inflation, see Henry J. Aaron, ed., *Inflation and the Income Tax* (Brookings Institution, 1976).

12. For a discussion of this rationale, see Alicia H. Munnell, *The Future of Social Security* (Brookings Institution, 1977).

will amount to $26.1 billion in 1983, or part of the $39.5 billion of the hospital insurance trust fund tax receipts in that year.[13]

ENERGY TAXES. The President's energy plan includes several major new taxes which are intended to promote conservation, more production from existing domestic sources, and conversion from oil and natural gas to more abundant fuels.[14] Most, but not all, of the tax receipts would either be refunded to individuals or would finance the energy program. The increase in receipts would amount to $4.3 billion in fiscal year 1981 and $7.9 billion in 1983. The prospects for congressional approval of this program are, however, poor.

Alternative Budgets

Tables 10-4 and 10-5 illustrate policy changes that could greatly affect future budgets. For fiscal year 1981, the President's budget would generate outlays of $574.8 billion, or 20.4 percent of the estimated gross national product of $2,814 billion (table 10-3). At 21 percent of the gross national product, outlays would amount to $590.9 billion, leaving room for additional spending of only $16.1 billion.[15] The revision of the estimates for current programs and the administration's proposals shown in table 10-4 add up to $22.8 billion,[16] which would bring total outlays to $597.6 billion or $6.7 billion more than the amount that would be consistent with the 21 percent target (see table 10-6). Furthermore, receipts should be revised downward to take into account the employment tax credit and the additional investment tax credit for distressed areas in the President's national urban policy and the possibility that Congress will not approve a major part of the President's tax reform program and may reduce payroll taxes. Assuming that two-thirds of the proposed reforms are rejected and half the 1977 payroll tax increases for 1981 are reversed, budget receipts would amount to $567.2 billion, leaving a deficit of $30.4 billion. As indicated earlier, a deficit may be needed in fiscal year 1981, but increasing outlays above the President's bud-

13. The rationale for a payroll tax is much weaker for hospital insurance than for the other social security programs, because the benefits are not related to earnings.
14. These taxes include a crude-oil equalization tax, a tax on industrial and utility use of oil and gas, and an automobile "gas guzzler" tax. The proposal would also provide individual tax credits for home insulation and installation of solar energy equipment and business tax credits for investment in equipment that is more energy-efficient or that produces electricity and steam simultaneously.
15. These figures are based on the alternative assumptions in table 10-1.
16. Table 10-4, lines 3, 5, 7, 8, 11, and 14–16.

Table 10-6. Revised Budget Projection, Fiscal Year 1981
Billions of dollars

Item	Outlays and receipts
Official outlay projection[a]	574.8
Adjustments	22.8
Welfare	3.0
Energy	4.7
Urban aid	2.9
Health	2.7
Education	1.5
Agriculture	5.2
State and local fiscal assistance	2.8
Total outlays	597.6
Official receipts projection[a]	585.8
Adjustments	−18.6
Individual income tax	−7.0[b]
Corporation income tax	−3.3[b]
Social security payroll tax	−8.3[c]
Total receipts	567.2
Margin	−30.4

Sources: Tables 10-3, 10-4, and 10-5.
a. Projections of current programs and those proposed in the 1979 budget (except for energy) under the alternative assumptions shown in table 10-1.
b. Assumes that urban tax incentives proposed by the President are enacted and that two-thirds of the proposed tax reforms are rejected.
c. Assumes elimination of one-half of the payroll tax increases enacted in 1977.

get or reducing taxes by much more than he recommends will make a deficit a certainty, whether it is needed or not.

There is more leeway for fiscal year 1983, because receipts will rise by about $80 billion a year between 1981 and 1983 under the tax system proposed by the President (see table 10-3). To illustrate the feasible budget policies, three sets of calculations are presented in table 10-7. In making these calculations, it was assumed that a balanced budget would be consistent with full employment in 1983 (which is defined as an unemployment rate of 4.7 percent) and that prices would rise by an average of 6 percent a year from 1980 to 1983.[17] Since a balanced budget can be achieved for a relatively wide range of outlays, it was also assumed that budget outlays will be within a range of 20–22 percent of the gross national product of $3,437 billion estimated for 1983. The high budget of 22 percent of

17. See the alternative assumptions in table 10-1.

Table 10-7. Alternative Budgets[a] for Fiscal Year 1983

Billions of dollars

Item	High	Intermediate	Low
Official outlay projection[b]	665.2	665.2	665.2
Adjustments	90.9	56.6	22.2
Defense	16.4	...	...
Welfare	9.2	9.2	−6.8
Energy	5.8	2.7	2.7
Urban aid	3.3	3.3	3.3
Health	31.8	21.3	5.1
Education	3.5	3.5	3.5
Agriculture	4.0	4.0	4.0
State and local fiscal assistance	7.5	7.5	7.5
Other	9.4	5.1	2.9
Total outlays	756.1	721.8	687.4
Official receipts projection[b]	747.2	747.2	747.2
Adjustments	8.9	−25.4	−59.8
Individual income tax[c]	0.8	−18.5	−33.3[d]
Corporation income tax[c]	0.2	−6.9	−13.5
Social security payroll tax	...	...	−13.0
Energy taxes	7.9	...	...
Total receipts	756.1	721.8	687.4

Sources: Tables 10-3 and 10-4.
a. High budget is 22 percent of gross national product, intermediate is 21 percent, low is 20 percent.
b. Projections of current programs and those proposed in the President's 1979 budget under the alternative economic assumptions shown in table 10-1.
c. Allocated in the ratio of three to one between individual and corporate taxes, and assumes that urban tax incentives proposed by the President are enacted and that two-thirds of the proposed tax reforms are rejected.
d. Assumes incremental welfare reform is substituted for comprehensive reform; therefore, the earned income credit remains unchanged.

gross national product is slightly lower than the average percentage since 1975, but higher than in any year between 1955 and 1974; the low budget of 20 percent of gross national product is equal to the average for the period 1965–74; the intermediate budget of 21 percent of gross national product is President Carter's target.

These calculations show the expenditure and tax decisions that would reconcile receipts with outlays at the assumed levels of government spending.[18] Two significant points may be noted about the basic assumptions.

18. The reader may wish to make his own combinations of expenditure and tax changes from the listings in tables 10-4 and 10-5.

First, the price index for government expenditures rises at a faster rate than the price index for the entire gross national product, because productivity growth in government is assumed to be zero in calculating the price indexes and because prices paid by government for the goods and services it purchases tend to rise faster than other prices. As a result, the 20–22 percent share in current dollars corresponds to 19–21 percent in 1972 dollars, which is roughly the range of the constant dollar share for the entire period 1955–78. This means that the share of the total available resources that would be used by the federal government under the three budgets would fall within the range of actual experience since 1955.[19]

Second, as indicated earlier in this chapter, a balanced budget or a surplus would be appropriate if private investment were strong enough to offset both savings of individuals and state and local governments and the payments deficit with the rest of the world; if this were not the case, a federal budget deficit would be called for. Under the circumstances, it would be prudent to rely on temporary tax cuts or expenditure increases to avoid the inflationary consequences of a federal deficit when private investment does recover. Thus, the assumed outlays and taxes should be regarded as the more or less permanent levels for each budget and not necessarily the levels that might be appropriate in the light of the economic conditions prevailing in 1983.

THE INTERMEDIATE BUDGET. The President's 21 percent target translates into outlays of $721.8 billion in fiscal year 1983. The official projections are that current programs and those proposed in the budget would amount to $665.2 billion (or 19.4 percent of the gross national product) in 1983.[20] But the administration itself raised the budget when it announced its new urban program. Even if the President's entire energy program is not enacted, the proposed one-billion-barrel petroleum reserve will add to outlays. The cost of federal education and health programs, the proposed comprehensive welfare reform, and grants-in-aid to state and local governments are probably understated in the official budget projection, and good crop con-

---

19. For a discussion of the reasons that the government's price index rises more rapidly than the GNP index and for data for the ratio of federal outlays to gross national product, see Joseph A. Pechman, ed., *Setting National Priorities: The 1978 Budget* (Brookings Institution, 1977), pp. 30–32.

20. As noted earlier, this estimate assumes that the President's energy program will not be enacted.

ditions will require higher outlays for agricultural price and income supports.

These changes and revisions would add $35.3 billion to the $665.2 billion projection for current and proposed programs, $21.3 billion below the 21 percent of gross national product. This would be enough to finance either catastrophic health insurance or a federalized Medicaid system, but not both. A 21 percent outlay total—$721.8 billion—in 1983 would cover the cost of current and proposed programs plus expansion of the federal health program, but it would not be sufficient to pay for comprehensive national health insurance or for any other major new initiatives, including greater defense growth, unless other expenditures were reduced.

Receipts under the tax system proposed by the President would amount to $747.2 billion in 1983, $25.4 billion more than the alternative projection of outlays. On the assumption that tax reforms accounting for only one-third of the revenue gains are approved by Congress—$11.7 billion below the level proposed by the President—and assuming also that the urban tax incentives are passed, there would be only $12.2 billion left for additional tax cuts or for a reversal of only half the 1977 payroll tax increases for 1983.[21] Even if the entire cut were allocated to individuals, receipts from the individual income tax would rise to 12 percent of personal income in 1983, which would be higher than any level reached since the end of the Second World War.

THE HIGH BUDGET. A budget of 22 percent of the gross national product would amount to $756.1 billion in 1983, or $90.9 billion over official projections. The excess would cover comprehensive welfare reform, catastrophic health insurance, federalized Medicaid, a 5 percent a year increase in real defense outlays over the next five years, the administration's energy program, and the increases for

---

21. Individual and corporation income tax cuts were calculated by subtracting the revenue loss resulting from rejection of two-thirds of the proposed reforms and allocating the remaining tax cuts between the two taxes, three to one. For the intermediate budget, the calculations (in billions of dollars) are as follows:

Tax source	Rejection of two-thirds of tax reforms	Urban tax incentives	Remaining tax cuts	Total revenue loss
Individual income tax	−8.2	−1.1	−9.2	−18.5
Corporation income tax	−3.5	−0.4	−3.0	−6.9
Total	−11.7	−1.5	−12.2	−25.4

urban aid, health, education, state and local financial aid, and agriculture enumerated in table 10-4, and would add $9.4 billion to other programs. But even at this level, there would not be enough room for comprehensive national health insurance or any other major initiative without cutting existing programs.

Outlays under this budget would exceed receipts under the President's tax program (except for two-thirds of the receipts from his proposed tax reforms) by $8.9 billion, thus forestalling any tax cuts beyond those that would be enacted this year. In a period of continued inflation, this would mean rapidly rising effective rates of taxation. Individual income tax receipts would reach 12.8 percent of personal income.

THE LOW BUDGET. To keep the budget for fiscal year 1983 to 20 percent of gross national product, outlays would have to be limited to $687.4 billion, or only $22.2 billion more than the projected cost of current and proposed programs. Given an atmosphere in which such a budget policy were acceptable, incremental welfare reform would be preferred to comprehensive reform. This would reduce projected spending by $6.8 billion, leaving $29 billion for other programs.[22] This amount would be adequate to cover the revised estimates shown in table 10-4 for education, health, grants-in-aid to state and local governments, agriculture, urban aid, and a one-billion-barrel petroleum reserve.

With outlays of $687.4 billion in fiscal year 1983, the margin for tax cuts would be enlarged to $59.8 billion. Even this would not be a large amount in the 1983 economy, particularly if some of it were used to reduce payroll taxes. For example, if half the 1977 payroll tax increases were eliminated ($13.0 billion), $46.8 billion would be left for income-tax cuts. Assuming that two-thirds of the President's tax reforms are rejected and that the remaining one-third is allocated in a three to one ratio between the individual and corporate income taxes, there would be enough to reduce the individual income tax to 11.6 percent of personal income ($33.3 billion) and the corporate tax to 25.4 percent of corporate profits ($13.5 billion). To cut the individual income tax below 11 percent, it would be necessary

22. The proposed increase in the earned-income credit might also be forgone, although some proponents of incremental reform support an increase in the earned-income credit to encourage work incentives.

to forgo a reduction in the payroll tax or the corporate tax or part of each, or to reduce budget outlays below the 20 percent level.[23]

Summary

The 1979 budget projects the cost of current programs plus those proposed by President Carter at 20.4 percent of the gross national product in fiscal year 1981. Since the budget was submitted, the administration has made a number of decisions that will increase expenditures; Congress may raise them even more. Moreover, the projections for education, welfare, and farm programs are probably underestimates. A realistic estimate of the cost of current and proposed programs would put the 1981 outlay total at 21.2 percent of the gross national product. Thus, outlays can be kept to 21 percent only if some reductions are made *and* no additional spending programs are approved without offsetting reductions.

The revenue picture for 1981 is also not encouraging. Even if this year's tax cut is held to $25 billion, taxes would generate receipts slightly below the 21 percent of gross national product required to balance the budget in 1981. If Congress rejects proposed tax reforms without reducing the tax cuts correspondingly, and reverses some of the payroll tax increases enacted last year, the 1981 budget could be in deficit by about $30 billion. Such a deficit may be needed in 1981 to keep the economy growing, but this year's budget will make a deficit a certainty and leave no room for any significant tax cuts between 1979 and 1981.

For the longer run, the budget can vary within a fairly wide range, depending on the relative emphasis placed on tax cuts and expenditure increases. If the budget rises to 22 percent of the gross national product in 1983, any tax reduction beyond the cuts now proposed by the President would lead to a budget deficit. If the budget is kept at 20 percent of the gross national product, small cuts could be made in individual and corporation income taxes and payroll taxes. At 21 percent of the gross national product, there would be no opportunity for any large new spending initiatives and the margin available

23. For example, if the real growth in the defense budget were reduced by 2 percentage points a year, the impact aid program were eliminated, and the public jobs program were phased down, outlays in 1983 would be reduced $20.7 billion (table 10-4, lines 2, 12, and 13). This would be enough to reduce the individual income tax to 10.8 percent of personal income.

for additional tax cuts would be slim. Thus, unless the budget is kept to the lower end of the 20–22 percent range, there will be no room to adjust income taxes for the effect of inflation or to moderate payroll-tax increases. On the other hand, limiting the budget to the lower end of the range would rule out higher defense budgets, long-promised social programs such as national health insurance, or any other major new initiative.

APPENDIX A

The Spending Shortfall

ROBERT W. HARTMAN

SINCE 1970, estimates of outlays for the current fiscal year,[1] presented in the President's January budget, have proved to be too high by an average of over 1 percent (see table A-1). The spending shortfall for fiscal 1977, moreover, was nearly 3 percent, and for fiscal 1978, the Office of Management and Budget has already acknowledged that another shortfall is developing. The 1978 reestimate released on March 13, 1978, less than two months after the budget was submitted, revised estimated spending downward by $8.7 billion in 1978 and by $0.8 billion in 1979.

The 1978–79 shortfalls—if limited to the level estimated in March 1978—would change the fiscal policy outlook somewhat. During fiscal year 1978, fiscal policy, instead of growing slightly more stimulative, would be moving in a restrictive direction compared to the last half of fiscal 1977 (table A-2). This means that demand from nonfederal sources in 1978 will have to show greater strength than anticipated if the administration's forecast of real growth in 1978 is to be realized. As suggested in chapter 2, such strength could plausibly come from reduced state-local government surpluses or international trade deficits. If nonfederal demand does not pick up the slack, the shortfall could lower real economic growth by between 0.3 and 0.5 percent during 1978.

The author thanks James Blum and the staff of the Budget Review Division of the Office of Management and Budget for advice on previous drafts of this appendix.
1. The fiscal year under way when the January budget is introduced.

301

Table A-1. Difference between Current-Year Estimates of Outlays and Actual
Outlays, Unified Budget, Fiscal Years 1970–78

Amounts in billions of dollars

Fiscal year	Current-year estimate	Actual	Difference	
			Amount	Percent
1970	197.9	196.6	−1.3	−0.7
1971	212.8	211.4	−1.4	−0.7
1972	236.6	231.9	−4.7	−2.0
1973	249.8	246.5	−3.3	−1.3
1974	274.7	268.4	−6.3	−2.3
1975	313.4	324.6	11.2	3.6
1976	372.3	365.7	−6.6	−1.8
1977	413.4[a]	401.9	−11.5	−2.8
1978	462.2	453.5[b]	−8.7	−1.9

Sources: Office of Management and Budget, "Overview of the Current 'State-of-the-Art' of Federal Outlay Estimating," Technical Paper Series BRD/BPB 77-1 (December 15, 1977; processed), attachment A, and "Current Budget Estimates, March 1978" (March 13, 1978; processed), p. 1.

a. Estimate made in February 1977 budget revisions excluding $3.2 billion of outlays attributable to proposed tax rebates that were later withdrawn.

b. March 1978 reestimate.

For 1979, the revised OMB estimates are little changed from those made in January. But given repeated instances of significant budget shortfalls in recent years, these early estimates of outlays must be taken warily. Whether the substantial 1978 shortfall will be repeated in 1979 can only be analyzed by examining the individual items that account for the shortfall and such analysis is in a very confused state.

The OMB has recently reviewed the basis for the outlay estimates it presents in the January budget.[2] According to this study, estimates of outlays, though reviewed by the OMB, are primarily the responsibility of the agencies that operate federal programs. This decentralized process causes several problems. One is that many agencies apparently devote few resources to making the estimates; they do little more than apply fixed formulas to past data or simply pass on the estimates of state agencies (which may devote even fewer resources to the effort). Second, program managers—especially in the case of new activities—tend to be optimistic about the rate at which they will obligate funds,[3] especially when they have reached an understanding

2. Office of Management and Budget, "Overview of the Current 'State-of-the-Art' of Federal Outlay Estimating."

3. It should be remembered that outlays are merely the last step in the execution of a program. First, the Congress creates budget authority (usually an appropriation) for an authorized activity. This establishes the legal basis for an agency

Table A-2. Original and Revised Estimates of Full-Employment Surplus,
Fiscal Years 1977–79[a]

Billions of dollars

Period	Original full-employment surplus[b]	Revised full-employment surplus
1977:II	−19.1	−19.1
1978:I	−28.8	−22.2[c]
1978:II	−20.9	−14.3[c]
1979:I	−34.4	−33.7[c]
1979:II	−20.9	−20.2[c]

Sources: Office of Management and Budget, unpublished estimates of March 21, 1978, and table 2-9.
a. National income accounts basis; semiannually at annual rates.
b. From table 2-9.
c. Revised by subtracting the March 1978 budget revisions on an NIA basis from the first column. Includes small changes in estimates of receipts. Equal shortfall arbitrarily assigned to each half-year.

with a congressional committee that they will make speedy progress.[4] Finally, it is clear that agencies use their estimates of progress to impel subordinate offices to meet targets and to demonstrate to congressional committees (and to the OMB) why they need more funds in the next year. This is illustrated by the procurement (of major military equipment and systems) accounts in the Department of Defense. Since 1975, these accounts have received huge increases in budget authority and Defense has published ambitious estimates of outlay growth, which proved too high in 1976 and 1977. Most recently, in March 1978, the OMB cut back procurement outlay estimates to show only a 13.6 percent rate of increase versus the 18.6 percent estimate of January 1978 (see table A-3).[5] Naturally, the Department of Defense would like to maintain the high growth estimates, which are really their planned (hoped-for) amounts, whereas for budget estimation purposes what is needed is realistic (best estimate) projections.

to obligate funds (that is, write a contract, hire somebody, order pencils). Once the service contracted for has been performed, the agency is billed and a check is issued and cashed. This last step is the outlay.

4. The Council of Economic Advisers illustrates this optimism with the increased local public works authorization requested by President Carter in 1977: "it was originally estimated that $0.6 billion would be spent on public works in 1977 under the . . . stimulus package. In fact spending was negligible." *Economic Report of the President, January 1978*, p. 65.

5. Even the March 1978 revisions may prove too high. In the first five months of fiscal 1978, outlays for military procurement were only 2.9 percent above the total for the first five months of 1977. Should growth continue to be so low, 1978 outlays would fall below $19 billion. However, bad winter weather may have slowed operations, and some speedier growth in spending should occur later in the fiscal year.

Table A-3. Budget Authority and Outlays for Military Procurement, Fiscal Years
1975–78

Amounts in billions of dollars

		Outlays			
Fiscal year	Budget authority	Current-year estimate	Actual	Predicted growth (percent)[a]	Actual growth (percent)
1975	16,729	14,785	16,042	...	...
1976	21,206	16,486	15,964	2.8	−0.5
1977	27,672	18,710	18,178	17.2	13.9
1978	29,545	21,552	20,652[b]	18.6	13.6

Sources: *The Budget of the United States Government, Fiscal Year 1979*, p. 328, and preceding issues.
a. January estimate for current year compared to actual outlays for preceding year.
b. Office of Management and Budget, "Current Budget Estimates, March 1978."

To the extent that the OMB outlay estimates are biased by these factors, it is impossible to project future shortfalls since the mix of new and rapidly expanding programs is constantly changing. Moreover, widespread attention to the spending shortfall has impelled the OMB to scrutinize some agency budgets closely, and this may have forced more realistic estimates for fiscal 1979. In short, the official 1979 estimates contain an unknown combination of some upward-biased estimates and some more realistic estimates, all subject to ordinary forecasting errors, making a simple extension of the fiscal 1978 shortfall an unlikely outcome. Fortunately, there is an alternative data source.

The United States is probably the only country in the world whose legislative branch has an independent capability for estimating government expenditures. Since 1976, the Congressional Budget Office has been making its own outlay estimates of the President's program as well as of congressional alternatives. The CBO's estimates are relatively free of the upward bias that comes from having spending agencies prepare the estimates, because the CBO makes its own estimates.[6] These estimates are based on a number of methodologies, the predominant one being the consistent application of historical "spend-out rates"[7] to past and present budget authority. In the case of entitlement programs, the CBO estimates the eligible population, participation rates, average benefits, and so on, using economic

6. The methodology is described fully in CBO, *Five-Year Budget Projections, Fiscal Years 1979–1983: Technical Background* (GPO, 1978).
7. The fraction of the budget authority of a given year t spent in years $t, t + 1$, $t + 2$, and so forth.

models of varying degrees of complexity.[8] Naturally these estimates are subject to purely statistical errors, since the equations are simply averaging the past behavior of scores of government units or millions of people.

The upshot is that the CBO's recent track record on predicting federal outlays is better than the OMB's. In fiscal 1977, the CBO came closer, sooner, to the actual outlay level realized. In January 1978, the CBO's estimate of outlays for fiscal 1978, based on President Carter's budget proposal, was $450 billion to $455 billion,[9] a range that includes the OMB's March revision of the shortfall.

Under these circumstances, it may be advisable to use the CBO's estimate for President Carter's budget proposal for 1979. As of March 1978, the CBO estimated that the President's budget would result in outlays of $495.2 billion, about $4.2 billion below the OMB's March reestimate.[10] This lower estimate may provide Congress with additional elbow room to add to the President's spending proposals without a commensurate increase in the projected budget deficit for 1979.[11] For the longer run, as discussed in chapter 10, the shortfall is likely to be a small fraction of outlays and is therefore disregarded in the calculations of budget margins.

8. For entitlement programs the OMB uses agency estimates that seem in many cases also to be based on fairly sophisticated models. See OMB, "Overview of the Current 'State-of-the-Art' of Federal Outlay Estimating," attachment B.

9. Congressional Budget Office, *An Analysis of the President's Budgetary Proposals for Fiscal Year 1979* (CBO, 1978), pp. 27–28. The CBO had intimated as early as July 1977 that a shortfall was in store for fiscal 1978. See CBO, *Recovery with Inflation* (CBO, 1977). However, in the second concurrent resolution on the 1978 budget, passed in the fall of 1977, the outlay estimate was over $458 billion. There is reason to believe that the outlays estimated in the concurrent resolutions are subject to the same upward biases that affect the OMB's official estimate.

10. Congressional Budget Office, "CBO Reestimates of 1979 Spending" (March 7, 1978; processed), p. 1.

11. The outlay estimates are not the only constraint on congressional action. The President's budget and the concurrent resolutions also set limits on budget authority, which in many cases is unaffected by outlay shortfalls. Thus leeway that results from a reestimate of outlays does not necessarily create any leeway in budget authority. However, since the administration's 1979 budget authority proposals contain some recommendations, such as advanced funding for several grant programs, that inflate the budget authority requests, Congress can create elbow room by simply refusing to accept such recommendations.

Multiyear Budget Planning

ROBERT W. HARTMAN

THE YEAR 1978 may go down in history as the one in which government officials began talking seriously about multiyear budget planning. Awareness was growing that "it has become very difficult for either the Congress or the President to plan budgets effectively just one year in advance."[1] This is due primarily to large built-in expenditure growth in the one-year-ahead budget, which limits the amount of reallocation possible (see chapter 2). Accordingly, each branch was being urged to take steps to make current decisions with the longer run—where there are more options (see chapter 10)—in mind. Whether these new procedures will actually lead to multiyear planning seems problematic.

The Executive Branch

In early January, President Carter directed all agencies to prepare their 1980 budget requests in a multiyear framework. As a later OMB bulletin explained, the purpose of this directive was to "expand the planning horizon to cover the three years following the budget year and fully integrate long-range planning into the executive budget cycle" and to "ensure that long-term consequences are

The author thanks James Blum, Darwin Johnson, Dale McOmber, and John Palmer for criticism of previous drafts of this appendix.
1. Jimmy Carter, Memorandum for the Heads of Executive Departments and Agencies, January 12, 1978 (Subject: Multi-Year Budget Planning).

identified and highlighted when decisions are made." The OMB
bulletin insisted that even before the 1980 budget cycle came into
effect "all significant program and tax policy proposals . . . include
an analysis of budget costs that identifies the long-term effects of the
proposals."[2]

The mechanism for such multiyear reviews centers around a "planning base." Early in 1978, the OMB furnished each agency with
budget authority and outlay targets for fiscal years 1980–82 that
were consistent with the 1979 administration budget. These projections are intended to be the starting point for any subsequent
budget decisions or program initiatives.[3]

This kind of system is needed by an administration, such as Carter's, that is deliberately setting long-term spending targets (chapter
10). It permits the administration to set outlay targets for the future
and to assess the compatibility of new proposals with the targets.

But there are also two other reasons for the multiyear planning
system. The first is to establish a common base of numbers so that
the cost of new proposals can be realistically weighed. This would
avoid the kind of numerical gamesmanship that characterized the
administration's welfare reform proposals of 1977, in which all sorts
of costs were used as offsets to the gross cost of the proposal so as to
make its net cost appear small (see chapter 3). This would not be
possible (or it would be more difficult) if there were a common base
of built-in budgetary costs; offsets would not be legitimate unless
they were part of that base.

The second reason seems to be an attempt by the OMB to regain
a central role in program planning in the administration. Certainly
the OMB played no major role in many of the Carter administration
initiatives in 1977.[4] But if every proposal had to be accompanied by

2. Office of Management and Budget, "Establishment of a Multi-Year Planning
System," Bulletin 78-7 (January 16, 1978; processed).

3. There is a sharp contrast between planning with a sharply defined planning
base and planning with the zero-base budget used in 1977; the latter denies that there
is a base. On the other hand, a planning base does not preclude future attempts to
reduce items contained in the base. For a discussion of zero-base budgeting, see
Joseph A. Pechman, ed., *Setting National Priorities: The 1978 Budget* (Brookings
Institution, 1977), chap. 11.

4. For a discussion of the development of three major initiatives, see Richard
Corrigan, J. Dicken Kirschten, and Robert J. Samuelson, "Jimmy Carter's Energy
Crusade," *National Journal*, vol. 9 (April 30, 1977), pp. 656–72; Linda E. Dem-
kovich, "Carter Gets Some Outside Advice for His Welfare Reform Package,"
National Journal, vol. 9 (April 30, 1977), pp. 673–75; and James W. Singer, "Carter
Is Trying to Make Social Security More Secure," *National Journal*, vol. 9 (June 11,
1977), pp. 893–95.

multiyear budgets, the OMB would have a central role in reviewing such estimates.

Thus far in 1978, the portents for multiyear planning are not good. In two major policy decisions by the Carter administration—on higher education student aid and on urban policy—the documents released to the public show no evidence of an explicit multiyear framework built on an existing planning base. Indeed, from the available evidence, neither decision seems to have been subjected by the OMB to intensive scrutiny.[5] The future will tell whether multiyear planning is ever really used in the executive branch.

The long-awaited Humphrey-Hawkins bill,[6] if it is enacted, will place strong multiyear planning requirements on the President. The bill requires that the Economic Report of the President set out a five-year plan for GNP to reach (by the fifth year after the first such report) a level consistent with an unemployment rate of no more than 4 percent. Moreover, the act requires that the "President's budget shall provide five-year projections of outlays and receipts consistent" with achieving the unemployment goal.

This requirement is quite different from current OMB practice. In fiscal 1979, although the President's budget projection is based on an assumed 4 percent unemployment rate in 1983, there is no explicit plan for how fiscal policy would be conducted to attain such a goal. The budget simply projects outlays and receipts under current law and indicates that the administration will take steps to ensure that its goals are met. It does not say what those steps will be. The long-range fiscal planning envisioned under Humphrey-Hawkins raises a number of thorny issues that also pertain to a new CBO planning system.

The Legislative Branch

In a series of publications since early 1977, the Congressional Budget Office has been trying to change the way Congress (and the public) views the federal budget.[7] This is a two-pronged effort: the

5. See Rochelle L. Stanfield, "The Carter Urban Strategy—Principles in Search of a Policy," *National Journal*, vol. 10 (February 25, 1978), pp. 304–08; David S. Broder, "Chaos, Reshuffled," *Washington Post*, March 29, 1978; Joel Havemann, "The Budget—A Tax Cut, Little Else," *National Journal*, vol. 10 (January 28, 1978), pp. 124–32.

6. The Full Employment and Balanced Growth Act, H.R. 50 and S. 50.

7. See Congressional Budget Office, *Budgetary Strategies for Fiscal Years 1979–1983: A Report to the Senate and House Committees on the Budget—Part I* (CBO,

Table B-1. Five-Year Budget Projections, Fiscal Years 1979–83

Billions of dollars

Item	1979	1980	1981	1982	1983
Current policy receipts	457	519	590	668	751
Current policy outlays	495	529	565	606	655
Current policy margin	−38	−10	25	62	96
Fiscal drag offset	29	51	74	101	115
Deficit (−) or surplus	−67	−61	−49	−39	−19

Source: Congressional Budget Office, *Five-Year Budget Projections: Fiscal Years 1979–1983* (CBO, 1977), p. 4.

first tries to show the required fiscal policy for reaching long-term goals and the second is an effort to integrate goal-setting into the annual budget process.

The CBO's attempt to prescribe long-term fiscal policy can best be explained by an illustration from its December 1977 report on five-year projections. Table B-1 comes from that report. The CBO first sets out its economic assumptions, which are similar to those used in chapter 10 of this volume.[8] It then projects outlays and receipts under current policy (first and second lines of table B-1).[9] The conventional analysis at this point (for example, see chapter 10 of this volume) would be as follows:

Under current law, receipts would grow much faster than outlays, producing a "current policy margin" (third line of table B-1). Such a tightening of fiscal policy would be inconsistent with the economic assumption of strong GNP growth. The government should plan for an approximate budget balance at full employment. This means that some combination of spending increases or tax cuts totaling $96 billion (the fiscal 1983 margin) will be possible by 1983.[10] As 1983 draws closer we will have a better idea whether a balanced budget is, in fact, compatible with full employment. Until then, it would be unwise to undertake permanent spending programs or tax cuts that would use up more than the projected margin.

1978); *Five-Year Budget Projections: Fiscal Years 1979–1983* (CBO, 1977); *Advance Budgeting: A Report to the Congress* (CBO, 1977); *Closing the Fiscal Policy Loop: A Long-Run Analysis* (CBO, 1977); *Budget Options for Fiscal Year 1978: A Report to the Senate and House Committees on the Budget* (CBO, 1977).

8. The CBO assumes real growth to 1983 of about 4.5 percent, inflation of about 5.8 percent, and an employment rate falling to 4.5 percent in 1983.

9. The CBO includes an inflation allowance for virtually all spending programs. The projections in the table do not include the December 1977 social security amendments or President Carter's 1979 tax and spending initiatives.

10. This assumes that federal taxes will not be raised by legislation in the period.

By contrast, the CBO introduces a new concept, which it calls "fiscal drag offset." This can best be understood as follows. For each year of the projection, the CBO makes a set of assumptions about nonfederal demand[11] and then calculates what federal surplus or deficit would be needed to attain the assumed rate of economic growth. This deficit is shown in the bottom line of table B-1. The CBO's analysis goes as follows:

In 1983, for example, the estimates show the need for a $19 billion budget deficit, but if current laws are simply left unchanged a $96 billion surplus would accrue. Some combination of additional spending and tax reduction of $115 billion (which converts a $96 billion surplus into a $19 billion deficit) would therefore be necessary by 1983 to offset growing fiscal drag.[12] Thus federal spending or tax cutting can be geared to fulfilling the economic assumptions by planning for a budget deficit at full employment.[13]

These two ways of looking at a long-term budget strategy obviously give different signals. The traditional approach is quite cautious in that it warns against overcommitting resources that may be needed in the future. It implicitly assumes that if and when full employment arrives, nonfederal demand will probably be so strong that a proper fiscal policy will be budget balance or that, if a deficit is required, it will be relatively easy to introduce stimulation measures. Nonetheless, the principal risk of this strategy is that it may make decisionmakers so cautious that fiscal policy will restrain the economy so much that full employment will never be reached.

The CBO approach is different. It makes explicit assumptions about nonfederal demand and then draws conclusions from its model of the economy.[14] Thus, in its five-year projections, the CBO assumes such chronic weakness in nonfederal demand that a federal government deficit will be needed to achieve full employment.[15] If this ap-

11. The assumptions are that the personal saving rate will be 5.9 percent, real investment will average 7 percent growth, real state-local government purchases will average 3 percent growth, and net exports will be nearly zero over the period 1979–83. See Congressional Budget Office, *Five-Year Budget Projections*, p. 5.

12. The CBO's terminology is somewhat confusing in that the fiscal drag offset is intended to counter not only a built-in fiscal policy drag but also to take into account a particular state of nonfederal demand.

13. For an example of a five-year budget plan based on this line of argument, see Congressional Budget Office, *Budgetary Strategies for Fiscal Years 1979–1983— Part I*, especially pp. 30–32.

14. See Congressional Budget Office, *Closing the Fiscal Policy Loop*.

15. To be fair, the required deficit of $19 billion is only 0.6 percent of GNP, which is smaller than it was in 1972–73, the last period of full employment. See table 2-7.

proach is persuasive and spending increases or tax cuts are instituted to put federal finance into deficit at full employment, the principal risk is inflation. If it turns out that nonfederal demand is stronger than the CBO's assumption, the federal budget will be in direct competition with the private sector for scarce resources, and, barring an emergency tax increase or credit crunch, this will raise prices and wages.[16]

There is no absolutely right way to devise a long-run budget strategy. The fact is that economists do not know what the state of nonfederal demand will be over the next five years. The set of plausible levels of nonfederal demand imply a range of required long-run full-employment policies—a range that includes surplus, balance, and deficit for the federal budget.[17] Basing long-run fiscal plans on a best estimate is not necessarily the best strategy. The best strategy can only be found after weighing the costs of pursuing a budget target that proves to be wrong. Such an evaluation depends on the priority assigned to inflation and unemployment and on the feasibility of introducing corrective fiscal measures such as tax rebates or surcharges.

This issue will have to be faced by the administration if the Humphrey-Hawkins bill is enacted. In setting out a budget compatible with the full-employment target in Humphrey-Hawkins, administration planners will come up with a range of budget alternatives over the next five years. If a single target is adopted—as the Humphrey-Hawkins bill seems to require—the choice will reveal a lot about how the administration evaluates economic risks. A large, planned budget deficit will invite spending increases and tax cuts and risk inflation. A planned surplus or balanced budget will invite caution and risk nonfulfillment of the full-employment goal. Like it or not, there is no scientific way to set out *the* budgetary strategy for full employment and balanced growth. Congress will have to grapple with whatever strategy the administration adopts—and there is no way for it to avoid taking a stand on underlying economic goals.

At present, the congressional budget process does not explicitly

16. On the other hand, had the CBO assumed very strong nonfederal demand, its scheme would have risked recession.

17. The CBO's most recent publications have shown a range for the fiscal drag offset. For 1983, for example, they now show a required surplus/deficit of +$6 billion to −$19 billion. See *Budgetary Strategies for Fiscal Years 1979–1983— Part I*, p. 4.

incorporate a multiyear framework. Although the CBO provides Congress with aggregate budget projections and with five-year projections of the cost of every bill reported out of committee, these projections are not part of the concurrent resolutions that guide the congressional budget. For this reason, the CBO has advocated "advance targeting."[18] The proposal is for the first concurrent resolution on the budget, which is voted on in May, to include targets for outlays and receipts up to five years in advance. Such targets would not be binding, but the CBO would "keep score,"[19] and Congress would be reminded, for each piece of pending legislation, how adoption of the law would affect other congressional goals. This procedure would allow Congress, for example, to defeat a farm bill because its enactment might jeopardize future spending for mass transit. Such trade-offs become clear only in a multiyear context.

So far, this procedure has not been adopted.[20] There are many evident problems. One is deciding on the nature of the future year targets. Should they be best estimates of the budget needed for full employment? Whose best estimates? Or should the targets show a balanced budget? At what percent of GNP should the budget be balanced? Congress has never confronted these kinds of issues head-on. But in requiring the administration, through Humphrey-Hawkins, to take a stand, they may be forcing themselves to explicitly consider a congressional alternative multiyear budget. If that is to be taken seriously, congressional budget procedures will have to change along the lines the CBO recommended.

While there is much to be said in favor of multiyear planning and budgeting, the British experience[21] should remind one that there is no such thing as a free high tea. For several years the British government committed itself to multiyear spending targets fixed in real

18. See Congressional Budget Office, *Advance Budgeting;* and CBO, *Budgetary Strategies for Fiscal Years 1979–1983—Part I,* pp. 34–37.

19. That is, the CBO would periodically report on how laws thus far enacted in a congressional session would affect the expenditure and receipts targets in future years. This is already done periodically for the current fiscal year. See, for example, Congressional Budget Office, *1978 Congressional Budget Scorekeeping Report,* Report 5 (CBO, December 1977).

20. In its drafting of the first concurrent resolution for 1979, the Senate Budget Committee experimented with a multiyear approach. In that committee, at least, the procedure seems to have worked successfully. For an example of how the multiyear approach affected the committee's 1979 decision, see *First Concurrent Resolution on the Budget, FY 1979,* S. Rept. 95-739, 95:2 (GPO, 1978).

21. Hugh Heclo and Aaron Wildavsky, *The Private Government of Public Money,* 2d ed. (University of California Press, 1978).

terms. When inflation exploded, so did public spending. If multiyear budgets are rigidly made—if the government commits itself more or less firmly to a given course—the chances are that the system will break down. Too many things can change to upset the assumptions that feed into any plan, and at that point the plan becomes the enemy of progress. For the long-run survival of planning, not to mention the economy, multiyear plans and budgets should be flexible. Future budgets in which a range of expenditures is shown should therefore be welcome, implementation of Humphrey-Hawkins should allow a president some leeway for adjusting programs and goals, adoption of a goal for federal spending should be explicitly conditional and broad (20.5 to 21.5 percent of GNP is every bit as good as 21 percent of GNP) to allow for unanticipated events and the probability that we do not know everything right now. If history teaches anything, it is that such surprises and revisions of plans are the rule.

APPENDIX C

Tax Expenditures

JOSEPH A. PECHMAN

SPECIAL PROVISIONS of the income tax laws reduce the tax liability for those who make payments or receive incomes in certain designated forms. Many of these tax subsidies are, in effect, direct federal expenditures. But direct expenditures are shown in the budget as outlays, whereas tax subsidies are reflected in lower income tax receipts. The Congressional Budget Act of 1974 applies the term "tax expenditures" to tax subsidies to emphasize the similarity between them and direct outlays. The law requires a listing of tax expenditures in each budget and directs all congressional committees to identify any changes made in tax expenditures by new legislation.

Tax expenditures in fiscal year 1978 are estimated at $124.4 billion. If they were counted as direct expenditures, both outlays and receipts would be raised by $124.4 billion; thus outlays in 1978 would be $586.6 billion, instead of the $462.2 billion reported in the budget, and receipts would be $524.8 billion, so that the deficit would remain at $61.8 billion (table C-1).

Tax expenditures are defined by the 1974 budget act as "revenue losses attributable to provisions of the federal tax laws which allow a special exclusion, exemption, or deduction from gross income or which provide a special credit, a preferential rate of tax, or a deferral of tax liability." A tax expenditure, then, is a result of any deviation from the normal tax structure. The normal tax structure is not defined by law, but it is generally regarded as being as close to economic

Cynthia E. Nethercut provided research assistance.

Table C-1. Effect of Tax Expenditures on the Federal Budget, Fiscal Year 1978
Billions of dollars

Item	Outlays	Receipts	Deficit
Official 1978 budget	462.2	400.4	−61.8
Tax expenditures[a]	124.4	124.4	...
Revised totals	586.6	524.8	−61.8

Sources: *The Budget of the United States Government, Fiscal Year 1979*, p. 488; and *Special Analyses, Budget of the United States Government, Fiscal Year 1979*, pp. 158–60.
   a. See table C-2.

income as possible. (Thus, capital gains are included in full, but imputed incomes such as rental values of owned homes are not because they are difficult to measure.) The normal tax structure includes the personal exemption and personal tax credit, the standard deduction, and the rate schedules.

The major tax expenditures include personal deductions under the individual income tax (for state and local income, sales, property, and gasoline taxes, charitable contributions, medical expenses, and interest paid); exclusions from taxable income (state and local bond interest, employee benefits, and transfer payments such as social security, unemployment compensation, and welfare); preferential treatment of long-term capital gains; and tax credits and accelerated depreciation for investment. A list of the major tax expenditures is given in table C-2.

Including tax expenditures in the budget encourages the administration and the Congress to take them into account in budget decisions. Tax expenditures constitute 26 percent of budget outlays (see table C-3), and in recent years they have grown faster than outlays. For some budget functions, tax expenditures (for example, commerce and housing credit, and revenue sharing) exceed direct outlays. The distributional effects of tax expenditures are often quite different from those of direct expenditures. For example, homeowner tax preferences provide little benefit to the poor, while housing allowances do.

The current discussion of alternative methods of providing financial assistance to college students illustrates the usefulness of the tax expenditure concept. Congress is considering bills to give tax credits to families with children going to college. President Carter has proposed grants instead (raising those under existing programs for

Table C-2. Major Tax Expenditures, Fiscal Year 1978

Millions of dollars

Tax expenditure	Individuals	Corporations	Total
Deduction of state and local nonbusiness taxes	13,930	...	13,930
Deduction of charitable contributions	5,830	730	6,560
Deduction of mortgage interest and interest on consumer credit	7,105	...	7,105
Deduction of medical expenses	2,435	...	2,435
Exclusion of employer contributions to pension, health, and welfare plans[a]	18,930	...	18,930
Exclusion of benefits and allowances to armed forces personnel	1,260	...	1,260
Exemptions for age and blindness	1,175	...	1,175
Credit for the elderly	250	...	250
Exclusion of transfer payments	9,485	...	9,485
Job credit	985	1,475	2,460
Exemption for parents of students aged nineteen and over	770	...	770
Credit for child and dependent care expenses	525	...	525
Preferential treatment of capital gains	17,020[b]	775	17,795[b]
Exclusion and deferral of interest payments[c]	4,800	3,925	8,725
Exemption for corporate surtax	...	3,885	3,885
Investment tax credit	2,390	10,735	13,125
Asset depreciation range	115	2,245	2,360
Excess of first-year depreciation and depreciation on buildings over straight line	570	255	825
Excess of percentage over cost depletion and expensing of exploration and development costs	640	2,005	2,645
Expensing of research and development expenditures	30	1,450	1,480
Deferral of income of domestic international sales corporations	...	1,135	1,135
Deduction of excess bad debt reserves of financial institutions	...	705	705
Other	4,355	2,495	6,850
Total[d]	92,600	31,815	124,415

Source: *Special Analyses, Budget of the United States Government, Fiscal Year 1979*, pp. 158–60.

a. Includes Keogh plans for the self-employed and contributions to individual retirement accounts.

b. Includes revenue effect of deferral of tax on capital gains transferred by gift or at death.

c. Includes exclusion of interest on state and local debt and life insurance savings and deferral of interest on savings bonds.

d. The totals are the arithmetic sums of the columns. The separate estimates assume no other changes in the tax law; consequently, the aggregate revenue effect will not equal the sum of the revenue effects of the individual items shown.

Table C-3. Estimated Federal Budget Outlays and Tax Expenditures, by Function, Fiscal Year 1978

Dollar amounts in billions

Budget function	Outlay[a]	Tax expenditures	
		Amount	Percent of outlay
National defense	107.6	1.4	1.3
International affairs	6.7	2.1	31.3
General science, space, and technology	4.8	1.5	31.2
Energy	7.8	2.7	34.6
Natural resources and environment	12.1	0.5	4.1
Agriculture	9.1	1.2	13.2
Commerce and housing credit	3.5	51.2	1,462.9
Transportation	16.3	0.8	4.9
Community and regional development	9.7	*	0.2
Education, training, employment, and social services	27.5	10.8	39.3
Health	44.3	9.8	22.1
Income security	147.6	26.2	17.8
Veterans' benefits and services	18.9	1.1	5.8
Administration of justice	4.0	0.0	...
Interest	43.8	0.6	1.4
General government	4.1	0.1	2.4
General purpose fiscal assistance	9.9	14.4	145.5
Total	477.9	124.4[b]	26.0

Sources: *The Budget of the United States Government, Fiscal Year 1979*, pp. 456–68; *Special Analyses, Budget of the United States Government, Fiscal Year 1979*, pp. 158–60. Figures are rounded.
* $0.05 billion or less.
a. Excluding undistributed offsetting receipts and allowances.
b. The totals are the arithmetic sums of the columns. The separate estimates assume no other changes in the tax law; consequently, the aggregate revenue effect will not equal the sum of the revenue effect of the items.

eligible families with incomes up to $16,000 and giving a flat $250 to eligible families with incomes between $16,000 and $25,000; see chapter 4). The major difference between the two approaches is in the distribution of the benefits by income class. Most tax credits help only families that pay taxes, while grants help all families. However, if tax credits are refundable, that is, if families with little or no tax liability are paid the excess of the credit over their liability, the distributional effects of both schemes are identical (provided they have the same features—income limits, amounts, eligibility, and so on). To avoid favoring high-income families, most serious proposals for higher education credits have the refundable feature.

Naturally, congressional appropriations committees prefer direct outlays, and the tax committees prefer tax credits. The budget committees, recognizing the similarities and differences between the two approaches, are trying to focus the attention of the Congress on their merits rather than on the choice of committee that originates the legislation. Only when it is understood and accepted that a vote for a tax expenditure is equivalent in budget terms to a vote for a direct expenditure can the budget process be said to work.

TYPESETTING *Monotype Composition Company, Inc., Baltimore*
PRINTING & BINDING *R. R. Donnelley & Sons Company, Chicago*